HOUSTON: A History

HOUSTON: A History

By David G. McComb

 UNIVERSITY OF TEXAS PRESS Austin

Requests for permission to reproduce material from this work should
be sent to Permissions, University of Texas Press, Box 7819, Austin,
Texas 78712.

Library of Congress Cataloging in Publication Data

McComb, David G.
  Houston, a history.
  Previous ed. published in 1969 as: Houston, the Bayou City.
  Bibliography: p.
  Includes index.
  1. Houston (Tex.)—History. I. Title.
F394.H857M32   1981   976.4'235   81-10350
ISBN 0-292-73018-7   AACR2
ISBN 0-292-73020-9 (pbk.)

To my mother, Mrs. John F. McComb,
and to the memory of my father, John F. McComb

CONTENTS

TABLES AND FIGURES

PREFACE

This urban biography is the result of a doctoral dissertation at the University of Texas completed in June 1968. When I began work on the history of Houston the suggestion to contact famous urban historians for information about research techniques and organization was included with the advice I received. When I mentioned this idea to Joe B. Frantz, my supervising professor, he counseled against such a tactic, and commented, "I want this to be your work, and want you beholden to no one." Consequently, this book is my own—for better or worse.

To an extent, however, I am indebted to certain persons for their aid: to librarians Llerena Friend of the Texas History Center and Mrs. Raymond Ulmer of the Houston Public Library; to archivist Chester V. Kielman of the University of Texas; to historians Andrew Forest Muir of Rice University for some helpful information and Marilyn M. Sibley of Houston Baptist College for the generous use of her manuscript on the port of Houston (published as *The Port of Houston: A History* by the University of Texas Press in 1968); to readers John E. Sunder, Barnes F. Lathrop, and Stanley A. Arbingast of the University of Texas; and to critic and typist, Mrs. David G. McComb. Ironically, I am beholden to Dr. Frantz himself—for a timely summer grant from the Texas State Historical Association, for friendly encouragement, and for his commentary on the final draft.

D. G. M.
Houston, Texas

PREFACE TO THE REVISED EDITION

How often have we said, "Now, if I had to do that again, I would have said . . ." Well, I have had a second chance, and I hope this is a better book. Houston has changed much in the past ten years, and these developments have been incorporated in Chapters 6 and 7. The epilogue is an attempt to answer a question I have pondered in the past year during the preparation of this new edition: What is the significance of Houston in the history of cities; has it made any difference? There are only hints of an answer. They are only glimmerings through the myopia of the present about what was, what is, and what can be.

David McComb
Fort Collins, Colorado

HOUSTON: A History

Introduction

On a day late in March 1858, Edward H. Cushing, the energetic editor of the Houston *Tri-Weekly Telegraph*, clambered to the roof of the uncompleted Academy Building, a two-story brick schoolhouse occupying the block Rusk-Capitol-Caroline-Austin, for a view of his town and observed:

> From the feet of the beholder, the city stretches away for a mile in three directions, while in the fourth the green prairie, dotted here and there with white houses, and covered with the beauties of spring, is bounded by the timber of Bray's bayou. The young shade trees in our streets and gardens, scarcely large enough yet to attract attention from the ground, here show to a better advantage, and give the town the appearance of a forest city, the house-tops everywhere peeping out from green bowers and luxuriant gardens. . . . The scene is still more satisfactorily set off to the citizen of Houston, if he is looking upon it at three in the afternoon, when the rumbling of the approaching train of the Central road, and the whistling of the boats in the Bayou salute his ears, while just below him the cars of the Tap [rail]road are running by with the speed of the wind. The hum of business barely reaches him from Main street.[1]

Taking Cushing's advice, I ascended by elevator, on October 9, 1967, at three o'clock, to the enclosed observation floor at the top of the forty-four–story Humble Building, located at the growing edge of the central business district. Although the only noticeable sounds were a moving elevator, air conditioning, piped music, and the voices of tourists, the view was unusually clear. To the north, enclosed by freeways leading to the central city, lay the melange of downtown office buildings, the very names of which designated the purpose of the community. Among the newer structures, with their rectangular symmetry, the dark-gray metallic Tennessee Building and the First City National Bank with its white, eye-catching exoskeleton predominated. Other buildings—the Sheraton-Lincoln, Houston Natural Gas, Bank of the Southwest—added to the building-block appearance. More subdued were the older edifices: the buff-colored Neils Esperson Building, topped with a circular cupola supported by Corinthian columns; the E-shaped Rice Hotel, located on the site of the capitol of the republic; and the thirty-seven–story Gulf Building, once the tallest in the city, its dignity now diminished by an orange-and-white, fifty-eight–foot–wide "lollipop," the trademark of the Gulf Oil Company, rotating on top.[2]

By 1980 the "lollipop" had been taken down and the view to the north changed by a line of new buildings. Unfortunately, there was no available new observation deck on the taller structures from which to view the city. The business area, where most spare land has been dedicated to the automobile, offered almost no greenery. Cars, crowded onto numerous lots, seemed to spatter the ground with color, demonstrating Houston's commitment to private transportation—a commitment that absorbs 62.5 percent of the downtown area.[3] Over all, however, the panorama of the business segment, with the bold rectilinear office towers tending to mask the older parts of the city, presented a bright, fresh-scrubbed picture. The contemporary architecture invoked fascination with its cold beauty, efficiency, and sense of strident power.

The view to the south revealed the straight line of Main Street reaching almost to the horizon. It led past the high-rise apartment Twenty-Sixteen Main; the dark-colored office of Southwestern Bell Telephone; the recently redecorated Warwick Hotel; the Texas Medical Center; and on through a cluster forming uptown Houston—the Prudential Building, the Fannin National Bank, the Siteman Building, and the Shamrock Hilton Hotel. Slightly east of this line, in the far distance, glittered the plastic top of the Harris County Domed Stadium and more to the southeast could be seen the University of Houston. To the southwest lay the Richmond Avenue office complex and almost on the horizon were the buildings in the Sharpstown suburb.

The southward view, in addition, disclosed a forest city, as Cushing had noted in 1858. The almost overwhelming greenness of the land emphasized Houston's forty-six–inch annual rainfall and its semitropical climate, with a January average of forty-five degrees, a July average of ninety-three degrees, and a three-hundred-day growing season.[4] Precipitation, however, has rarely been evenly distributed, and the change in seasons has generally been abrupt. As

Andrew Forest Muir, a Rice University history professor, once explained to a reporter who had asserted that Houstonians experience no distinct seasons: "Oh, yes, we do. We have dry spells and wet spells."[5]

The high temperature, often combined with high humidity, has impressed and oppressed inhabitants of the city since its founding. Ashbel Smith, for example, a leader in Texas medicine, education, and politics, wrote in 1838, "Heat is so severe during the middle of the day, that most of us lie in the shade and pant."[6] The editor of the *Morning Star* may well have expressed the complaint for all Houstonians when he commented in 1839:

> Oh for a good cold norther! one of your real old-fashioned ones, early though it be for them. We are tired of gazing upon burning, brassy skies; upon hot looking clouds, and the parched earth. We are weary of throwing open all the doors and windows, and placing ourself in the draught, in hopes to catch one breath of cool air to cool our fevered brow. We are weary of staying at home in the day time, lest we should be scorched with the intense heat; and of being obliged to remain within our mosquitoe-bar at night, lest we be devoured by the mosquitoes. We are weary of feeling the perspiration coursing down our cheeks as we sit at our desk puzzling our brains, or rummaging over the mails, in order to present something interesting to our readers. We are weary of this lassitude, and languor; this constant relaxation of mind and body, which incapacitates us alike for mental and physical labor. We want something to brace us up. And what is better for that purpose than a good cold norther?[7]

Even with the relief of air conditioning, which spread throughout the city after its introduction at the Second National Bank in 1923, the heat can still be impressive, especially to visitors. As A. D. George, advertising controller of the *Guardian* (of Manchester and London), expressed it, "Everything is so new, clean, fresh looking, as compared with the cluttered, gray life in England. But it's rather warm outside, isn't it?"[8] It is for good reason that Houston has been the leading market for air conditioning in the past decade.

During the heat wave that struck the entire Southwest in the summer of 1980, Houston broke 100 degrees on fourteen consecutive days and recorded a record high of 107 degrees. Water resources dropped, which required a restriction on outdoor usage except from midnight to 5:00 A.M. Foundations and walls cracked due to the contraction of the notorious gumbo soil.[9] C. J. Haynes summed up Bayou City summer weather with a verse sent to *Houston Post* writer George Fuermann:

> When Satan came to Houston,
> He beat a quick retreat;
> He loved its wicked people,
> But he couldn't stand the heat.[10]

The cityscape southward from the Humble observation floor portrayed not only the nature of the climate but also the extreme flatness of the land. It appears almost as if Houston stands on a level surface—a tangible illustration of August Lösch's contention that, because of economic advantages, metropolitan centers would develop on a uniform plane.[11] This, of course, is not quite the case. Houston, located in the south-central portion of Harris County, is fifty-five feet above sea level, with the land sloping about five feet per mile to the southeast.[12] There are seven active geological fault lines crisscrossing the urban area. These have provided some slight tremors, which have caused cracks in roads and buildings but no earthquake of significance. Slippage is one inch or less per year but becoming worse.[13] Historically, Buffalo Bayou as well as various gullies and small bayous which cut through the city, some now filled over, served as barriers to development, but these were minor. Houston today can expand physically in any direction, the ultimate limits being only Galveston Bay, the Gulf of Mexico, neighboring cities, and the imagination of the inhabitants.

Under such circumstances there has existed a temptation to spread, or sprawl, as it may be interpreted. In 1980 Houston encompassed within its boundaries a little over 556 square miles. Its population of 1,573,847 gained 656 people per week, placing it fifth in the nation. Such a ranking is misleading. The metropolitan population, including Harris, Brazoria, Fort Bend, Liberty, Montgomery, and Waller counties, which numbered 2,286,247 in 1975, was 2,891,146, ninth among urban centers of the country.[14]

The city, nevertheless, is the largest in Texas and in the South. Its growth pattern, which parallels that of the state, suggests three major chronological divisions: 1836–1875, a period of frontier life; 1876–1930, an era of transition; and 1930–1980, a time of rapid growth. In the first phase the city served an expanding hinterland and there was some improvement in transportation facilities, but only in the second period did Houston gain a semblance of "maturity," a point which Walt W. Rostow defines as "the period when a society has effectively applied the range of (then) modern technology to the bulk of its resources."[15] Although Rostow was referring to the society of a nation, his model of development, as outlined in *The Stages of Economic Growth*, possesses some application to the growth of an individual city. Houston, for instance, at the beginning of the twentieth century, gained this maturity with a rapid rise in bank deposits, the full development of its railroads and ship channel, the discovery of nearby oil fields, and a new, more efficient municipal government which solved a major problem of fresh water supply. For the Bayou City, in Rostow's terms, it was a time of both "maturity" and "take-off." It was, in essence, a moment when the develop-

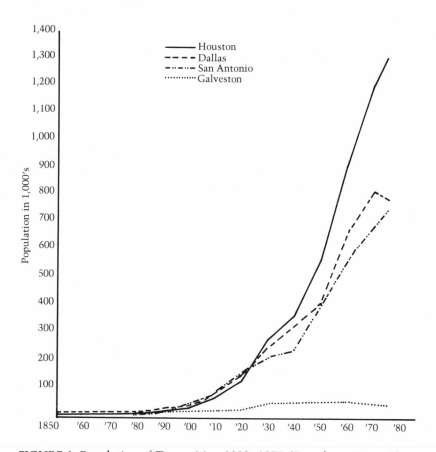

FIGURE 1. Population of Texas cities, 1850–1975. (Data from *Texas Almanac, 1978–1979*, pp. 189–192, and Bureau of the Census, *County and City Data Book, 1977*, p. 756.)

ment of the past, the discoveries of the present, and current knowledge converged to form the foundation of the modern metropolis. During the third period of development, especially after the 1930's, Houston underwent rapid expansion; a time of "post-maturity" and "high mass-consumption" as Rostow would phrase it.

In the following study, I am most concerned with causative aspects, essentially: Why and how has Houston grown? This, of course, involves many factors—geography, natural resources, technology, population, climate, and civic leadership. In a broad sense, as with most history, the study portrays the interaction of humans and their environment over a span of time. Unfortunately, because of the multifaceted nature of urban life, the biography of a city runs a danger of becoming, according to Roy Lubove, "a kind of historical variety store."[16] Somehow, a writer must avoid the Scylla of attempting to include everything and thus failing to emphasize the major themes, and the Charybdis of following too narrow an outline and thereby missing the rich variety of urban existence. This study, consequently, attempts primarily to analyze and relate those events which have contributed to the development of the city and, at the same time, to offer some minor reference to other incidents which have enriched urban life in Houston.

1

The Town of Houston

On August 30, 1836, the editor of the *Telegraph and Texas Register*, published by Gail and Thomas H. Borden in Columbia, Texas, commented: "We call the attention of our readers to the advertisement of the town of Houston, by Messrs. A. C. & J. K. Allen. . . . From all we can learn, the locatin they have selected possesses as many advantages as any other interior town in Texas, and on account of the easy access to Galveston and the facility in procuring timber, as well as its central position, this town, no doubt, will be a rival for the present seat of Government in Texas."[1]

The unusually detailed and lengthy advertisement the editor referred to read as follows:

The Town of Houston

Situated at the head of navigation, on the West bank of Buffalo Bayou, is now for the first time brought to public notice because, until now, the proprietors were not ready to offer it to the public, with the advantages of capital and improvements.

The town of Houston is located at a point on the river which must ever command the trade of the largest and richest portion of Texas. By reference to the map, it will be seen that the trade of San Jacinto, Spring Creek, New Kentucky and the Brazos, above and below Fort Bend, must necessarily come to this place, and will warrant the employment of at least *One Million Dollars* of capital, and when the rich lands of this country shall be settled, a trade will flow to it, making it, beyond all doubt, the great interior commercial emporium of Texas.

The town of Houston is distant 15 miles from the Brazos river, 30 miles, a little North of East, from San Felipe, 60 miles from Washington, 40 miles from Lake Creek, 30 miles South

West from New Kentucky, and 15 miles by water and 8 or 10 by land above Harrisburg. Tide water runs to this place and the lowest depth of water is about six feet. Vessels from New Orleans or New York can sail without obstacle to this place, and steamboats of the largest class can run to Galveston Island in 8 or 10 hours, in all seasons of the year. It is but a few hours sail down the bay, where one may take an excursion of pleasure and enjoy the luxuries of fish, foul, oysters and sea bathing. Galveston harbor being the only one in which vessels drawing a great draft of water can navigate, must necessarily render the Island the great naval and commercial depot of the country.

The town of Houston must be the place where arms, ammunitions and provisions for the government will be stored, because, situated in the very heart of the country, it combines security and the means of easy distribution, and a national armory will no doubt very soon be established at this point.

There is no place in Texas more healthy, having an abundance of excellent spring water, and enjoying the sea breeze in all its freshness. No place in Texas possesses so many advantages for building, having Pine, Ash, Cedar and Oak in inexhaustible quantities; also the tall and beautiful Magnolia grows in abundance. In the vicinity are fine quarries of stone.

Nature appears to have designated this place for the future seat of Government. It is handsome and beautifully elevated, salubrious and well watered, and now in the very heart or centre of population, and will be so for a length of time to come. It combines two important advantages: a communication with the coast and foreign countries, and with the different portions of the Republic. As the country shall improve, railroads will become in use, and will be extended from this point to the Brazos, and up the same, also from this up to the head waters of San Jacinto, embracing that rich country, and in a few years the whole trade of the upper Brazos will make its way into Galveston Bay through this channel.

Preparations are now making to erect a water Saw Mill, and a large Public House for accommodation, will soon be opened. Steamboats now run in this river, and will in a short time commence running regularly to the Island.

The proprietors offer the lots for sale on moderate terms to those who desire to improve them, and invite the public to examine for themselves.[2]

Augustus C. Allen and John K. Allen, whose names appeared at the bottom of the advertisement, had arrived from New York in 1832. After a brief sojourn in San Augustine, the two brothers settled in Nacogdoches where they occupied themselves mainly with land speculation. Augustus, a small, "taciturn and settled" man, married Charlotte M. Baldwin, a tall, commanding woman who possessed the strong face of a pioneer. With his younger brother, John, described as intellectual, suave, "bright," and "quick," Augustus invested her inheritance money.[3] Their vocation must have been worthwhile, for Ashbel Smith wrote about John: "In regard to Major Allen, I have lived in the same house with him, most of the time since my arrival here. He is an astute financier, I believe his house and honesty can be safely depended upon. He is a leading member of Congress, and stands very high in the confidence of the Government. His private wealth is very great, his landed interest immense, as great perhaps or greater than that of any other man in this country."[4]

Following the Texas revolution, in which the Allens had apparently served as supply agents, they entered the scramble to attain the seat of government, a bright prospect for speculation since the land around the capital would certainly increase in value. After failing to purchase Harrisburg because the title was fouled in litigation, the brothers, on August 26, 1836, bought from Elizabeth E. Parrott, wife of T. F. L. Parrott and widow of John Austin, the south half of the lower league granted to her by her late husband. They paid $5,000 total, but only $1,000 of this in cash; notes made up the remainder.[5]

The site, at the head of tide on Buffalo Bayou, reflected a particularly shrewd choice. Pioneer Texans needed supplies from the outside, and the cheapest manner of transport was by water. Location of a town on a navigable stream, therefore, was helpful. But most Texas rivers were unreliable. They meandered; they had too much water in the spring and not enough at other times; they possessed log jams, snags, sand bars, and muddy water. Buffalo Bayou, however, was exceptional. It was comparatively deep, fairly wide, clear with substantial banks, and relatively constant in depth. Moreover, it ran east and west, pointing to the heart of the fertile Brazos valley.[6] It had greater potential usefulness than did the Brazos River itself. As Nan Thompson Ledbetter has explained: "The Brazos is an eccentric river. In flood stage it sweeps its precious water out to the Gulf, washing out crops and buildings on the bottom lands; yet mostly, between these rampages, the muddy Brazos winds slowly down its flat valley, a river without much water."[7]

Buffalo Bayou, moreover, flowed into Galveston Bay, and Galveston Island at the mouth of the bay offered one of the more promising harbors of the Texas coast. All was not perfect, however. Red Fish Bar, an oyster reef stretching across the bay, and Clopper's Bar, a sand bar at the confluence of the bayou and the San Jacinto River near Morgan's Point, obstructed traffic.[8] There could be, in addition, some doubt concerning the usefulness of Galveston. Stephen F. Austin, who had recommended a customs house for the island in 1825, shortly had misgivings due to the lack of timber and the tendency to flood.[9] Galveston lay at the mercy of the sea. "In the month of October [1837], during the storm which laid waste the whole southern coast, from Mobile to Vera Cruz and still further south, it was my lot to witness vessels of considerable tonnage floating over the foundations of the future city," commented an unknown writer for the *Hesperian* in 1838.[10]

For the Allens, nonetheless, the area seemed promising. Augustus Allen invested in Galveston land, once tried to buy Morgan's Point, and together with his brother attempted to purchase Harrisburg on Buffalo Bayou, a town destroyed by Santa Anna during the Texas revolution, before establishing Houston eight miles farther upstream.[11] Located at the "head of navigation" on the bayou, Houston was at a break in transportation—a point where goods required transfer from one mode of transport to another, in this case, from steamboat to ox-wagon. Since, as it evolved, there often occurred a change in ownership and storage of goods at this same place, Houston formed a commercial break, which, according to the theory of Charles H. Cooley, is most important as a foundation for later manufacturing and political development.[12]

The brothers named the town after their friend and hero of the moment, Sam Houston, the victorious general at the decisive battle of San Jacinto and a leading candidate for president of the republic. Although there exists some legend about the selection of the name—Charlotte Allen at a dinner saying, "General Houston, I shall claim the honor of naming the place, and I shall call the new town after the gentleman who sits at the head of the table, or 'Houston'"; and the gallant general replying, "May our hostess, Mrs. Allen, live to see the city of Houston the [first] city of Texas and the pride of the Lone Star Republic!"—it was undeniably a clever choice.[13] Legend

FIGURE 2. This is the earliest map of Houston extant, and it illustrates the grid pattern of the streets. Various parts of the map had to be darkened for reproduction purposes, and part of the upper portion has been torn away. The map bears a printed date of 1836 and a handwritten notation dated January 18, 1837. (Copied from the original in the Texas Room of the Houston Public Library.)

also holds that Augustus Allen, while seated on a bank of the bayou, sketched a plat, using his top hat for a table.[14] Be that as it may, the brothers hired Gail Borden and Thomas H. Borden to survey and map the site. Moses Lapham, an employee of the Bordens, did most of the work, apparently, and received for his effort mainly a "bad case of chills."[15] Typically, as in other such enterprises, the surveyors platted the site in gridiron fashion with broad streets running parallel and perpendicular to the bayou. Although it sometimes sacrificed beauty for order, the grid pattern, popularized by Philadelphia, was most efficient for commercial purposes. As in many other towns, Houston originally possessed a Water Street along the riverfront.[16]

With their site purchased, named, and being mapped, the promoters, with John Allen as a member of the Texas legislature, pushed for the selection of Houston as the temporary seat of government—an action that could bless the embryonic town with immediate success. They boomed it as healthy, beautiful, plentiful in food and natural resources, and in an advantageous location for Texas and for communication with the United States. More important, perhaps, they offered to the government free lots and buildings to be rented on credit.[17] At a session on November 30, 1836, the forty-nine–member legislature chose Houston on the fourth ballot over fifteen contenders, "whereupon, the Speaker proclaimed that the town of Houston was duly selected by joint vote of both houses of congress as the seat of government for the republic of Texas until the year 1840."[18] The speculators' dream thus became reality and the immediate future success of the enterprise was ensured.

Migration to the "City of Houston" and "The Present Seat of Government of the Republic of Texas," as the Allens' advertisement had now been altered to read, began around the first of the year 1837.[19] One of the early arrivals was Francis R. Lubbock, who with John Allen traveled on board the *Laura*, supposedly the first steamboat to penetrate the bayou above Harrisburg and reach the townsite. As Lubbock recalled in *Six Decades in Texas*, navigation up the bayou to Harrisburg was easy, with "plenty of water and breadth," but it required three days to push through the various snags and other obstructions to reach Houston. About "the first of January, 1837," Lubbock wrote: "Just before reaching our destination a party of us, becoming weary of the steamer, took a yawl and concluded we would hunt for the city. So little evidence could we see of a landing that we passed by the site and run into White Oak Bayou, realizing that we must have passed the city when we struck in the brush. We then backed down the bayou, and by close observation discovered a road or street laid off from the water's edge. Upon landing we found stakes and footprints, indicating that we were in the town tract."[20] Upon further inspection he discovered a few tents, one of which served as a saloon, and several small houses under construction.[21]

Although Sam Houston, who arrived April 26, 1837, may have been biased, he thought the site to be "far superior" to others for business and government. "On the 20th of January," he wrote, "a small log cabin & 12 persons were all that distinguished it from the adjacent forests, and now there are upwards of 100 houses finished, and going up rapidly (some of them fine frame buildings) and 1500 people, all actively engaged in their respective pursuits."[22] The town of Houston, Texas, conceived for land speculation, its site chosen in part through logic and in part through chance, with the unusual advantage of being a political focal point, thus began life as a frontier community.

2

The Commercial Emporium, 1836-1875

The stimulus provided by the presence of the government, which attracted not only politicians but also businessmen to the Bayou City, was of short duration. Prompted by the bad weather, mud, sickness, discomfort, and perhaps the desire for fresh land speculation, legislators even in October 1837 began discussing a move.[1] As one man, Kelsey H. Douglass, explained to his wife, "I find this the most miserable place in the world we had bad weather to come Down in and Iam Sum what un well at presant"; and in another letter, "I am badly situated hear the room that I occupy has no fire and I all most frose Last night."[2] The government early in 1839 appointed a joint commission to locate a new site, and in a few months the *Morning Star* noted the selection of a village to the west populated by only four families.[3] The editor of this Houston newspaper grumbled through the summer that the expenses at the new site would be high, the selection commission was illegal, the only reason to move was for "making speculation," and the new location lacked wood, water, and accessibility.[4] In spite of arguments, however, the government moved.

Somewhat bitterly and somewhat in jest the editor commented in August: "But let it not be supposed that we in Houston are going to sit down like children, and cry because we have dropped our bread and butter, although it *has* fallen on the 'buttered side.' Not we, nothing can be farther from our thoughts than this. We *will* have a great city, in spite of them, and if they dont behave very well up there in Austin, we will *cut off their supplies*, and throw them upon corn bread and beef."[5]

In September, with the removal of the furniture and the archives, the government completely abandoned Houston for the new location. Sadly, the *Morning Star* noted that the Capitol Building, constructed by the Allens to house the officers of the republic, stood "desolated and empty" like a "banquet hall deserted."[6] The town consequently was left to its own resources, to live or die on the basis of its commercial usefulness to the region of south Texas.

Few statistics exist for the period to analyze business activity thoroughly, but it seems obvious that trade, rather than manufacturing, was most important for Houston. There was, nonetheless, some manufacturing throughout the period. In 1841 the *Telegraph and Texas Register* noted two new sawmills and a brick establishment on the outskirts of town.[7] The following year the editor reported that bricks previously made in Houston were not too satisfactory, but that those currently produced by N. K. Kellum compared favorably to any that could be imported.[8] Schmidt and Wilson demonstrated foundry skills by casting a 218-pound bell for the St. Vincent de Paul Roman Catholic Church in town; the *Telegraph and Texas Register* thought the bell the finest piece of such workmanship in the republic.[9] Shortly thereafter, J. Wilson opened a brass foundry and fabricating shop for the making of stills, bells, stirrups, and spurs.[10] A saddlery, lard-oil factory, corn mill, pottery establishment, and even a bookbinder offered services during the 1840's.[11] In 1850 J. Thompson started a sash and blind shop with machinery powered by horses, and in 1860 John Kennedy erected a flour mill that could produce twenty-four barrels per day.[12]

The flour mill continued to produce during the Civil War, a period which inspired the manufacture of cartridges at the courthouse and local production of candles, drugs, leather goods, and printer's ink.[13] In 1869 the Houston City Mills, a textile factory which employed eighty people and paid $1,500 per month in wages, began production in a three-story building on the southern bank of the bayou near the eastern edge of the town. The mill operated fifty looms on the first floor, 2,200 spindles on the second, and a wool department on the third. An eighty-horsepower engine provided power for the whole factory.[14] The Eureka Mills, five miles northwest of Houston and owned mainly by Houstonians, began operation in 1870. It was a $125,000 investment and used 1,700 pounds of cotton per day.[15] In addition, after years of dreaming of such an event, the people began to enjoy gas lighting in 1868. By producing gas from oyster shells and coal, the Houston Gas Light Company supplied churches, hotels, and private homes; the city street lamps were only occasionally in service because of disputes over the gas rates.[16]

Manufacturing in Houston, however, was still a secondary aspect of business life. Harris County listed only twenty-one manufacturers in 1860 and sixty-four in 1870. In 1860 they employed 158 persons and added $240,868 in value to products, while in 1870 they employed 583 persons and added $305,359 in value to manufactured items.[17] In contrast, the *Tri-Weekly Telegraph* reported for Houston, in 1860, 150 to 175 mercantile establishments, including 25 dry goods houses, 30 retail groceries, 5 hardware stores, 10 warehouses, 15 commission merchants, 5 drugstores, 20 mixed wholesale and retail merchandise houses, and 3 bookstores.[18] The sources of the period—newspapers, journals, and letters—all emphasize the commercial nature of activity. In Houston, therefore, as elsewhere on the frontier, commerce was the "nexus of urbanization."[19]

The general pattern of trade, although influenced by continually improved transport facilities, remained much the same from 1836 to 1875. The merchants, who occupied a middle position, exchanged a variety of goods, including furniture, groceries, clothing, hardware, farm implements, weapons, books, medicine, soap, jewelry, and liquor, for the products of the countryside, mainly cotton, hides, lumber, corn, unrefined sugar, livestock, and pelts. Though most merchants maintained stores, advertised in the newspapers, and sold on credit, there existed also an active auction business until about 1865. Items of all kinds—real estate, livestock, dry goods, "segars," books, and slaves—appeared at the auctions held by such firms as Obrien and Everrette, Hedenberg and Vedder, and Davison and De Cordova.[20] Auctioning, as in early New York, probably contributed to Houston's attractiveness as a market.[21]

The trading season lasted approximately from September until April, with country products moving by ox-wagon, and later by railroad, to Houston after the harvest. Bought by Houston merchants, the goods then traveled down Buffalo Bayou on shallow-draft steamboats to Galveston for transfer to oceangoing vessels. During the off-season months, from May to August, merchants often journeyed eastward to replenish stocks and arrange for shipment at such places as Boston, New York, Baltimore, Mobile, and New Orleans. Observations from the period reflect this rhythm of commerce. In May 1839, for example, the editor of the *Morning Star* commented: "Weather dry, hot and oppressive. Streets dusty and disagreeable. Money scarce and getting scarcer. Business dull, and growing duller. Loafers have increased, and are increasing, and ought to be diminished. District Court in session—crimes and criminals are undergoing its scrutiny—hope it will have some effect on the loafers. Such are the principal items about this city at present—hope to have something more agreeable in our next."[22]

The following September the editor noted, "Our city is quite dull; money scarce; and when obtained, of comparatively little value, both on account of its depreciation and of the high prices of everything."[23] In October, with an unusually late business season, he complained, "We do not remember to have seen duller times in Houston than at present. Business seems almost at a stand."[24] Ashbel Smith, however, observed in December, "Business is become very brisk in Houston, and is much greater than in any previous year."[25] During April 1840, the editor of the *Morning Star*, after commenting on the brisk trade, stated with apparent satisfaction, "Houston is advancing with giant strides to her destined greatness."[26]

At moments of heavy trading, remarks like the following were common: "Hundreds of baggage wagons have been constantly arriving from the upper country, and return loaded with merchandise"; "Our streets are often thronged with wagons"; "For the last three or four weeks all our streets in the business part of the city have been so blocked up with wagons and teams that it is almost impossible to pass between them, even on foot, in any direction"; and "Main street was, for some distance, lined with ox teams from the country."[27] The commentary of the *Tri-Weekly Telegraph* about warehousemen reflected the same seasonal phenomenon. During the summer, according to the editor, the men became fleshy and assumed a "genteel, indolent, lazy sort of way," but with the rush of work in the fall some appeared as if "drawn through a knot hole," and "as for getting a civil word out of them, it is out of the question."[28]

The hinterland served by Houston mainly stretched eighty to one hundred miles toward the west and northwest to Bastrop, La Grange, Navasota, Caldwell, and other small settlements. About Milam County in 1840, Susan Turham McCown recalled, for example: "We had to send to Houston for any supplies the woods did not furnish. As we raised nothing to sell, we had to hunt for wild honey and all sorts of skins of wild animals that had any value as fur, and these, with buffalo tallow, were our only medium of exchange. When the trader reached Houston and began to barter, his first purchases were for powder and lead, next some calico, some sugar and coffee, and always some castor oil and rhubarb for the children."[29]

Typical of the successful merchants of early Houston was Thomas W. House, an Englishman who arrived in 1838. He tried his hand at baking and making candy, lent money as a sideline as early as 1840, and eventually became a dry goods merchant, cotton factor, banker, and investor in railroads and public utilities.[30] His business correspondence reveals the nature of his work. Thomas P. Collins in Crockett, Texas, for example, wrote to arrange an exchange of eleven bales of cotton for small amounts of flour, sugar, whisky, iron castings, dry goods, and percussion caps. Collins expected to travel to Houston to pick up the items.[31] Similar letters came from Bastrop, Caldwell, Nolansville, Cameron, Springfield, and Columbus. One irrepressible man, E. N. Clarke, of Cat Spring, wanted to know the amount of his two-year-old debt, because he was changing his business back to Houston from San Felipe and needed many items.[32] The business letters disclosed that House purchased goods from New York, Boston, and New Orleans, but that he shipped his cotton to Liverpool, England. He first explored such cotton shipment in 1838 and was involved in it by the late 1850's.[33] During the Civil War, he avoided Confederate currency, amassed gold reserves in England, and attempted to run cotton through Matamoros on British vessels. After the war, he resumed shipments to Liverpool and broadened his interests in banking, railroads, and utility companies. At his death in 1880 he left an estate of $1 million.[34]

Sharing the period with House was another merchant of similar nature—William Marsh Rice. He arrived in Houston in 1839, worked temporarily as a barkeeper, established a general store, became the most prominent cotton factor in Texas, and invested in real estate, railroads, and local enterprises. He possessed a fortune of $750,000 in 1860 and emerged a millionaire from the Civil War, after running cotton through Mexico. Although he left Houston in 1863, he later provided for the founding of Rice Institute in the city. He is famous, moreover, as the unfortunate victim in a sensational murder at the turn of the century.[35]

Rice and other merchants depended, of course, on cotton as the main item of commerce, and they once presented several silver cups and a gold one for the first cotton of the season that came to Houston.[36] The amount of cotton moving in trade is difficult to assess because of the lack of statistics, but the *Telegraph and Texas Register* claimed in 1845 that Houston had received more than 14,000 bales the preceding year. Five years earlier, shipments had amounted to scarcely 1,000 bales.[37] Shipments in 1854 equaled 38,923 bales; in 1857, 46,220 bales; in 1860, 115,854 bales; and, with the pinch of war, 70,854 bales in 1861.[38] The Civil War, of course, with the Union blockade of the coast and the Confederate need for foodstuffs, disrupted the whole pattern of trade and also cotton cultivation. Hearing that farmers were planning to grow cotton, the *Weekly Telegraph* pleaded: "We appeal to the patriotism of the country to plant Corn! Corn!! Corn!!! Let us have corn to feed the soldiers, to feed the people. Let cotton be let alone while our soldiers are hungry."[39] The end of the fighting, however, brought a seemingly quick return to the normal trade pattern:

We are glad to see so much activity and bustle in our streets and among our merchants. It is a sure indication that business is rapidly reviving. Almost every day we see wagon trains in our streets loaded with cotton, and goods are being packed up in bales and boxes and those trains loaded back to the country. It is difficult to pass on either walk on Main street without finding it obstructed with packages of goods just being received or sent away. We are assured that some of our merchants are making sales to the amount of a thousand dollars daily.[40]

Since commerce was all-important to Houston, it was inevitable that merchants, such as Rice and House, would be interested in the improvement of transportation facilities. The businessmen thus invested in roads, railways, and the clearing of Buffalo Bayou as a necessary part of successful enterprise. As explained by a newspaperman, "Of what advantage would it be to us if our streets could be paved with granite, our sidewalks laid in Mosaic work, if the city were surrounded with a morass that excluded the trade of the interior settlements!"[41]

The roads for the most part were dirt pathways, largely unimproved, marked by wheel ruts and hoofprints left by previous travelers, and sometimes of uncertain destination. Frederick Law Olmsted, journalist, traveler, and landscape architect, journeyed through the area in 1854 and noted: "We were unable to procure at Houston, any definite information with regard to our proposed route. The known roads thence, are those that branch northward and westward from their levee, and so thoroughly within lines of business does local knowledge lie, that the eastern shore is completely terra incognita." Olmsted nevertheless traveled to Harrisburg, but "taking a road here, by direction, which, after two miles, only ran 'up a tree,' we were obliged to return for more precise information." By following a trail that continually broke into cow paths, he finally reached the San Jacinto Battlegrounds and Lynchburg.[42] His comments underscore the direction of Houston's trading area, but if the unhappy Abbé Domenech can be trusted, even the known roads in that direction were not much better.

In the summer of 1848 the Abbé traveled by "poste," an open wagon drawn by four horses, from Houston to San Antonio. It left Houston at a gallop and proceeded over Buffalo Bayou on a bridge six or seven feet wide, "constructed of two planks and branches of trees joined together." About this experience, he wrote:

We crossed this bridge at full speed. I was filled with alarm; for the slightest accident would have precipitated us into the river. I had not, however, much time for reflection; for the jumping and jolting of the waggon knocked me about so, and put me in such imminent fear of capsize, that I laid hold of the vehicle with the desperation of a shipwrecked mariner clinging to a rock despite the waves which dash about and buffet him on all sides. In a short time, however, I relaxed my grasp, bruised and exhausted, and abandoned myself an unresisting victim to the jolts and tossings of the waggon.[43]

The roads, according to this French missionary, had been marked by notches on trees, but stumps had been left in the pathway, "with the intention, it would appear, of insuring a jolt here and there." Through forests the "poste" traveled at full tilt, careening off stumps and trees, but on the hot, shadeless prairie it moved only at a slow pace. The Abbé was none too pleased with that, but he became altogether miserable after being dumped into a ravine when the driver fell asleep, tumbled head over heels in the wagon when a panther leaped on the foremost horse, and soaked during a rainstorm when a female traveler held erect an umbrella which "sent down upon my neck and knees two torrents of ice-cold water."[44]

Although horses, as with the Abbé's "poste," and mules were used, ox-teams hauled much of the commerce of Texas. Oxen cost less than draft horses, could exist on prairie grass, possessed broad hoofs that did not sink so deeply in the mud, and with decent roads could cover ten to fifteen miles a day.[45] According to one observer:

The loading of a wagon was regulated by the number of oxen composing the team; five yoke carrying five bales [of cotton] and six yoke six bales, and so on. A round trip [Washington County to Houston and back] was made in good weather and good roads in fourteen days. And on bad roads in bad weather it took nearly a month to make the trip. Each wagoner was provided with a complete camping outfit and always took with him a Spanish pony to ride when driving his oxen. In this way he made towpaths along each side of the main road, as in the case on canals.[46]

The teamsters, apparently, did not rush their work. They set up camp an hour or so before dark, slept until the sun had long arisen, and began the day's drive at ten to ten-thirty in the morning.[47] The driving, which required some skill, was on occasion handled by blacks. According to Ferdinand Roemer, "It almost seemed to me as if they understood it better than the whites . . ."[48] Accompanied sometimes with hallooing in the streets and the cracking of whips, the wagoners reached Houston, deposited their freight with the appropriate merchant, and proceeded to a wagon camp until time to reload for a return trip.[49] The wagon camps, of which Houston had at least two, generally consisted of an acre or so of land, enclosed by covered stalls on two sides for the teams, and cabins on the other two sides for the drivers. A large well and a jug of whisky provided by the management made these yards a mecca for the wagoner.[50]

Not only planters occupied the roads, but also freight and stage lines. The Texas Stage Line, for example, offered service from Houston to Richmond, a one-day trip, for $5.00, in 1839.[51] Smith and Jones started a Houston-Austin line in 1841 and R. T. Kane opened stage service to Washington, Texas, in 1843.[52] Tarbox and Brown advertised twice-weekly connections with Austin in three days at $15 cost and six cents per pound on baggage over thirty pounds. This firm, one of the more successful of the period, later offered trips to San Antonio and tri-weekly service to Austin.[53] For the most part, no regular firms handled freight; it was an off-season occupation for farmers with idle teams and wagons. A. M. Gentry and Company, however, did advertise express and forwarding service for letters and packages between Texas and the United States or Europe, a service offered, incidentally, by most merchants.[54] The cost of freight, of course, varied with the times, ranging from $10 to $15 per hundredweight in 1839, to $5.00 in 1842, and $2.00 to $2.25 in 1856 for items moved between Houston and Austin.[55] In 1840 a pound of coffee cost forty-five to fifty cents in Houston and one dollar in Austin, due in large part certainly to the high cost of transport.[56]

One cause of expense was the obstruction of the roads by mud and water, especially in the winter months when, unfortunately, much of the freight was dispatched. The *Morning Star* noted in 1842, for instance, that although teams arrived daily, they could travel only six to eight miles per day. They had to wait at flooding streams eight to ten days, and one wagon from Independence had been so detained for thirty days.[57] Wagons sank one to two feet in mud in bad spots and at times rain inundated the prairie. In 1846, sheets of water, two to three feet deep and four to five miles wide, covered the Richmond road.[58] The Washington road, too, could be "literally a bog for miles."[59] In the Brazos bottom on the road from Houston, Ferdinand Roemer, who traveled in Texas from December

1845 to April 1847, described a day's trip of six miles in which the wagons stuck in the black mud about twenty times and had to be unloaded five times in order to free them.[60]

ιhe merchants of Houston, well aware of the problem, lacked sufficient money for much improvement.[61] They nonetheless demonstrated interest in turnpikes and road betterment and at a mass meeting in 1846 resolved to improve conditions.[62] Little happened, however, until 1849. After losing Austin trade to a rival town, Lavaca (now Port Lavaca), Houston began improvement of roads toward Montgomery and Washington counties, financed in part by local funds and, apparently, by a loan from New York.[63] Most of the people concerned agreed that the roads should have ditches and that dirt and logs should form causeways over the often-flooded prairie. A minority contended that, if dirt were piled up, it would only make deeper mud, but observation of dry hillocks rounded by water disproved the allegation. After some experimentation, the road workers devised a primitive grading machine consisting of two seventeen-foot-long planks hinged to form a wedge and shod with iron. Pulled by oxen, the grader, with six to eight successive furrows, swept the dirt to the center of the roadbed and left a wide, deep ditch. Six completed miles of the Washington road cost $1,500.[64]

Discussion about a road to be made of two-inch oak or three-inch pine planks, at an estimated cost of $1,000 per mile, started in 1850. A committee, including Mayor Francis Moore, Jr., investigated, and in May a group of businessmen, among them Paul Bremond, William J. Hutchins, William M. Rice, B. A. Shepherd, Thomas M. Bagby, A. S. Ruthven, and Thomas W. House, formed the Houston Plank Road Company. It possessed eminent domain for a fifty-yard-wide roadbed to the Brazos River, $150,000 capitalization, and the right to charge a toll.[65] Although by September $50,000 had been collected in subscriptions at home and in loans from Boston and New York, growing interest in railroads apparently brought about the cancellation of the project.[66] Conditions remained unchanged and after a rain in 1872 the *Weekly Telegraph* echoed the old complaint: "And the roads! They are indescribable. If anything, those leading into the city, from the prairies, are equisitely and excrutiatingly horrid."[67]

The problem, of course, did not halt at the city limits but continued to the heart of the business district. "Rain! why it falls in torrents," wrote the Methodist cleric C. H. Brooks. "And muddy! whoppee!! If there is a town in Texas more muddy than this pleas tell the Bishop not to send me to it."[68] Mud did have a certain egalitarian influence, however, as the *Tri-Weekly Telegraph* observed:

"The light, but continued rains have thoroughly moistened the soil and worked it up into as beautiful a loblolly as ever a poor wagoner hated. For a day or two, the 'kid glove gentry' were able to pick their way from brick to brick, and from one dry stepping place to another, but at last all hands came down to the same level, and heavy mud boots, etc. became the order of the day."[69]

Mud, naturally, has a dry counterpart—dust. The dirt, pulverized by wagon wheels to a powder, would blow in clouds through the town.[70] Houstonians attempted at various times to drain off excess water, to lay the dust by sprinkling, and to pave the streets with white oyster shells. In February 1858, the *Tri-Weekly Telegraph* suggested shell paving, and by the end of the first week in April the townspeople had raised $2,000 for the ill-fated project. In July the shell on Main Street made the thoroughfare handsome and smooth,[71] but in September dust became all-pervasive: "The amount of dust now prevailing in the city is enormous. We have dust everywhere. Dust in the street, dust in the air, dust in the houses. The streets are filled with dust. We eat dust, breathe dust, walk in dust, sit in dust. Dust rises in clouds on every puff of air, and floats about as though it had no gravity. It settles on everything. . . . If never before, our dusty citizens can now realize the meaning of the words dust thou art, and unto dust thou shalt return."[72]

The following spring the editor of the *Tri-Weekly Telegraph* complained: "Something will soon have to be done to lay the dust on the shell road. At present the glare of the shells is almost blinding. A good sprinkling twice a day would help the street amazingly."[73] But the nuisance of mud and dust did not abate until the latter part of the century, when better drainage and paving became effective.

Meanwhile, the streets caused additional problems. The numerous gullies and bayous required the construction and maintenance of bridges, beginning in 1838 and continuing thereafter.[74] In 1839 individual merchants installed sidewalks, and later an ordinance prompted other Main Street businessmen to do the same.[75] Stray animals—hogs, goats, cows, and dogs—roamed the streets, despite ordinances and periodic campaigns against them. "We propose," said the *Weekly Houston Telegraph* after two children had been bitten, "that every man in town contribute a dime's worth of poisoned sausage and an hour's time to the work of canine extermination tonight."[76]

For better transportation around early Houston the answer was not improved roads, but the railway, which was faster, cheaper, and much more dependable. Since Houstonians were among the first to develop railroads in the region, they brought to their town a prestige and prominence that provided not only a competitive advantage but also a foundation for manufacturing.

The legislature of the Texas republic chartered four railroad companies. In 1836 it authorized the Texas Railroad, Navigation and Banking Company for improving waterways, building railroads, and establishing a bank. Even though Augustus Allen was a charter member, the *Telegraph and Texas Register* and others opposed it because of its unlimited right of eminent domain and its banking privileges. The company advertised stock but sold none, and failed.[77] The Brazos and Galveston Railroad Company, chartered in 1838, which intended to connect the recently founded island city with the Brazos valley, inspired Augustus Allen to counter with the Houston and Brazos Rail Road Company, authorized in 1839. In order to revive Harrisburg, Andrew Briscoe surveyed a westward route in the spring of 1840, advertised for black laborers and, backed by Galvestonians who disliked Houston rivalry, received a charter for the Harrisburg Rail Road and Trading Company in 1841.[78] Meanwhile, the Houston enterprise faltered, despite a grand celebration with speeches, salutes, and blessings to mark its commencement. After constructing embankments and purchasing crossties, the Harrisburg firm also stumbled. In the end, the four companies completed nothing.[79] Around Houston capital was unavailable, and although shares were spoken for, "when the money was wanted, it was ascertained that those who had taken 'lots of shares' had nothing but *lots*, and no value for them: consequently the roads were never finished."[80]

In 1850–1851, however, Sidney Sherman, allied with a group of Boston capitalists, acquired the Harrisburg Town Company and began construction of the Buffalo Bayou, Brazos and Colorado Railway along the route earlier surveyed by the Harrisburg promoters.[81] The construction, contracted to W. J. Kyle and B. F. Terry (Civil War commander of Terry's Texas Rangers), proceeded steadily without much publicity at a cost of $18,400 per mile. As the *Telegraph and Texas Register* explained, "They talk but little and do a great deal."[82] Railroad fever spread the following year, inspiring public meetings, not just in Houston but elsewhere in Texas as well. Wagoners argued that nothing could travel so fast as trains were supposed to and that they would destroy life along the right-of-way. But Texans demanded railroads.[83]

Some recognition of the commercial threat to Houston of the Harrisburg enterprise came when advertisements in northern newspapers said that Harrisburg was the head of navigation on Buffalo

Bayou and that the railway would cause Houston to decline.[84] When the line reached the Brazos in 1856, Houstonians voted to construct a railway to tap the Buffalo Bayou, Brazos and Colorado in order to divert the traffic and thus prevent the resurgence of Harrisburg. Under the heading "Every Man for Himself and the Devil take the Hindmost," the editor of the *Weekly Telegraph* remarked, "The construction of the Tap Road will secure to Houston the '*lion's share*' of the benefits resulting from the entire cost of the Harrisburg road!"[85]

Work began on the seven-mile line on April 7, 1856, under a contract to Kyle and Terry, who utilized slave labor.[86] Although the president of the B.B.B. & C. thought it an "illiberal" act, he could not prevent it, and the Tap Road connected in October at Pierce Junction, thus robbing Harrisburg of its future.[87] Houston, which had spent $130,000 building the Tap, sold it in 1858 to a group of Brazoria planters for $172,000. They extended the rechristened Houston Tap and Brazoria into the sugar-cane area to the south, which resulted in an initial shipment of sugar and molasses to Houston over the "Sugar Road" in 1859.[88]

Paul Bremond, the promoter of the Houston and Texas Central Railroad (known as the Galveston and Red River Railroad until 1856), meanwhile began construction of a northwesterly line toward the upper Brazos. Bremond, a Houston merchant, had acquired the charter from Ebenezer Allen and turned the first spadeful of dirt for the railway on January 1, 1853. He at first planned to build to Austin but shortly turned northward because another company proposed also to connect with the capital. Due to lack of funds the H. & T.C. grew slowly. Bremond had exhausted his finances in the initial work, but was kept going with small amounts of $100 each from Thomas W. House and William J. Hutchins. He strung out his laborers to impress passing teamsters. In 1856 the H. & T.C. passed the twenty-five–mile mark at Cypress Creek and in 1858 it reached the fifty-mile mark at Hempstead.[89] The line began hauling freight while under construction and by February 1857 it had earned almost $18,000 carrying mainly cotton and passengers but also hides, pecans, turkeys, hammers, washboards, plows, and tombstones.[90] The building costs amounted to $22,650 per mile.[91]

As Bremond successfully moved into the region northwest of Houston, the Galveston, Houston and Henderson Railroad Company, chartered in 1853 and financed primarily by Galvestonians and Europeans, attempted to tap the H. & T.C. by building from Galveston to Houston. It sought to construct its line through the Bayou City, but the city council required its depot to be located on the south side of Main Street, thus preventing connection of the two railways. Seemingly, the town fathers feared that cotton from the upper Brazos would travel through Houston directly to Galveston.[92] This became a distinct possibility early in February 1860 when the first train crossed a causeway linking Galveston to the mainland. Soon there were daily runs between the two towns, with tickets costing $2.50 each for the two–and–one-half to three-hour ride. It saved about twenty hours' travel time for persons journeying inland from the island.[93] Some Houstonians still opposed a rail connection, however, asserting that it was "neither fair nor right" for Galveston to tap Houston trade at the mere expense of a "few thousands."[94] The editor of the *Tri-Weekly Telegraph*, on the other hand, after noting the concern about the possible ruin of Houston's commerce, pointed out that all trade had to flow to Galveston anyway.[95]

This was not necessarily the case. The Texas and New Orleans Railroad, originally chartered as the Sabine and Galveston Bay Railway and Lumber Company, broke ground in 1857 under A. M. Gentry but did not accomplish much until 1858.[96] In 1861 the T. & N.O. reached Beaumont, and had its potential been realized, it is possible that trade, flowing east and west, might have bypassed Galveston. Discussion about such grandiose schemes had emerged in the 1850's when Galvestonians suggested a state rail network radiating like a fan from Galveston. Houstonians supported a plan for connecting private railroads with the transcontinental lines moving east and west. The state rejected Galveston's plan and decided for Houston's in 1856.[97]

When the Civil War began, the Bayou City was quickly becoming the railroad center of south Texas. In September 1861, the Houston and Texas Central stretched over eighty miles to the northwest; the Houston Tap and Brazoria, fifty miles to the southwest; the Galveston, Houston and Henderson, fifty miles to the southeast; the Texas and New Orleans, one hundred miles to the east; and the Buffalo Bayou, Brazos and Colorado, seventy-five miles to the west. Only the Houston Tap and Brazoria and the Buffalo Bayou, Brazos and Colorado possessed a four-foot, eight–and–one-half–inch (standard) gauge; the others were all five feet, six inches between the rails.[98]

The war, however, halted railroad construction and left the Houston Tap and Brazoria in such poor condition that at the end of the fighting its owners abandoned it.[99] William J. Hutchins bought it for $500 at a sheriff's sale in 1869 and managed to transport some sugar to market, but the editor of the *Weekly Telegraph* thought he would not recover his investment in the current year. The road owed the state $402,000 when taken over by Hutchins. Texas sold it in 1870 to Masterson and Wagley of Houston who in turn sold it in 1871 to the Houston and Great Northern. It became part of the International and Great Northern in 1873.[100] In 1870 the Buffalo Bayou, Brazos and Colorado also had to be sold. It brought only $25,000 and was subject to a state lien of almost $1 million at the time. Its name was changed to Galveston, Harrisburg and San Antonio Railway the same year and it eventually became a part of the Southern Pacific.[101] The Texas and New Orleans ceased to operate during the war. It was characterized afterward as "a lifeless, and rotting and rusting apology for a railroad," and "a shameful ulcer on State enterprise."[102] The line barely kept alive in the postwar years, due to only partial operation and a series of abortive reorganizations. It was ultimately linked with other railroads, however, and the first train to New Orleans left Houston on August 29, 1880. The following year it became a part of Collis P. Huntington's growing railway empire, the Southern Pacific.[103]

Not all railroads, however, had such difficulty. The Galveston, Houston and Henderson completed a $100,000 drawbridge over Buffalo Bayou in 1865 and at last connected with the Houston and Texas Central.[104] The latter line, which recovered rapidly from the war, took up its northwesterly course again. In June 1868, its tracks reached Bryan; by November 1871, it had thrust to Corsicana; and in March 1873, it connected with the Missouri, Kansas and Texas Railway at Denison near the Texas-Oklahoma border.[105] At last rail connections existed between St. Louis and Galveston; Houston thus joined the national railroad network.[106]

Several other railroad enterprises meanwhile started. The Houston and Great Northern, chartered in 1866 to build northward, received needed motivation from William E. Dodge, who had learned of the languishing project while visiting the town. Impressed by local enterprise and the closing of stores on Sunday, Dodge, who was president of the National Temperance Society, secured the necessary capital from friends to get the project under way.[107] In 1873, however, the Great Northern merged with the International and became part of Jay Gould's southwestern rail properties.[108] The Texas Western Narrow Gauge Railroad, construction of which was to have started in 1872 after its president, Ingham S. Roberts, threw up the first spadeful of earth, was not so fortunate.[109] Due to financial problems, actual construction of the three-foot-gauge line did not begin until 1875. Thomas W. House was president at that time and the city provided bonds to pay for the enterprise.[110] Forty-two miles westward to

Patterson opened in 1877, but business proved unprofitable. After several changes in ownership and reorganization, it was abandoned in 1899.[111]

A side product of all the railroad activity was the development of a street-railway system for Houston citizens. In 1868 a horse car was operated over the Tap rails, and in April of that same year the Houston City Railroad Company began sending mule cars over its wooden tracks.[112] By 1874 eight cars were in service, and the standard complaint about public transit could be heard: "If you are a block and a half away from the street railway, a car is sure to pass and leave you a hot walk."[113]

More significant, however, was that the railroad activity extended Houston's commercial influence. As the *Weekly Telegraph* exulted in 1856, "Every mile of railroad built extends the trade of Houston a circumference of at least ten miles."[114] Railroads, especially the Houston and Texas Central, developed the north side of Buffalo Bayou and brought outsiders to town for shopping. As might be expected, each new advance in the network inspired local celebration. When the H. & T.C. reached Hempstead, for example, six to eight hundred Houstonians boarded the train, a few even on the cowcatcher, and rode to Hempstead for a jubilee. Whistles blew, cannons fired, and people cheered. There were speeches, music, and barbecue. Suggested toasts for the occasion included "The Union of the Town with the Country; produces happiness and well-being in both" and "The Memory of Wagoners and teams martyred in the mud of the Houston Prairies."[115] The ox-teams, indeed, began to fade into memory as the railways supplanted the uncertain stage and freight companies. John Washington Lockhart summarized the effect of the railroads on the region, saying: "Soon the tumble-down log cabins gave way to nice comfortable dwellings, painted, and in most instances supplied with new furniture. And many of the old settlers went so far as to have carpets on their floors. The old time wagoner, with his long string of oxen and his long whip, disappeared from the land forever."[116]

The usefulness of roads and railways, however, depended, at least in part, on a third commercial artery—Buffalo Bayou, Houston's link to the outside world until the rail connections of 1873. When the Allens advertised Houston's location as the "head of navigation," they did not precisely prevaricate, but they certainly did exaggerate. The narrow, tortuous bayou, as it existed above Harrisburg, possessed overhanging trees along the banks and dangerous snags in the water. Only small steam vessels could navigate, and these, in order to turn about, had to back into White Oak Bayou, which joined Buffalo Bayou at the foot of Main Street, or move to some other wide spot, such as Constitution Bend. Marilyn Sibley, in fact, claims that the Allens hired the *Laura* to prove the veracity of their statement.[117] Lending support to that contention, the *Telegraph and Texas Register*, under the heading "*The Fact Proved*," noted, on the arrival of this first vessel, "The steamboat Laura, captain Grayson, arrived at the city of Houston some few days since without obstruction, thus it is proved that Houston will be a port of entry."[118]

The bayou was not without beauty. As Abbé Domenech, the missionary who found the roads such a menace, observed: "Arrived at the extremity of the bay, we entered the little Buffalo river, bordered with reeds and bulrushes, in the midst of which heron, and cranes, and thousands of ducks were disputing. By-and-by the banks increasing in height, approached so near each other, and formed so many and tortuous windings that at every instant the boat was caught either by the bow or by the stern. At length the high lands appeared, covered with magnolias with their large white flowers and delicious perfumes. Grey and red squirrels leaped from branch to branch; while mocking-birds and cardinals imparted life and language to these wonderful solitudes."[119]

Millie Gray, who noticed the same beauty and narrowness of the stream, also found in the numerous floating logs a ready explanation for the steamboats she had seen with paddles on only one side rather than on both as was customary.[120] Matilda Charlotte Houstoun, moreover, discovered the channel so distressingly restricted that both the bow and stern touched the banks at the sharp turns and, while on the hurricane deck, "I was at last . . . warned of the danger of my position, by receiving a pretty smart blow from the branch of one of the trees which nearly met over the stream."[121] She found, however, the "egg-noggy" on board palatable and the gentlemen who would politely ask, "Do you liquor, ma'am?" also enjoyable.[122]

The experience of the newsmen who moved the *Telegraph and Texas Register* to the new capital in the late spring of 1837 underscored the difficulty of the water route. After going aground on Clopper's Bar, "groping" to Houston at one to two miles per hour, and then discovering their quarters as yet unfinished, the editor commented: "This place is yet merely a city in embryo, but the industry, enterprise and amount of capital which are now ministering to its greatness will soon elevate it to a prominent rank among the cities of older countries. . . . The principal objection to this place is the difficulty of access by water; the bayou above Harrisburg being so narrow, so serpentine and blocked up with snags and overhanging trees, that immense improvements will be required to render the navigation convenient for large steamboats."[123]

In 1839 a group of businessmen and boat owners assumed responsibility for clearing the bayou, formed the Buffalo Bayou Company, and selected John D. Andrews president.[124] They collected money, as much as $200 from merchants League and Andrews, contracted with L. J. Pilie, and cleaned five miles of channel so that by mid-April ships could travel from Harrisburg without fear of being snagged or losing their upper works to a tree.[125] Snags remained an ever-present danger, however, and in early 1840 two ships, *Emblem* and *Brighton*, so damaged, sank and partially blocked the channel. The *Emblem* apparently remained on the bottom, but after a public subscription, the *Brighton*, salvaged and renamed *Sam Houston*, sailed again. It sank once more, however, the next year.[126]

Official control came when the Texas congress in 1840 authorized the town to build and maintain wharves and in 1842 when it allowed city officials to inspect and remove wrecks after twenty days. With wharfage funds available, the city council established in 1841 the Port of Houston, which encompassed all wharves, landings, slips, and roads along Buffalo and White Oak bayous. Taxes on boats using the channel permitted the municipality to issue contracts for bayou maintenance in 1843 and 1844, but after 1845 the city simply allowed free wharfage to certain ship owners for keeping the bayou clear.[127]

In time Houstonians lined the bayou at the foot of Main Street with docks, but by the 1850's dredging had become necessary to combat silting in the channel. Houston and Harris County provided funds for bayou improvement and Texas allocated money for dredging Clopper's and Red Fish bars, but, nonetheless, through the Civil War only shallow-draft vessels of relatively small dimensions could utilize the bayou.[128] In 1865 a newsman advised: "Did any one ever look at the small incomparable creek called Buffalo Bayou and wonder how such a thing as a steamboat could navigate it? . . . But nevertheless, it is navigable, and is expected to be so, and would be so if the people would take hold of it and push forward an improvement—Dredge it out!—*dredge, dredge, dredge*. Five boats are now waiting for more water, or some other circumstance which will allow them to get away from the wharf."[129]

The dream of a deep-water channel sufficient for oceangoing vessels was perhaps as old as Houston itself, but it began to provoke action shortly before the Civil War. The Galveston Wharf Company, which controlled the island's waterfront and charged monopoly rates, inspired Bayou City shippers to bypass Galveston docks by transferring goods in mid-channel. The Galveston company struck back, however, with an additional charge on the ships involved when they stopped at the island to fill out a return cargo.[130] Interrupted by warfare, the intercity strife reopened in 1866 when Houston municipal officials encouraged the formation of the Houston Direct Navigation Company to promote barge transport of cotton to mid-channel positions and to improve bayou navigation.[131] Incorporated by John H. Sterrett, Thomas M. Bagby, Alexander Sessums, William M. Rice, Charles S. Longcope, and others, the company prospered, advertised a through bill of lading to New York and elsewhere by 1869, and by 1871 reduced costs for shipment down the bayou from $1.16 per barrel to $.40 per barrel.[132]

Colonel Hugh Rice, meanwhile, demonstrated in a report to the city council the feasibility of a ship channel. The city fathers appropriated $75,000 for work on Clopper's and Red Fish bars, and composed a memorial for congress requesting designation of Houston as an official port of entry and for the authority to construct a channel. The memorial, although not forwarded to Washington, D.C., argued that the Houston project was necessary for immigration and that "Galveston . . . (without intending to disparage the Same) is not a harbor that affords the protection so necessary to shipping . . . on the contrary from its exposed situation vessels are in constant danger of disaster."[133] At the same time the *Weekly Telegraph* warned, "Houston, with the ship channel, is the favorite commercial point in Texas; without it she is a small commercial town gradually growing up by her railroads and manufactories, but destined never, in our life-time, to grow very much beyond what she now is."[134]

To convert the dream to reality, Thomas W. House, Abram Groesbeeck, William M. Rice, William J. Hutchins, and others founded the Buffalo Bayou Ship Channel Company in 1869. Financially supported in part by the city and in part by a toll, the company sought to dredge a nine-foot channel from Houston to Bolivar Roads, the opening into the Gulf, in three years' time. The most important phase of the project was to dig a canal through Morgan's Point in order to avoid Clopper's Bar.[135]

In 1870, the same year that the Buffalo Bayou Ship Channel Company commenced dredging, the federal government declared Houston a port of entry, authorized a customs house, and ordered a survey of the proposed water route.[136] Lieutenant H. M. Adams of the United States Engineers, as a result, reported in 1871 that improvement above Harrisburg would be expensive, but that a channel, six feet deep and one hundred feet wide, might be possible.[137] The federal government consequently allocated its first grant in 1872. The $10,000 thus provided was utilized to improve the crossing at Red Fish Bar while the Ship Channel Company continued its work on Morgan's Point and elsewhere on the bayou.[138]

Although the panic of 1873 disrupted work on the project, outside circumstances provided an impetus. Charles Morgan, the chief shipowner on the Gulf coast, decided to shift his trade terminals in order to meet the competition of the through railroads.[139] The *Weekly Telegraph* reported in April 1873 that several men, one of whom was affiliated with Morgan, hired a tugboat to inspect the work on the channel. Their purpose was unknown at the time.[140] The following year, however, Morgan purchased the Buffalo Bayou Ship Channel Company and promised to complete its work.[141] He then successfully promoted a twelve-foot-deep channel with army engineers, acquired control over the Houston Direct Navigation Company, and purchased the Texas Transportation Company, which possessed as its main asset the right to run a railroad from Houston to the vicinity of Brays Bayou. Next, below Harrisburg and opposite the juncture of Buffalo and Sims bayous, he founded the town of Clinton, with rail service to Houston.[142]

In April 1876, the first ship through the new channel, the *Clinton*, an iron-hulled, schooner-rigged side-wheeler, reached the new terminal carrying 750 tons of freight, including 500 tons of steel rails for Morgan's transfer line. The vessel left with a return cargo of 250 cattle from a nearby ranch.[143] In 1878 a reporter traveled twenty minutes over the Texas Transportation Company Railroad to Clinton and noted two eighty-by-three-hundred-foot storage buildings filled with cotton and merchandise, a cotton compress that could process fifty to sixty bales per hour, livestock pens, and one hundred employees earning $1.50 average wages per day.[144] The opening of Clinton and the channel to that point marked a turning point in the history of Buffalo Bayou, but unfortunately it meant also a near monopoly of the carrying trade by Morgan.

Such trade on the bayou had commenced with the voyage of the *Laura* in 1837. Shallow-draft boats, using high-pressure, wood-burning steam engines and paddle wheels on the side for maneuverability, carried freight, passengers, and mail between Houston and Galveston. They suffered frequent accidents but nonetheless on occasion indulged in races. Henry Woodland, a worker on the *Sam Houston*, recalled a contest with the *Courrier* at the end of which the victorious *Sam Houston* possessed boilers so hot and with such high pressure that the "whole boat trembled like a man with a violent ague." No one apparently worried, however, and nearly all on board got "stewed" on champagne in celebration.[145]

Steamboat captains may well have competed in speed of transit, but they apparently saw little reason for competition in freight rates. The owners of the *Sam Houston, San Jacinto, Correo,* and *Friend* announced in 1838, for instance, that they had agreed not only on similar rates but on higher ones as well.[146] Regular packet service with Galveston commenced in 1841 with an arrangement between the captains of the *Dayton* and *Gallatin,* but rates, frequency of service, and cargo varied from time to time.

Just as steamship lines, stagecoach and freight companies, and railroad corporations arose to aid the merchant, other ancillary businesses and facilities emerged also. The Texas Telegraph Company, for example, which was financed in Louisiana, strung wire from Shreveport to Marshall, Henderson, Palestine, Montgomery, and Houston during 1853–1854. The local representative, L. K. Preston, succeeded in completing contact between Galveston and Houston in 1854 with a wire under Galveston Bay. Service proved faulty, however, since Preston, acting as general manager, operator, and maintenance man, could not keep the frequently severed line in repair. The telegraph failed in 1855, but Edward Cushing reestablished service in 1859–1860, allowing Houstonians to receive reports from the island about weather, ship arrivals, and prices in New Orleans. The telegraph system consolidated under Western Union in 1869.[147]

Small-scale, simple banking, moreover, commenced when merchants Thomas W. House, William M. Rice, Benjamin A. Shepherd, and others acquired excess funds that could be lent. Andrew Briscoe, for example, advertised in 1838, "Money to Lend. . . . In small sums, on short time, at good interest, on good endorsed notes, or special mortgage of real estate or negroes."[148] Neither the Texas Railroad, Navigation and Banking Company nor a movement in 1841 to establish a bank of exchange succeeded.[149] Formal banking institutions, prevented by popular prejudice and by the state constitution before the Civil War, emerged with the First National Bank, started by Thomas M. Bagby in 1866. The bank failed after a year, but Benjamin A. Shepherd assumed control and brought it success.[150] This institution, the third national bank established in Texas, was the first to operate exclusively as a bank, although Thomas W. House may have separated his monetary activities as early as 1852.[151] Created through a special enactment of the state, the City Bank of Houston opened in 1870, only to become insolvent in 1886. Meanwhile, the National Exchange Bank had started in 1873, followed by the Houston Land and Trust Company in 1875, the latter founded by a colorful lawyer, Decimus et Ultimus Barziza.[152] Also through special legislation, the Young Men's Real Estate and Building Association of Harris County started in 1866, a precursor of the later building and loan associations.[153] Altogether, by May 1874, there existed a $1,300,000 capital investment in Houston's financial institutions.[154]

A. S. Ruthven, "distinguished for accurate business habits, strict integrity, and great discernment," began in 1850 to offer for Southern Mutual Life Insurance Company policies to cover not only white people but also slaves.[155] In 1856, W. L. Withers, a subagent for Miller and Russel of New Orleans, advertised life, fire, and marine insurance, but in 1858 a local concern, Houston Insurance Company, began to provide insurance for the Bayou City merchants. The local enterprise was apparently a success, for it paid a $10 dividend and possessed $250,000 capital in 1869.[156]

Perhaps the most significant ancillary organization for the benefit of business, however, was the Board of Trade, similar to a chamber of commerce. Earlier, in 1840, Thomas M. League, Henry R. Allen, George Gazley, John W. Pitkin, Charles Kesler, DeWitt C. Harris, and E. S. Perkins had formed a chamber of commerce in response to Houston's expanding trade.[157] Oriented to wholesale commerce, its main achievement was to set standard rates for freight handling and storage.[158] It lacked viability, however, and after several years the organization apparently ceased to exist. The *Weekly Telegraph*, in 1869, repeated several times that Houston had no chamber of commerce.[159]

In May 1874, however, a delegation from Kansas City passed through Houston on a tour of coastal towns to encourage trade with that midwestern city. They were especially interested in the shipment of grain by railroad to the port of Galveston.[160] The editor of the *Houston Daily Telegraph* hoped that this event would inspire the formation of a Houston commercial association, and, as desired, on May 15, 1874, a group of businessmen met in the offices of the Planter's Insurance Company, selected C. S. Longcope as chairman, and created the Houston Board of Trade. They set dues at $1.00 per month with an initiation fee of $5.00.[161] The following June the board sent a ten-member delegation, which joined with representatives from Galveston, Sedalia, and Denison, to visit Kansas City and Denver in response to an invitation from the Kansas City group and to promote business for south Texas.[162]

The formation of the Houston Board of Trade and of the Cotton Exchange, an organization started at the same time, which worked in conjunction with the board, symbolized Houston's dedication to commerce and marked the culmination of the Bayou City as a commercial emporium. For the years that followed, the economy, although remaining commerce oriented, became less devoted to trade as other developments, including the exciting discovery of oil, encouraged diversification.

3

A Frontier Society, 1836-1875

The nature of its society as well as the characteristics of its economy indicate that Houston was a town of the South. It possessed a typical extractive economy which depended mainly on slaves, plantations, and agricultural products. The population, although it had a strong German element, migrated for the most part from the South. The census of 1850 revealed 48 percent of the free inhabitants born in the southern region and 33 percent foreign born. Twenty years later the census disclosed 67 percent born in the South and only 17 percent born abroad.[1] If it can be said that people tend to adopt the culture of the society into which they are born, then these statistics underscore Houston's southern orientation.

The town, however, was on the western edge of the South and consequently exhibited many frontier qualities, such as rapid growth, leadership by merchants, and emphasis on commerce.[2] "We frequently notice on our way to breakfast," the *Telegraph and Texas Register* commented in 1837, "a quantity of lumber thrown carelessly in a heap, and, upon returning in the evening, are greeted with the surprising appearance of a house."[3] More than twenty years later, a newspaper could still remark: "The mania for building seems still [to] possess our people. Dozens of new dwelling houses are now going up in every part of town. In every direction the sound [of] the carpenter's hammer, and the bricklayer's trowel is heard. Each new day seems but to add to the spirit of improvement among us."[4]

The Bayou City, moreover, demonstrated that surprising early interest in cultural development which appeared in other frontier townships.[5] On June 11, 1838, Henry Corri presented a comedy by Sheridan Knowles entitled *The Hunchback*, plus a farce called *The Dumb Belle—or I'm Perfection*, to an overflowing crowd. The actors "exceeded the expectation of their most sanguine friends."[6] From that time onward, Houston theaters presented sporadically not only plays but also the special acts of ventriloquists, comedians, minstrels, trained animals, singers, local amateurs, bell-ringers, and phrenologists.[7] Although Corri tried to retain actors on contract for a season, troupes which stayed for only brief periods presented most performances.[8]

The town also could boast of a "natural painter," Jefferson Wright, of whom it was said, "The portraits of this gentleman bear the evidence of much genius and application."[9] Mattie Austin Hatcher, who saw Houston in 1837, noted the portrait gallery at the capitol and wrote, "You see, the arts flourish in this new land already."[10] In 1857 there were music- and dancing-teachers and a Houston Brass Band.[11] Citizens took delight in popular tunes, such as "Shoo Fly" and "If I Ever Cease to Love," but those with the greatest musical interest were the German immigrants.[12] They formed a *verein* in 1840 to aid newcomers like themselves and founded the Houston Turnverein in 1854. The long-lived Turnverein stressed gymnastics and music and organized social events. At a *liederkranz* in 1874, for example, Aurelia H. Mohl enjoyed the solos and impromptu *volkslieder* presented by male singers for the entertainment of friends and guests.[13]

The Philosophical Society of Texas was formed in 1837 for the "collection and diffusion of knowledge," with Mirabeau B. Lamar president, Ashbel Smith vice-president, and William Fairfax Gray recording secretary. Smith, who presented a paper to the organization relating to health in the Texas climate, thought that the society would bring Texas cultural recognition from the nations of the world.[14] Debating clubs, the Franklin Debating Society in 1837 and the Houston Young Men's Society in 1839, also existed and discussed such questions as "Was Queen Elizabeth justifiable in her conduct towards Mary Queen of Scots?" and "Can the treatment of the Indians by our ancestors be justified?"[15] For Houston the groups proved ephemeral, as the Philosophical Society and the others shortly ceased to meet.[16]

More enduring was the Houston Lyceum, which started in 1854 and survived periods of quiescence and reorganization until the end of the century. It sponsored at various times lectures, debates, and musical programs, and, most important, it supported a library. Along with his stationery and bookstore, Henry F. Byrne had operated a 1,300-volume subscription library as early as 1839. It failed because of a law suit and the change in the seat of government, but similar facilities, started by Martin K. Snell in 1844, may have lasted until 1849.[17] The Lyceum library, operated free for the benefit of members, naturally shared the vicissitudes of the sponsoring organization. Although it did not function at all between 1869 and 1874, the Lyceum did endure long enough to help establish a free public library in the early twentieth century.[18]

Most important for the benefit of the literate public, however, were the local newspapers, the *Telegraph and Texas Register* (1835–1853), *National Intelligencer* (1838–1840), *Morning Star* (1839–1846), *Weekly Telegraph* (1852–1873), *Tri-Weekly Telegraph* (1855–1864), *Daily Telegraph* (1864–1877), *Houston Union* (1868–1869), *Tri-Weekly Houston Union* (1869–1871?), and *Houston Daily Union* (1870–1874).[19] Although the editor of the *Morning Star* once complained about "reading room loafers" who would use the paper in the file rather than purchase a copy, the subscription rates do not seem exorbitant.[20] In 1838 the *Telegraph and Texas Register*, a weekly publication, charged $5.00 per year for a subscription paid in advance and $1.00 for eight lines of advertising. In 1844 it still charged the same rates, but the *Weekly Telegraph* in 1861 demanded only $3.00 per year and $1.00 for ten lines of advertising. The *Weekly Telegraph* failed during the months of national financial panic in 1873, but the *Weekly Houston Telegraph* in 1874 received $3.00 for a subscription per year and $2.00 per inch for advertising.[21]

The editors offered stories and jokes: "A young lady taking a walk one morning, met a gentleman of her acquaintance to whom she said, 'you see sir, I am out for a little *sun* and *air*.' 'You had better get a *husband* first' was the ready response."[22] They also gave their opinions concerning various matters and printed a variety of local and national news items. Including several pages of advertising, the newspapers generally extended from four to eight pages in length. Even though quality varied and the editors frequently revealed bias, Houston newspapers, as those elsewhere, were apparently widely read and informative. They provided a unifying force for the town.[23]

As might be expected in a place where newspapers existed, there was also some interest in education. From the first years small private schools existed, among them the Male and Female City School, Classical School, Houston Female Seminary, and Houston Academy.[24] They subsisted on monthly tuition. James A. Bolinger charged for primary courses in spelling, reading, geography, and arithmetic a fee of $3.00 at his Houston Male and Female Academy. Senior courses in reading, philosophy, chemistry, trigonometry, and rhetoric cost $6.00.[25] Attendance was not heavy, and the *Weekly Telegraph* mentioned in 1856 that only 175 out of 700 youths sixteen to seventeen years old were in school.[26] Until that point the schools were temporary affairs and indifferently attended, but in 1857 James H. Stevens left the city $5,000 to help construct a permanent schoolhouse. A fund drive increased the amount to $20,000, which financed the construction of the two-story brick Academy Building.[27] Late in 1858 the Academy opened, and shortly thereafter Ashbel Smith became its superintendent.[28] With 140 students and five teachers the institution was a "noble ornament" to the town.[29] As time passed, however, attendance decreased and in the summer of 1864 the C.S.A. commandeered the structure for a soldiers' hospital.[30]

Following the war, educational institutions revived with a black school operating at the African Methodist Church.[31] The catechetical method in use by the blacks, which offered such questions as "To whom are you indebted for your freedom?" answered by "To the Yankee soldiers," proved to be disturbing to one newsman and perhaps to other people.[32] The movement for free public schools began in the early 1870's, partially inspired by the announcement that the Peabody Educational Fund might aid Texas.[33] Authorized at a public meeting, a committee of citizens drew up a bill to present to the legislature that would permit the town to inaugurate free public education.[34] This failed, but the children did attend a free county school system supported by state funds. In 1873 Harris County operated twenty-four schools for 1,561 pupils. They were taught by thirty-seven teachers, who earned an average of $65.64 per month.[35] Schools met in 1874 for only four months and in 1876 for possibly as little as two to three months.[36] As one newspaper concluded, "The present method is an improvident waste of money, almost totally barren of results, and a reproach to the fair fame of this great State."[37]

In 1876, when the legislature granted municipalities the opportunity to direct the schools and to receive a pro rata share of the educational funds, Houston voted 65 to 9 in favor of local control. Given authorization by that rather small election, the city council provided in 1877 for free public schools for all children eight to fourteen years old. Three trustees and a superintendent, all appointed by the mayor with approval of the council, would direct the system, which would be intentionally segregated by race.[38] Houston thus assumed responsibility for the formal education of the young.

Though higher cultural pursuits, such as painting, music, and even education, yielded some entertainment value, for outright amusement the townsfolk enjoyed most of all the holidays, parties, fairs, and traveling shows. The circuses, which visited in the 1850's and later, were a constant delight. Men, women, and children from all stations in life appeared at the circus tent to enjoy what was considered "capital entertainment."[39] Most of the same holidays observed by other Americans found favor: Christmas, New Year's Day,

Washington's Birthday, and May Day. The Fourth of July was celebrated even while Texas was still an independent nation, for, as the
Morning Star explained, "All seemed to forget that it was the national holiday of a foreign country . . . our citizens forgot that they
were Texians and *transported* with an unpatriotic ardor celebrated
as Americans, the national festival of the parent republic."[40] This
particular holiday naturally lost favor during the Civil War but
slowly regained popularity afterward. In 1869 the *Weekly Telegraph*
commented: "We look back and mourn for our dead. They rest upon
five hundred battle fields. We look up and see the same flag waving
over us, the flag we tried to pull down. We look back and remember
how we loved it, and the power of the first begins to assert its sway,
and the old love revives and even tempers our bitter memories."[41]

Houstonians recognized other special occasions like Texas Independence Day and Saint Patrick's Day. The citizens celebrated
the holidays with band music, fireworks, performances of military
groups, dinners, speeches, picnics, and drinking. On Christmas Eve
1871, the *Daily Telegraph* observed many homes which served sparkling wine to guests, so that "in consequence, not a few gents went
home a little 'how come you so,' if not with active *bricks in their
hats.*"[42] Toasts were often in order, as at a special dinner for Sam
Houston in 1845. Among the pledges were "San Jacinto: When Victory perched on our banner, Opposition fled howling from the field"
and "His Excellency the President, Anson Jones. Chief ploughman
in the cornfield, he turns his furrows handsomely, and never looks
back."[43] At a Washington's Birthday dinner in 1858 they toasted:
"The memory of George Washington" (drunk in silence with people
standing); "The President of the United States—The office and the
man" (followed by applause); "The Constitution, the rock of liberty"
(followed by applause); and "The heroes of Texian Independence—
they need no eulogy, their country is the monument of their glory"
(followed by loud applause).[44]

Local military groups, such as the Milam Guards, Davis Guards,
Washington Light Guards, Turner Rifles, and, after the Civil War,
the Houston Light Guards, often sponsored social events. Wearing
elaborate uniforms, the units conducted dances, picnics, shooting
contests, and drill competition. Occasionally they acted as an armed
force to police the city, guard a prisoner, or quell disturbances. With
the outbreak of the Civil War, the groups provided partially trained
men for service.[45]

As sports activity the citizens enjoyed target shooting, boxing,
sailing on Galveston Bay, baseball, bowling, and horseracing. Horse-

racing was one of the most popular as well as one of the earliest sports. The Houston Post Oak Jockey Club was formed in 1839 to sponsor races, but that organization, apparently like most others, lasted only a few seasons.[46] The sport itself, nonetheless, endured and attracted interested fans whenever someone would sponsor the competition. "Equine" in the *Weekly Telegraph* in 1869, for example, eagerly anticipated the opening of the "Houston racing and trotting park," where "the grandstand will be a vast bouquet of sweet smiles and bright eyes set in banks of rustling silk and snowy muslin."[47]

The Houston Base Ball Club, with F. A. Rice as president, started in 1861, and, in time, competition arose with other towns. Because of inaccurate throwing, the Houston Pioneers lost to the Galveston Island Cities nineteen to fifteen in 1871.[48] A group of boxing enthusiasts quietly conducted the "light weight championship of the road" between red-haired Tim Donovan and Nick Murphy, "an ugly cuss," in 1875. Murphy won the $100 prize in eighteen minutes after he held Donovan's head under his arm and gave him "fearful licks."[49] In another sport, "Colorado Boy" Craft from Bastrop defeated Mr. Herring in a fifty-yard foot race. Although skeptics might doubt the impossible time of three seconds for the event, they might consider Craft's reputed ability to run down rabbits in the open prairie.[50]

Sporting events were often a part of the fairs sponsored by Houstonians. The Germans, from 1869 to the mid-1870's, presented an annual late-spring celebration called Volksfest, which attracted thousands of visitors from south Texas. A parade featuring floats and King Gambrinus, the German Bacchus, usually led the way to the fairgrounds. Here, on an acre of land decorated with flags and evergreens, would be swings, dancing circles, seats, benches, and booths for the sale of lemonade, ice cream, sherbet, venison, beer, pies, and perhaps "solid shot" for the older people. The Germans offered speeches, gymnastics, music, dancing, and baseball contests for entertainment.[51] At an elaborate, two-day Volksfest, in 1874, a group dressed in armor and helmets and equipped with swords presented a sham battle described as follows:

> The buglar said "toot'ty'toot'ty'too!" and the knights said "H-ya! Git up!" and driving spurs into their horses' sides, flew over the plain like cavalry in a funeral procession. They drew their swords and flourished them aloft, and then put them back into the scabbards unwet with any considerable amount of gore. Thrice they repeated this manouvre, neither party dar-

ing to come within reaching distance of the other's awkward-
ness. The man with the big axe skirmished around in the high
grass, and hunted for a cherry tree to cut down with his little
hatchet. The buglar blowed until he said "he'd be blowed if
he'd blow any longer."

Soon the knights saw that neither of their sides wanted to
fight, they declared an armistice, an[d] agreed to settle the matter at Japhet's lager beer stand. Thereupon they mixed and
rode triumphantly from the field, to the music of "See, the
Conqu'ring Heroes Come!" from the band.[52]

Sharing the period with the Volksfest was the state fair of the
Agricultural, Mechanical and Blood Stock Association of Texas. A
charter for the organization had been granted shortly after the Civil
War, but nothing resulted until 1870, when a four-day exposition,
supported by local business people, opened, with exhibits of machinery and farm products and contests for hundreds of prizes. Even
though there were complaints of unfair judging in the bread-baking
competition, Houston profited, according to the *Galveston Bulletin*,
by an estimated $250,000.[53]

The association laid out a fairgrounds on the outskirts of town
off Main Street in 1871, with a one-mile race track, grandstand, and
exhibition halls. The seven-day fair of 1872 featured not only the
various exhibitions but also horse races, music by Madden's Fair Orchestra, and a baseball game in which a Houston team defeated a
Galveston squad by four runs. Perhaps most delightful were the
ladies, dressed in a colorful new fashion, the "mysterious, incompre-
hensible, and now celebrated Dolly Vardens!"[54] The annual festival
was a success until 1878. In that year the weather was unfavorable, a
yellow-fever scare occurred, and, worst of all, the citizenry lost interest. "The fair was a grand success—as a failure. The exhibits were
wonderful—scarce, and the financial result no better," recorded the
Houston Daily Telegram.[55] That ended the state fair for Houston,
but later the city of Dallas took up the project and made it successful
once more.

Just as the fairs and the emphasis on education demonstrate a
growing urbanization, so also does the subsidence of rowdiness and
outright lawlessness. In its early days Houston could rival the worst
of frontier communities in flagrant drunkenness, gambling, pros-
titution, thievery, and violent death. Littleton Fowler, a Methodist
minister sensitive to such matters, recorded, when he arrived in
1837, "Here I find much vice, gaming, drunkenness, and profanity

the commonest."[56] While on a trip to Galveston the next year he observed:

So soon as I recovered from my serious illness I took a trip to Galveston Island with the President and the members of Congress, and saw *great* men in *high* life. If what I saw and heard were a fair representation, may God keep me from such scenes in [the] future. . . . On our return on Sunday afternoon, about one-half on board got mildly drunk and stripped themselves to their linen and pantaloons. Their Bacchanalian revels and blood-curdling profanity made the pleasure boat a floating hell. The excursion to me was one of pain and not pleasure. I relapsed from this trip and was near the valley of death.[57]

Fowler's experience was no exceptional affair. Barrooms, billiard halls, and faro banks ran unrestricted, even on Sundays.[58] As that anonymous writer stated in the *Hesperian* about drunkenness:

While there were a few who did not exceed the limits of moderation, a large majority knew no restraint of their appetites. The extent to which this vice was carried, exceeded all belief. It appeared to be the business of the great mass of people, to collect around these centers of vice and hold their drunken orgies, without seeming to know that the sabbath was made for more serious purposes, and night for rest. Drinking was reduced to a system and had its own laws and regulations. Nothing was regarded as a greater violation of established etiquette than for one who was going to drink not to invite all within a reasonable distance to partake, so the Texians being entirely a military people not only fought but drank in platoons.[59]

As might be expected, all sorts of public disturbances occurred. In 1839 a mob of drunken gamblers and loafers armed with Bowie knives and pistols halted a play, beat the theater manager, attacked some unarmed people at the Exchange Hotel bar, and then intruded on a dance in progress on the hotel's second floor. The Milam Guards finally suppressed this minor riot in an atmosphere of "horrid yells and curses."[60] Shortly afterward the *Morning Star* complained about a mysterious Calithumpian Society that traveled the night streets to the music of a fife and fiddle, pausing periodically to vent three cheers.[61] In 1837, John James Audubon, the naturalist, found "drunk and hallooing" Indians stumbling about in muddy Houston streets, while the following year John Herndon judged the town as "the greatest sink of disipation and vice that modern times have known."[62]

The nature of early Houston was enough to repulse newcomers and to inspire flight among the less bold. Charles Hedenberg told Francis Lubbock that he had once persuaded an uncle to migrate to Houston to set up a carriage shop. The uncle arrived from New Jersey in the morning and transferred his trunks to the nephew's business house, Hedenberg and Vedder. Charles, busy at the moment, suggested to his relative that he visit the capitol and observe congress in action. While there, the uncle, attracted to a hallway by resounding gunshots, witnessed the carting off of Algernon Thompson, severely wounded by a fellow clerk of the Senate. The uncle, apparently shaken, promptly left and quickly walked down the west side of Main Street. A soldier, shot by another, almost fell upon him as he passed the Round Tent Saloon. The uncle then ran across the street and arrived in front of John Carlos' Saloon just as a man rushed out the door with his bowels protruding from a gigantic Bowie-knife wound.

Reaching his nephew's store, he gasped, "Charley, have you sent my trunks to the house?"

"No, uncle; not yet."

"Well, do not send them. Get me a dray so I can at once take them to the boat that leaves for Galveston this afternoon."

"Why, uncle what do you mean? Why, you have seen nothing; have not had time to look at the town."

"Charley, I have seen enough. I wish to return home immediately. I do not wish to see any more of Texas."

With that, the man left and never returned.[63]

As time went by, the city government, police, and society managed to suppress extreme lawlessness, but crime and vice continued in Houston, a part of life as in other communities. In 1856 the *Weekly Telegraph* complained, "One can hardly walk through the bye-streets, or about the wharves, of the city, without hearing oaths and blasphemy enough to chill his blood with horror."[64] Shortly before, the paper noted: "Rows are getting to be common occurrences in Houston. Black eyes and bloody noses are worn about through the streets with an air of *sang froid* which would do credit to the participants in the convivialities of Donnybrook Fair."[65]

Crimes and vice of all kinds, of course, are evident in Houston history. Drunkenness persisted and saloons flourished. Among the most famous establishments of that sort was the Bank of Bacchus started by a popular Irishman, Dick Dowling, in 1860. He sold "sight checks on Inebriety at 10¢, for cash," and garnered publicity by sending a new drink called "kiss me quick and go" to a local editor. The saloon, closed during the Civil War, reopened afterward, but Dowling, a hero of the Battle of Sabine Pass, died of yellow fever in 1867.[66]

With the uncertain currency of the Texas republic and the United States, counterfeiting was especially prevalent before 1875. The newspapers diligently warned people about current fakes and how to recognize them.[67] Newspapers also referred occasionally to problems with prostitutes. A city constable, for example, was stabbed in the chest with a sword cane while breaking up a commotion at a house of ill-fame occupied by "Nelly."[68] After another affray at such a house, in which a man was cut with a Bowie knife, the *Morning Star* suggested that officials or, if necessary, citizens should move to assure the safety, peace, and purity of the town. The next day the paper hastily added that the occupants should not suffer loss of property or be turned "naked and pennyless" upon the world. They should simply be forced to leave without harm.[69]

In 1840 a city ordinance provided a fine of not less than $50 and a jail term of ten to thirty days for any woman committing lewd actions or exhibiting herself in a public place in a style "not usual for respectable females." Brothels within the city limits could not be located closer than two squares to a family residence. A supplementary ordinance in 1841 required a $20 bond for a "female of ill fame" found in a public place after 8:00 P.M., in order to ensure good behavior.[70] Although perhaps not a prostitute, one of the most notorious female characters from the period was Pamelia Mann, an expert at firearms, knives, horseback riding, and profanity. She appeared in court at various times charged with counterfeiting, forgery, fornication, larceny, and assault. According to William Ransom Hogan, she ran the Mansion House hotel in such fashion that "Mrs. Mann and her 'girls' achieved a satisfying success" providing Houston with female companionship of "a robust and none too virtuous nature."[71]

A Texas law that prohibited faro, roulette, monte, rouge et noir, and all other games of chance suppressed gambling as early as 1837.[72] For the reduction of violence in Houston, the elimination of dueling represents a forward step. The custom, popular in the town, especially offended the one-armed editor of the *Telegraph and Texas Register* and sometime mayor of Houston, Dr. Francis Moore, Jr. His indignation particularly boiled in regard to the Laurens-Goodrich affair. Chauncy Goodrich accused Levi L. Laurens of stealing $1,000. Though he later realized the falseness of the charge,

Goodrich refused to retract the statement and Laurens issued a challenge. In a duel calling for rifles at twenty paces, Goodrich escaped untouched, but hit his opponent in both thighs at first fire. Laurens, a likeable young man, died at the home of Moore after forty-seven hours; "the wound of the spirit was more fatal than that of the body."[73]

Goodrich fled the city, apparently fearing the wrath of the citizenry and particularly of Francis Moore, Jr. But from a safe distance, in a letter to Ashbel Smith, he threatened to whip Moore if the editor said anything in the newspaper.[74] The *Telegraph and Texas Register* eulogized Laurens and demanded a means to prevent such future slaughter.[75] Goodrich shortly met violent death in San Antonio after an argument with a gambler, which allowed Moore to intone, *"Whoso sheddeth man's blood, by man shall his blood be shed."*[76] The editor, nevertheless, continued his fight against dueling and carrying weapons in general. Brave men need no such arms, he contended. Those carrying weapons insulted a peace-loving community; such "blackguards and knaves" should be "frowned down" by respectable people.[77]

Moore seemingly gained success. In February 1838, he reported that a dozen challenges had been settled peaceably in the preceding three months.[78] In 1840 the city council approved an ordinance which prohibited carrying deadly weapons, and through the efforts of Moore, Texas passed a revised antidueling law to penalize not only combatants but also seconds.[79] A grand jury reported in 1841 that the moral tone of the town had improved, vice had diminished, and dueling was considered ungentlemanly.[80] In 1842 the *Telegraph and Texas Register* reported that no duels had occurred in four years and concluded that "reason has at length asserted her supremacy."[81] The *Morning Star* observed in 1844: "The ladies who invariably shun scenes of violence and disorder, now daily walk the public streets without fear that they will be disturbed by any brawl or riotous assemblage. Harmony and good order every where prevail."[82]

After six to eight years, Houston had lost the extreme lawlessness so noticeable in the first years. This came about through civic action, public desire, and perhaps the civilizing influence of the churches. City police work began at least as early as 1838, when the council appointed two constables at a salary of $60 per month.[83] Protection, however, was inconsistent until after the Civil War. There was often no protection at night except that offered by volunteers or private guards; the amateur policemen were perhaps of mixed value. As the *Tri-Weekly Telegraph* observed in 1860: "If the gentlemen who have nobly volunteered upon the night police in Houston, and whose services have already been of no little importance in arresting vicious negroes, would be a little more careful of their fire-arms, and bear in mind that their business is not to shoot cats and dogs *ad libitum* as they pass about, they would enhance the appreciation of their services in the minds of the people."[84]

To add to the inconsistency of the work, law enforcement officers sometimes lacked public support. "What . . . is the use of paying a parcel of policemen better wages than they could make at hard work, and all for loafing about our streets with big sticks in their hands, hunting in vain for some official duty to perform?" questioned the *Tri-Weekly Telegraph* in 1860.[85]

Criminals, when caught and convicted, faced possible fines, jail terms, whipping, hanging, and, in early days, branding. In 1838 the *Telegraph and Texas Register* noted that a thief had been *"convicted, whipt, and branded!"*[86] Whipping could be excessive, as in the case of Abe Stanley, a black who was caught with stolen goods and in the act of theft. His sentence consisted of 750 lashes on the bare back—100 the first day and 50 three times per week thereafter until completed.[87] Life in jail was none too pleasant since poor food and lack of sanitation were common. On the other hand, the jails were not always well guarded and escapes were frequent.[88] Officials administered punishments in public, supposedly as a warning to potential transgressors, but the popularity of hangings indicates that perhaps the populace enjoyed such affairs. John H. Herndon claimed that two thousand to three thousand persons witnessed the hanging of David Jones and John C. Quick, both convicted murderers, in 1838. Herndon and several others severed the heads for purposes of dissection after the execution. Herndon then recorded that he enjoyed a good supper that evening.[89]

One of Houston's two recorded lynchings occurred in 1859. George White, a "stout two fisted man standing over six feet high" supposedly committed a "hellish" rape on twelve-year-old Agnes Hyde near Harrisburg. Captured in Galveston, White was sent to Houston for trial under the guard of a constable and deputy sheriff. About one and one-half miles from Harrisburg, however, forty to fifty disguised men "seized upon the prisoner and hung him to the branch of a tree." The reporting newspaper condemned such action, preferring the law to take its due course.[90] Houstonians, except on one other occasion in 1928, agreed.

The role of churches in the suppression of crime and the betterment of town life is difficult to assess. Almost from the beginning, Houston received the benefit of itinerant preachers and ministers who came to organize churches. One of the earliest was Littleton

Fowler, the tall, dark-eyed Methodist who was so impressed with local drinking. He arrived on November 19, 1837, preached that same
afternoon, and two days later became chaplain of the senate.[91] There
were others, of course, such as Q. N. Morrell, a Baptist who apparently preceded Fowler; W. W. Hall, a Presbyterian who also became a
chaplain to Congress; Jesse Hord, a Methodist; and William Y. Allen, a Presbyterian who held the first local temperance meeting following a suggestion by Sam Houston.[92]

The churches grew slowly. Ministers co-operated with each
other, preached in the Capitol Building, boarded among the people,
and shared communicants. William Y. Allen once administered the
sacrament to a small mixed group of Presbyterians, Baptists, Methodists, and at least one Episcopalian.[93] Church building came tardily.
"It is a source of much astonishment, and of considerable severe
comment upon the religious character of our city, that while we have
a theatre, a court house, a jail, and even a capitol in Houston we have
not a single Church," lamented the *Morning Star* in 1839.[94] Later,
the same paper stated: "It is a truth, the mention of which should
call a blush of shame to the face of every good citizen, that in a city
like ours with more than three thousand inhabitants and with so
much wealth, there is no place for public worship, and not one resident minister. The people seem to have forgotten that 'Righteous-
ness exalteth a nation.'"[95]

Various groups, however, soon opened churches—the Presbyterians in 1841, the Roman Catholics in 1842, the Methodists in
1844, the Episcopalians in 1847, the Baptists in 1847, and the Jews, a
synagogue, in 1854.[96] Possibly Houston society was so lawless in the
first years that men of God found little sympathy. Recklessness, nevertheless, began to abate when the churches became permanent.
The wild members of society perhaps left, allowing churches to
grow, or maybe religious groups wrought a transformation, thereby
proving an editor's assertion that a church could do more for peace
and order than a "whole volume of ordinances."[97]

The role of ordinances and city government in maintaining
order in society, of course, cannot be denied. Houston, with sixteen
other towns, was incorporated on June 5, 1837. The charter authorized the power to sue or be sued, own and sell property, pass laws,
tax, establish schools, and maintain streets. Elected officers included a mayor, eight aldermen, a secretary and treasurer, tax collector, and constable. The chief justice of the county was designated to
call for their election.[98] Andrew Briscoe, the chief justice of Harrisburg County, accordingly initiated the election, and on August 14,
1837, the voters elected James S. Holman as mayor. The total votes

cast amounted to twelve for Holman, eleven for F. R. Lubbock, and ten for Thomas W. Ward. Holman took the oath of office as mayor on August 28, 1837.[99]

Another charter in 1839 and a supplement in 1840 provided a more detailed account of powers and limitations. The town was to encompass nine square miles with the courthouse in the center, and two aldermen were to be elected from each of four wards. The boundaries of these political divisions ran as follows: First Ward, north of Congress Street and west of Main Street; Second Ward, north of Congress and east of Main; Third Ward, south of Congress and east of Main; Fourth Ward, south of Congress and west of Main. Later the Fifth Ward was formed north of Buffalo Bayou and White Oak Bayou. The body politic included free white inhabitants who were citizens of Texas, had resided in Houston for at least six months, and had held more than $100 in real estate for three months. The mayor and council, moreover, gained the power to erect wharves and to regulate the price of wheaten bread.[100] In 1841 the town received the power to levy a 0.5 percent ad valorem tax on real and personal property.[101] Although subjected to various adjustments from time to time, these early incorporation acts provided the outline for city government until the early twentieth century.

Before 1860 the sources of income were wharfage, license fees, bond issues, and special taxes. In 1857, for example, the total receipts for the city were $59,635.95, which included $22,380.35 from bonds, $20,178.98 from wharfage, and $2,264 from licenses.[102] Though wharf charges constituted the major tax, the town abolished the charges in 1860. Wharfage originally had been charged for the construction and maintenance of roads and docks for the benefit of outside merchants and wagoners. As time passed, however, the town used the fees for other purposes, and the railways made good roads and bayou improvement less important. Wharfage was no longer defensible. Houston, consequently, for that reason and also for the sake of bayou trade which faced railroad competition, eliminated wharfage.[103] After 1860 the ad valorem tax on property was the chief source of revenue.

Major expenses for the town involved those for streets and bridges, salaries, the city hospital, and, after the Civil War, city indebtedness. The municipality, moreover, allocated some funds for schools, cemeteries, paupers, sanitation, fire protection, police protection, and market control.[104] The government obviously operated for the general benefit of the public and for business. There exists no evidence of great scandals or calculated misuse of funds. Alderman R. G. Rawley, however, provided some minor excitement in 1868 when he gave to a woman for "illicit intercourse" a $10 note drawn on the city treasury. Upon exposure, Rawley resigned.[105] For the period, however, the greatest turmoil in city government came during the Reconstruction era.

Houston reacted as did many other Southern communities to the Civil War. Although some "submissionists" opposed secession, while others desired to restore the Texas republic, the people generally opposed Lincoln and voted heavily to secede in 1861.[106] The Bayou City never became the site of a battle, but it served as a point of administration and distribution. Houstonians eagerly volunteered for war service with such units as the Turner Rifles, Bayou City Guards, Gentry Volunteers, Houston Artillery, Texas Grays, Rough and Ready Guards, and Davis Guards. In April 1862, the *Weekly Telegraph* estimated that 12 percent of the county population had joined the service.[107] The Methodist church held prayer meetings, a newspaper warned dissenters to leave, and the people said farewell to departing warriors.[108] Commented the *Weekly Telegraph*: "We were called upon yesterday in common with the whole town, to say good bye to many friends who were leaving for Virginia. It was with a sad heart that we saw so many loved ones marching away to the danger. God protect them is the daily prayer of thousands in our city. We shall watch every mail with additional eagerness for tidings of them while they are gone."[109]

The townspeople collected money for the benefit of their soldiers in camp, helped nurse the ill and wounded, provided clothing, manufactured cartridges, and, on one glorious occasion, aided in the recapture of Galveston by preparing several steamboats armored with cotton bales.[110] Houston businessmen, of course, did not mind some profiteering mixed with patriotism. "Junior 2nd Lieutenant" in a letter to the *Weekly Telegraph* from a nearby encampment thanked J. T. Cyrus for a cask of molasses, P. W. Gray for a donation, and A. Whitaker and Company for a present. He then added, "but no thanks to the hide bound fellow that asked twelve dollars for one ounce of quinine, to break a soldier's chill."[111] The editor of that newspaper ranted about "gross outrages and impositions" when several merchants who had cornered salt and flour doubled the prices.[112] At about the same time, however, the editor, who had previously offered the services of the newspaper without cost to soldiers, said that there would be no more printing charged off to patriotism. Over $200 had been spent, and henceforth all deals were cash.[113]

Prices went up throughout the war, in part because of profiteering, in part through sheer scarcity. As early as 1861 a newsman noted markups of 300 to 400 percent and shortages of salt and lamp oil.[114] There were suggestions to use castor bean or Palma Christi bean oil for lamps and okra seeds for coffee.[115] A "Texas Housewife" offered in a letter to a newspaper a method of making candles from alum, saltpeter, tallow, and water. "If any one, after giving this recipe a trial, goes in darkness," she concluded, "it is because their deeds are evil."[116] Rents increased, labor costs more than doubled in certain instances, and currency cheapened.[117] As Gresham's Law began to operate, gold and silver disappeared from the marketplace, replaced by depreciated Confederate notes and "shinplasters" circulated by local merchants.[118]

Crowded with refugees, the city, nonetheless, maintained enthusiasm for the war. Eliza Ripley, one of those who came seeking safety in Houston, observed with "my heart almost bursting with proud emotion, my eyes dim with grateful tears," as General John B. Magruder received a sword from the hands of a young lady in a blue-silk evening dress for his action in saving Galveston from the enemy. Magruder, wearing a "gorgeous" uniform, accepted the sword and with an "unfortunate lisp" promised the crowd on Main Street that it would never be sheathed while the enemy trod on Confederate soil. After the speeches, music, and cheers, however, the sword, borrowed for the occasion from a Mexican War veteran, had to be returned to its owner—a sad commentary on the economic condition of Houston and the state.[119]

After the surrender of Robert E. Lee, a "large and enthusiastic" public meeting in Houston expressed a sentiment of "uncompromising resistance." Colonel C. C. Gillespie expressed this feeling when he told the crowd: "It is just as though the Yankees called on us to give up our faith in God, in Christ, in our souls, or our hope of heaven. The loss of Lee's army can have no effect to change the course of true men on such a question as this."[120] But demoralization, regardless of the fine words, commenced. The women refused to yield their silver, jewels, and gold as suggested by Aurelia Mohl for the aid of soldiers.[121] The *Galveston Daily News* wondered about the money from government cotton sales after observing many soldiers in homespun material.[122] The townspeople, moreover, became apprehensive with so many armed men nearby. As one soldier wrote to his wife:

> The Sitizens of Houston are becoming Very patriortick at this late Hour of the war they are Sending to Our Camp Every thing that we Could wish for to Eat Such as Coffee Sugar Flour Potatoes Tobacco Bacon Hams &c the Boys do Not refuse to Except of It at the Same time they give them No Credit for So

doing. They Eate what is donated to them and Curse them at the Same time for having been instrumental in bring this trubel upon us they are Now fearful that those Soldiers who are passing through the Town will distroy their ill gained property and they want Elmor es Mentto [Elmore's Men to?] protect them untill all the Soldiers Can. be Sent Home[.][123]

On May 23, 1865, soldiers, calmly, without violence but without orders, looted local government warehouses. They took what they considered already belonged to them. Other, late-arriving troops threatened to search private homes for stolen government materials, but at the request of a local officer and the city marshal, citizens turned over plundered supplies for distribution to the latecomers. This action quieted the soldiers, and afterward a voluntary guard of citizens watched the city.[124] The postal system collapsed in June as contractors abandoned their work, and trade practically halted.[125] With blacks and former soldiers loitering about the streets the town awaited the conqueror.[126] "Business is at a standstill," commented one newsman; "the machinery is out of gear, and every one appears to be waiting for the crack of the whip which is to start us—God knows where."[127] As an old man remembered:

> One day in June, 1865, when I lacked a month of being 4 years old, I was playing in the yard when I heard the noise—or music, if you could call it that—of a drum and fife corps, and knew soldiers were coming. I went to the gate and saw a body of troops (it must have been a full regiment) marching down Fannin Street. Somehow these soldiers did not look just right to me. Their uniforms were not ragged enough, were of a much darker color than any I had seen before, and their guns were too shiny. They had a flag, too, that was different from those to which I was accustomed.[128]

On the morning of June 20, 1865, part of the 114th Ohio Regiment along with the 34th Iowa Regiment arrived by special train from Galveston.[129] Only the violent death of a black working for the Union soldiers disrupted the occupation day. Seemingly, the black, pushing through a crowd, jostled either Bud or Lee Cotton as they watched the Northern troops march by. Tempers flared, and the black jumped into the street and picked up a brickbat, whereupon one brother harmlessly fired a pistol while the other plunged a Bowie knife through the black's throat. No legal action apparently resulted from the event.[130] Houston remained quiescent under military rule, and when some of the troops left in August, an editor commented, "Men actuated by such feelings and principles as have characterized their conduct, while here, cannot be other than brave men, to be relied on in an emergency."[131] Since the town remained orderly, there was no need for military rule and in November the office of provost marshal was closed.[132]

Trouble for the city government began, however, in 1867, when Brevet Major General J. J. Reynolds, military commander of Texas, asserted Radical power and arbitrarily replaced six aldermen and the assessor and collector. Although most of these initial assignments failed to work out, other appointments followed which kept the government in turbulence.[133] Among the appointees in 1868 was Thomas H. Scanlan, who became the most famous Radical in Houston.[134] Born in Ireland, he arrived at the Bayou City in 1853 and apparently worked as a merchant.[135] From 1870 to 1874, Scanlan served as mayor after appointment by Edmund J. Davis, the Radical governor of Texas. His administration managed to extend the sidewalks, build a market house, construct a large sewer on Caroline Street, improve roads and bridges, and welcome several blacks to the city council and police force.[136]

Tradition holds that Scanlan and the Radicals were profligate, corrupt, and sustained in office only through fraudulent votes.[137] An investigation of financial affairs after the Radicals had been removed from office by the newly elected Democratic governor, Richard Coke, placed the city debt at $1,414,000.[138] Though the evidence is not clear, the amount of debt in 1870 when Scanlan became mayor totaled approximately $200,000 to $300,000.[139] Revenue from March 1873 to January 1874 had been $87,800, and an estimated income in 1874 was set by the investigators at $110,000 per year. The interest due per annum was $103,500. "Enough . . . is known . . . to show that the annual necessary expenditures of the city and interest on its bonded debt far exceeds the annual resources of all kinds," noted the report, which concluded, "Heavy debt, an empty treasury, and a confused condition of city affairs, constituted the legacy of embarrassment handed down by the late radical administration to the council appointed in January."[140]

The most conclusive proof against Scanlan supposedly involves the extravagance of the market house. Interest in constructing market quarters had existed at least since 1866.[141] Scanlan toured New York, Philadelphia, New Orleans, Chicago, and Louisville looking at market halls and pavements in 1871. He returned and suggested a brick market house rather than an iron building previously recommended. The iron building, which would cost $250,000 to $300,000, was too expensive. Good ditches, sewers, and shell paving were satisfactory for the streets; the other paving he had seen was too costly. He advocated the purchase of three parks to avoid high prices for such land in the future.[142] These thoughts seem hardly suitable for a reputedly wasteful mayor.

The market house construction began in 1872, but plans changed in progress, and at completion not only stalls for vendors but also well-furnished city government offices and a 1,000-seat theater, "handsomely furnished, ornate and charming," were included. It measured 250 feet by 125 feet with a central portion 100 feet by 125 feet and three stories high. There were two towers, each reaching 35 feet above the roof; one housed a clock and the other a fire bell. The building was supplied with water and gas and cost about $400,000. It was insured for $100,000.[143]

On July 8, 1876, James Wood, a clerk in the assessor and collector's office, noticed smoke. He rushed to the fire tower, but the bell rope was gone, and he had to crawl down the steps, almost overcome with smoke. The fire, which apparently started under the stage of the theater, was beyond control by the time the firemen, summoned by scattered church bells, arrived. A crowd estimated at twenty thousand people watched this devouring blaze, which climaxed with the crash of the fire bell: "Mutely and sadly it swung above the leaping crackling flames, awaiting its fate until the last support gave way beneath it, and then as it fell down through the terrible abysm of fire, yawning and seething below; it peeled forth its own requiem in one wild, frenzied clanging, rising in a shrill alto above the hoarse bellowing of the hungry, maddened flames."[144]

Since insurance coverage was unclear, the city, after some controversy, accepted from the companies a compromise settlement of $82,500.[145] The town then used the debris of the market house to fill in mud holes and built a new structure, without a theater, upon the old foundation. The new building cost about $100,000, but, of course, Houston still had to pay off the old market house bond debt of $250,000.[146] Political opponents used the idea of a $100,000 structure replacing a $400,000 one as proof of Scanlan's wastefulness.[147]

The censure of Scanlan has been, however, somewhat unjust. Throughout the nation in the early 1870's the same sort of public construction went on, and a rise in city indebtedness was common.[148] For Houston, the debt actually began to rise before Scanlan's term and continued afterward.[149] County debt more than doubled in the same period.[150] In addition, a depression struck in 1873, which made debt payment difficult, cut city income, and deflated prices. Neither the deflation nor the fact that the new marketplace was less elaborate and utilized the old foundation was recognized by Scanlan's detractors. Corruption was never proved against Scanlan or his administration, although an alderman, Henry Hendricks, had to resign in October 1873 under an accusation of taking a $2,000 bribe to raise a yellow fever quarantine imposed by Houston on Galveston.[151]

In the first election in six years when Houstonians could select their own officials, interestingly enough they selected not only Scanlan for mayor but also a complete slate of Radicals, including two blacks, for aldermen.[152] The *Weekly Telegraph* claimed fraud, saying that large numbers of nonresident blacks came from the country to register and vote. According to the editor, there should have been about 2,000 white votes and 667 black ballots, but 3,010 votes had been cast and 1,419 blacks had registered.[153] Truth in this instance, however, is elusive. The population schedules of the census of 1870 indicate 793 male blacks twenty-one years of age or older living in the town.[154] How many more lived in Houston by 1872 and how many actually registered from the total eligible is impossible to say. The editor could not prove his allegation and admitted the vigilance practiced at registration and at the polls.[155] It is at least possible that Scanlan and his followers gained office in 1872 in a legitimate manner and thus reflected the will of the majority. The case against Scanlan and other Radicals in Houston is uncertain; they were not, however, the unmitigated scoundrels that historians and political enemies have pictured.

The Radicals, of course, depended on black support, and of all groups in Houston it was probably the blacks who experienced the greatest change as the result of the Civil War. Prior to that time, both slaves and free blacks lived in Houston. The *Morning Star* claimed in 1839 that there were only twenty to thirty free blacks in Texas and that most of them resided in Houston.[156] The census of 1860 listed 567 female slaves, 502 male slaves, and eight free blacks, seven of them female.[157] The free blacks could not vote, hold office, serve on a jury, or give testimony except against blacks. They were subject to the same punishment as slaves and were generally looked upon as a threat to civic tranquility.[158] According to a grand jury report, such persons were "worse than useless," a "mischievous influence," and "a very great evil."[159] Yet, even though Texas made it illegal to remain in the state without special permission, free blacks managed to move about, work, and otherwise live without a great threat to their freedom.[160]

State laws and local ordinances regulated the life of the urban slave by providing an 8:00 P.M. curfew and making it illegal to sell or deliver liquor to slaves. Slaves could not take independent employment without the owner's permission, nor could they have dances within the city limits without the mayor's approval.[161] Laws such as these suggest that they were necessary to check abuses, as the *Tri-Weekly Telegraph* indicated:

> The first thing that strikes an attentive observer on his arrival in Houston, is the immense latitude allowed to the negroes. No matter what time of night you pass through the streets you are sure to meet parties of negroes, who go where they please, unquestioned and irresponsible. Such thing as a "pass" is unheard of, and we doubt if they are even furnished. In certain quarters of the city there are large congregations of negroes, who hire their own time, and w[h]o live entirely free from the supervision of any white man. Speaking candidly and impartially, there is more insolence among the negroes of Houston, and more careless conduct, than in any other city or town South of Mason & Dixons line.[162]

It was apparently profitable to employ slaves in Houston. League-Andrews recorded in 1838 a receipt of $50 per month for the labor of "Black Boy Bob," and in 1856 Martha E. Wynns hired a black servant named Elizabeth for $12.50 per month.[163] Francis Lubbock, however, warned a friend against sending a slave, Ellen, to be employed in Houston: they become "spoiled" and acquire "bad habits," he said.[164]

Since Houston was a commercial center, there naturally existed some buying and selling of slaves, usually at auction.[165] No merchant who traded exclusively in slaves apparently operated in Houston over any long span of time, but local businessmen sometimes dealt with them in the course of their work. Frederick Law Olmsted in 1854 noticed many written advertisements posted about in public places and commented, "There is a prominent slave-mart in town which held a large lot of likely-looking negroes waiting purchasers."[166] In 1858, moreover, an editor referred to Riordan's slave depot where an unusual albino slave could be seen.[167]

The victory of the North, of course, ended such traffic, but some regulation became necessary to control the freedmen who crowded the town. The occupying military forces enforced a 9:00 P.M. curfew and threatened to put unemployed blacks to work without pay.[168] As E. N. Gray recalled, the blacks sang a song about the provost guard which said, "Run, nigger, run—the paterole will catch you! Run, nigger, run—it's almost day!" To Gray, a young boy at the time, the "paterole" was some monstrous animal kept in the county jail and turned loose at 9:00 P.M. to devour anyone found on the streets.[169] Local planters, meanwhile, tried to hire blacks on a basis of sharing the final crop,[170] and the *Weekly Telegraph* warned them about politics and the use of the franchise:

> Not even the Northern Republicans would allow you and a few white Radicals to take the rule over the white people of the State, and upon reflection, you will see that you should neither expect or ask it. If you should now demand it, the effect of it will be to lose it before long, and then the prejudice will become so strong that you may never again obtain the privilege, but if you take the proper course and leave it to the white people, it may be after awhile that they will adopt some plan by which at least a part of you can vote, but this would depend very much upon how you devote yourselves to learning, so as to become qualified for this great privilege. Some of you are now pursuing the very course to deprive you forever of the power to vote. You may not believe me, but you will do so before five years, and be sorry that you did not follow the advice we now give you.[171]

Houston blacks paid no heed, much to the chagrin of the newspaper, which admonished, "Now listen, colored men—the demanding of offices by your race, for which you are not qualified, is doing you more harm than all other causes."[172] Participation of blacks in local politics, however, was tolerated and apparently accepted without inspiring much extralegal activity in the vicinity.[173] This occurred, perhaps, because blacks did not predominate politically and because there was already a tendency for the races to shun each other socially.

Houston in 1870, in regard to residence, was fairly well integrated, as the census (shown in Table 1) indicated.[174] Such a balance, of course, would make it difficult for the minority race to elect aldermen except in the Fifth Ward. A half-century later, when there existed de facto residential segregation, the aldermen were elected at large. Black voting strength thus has been negated, perhaps without conscious planning. Segregated schools and teaching staffs came with the founding of the public system. Churches were separate, and black enthusiasm sometimes attracted criticism. The *Weekly Tele-*

TABLE 1. *White-Black Racial Distribution by Wards in 1870*

Ward	White Population	Black Population
1	488	250
2	1,164	474
3	1,737	1,075
4	1,741	1,314
5	561	578

graph mentioned complaints about the "howling, vociferous and muscular demonstration" of black Christians who attended church four times a week. One group even staged skirmishes in which "the pastor goes out and ranges his flock in line of battle, and then, torch in hand, leads a helter-skelter charge upon an imaginary Fort Devil, in the shape of a bonfire." The editor suggested that the "God of the sinner" was not so far away that he could not hear the cries of the wrongdoer in a more subdued tone.[175]

Black and white people celebrated separately the various holidays, with the black citizens adding "Juneteenth" to commemorate emancipation. There existed separate clubs, bands, and baseball teams.[176] Although races might intermingle in politics, in business, and in certain slums, such as Vinegar Hill, that "sinkpool of crime and pollution," on the north side of Buffalo Bayou near the Houston and Texas Central depot, segregation was entrenched in Houston by 1875.[177]

All humanity in the Bayou City, black or white, shared the diseases of the land. The warm, wet climate, poor drainage, sluggish bayous, and commercial intercourse all assured the town a full allotment of illness. Flies, rats, fleas, and mosquitoes swarmed over the city.[178] C. C. Cox, who in 1837 slept in the loft of a Houston house, commented:

> The fleas were as thick as the sands of the sea[.] Our clothes were actually bloody, and our bodies freckled after a night of warfare with the Vermine. And the Rats, I cannot convey an idea of the multitude of Rats in Houston at that time. They were almost as large as Prairie dogs and when night came on, the streets and Houses were litterly alive with these animals. Such running and squealling throughout the night, to say nothing of the fear of losing a toe or your nose, if you chanced to fall asleep, created such an apprehension that together with

the attention that had to be given our other Companions made sleep well nigh impossible.[179]

The town naturally was a gold mine for physicians and patent medicine salesmen. Ashbel Smith, a prominent doctor in early Houston, claimed a rate of income that amounted to $15,000 per year. He also noticed that drugs, which were scarce, could be sold at a 200-percent to 1,000-percent markup over normal retail prices.[180] For those who wished to be their own physicians there existed "Texian Universal Pills," useful "to thoroughly cleanse the stomach and bowels"; "Ramrod's Tincture of Gridiron," which carried a testimonial—"Walking, not long since, near the machinery of a mill, I was caught and carried between two cog-wheels and every bone in my body broken to pieces. A phial of *Ramrod's Tincture of Gridiron* being thrown into the pond, I found myself restored, and as whole and sound as a roach"; "Moffat's Life Pills and Phenix Bitters," for "renovating an exhausted and prostrated constitution"; and "Diggers' Specific" or "Dirt-Eaters' Cure," which at five dollars per bottle cured people of eating dirt and the effects of such a habit.[181]

Newspapers offered advice to the health-conscious person: to avoid excessive exertion and drinking of liquor in hot weather; to bathe twice a week; and to change one's personal linen twice a week.[182] For propriety and safety, bathing in the bayous was not recommended, yet it was a common affair throughout the period, despite ordinances against it.[183] The municipal government tried to promote good health by collecting fees to clean the marketplace, passing a pure-milk ordinance, establishing a board of health, hiring scavengers, isolating diseased persons, and supporting a hospital.[184]

Of the serious diseases affecting Houston, such as cholera, dengue fever, and smallpox, the most important was yellow fever, which hit Houston with epidemics in 1839, 1844, 1847, 1848, 1854, 1855, 1858, 1859, 1862, and 1867.[185] Posing an annual threat against life, it brought business to a halt and prompted a summer exodus of population. "Yellow Jack" struck its victims suddenly, killed relentlessly and without discrimination, and could decimate the population. Millie Gray recorded in 1839 that one-third of the people had fallen ill with yellow fever.[186] According to one account, the city sexton reported 229 deaths from July 24, 1839, to December 3, 1839— about one-twelfth of the population.[187] Though all of these deaths may not have been due to yellow fever, the disease was epidemic at the time. It was a fearful type of illness, as illustrated by this case in 1847 treated by Dr. William McCraven, one of the most experienced physicians in Houston:

Mr. T. . . . was ill in the house at the same time; he was taken with the same symptoms on the morning of the 4th [October 1847]. Sick 24 hours when I saw him. His eyes were quite red; pulse frequent, quick and compressible; tongue fiery red on the edges and tip, partly coated and partly as though it had been scalded and the epithelium peeled off; restless and thirsty. His was a well-marked case of yellow fever of a bad type, and as his constitution was very delicate, I augured unfavorably of its termination. It did not run a regular course however. Fever declined gradually, but did not leave him till the 6th day. His tongue at one time had been very dry and almost black, especially on the denuded portions, became moist and looked well. He had become very yellow—had some appetite and no thirst. He was cheerful, and I thought almost out of danger on the 10th. But that night he grew worse. I found him on the morning of the 11th, much to my surprise, with dry hot skin, great thirst and restlessness; tongue again dry. He died on the evening of the twelfth, with all the characteristics of yellow fever, including black vomit, which occurred just before his death.[188]

Treatment for the illness included keeping the patient in a perspiring condition, avoiding drafts and chills, and periodically administering quinine, castor oil, brandy, orange leaf tea, and sometimes beef tea.[189] Although the cause of the sickness was unknown, it was connected with poor drainage, lack of sanitation, and contact with the disease.[190] People well understood that frost would dramatically halt the spread of the illness. Though they did not realize that the cold weather killed the fever-carrying mosquitoes, they greeted its coming as a time of delivery and jubilation. In November 1859, after yellow fever had struck 1,200 to 1,500 persons and killed at least 246, the *Tri-Weekly Telegraph* joyously announced:

The wind continued all Saturday night, and Sunday morning found ice everywhere, ice in the prairie, and ice in town, ice in the gutters and ice in the houses[,] ice in the kitchens and ice in the bedrooms, and cold?—guess it was cold! Cold enough to keep lazy people and invalids in bed half the morning; cold enough to drive the frightened blood away from the blue and purple fingers; cold enough to make a man dance a hornpipe;—cold enough to freeze the horns off from a Billy goat! And of course, cold enough to freeze Yellow Jack's ears off. Runaways can come back now. The frost we have had has killed the fever if frost will do it. Last night we had another heavy frost. And to-day is bright and beautiful, but not brighter or more cheerful than the faces of our citizens, who are all rejoicing that the dark days ar[e] over.[191]

Besides cold weather, the greatest weapon against yellow fever was a quarantine against infected places and persons. In 1839 the *Morning Star* suggested that Galveston set up a quarantine against New Orleans, but it was not utilized to any extent by Houston until 1870.[192] During the epidemic of 1867, Columbus set up a barrier against Allyton, several miles away, and escaped the pestilence; Gonzales, on the Guadalupe River, escaped by the same means, while others suffered.[193] This established the efficacy of quarantine. Although such action might disrupt trade, the fear of yellow fever was justifiably deep-seated. "It is far better for us to suffer inconveniences, than for our citizens, our friends, our loved ones to die," stated the *Weekly Telegraph*.[194]

Houston attempted in its quarantines to halt all movement of passengers and goods between its boundaries and the point of contagion. In turn, other places erected barriers against the Bayou City when fever appeared at that location. The quarantines could be vicious:

> When a suspected person is found on the train going to Galveston, he is summarily seized at the muzzle of the six-shooter and tumbled off the train on the open prairie. If he is sick there is no shelter, no hospital, no bed, no preparation for medical treatment, no anything to keep him from dying like a dog. If he is well there is no house, no food, no place where the necessities of life are to be had, and if he approaches a human residence he is driven off by an excited and fear stricken people armed with shot guns. Every house has its separate quarantine, any hamlet or village takes the responsibility of turning back trains, stopping the mails and disorganizing the commerce of an entire State. Human pity is extinguished, human mercy abolished, and insane panic armed with a shot gun rules supreme.[195]

Quarantines, made more efficient with state control after 1878, however, were successful.[196] The *Houston Daily Post* noted in 1887 that the town had experienced no case of yellow fever in fourteen years.[197] Anxiety and panic were now a past phenomenon.[198]

Houston, therefore, by the middle of the 1870's had lost much of its roughness. It was a well-established commercial town with a network of railroads and a useful bayou. Its population had grown in number, suffered through the consequences of Civil War, and witnessed the practical elimination of yellow fever. The next half-century was a period of transition from a somewhat minor town on the western edge of the South to a city of diversified interests, a leader of the Southwest.

4

The Bayou City, 1875-1930

Between the end of Reconstruction and the Great Depression, the transportation network composed of roads, ship channel, and railroads reached maturity. This network, although inspired by the demands of trade, attracted enough manufacturing to dilute the strong, commercial orientation of business. Still, the economy depended on the extraction of products from the surrounding country—mainly cotton, oil, and lumber. Of the three, oil was most significant, for with it came construction of a refinery complex and a local oil-field equipment industry. First, however, the transportation system had to be completed.

Charles Morgan, the ship master who had flanked Galveston and constructed Clinton, died in 1878. His successors adhered to his long-range plans and diverted Clinton traffic when they completed rail connections between New Orleans and Houston in 1880. Though the Houston Direct Navigation Company continued barge operations, the bayou became less important, especially after the new rail connections and also after an improvement of the harbor at Galveston.[1] Morgan and his successors, in addition, collected a toll for the use of the cut through Morgan's Point. The heavy chain stretched across the channel to enforce the payment was a symbol of the monopoly control and decline of bayou traffic. In response to local protest, the United States government agreed to purchase Morgan's improvements in order to liberate the stream. A formal contract for that purpose was drawn in 1881, but because of an adverse report by an army engineer about bayou conditions in 1883 and other delays, possession did not transfer until 1892. Then the government removed the notorious chain and freed the channel.[2]

Despite the decline of water-borne trade, the idea of a serviceable, deep-water ship channel survived. Among the dreamers were John T. Brady, Eber W. Cave, George W. Kidd, William D. Cleveland, Joseph C. Hutcheson, Thomas W. House, Captain H. W. Garrow, and Captain Sinclair Taliaferro.[3] When Galveston obtained a twenty-five–foot–deep channel through her obstructing bar in 1896, she negated Houston's competitive advantage. Large vessels, which formerly had been forced to unload beyond the bar, giving opportunity to Houston barges, could now unship cargo at Galveston docks.[4] That same year, however, U.S. Representative Joseph C. Hutcheson introduced into Congress a bill proposing a twenty-five–foot channel for Buffalo Bayou. The measure passed and Hutcheson arranged for a visit by the Rivers and Harbors Committee.[5] At the end of January 1897, the visitors traveled by tugboat over the rain-swollen bayou, accompanied not only by local channel enthusiasts but also by Thomas H. Ball, Houston's new congressman, who had replaced Hutcheson in the House of Representatives. A grand reception duly impressed the committee, but delays came to the project the following year after inspection by army engineers.[6]

The engineers expressed reservations about the usefulness of the bayou above Harrisburg and the need for the project since Galveston could serve as a port. A temporary intransigence of Congress in regard to river and harbor bills and opposition by Theodore Burton, chairman of the House committee for such projects, added more delay, despite efforts by Houstonians.[7] In 1902, however, through the work of Ball, Congress allocated $1 million for the bayou. Work on the channel continued through 1903, and in 1904 engineers placed a turning basin at the head of Long Reach, a straight stretch of the bayou just above Harrisburg.[8] Although the basin was more than four miles away from the foot of Main Street, where the Allens had located the head of navigation, it made little difference, because the city absorbed the area in 1926.[9]

Workmen completed an eighteen–and–one-half–foot channel in 1908, and on August 10, amid celebration, the United States revenue cutter *Windom* entered the turning basin escorted by the boats of the Houston Launch Club.[10] Houston assumed legal authority over the basin shortly thereafter.[11] National stringency in 1908 prevented appropriations to dredge the bayou to twenty-five feet, the depth necessary for the vessels then in common use along the Gulf coast.[12] In order to push the project forward, Major H. Baldwin Rice, nephew of William Marsh Rice, and Thomas Ball suggested the creation of a navigation district. Such a district could control the watercourse, sell bonds, and offer matching funds to the federal government. Texas City moreover had recently shared costs successfully with the government in a similar undertaking.[13]

Congress approved Houston's plan, and the thought about matching funds helped to set a precedent for such programs.[14] After a spirited campaign, county voters sanctioned the creation of the Harris County Houston Ship Channel Navigation District and a $1.25 million bond issue.[15] Because the bonds offered poor commissions, lacked proper publicity, and demanded a price which could be no less than par value plus accrued interest, the district could not sell them. Houston banks, under the urging of Jesse H. Jones, however, solved the problem by purchasing the securities in proportion to their capital and surplus. This was a tribute not only to the civic interest of the bankers but also to the strength of the financial institutions which now possessed sufficient funds to aid the city.[16] In 1913 voters approved $3 million in bonds for port facilities and the city council established a city harbor board. This organization merged with a district board in 1922 to create a five-member Port Commission with the power to acquire wharves, warehouses, and other facilities for the benefit of the ship channel. Such an arrangement was similar to those of New York, Boston, Philadelphia, San Francisco, Seattle, and New Orleans.[17]

During 1914 the ship channel was dredged to the desired depth of twenty-five feet and in September the *William C. May*, a four-masted sailing vessel drawing eighteen feet of water, arrived at the Clinton docks with a cargo of cast-iron pipe. In October, the *Dorothy*, 310 feet long and drawing nineteen and one-half feet of water, delivered three thousand tons of anthracite coal at Clinton. The official opening of the ship channel came on November 10, 1914, with appropriate celebration. Thousands of spectators witnessed the ceremonies, which included a twenty-one–gun salute, a cannon fired through remote control by Woodrow Wilson in Washington, D.C., a band playing the national anthem from a barge in the center of the turning basin, and Sue Campbell, daughter of Mayor Ben Campbell, dutifully dropping white rose petals into the greasy water from the top deck of the *Windom*. She pronounced, "I christen thee Port Houston; hither the boats of all nations may come and receive hearty welcome."[18]

Unexpectedly, channel traffic decreased in the following years with customs receipts dropping almost 50 percent between 1913 and 1914.[19] Although some blame could be placed on inadequate harbor facilities, the main cause of the faltering trade was World War I, which forced an over-all decline in United States commerce abroad.[20] There was also some difficulty in breaking traditional trade patterns. As J. W. Williams, manager of the Traffic Bureau of the chamber of commerce, explained the situation to the Rotary Club in August 1914: "Now that we have it, what are we going to do with it?"[21] In April of the next year the editor of the *Houston Post* noticed 17,296 bags of sugar transported via Galveston to Sugarland, only twenty miles from Houston, and commented: "It is almost time to hold another dinner and enjoy a general discussion of the value of the ship channel to Houston. The channel has been ready for business since September 1, 1914."[22]

Despite efforts by businessmen and the chamber of commerce, traffic did not increase noticeably during the war years even though the Southern Steamship Company opened service between New York and Houston.[23] Harbor facilities meanwhile improved and in 1919 the port enjoyed its greatest volume since 1914.[24] Tonnage increased through the 1920's with heavy exports of cotton. By 1930 the channel had been deepened to thirty feet, and 7,400 feet of public docks with 17 berths and 72 miles of service railroads existed around the port.[25] Houston ranked as the eighth port in the nation in 1929 and led the country in cotton exports the following year.[26]

While the ship channel evolved to a point of maturity, the railroads completed a web of lines. Between 1875 and 1890, Texas increased trackage from 1,650 miles to 8,486; Houston as the center in south Texas shared this activity.[27] Paul Bremond and others formed in 1875 the Houston East and West Texas Narrow Gauge Railway to penetrate the timber regions to the northeast, a plan often considered before.[28] Bremond, the leader of the venture, had come to Houston in 1842, prospered as a merchant, and successfully constructed the Houston and Texas Central. Work commenced on the new project in 1876, and in 1878 the line reached forty-three miles to Cleveland on the Trinity River.[29] When it connected with Livingston in 1879 and Moscow in 1880, the H.E. & W.T., nicknamed "Hell Either Way Taken," touched the east Texas pine forests.[30] The *Houston Daily Post* reported in 1881 that the three-foot-gauge railroad was transporting twenty carloads of lumber daily to Houston (5,000 feet of lumber per car) and thus earning $400 per day.[31] It connected with Nacogdoches in 1883, but as it reached the Sabine River in 1885, Bremond died and the enterprise fell into receivership. After reorganization in 1892 and conversion to standard gauge in 1894, "Bremond's Road" became part of the Southern Pacific in 1899.[32]

The Houston and Texas Central changed to standard gauge in 1876, which meant that cars from other sections of the nation could roll all the way to Houston,[33] and in November a car of the Chicago, Burlington and Quincy was seen in the Bayou City.[34] Charles Morgan bought this important line in 1877, but the Southern Pacific took it over in 1883.[35] The H. & T.C. ran the most important of the four depots in Houston, Grand Central Station, a "handsome" brick structure, which served nine railways in 1900 and posted twenty arrivals and departures per day.[36] In 1904 the *Houston Post* reported that the various lines had moved 500 million tons of freight in and out of Houston during the preceding year; they paid $4 million to six thousand employees, and five railroads maintained their general headquarters in Houston.[37] In 1906, Colonel B. F. Yoakum, who was affiliated with the Rock Island–Frisco interests, constructed the Houston Belt and Terminal, which encircled the city to facilitate the transfer of cars. This company, which had its headquarters in Houston, placed a depot on Crawford Street.[38] By 1910 seventeen railroads, operated by thirteen companies, united in Houston. This represented the completion of the railroad network, with the exception of an eighteenth line, operated by the Missouri Pacific, which joined the others in 1927.[39] The railway concentration was such that at the end of the first decade of the twentieth century railroads constituted Houston's most important industry.[40]

The coalescent development of rail and water transportation facilities generated an enduring, acrimonious fight between Galveston and Houston over freight rates or, more specifically, over the "differential." Because Houston was foremost in railroad construction for about the first twenty years, most goods moved in and out of Houston, thus establishing it as a basing point for rates. This was reinforced in the 1880's as railroads took over the water-borne freight that traveled to New Orleans and New York.[41] Steamship companies in order to compete had "to bring Houston, so to speak, to the seaboard."[42] The shipping firms therefore minimized, when calculating freight costs, the difference between Houston and Galveston. To figure costs from an interior point, shippers customarily used the charge for shipment to Houston and then added an amount, the differential, to obtain the rate to Galveston. Because of competition offered by the ship channel, the differential was usually less than a railroad would normally charge for carrying freight a distance of fifty miles. The differential thus operated to equalize total freight charges and allowed Houston and Galveston to compete on the same basis for the trade of the interior. When created in 1891, the Texas Railroad Commission, which could control rates, recognized this balance and allowed it to stand.[43]

From 1891 to 1933, Galveston agitated to abolish or reduce the differential so that, in effect, railroads would haul freight to Galveston at little or no charge. Houston's advantage of inland location would thus be lost.[44] The completion of a deep-water channel and the utilization of the same rates for both ports by the Southern Steamship Company placed Galveston at a disadvantage. The fight continued through the 1920's until 1933 when the differential was eliminated on almost all items. By then, however, Houston had expanded southward so that the distance between the two was not so great as before. Galveston, moreover, had long since lost her supremacy, and the Bayou City had little fear of competition from the Island City.[45]

The development of the ship channel and the railroads in this period brought to a point of maturity two major elements of the transportation network. Three other elements—roadways, air transport, and pipelines—evolved but did not reach full effectiveness until after 1930. Early attempts to improve roads and streets by paving with shell or debris from the burned market house had been unsuccessful, and Houston mud remained "a proverb in the mouths of the people who stop in or pass through the city's precincts."[46] In 1879 a special committee of eighteen persons investigated the problem and recommended slab rock plus gravel and shell for a first-rate pavement, but nothing resulted from this.[47] Some plank roads were useful in the First and Fifth wards, but the plan for a twenty-foot plank roadway for Franklin Avenue proved stillborn, and until 1882 Houston amounted to "a huddle of houses arranged on unoccupied lines of black mud."[48]

·In the summer of 1882 the holders of adjoining property paid $10,000 to pave two blocks of Main Street with limestone squares on top of a gravel base. Merchants meanwhile financed at $500 each the laying down of fifteen blocks of gravel on Congress and Franklin streets.[49] With bad weather the following winter the stone pavement became mud covered, probably tracked by vehicles and people, and threatened to sink from sight.[50] The battle nonetheless continued with cypress blocks over a sand-and-gravel foundation for Congress Avenue in 1887 and planking for Washington Avenue in 1888.[51] After experimenting with a variety of materials, the city could boast of twenty-six miles of pavement by 1903. This included about nine miles of brick streets, six of asphalt, six of gravel, three of bois d'arc blocks, and one of macadam.[52] Dust and mud continued to be a nuisance even on these streets, until 1905, when the city employed sweepers and sprinklers to clean them.[53] In 1912 the citizens voted to split the cost of paving, with the city to pay one-third and the property owners two-thirds.[54] Material used was left to local option and in 1914 the city council was authorizing creosoted three-inch wooden blocks, bricks, asphalt, Westrumite, and cement at a maximum cost of $3.50 per square yard.[55] By March 1915, Houston possessed almost 196 miles of paved streets including those of shell or gravel; in 1922 the town began to replace wooden bridges with those of concrete and steel; and in 1926 Harris County voted by a ratio of 4 to 1 to improve the outlying roads.[56]

Main Street, looking north from Preston Avenue, 1890
(HMRC, Houston Public Library)

Sweeny-Coombs Opera House, 1890's (HMRC, Houston Public Library)

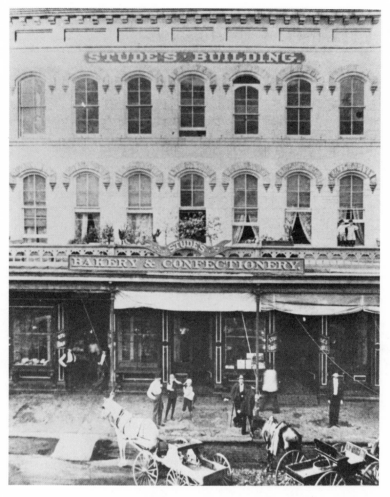

*Stude's Bakery and Confectionery, opposite Market Square, 1890
(HMRC, Houston Public Library)*

*Southwest corner of Main Street and Prairie Avenue, 1894
(HMRC, Houston Public Library)*

Buffalo Bayou at Magnolia Park, 1894 (HMRC, Houston Public Library)

T. W. House Banking Building, 1905 (HMRC, Houston Public Library)

*Main Street, looking south from the north side of Buffalo Bayou, 1915
(HMRC, Houston Public Library)*

Rice Hotel, 1910 (HMRC, Houston Public Library)

Magnolia Park construction, 1911 (HMRC, Houston Public Library)

Main Street, looking south from Preston Avenue, 1915
(HMRC, Houston Public Library)

Chronicle Building, 1915 (HMRC, Houston Public Library)

San Jacinto Battlefield, 1920's (Bank of the Southwest/Frank J. Schlueter Collection, HMRC, Houston Public Library)

Humble oil fields, 1920's (Bank of the Southwest/Frank J. Schlueter Collection, HMRC, Houston Public Library)

During the 1929 flood (HMRC, Houston Public Library)

Possibly the irritation of mud and dust was sufficient to inspire the paving of streets, but local bicycle and automobile enthusiasts also may have had some influence. In 1892 the *Houston Daily Post* noted the use of the shell roads in Houston Heights by the cyclists and commented that with the prospect of brick pavement "their hearts are full of joy." A large crowd, moreover, witnessed the first annual road race of the Magnolia Cycling Club that same year.[57] The use of the automobile also encouraged the building of durable roads and influenced the production of materials for their construction. As the car replaced the horse, the old argument that hard surfaces, such as brick, caused lameness to livestock was no longer heard.[58]

Houston's romance with the automobile began at the turn of the century and by 1905 there were about eighty cars in town.[59] Harris County counted 1,031 motorcars in 1911, 34,869 in 1922, and 97,902 in 1930.[60] With this multiplication came not only agitation for better roads but also problems.[61] The hit-and-run driver appeared: "A day or two ago one of these juggernauts running at high speed ran over a man and broke his leg. It is related that the driver, whoever he was, did not stop to learn how badly his victim was injured or to express regret for the accident. This was simply atrocious . . . it seems there are people here who disregard the rights of the public the moment they become the owners of these machines."[62]

The careless driver made his debut when J. L. Darragh, a young real estate agent who ten days earlier had been arrested for "fast running," struck the back of a slow-moving dairy wagon four miles from Houston. Darragh, who had been traveling at an estimated fifty miles per hour, a "fearful rate of speed," died with a crushed chest, but the young lady with him was only dazed.[63] Joining these other characters was that bane of all urban streets—the woman driver. After reporting that two young women had run down an aged pedestrian, the *Houston Post* stated:

The chivalry of American manhood has always extended to women the widest liberty of action consistent with the welfare of society, hence, whether driving along the public thoroughfares or perambulating the streets, gentlemen, whether clothed in rags or in broadcloth, always freely give her right of way. Appreciating this fact, she should be careful not to abuse the privileges extended her, as by so doing she inevitably loses some of the veneration that man is proud to bestow upon her. We can conceive of no spectacle more pitiable than a woman grown callous to the sufferings of others, and the evidence of such callousness finds its strongest exhibition in driving reck-

lessly through crowded streets and running down helpless pedestrians, without even halting at the cry of distress heard in
the wake of such mad driving.[64]

For those drivers who had trouble with the engine, an Oldsmobile instruction book advised: "We make only one kind—the motor that motes," and "Always consider that it has run, and will run
again if conditions are the same." The handbook went on to warn,
"Don't imagine that our motor runs well on equal parts of gasoline
and water," and, "Don't drive your Oldsmobile 100 miles the first
day. You wouldn't drive a green horse ten miles until you were ac-
quainted with him. Do you know more about a gasoline motor than
you do about a horse?"[65]

To inspire better country roads, the *Houston Post* sponsored a
535-mile race covering a route Houston–Victoria–San Antonio–
Austin–Houston. Jesse Illingsworth won over seven other entries
while driving a twenty-eight–horsepower Maxwell. The competi-
tors experienced good and bad roads, dogs which bit at the tires, and
farmers, "road hogs," who drove their wagons down the middle of
the highway. G. W. Hawkins, who placed second, found it advisable
to pass such wagons as fast as possible. The horses then had less
time to be frightened and the driver following behind could get the
credit for the scare. If nothing else, the race demonstrated the feasibility of cross-country travel by automobile.[66]

As city traffic increased, Houston started a program of control.
In 1907 the council passed an ordinance that required registration,
lights for night-time driving, observation of an eight-miles-per-hour
speed limit downtown and a fifteen-miles-per-hour speed limit elsewhere, driving on the right, passing on the left, a minimum age limit
of eighteen years, and yielding the right-of-way to horses. For violations, fines ranged from $5 to $100.[67] In 1914 the city banned jay-
walking with an ordinance that appropriately became effective on
April Fools' Day. City officials forgetfully violated the ordinance and
one stately gentleman, upon observing a policeman's outstretched
arm signaling him to return to the sidewalk and cross properly,
strode up to the officer, smiled, shook his hand, and said, "So glad to
meet you."[68] In 1920 Rusk and Walker became one-way streets, and
in 1921 the first traffic signals appeared. Operated by a twenty-
two–man traffic squad in khaki shirts and blue trousers, the signals
consisted of semaphore stop-and-go signs mounted on top of permanent umbrellas set in the middle of eleven downtown intersections
and rotated by hand.[69]

The city shortly replaced these awkward devices with an electric system controlled manually at a traffic tower placed in the center of the Capitol–Main Street intersection. The men in this tower could change the Main Street lights to the same color simultaneously.[70] Traffic congestion nonetheless worsened, and some places, such as the intersection of Polk and Dowling, were clogged to a point of paralysis.[71] In 1927 automatic traffic signals came in use and in 1929 the city began to restrict parking on Main Street.[72]

In company with the automobile, of course, was the truck. Trucking lines started in Houston in 1919, but the following year, by the time Governor Will Hobby declared "Ship by Truck and Good Roads Week," there existed twenty-two such firms. That same year the Houston Motor Truck and Trailer Dealers Association promoted a tour: Houston–Cypress–Hempstead–Navasota–Brenham–East Bernard–Eagle Lake–El Campo–Wharton–Bay City–Wharton–Houston, to publicize shipping services.[73] Although little information exists on the growth of the trucking industry, it appears important that a concrete highway to Galveston became available in 1928 and all-weather roads to the Rio Grande Valley by 1931.[74] During the 1930–1931 season, 696,169 bales of cotton moved to Houston by truck. This amounts to three times that of the previous year, but only 697 bales left Houston by truck in 1930–1931 and gross receipts amounted to 2,849,830 bales.[75]

Sharing the city streets with trucks and automobiles were the cars of the interurban railway and the trolleys. Until 1891 the streetcars of Houston moved by mule-power. This alliance between man and animal was not altogether happy, as illustrated in the story of the mule that landed on its back underneath a car after slipping on a curve. Thought to be dead, the mule demonstrated otherwise by kicking its way through the bottom of the car and standing up. The remainder of the night had to be spent finding a means to get the beast out of the car.[76] The mules did provide an excuse for surly drivers, however, as Julia Truitt Bishop explained, "Even with all other circumstances at their smoothest, no man's life can be called happy when it is passed in one long contest with the motive power of Houston street cars."[77] Tradition moreover died with difficulty, for after twenty years of electric cars a driver was heard to say sharply, if absentmindedly, "Git up!" and "Whoa!" when starting and stopping his car.[78]

In 1883 William H. Sinclair bought and merged the Houston City Street Railway Company, which had started in 1874, and the Bayou City Street Railway, which had formed in 1881.[79] In 1886 Sinclair's Houston City Street Railway utilized 41 cars, 119 mules, and 60 employees. It operated six lines, five of which ran on a loop, thus obviating a turntable, and it encouraged the spread of the town.[80] In 1889 William Boyd and his brother started to build a second Bayou City Street Railway Company, resulting in a small-scale track-construction race on Congress Street. Both teams built feverishly as managers exhorted and people cheered. Then the sheriff arrived with an injunction, forcing the Boyds to lay down their tools. Shortly, the sheriff returned with another court order to halt the other crew. With that the *Houston Post* commented, "In the meantime Congress street is all tore up, the rails and ties are promiscuously strewn along the surface, and for several blocks it looks as though it had been hit by a cyclone."[81]

The Bayou City company apparently won the injunction fight and went on to complete sixteen miles of track financed by Galveston capital.[82] In 1890 E. A. Allen and O. M. Carter, representing associates in Omaha, Nebraska, purchased the two lines and proceeded to convert them to electric power.[83] In June 1891, spectators saw the test of the first electric cars, the wheels of which would spark and sputter on rainy days.[84] In 1901, after several receiverships, Owen D. Young of Boston bought the line for the Stone-Webster syndicate. They extended the trolley system to fifty-one miles by 1910 and established a crosstown track in 1913.[85]

Private motorcars and jitneys began to affect streetcar profits as early as 1915 and in 1919 Luke C. Bradley, vice-president of the company, told the Kiwanis Club that the Houston Electric Company, because of its five-cent fare and $400,000 per year loss to jitneys, could neither afford to expand nor maintain the line.[86] The company insisted on paying an 8 percent return on investment, however.[87] Despite increases in fares, profits still declined, so, to help the traction concern, the city outlawed jitneys in 1924.[88] Profits increased then, but so did private auto usage.[89] In 1927 the streetcars and buses, which the company had started to operate in 1923, carried 152,000 passengers per day. They contributed only 9.5 percent of the number of vehicles entering the downtown area but carried 79.6 percent of the people. Still, with 224 trolleys, 90 miles of track, and 39 buses, it was already a crippled business hamstrung by a restrictive franchise, high investment and operating costs, and the popularity of private transportation.[90]

Suffering in somewhat similar manner was the Galveston-Houston Electric Railway, an interurban enterprise that stretched 50.47 miles over an almost straight, flat right-of-way from Houston to Galveston. It utilized fifty-four–seat cars, powered by electricity, and advertised eighteen trips per day each way. The cars, painted Pullman green and capable of moving fifty-five to sixty miles per hour, started operating in November 1911. In November 1936, however, the company quietly ceased to operate, its service taken over by buses.[91]

Somewhat more successful than the electric railways was the air-transport industry which began in this same period. Louis Paulhan, a dapper French pilot with a curled mustache, clad in oilskins and puttees, introduced the airplane to Houstonians with a demonstration in 1910.[92] That same year a local enterprise, the Charliss-Wendling Automatic Aeroplane Company, demonstrated its eighteen-horsepower aircraft. The plane left the ground only twice in seven attempts and finally plowed through a fence and into a car.[93] In the following years there occurred various air shows and exhibitions, but Houstonians did not become air-conscious until the initiation of an airmail route involving Dallas, Fort Worth, Oklahoma City, Wichita, Kansas City, St. Joseph, Moline, and Chicago, in 1925.[94] In 1926 a group of Houston businessmen, including Jesse H. Jones, T. P. Lee, George Noble, and W. S. Patton, along with Major B. M. Law from nearby Ellington Field, a World War I air base, conferred with Paul Henderson, the general manager of National Air Transport, Inc., about connections with Houston. The corporation, which held the mail contract from Dallas to the East, demanded extensive use but started service in November 1926.[95]

To accommodate the airships, Mayor Oscar F. Holcombe appointed a committee in 1927 to locate a flat, well-drained area 1,000 yards square. Shortly, the assistant postmaster-general announced a Galveston-Houston-Dallas route, and in 1928 the Houston Airport Corporation opened the 193-acre airstrip on Telephone Road which became the city's first municipal airport.[96]

The development of these transportation facilities not only aided in moving goods and people but also engendered other business activity. In 1906, for example, the Southern Motor Car Company began to market the "Dixie," assembled from parts shipped to Houston at cheap hardware rates. Because of debts caused by a bank failure, after three years and seventeen automobiles the enterprise failed.[97] In 1920 another company, Southern Motors Manufacturing Association Ltd., offered the "Ranger Four," a five-passenger, four-cylinder vehicle which proved in a 3,500-mile test that it was durable and could travel fifty miles per hour without vibration. This company also failed. It fell into receivership in 1922 and into an alleged mail fraud in 1924.[98] The Ford Motor Company maintained an assembly plant in Houston from 1919 until 1931 and at peak operation employed 1,300 people and produced 350 cars per day.[99] In addition, some attempt was made to produce tires in Houston, and, of

course, automobile dealers, service stations, and garages existed.[100]
More important, however, was the influence of the railroads.

The Houston and Texas Central, from its start, and the Southern Pacific, beginning in 1887, maintained repair shops in the Bayou City. Collis P. Huntington proposed the installation in 1882 but insisted on a bridge over the bayou at Fannin Street. City and county officials complied, and the S.P. shops created a construction boom in the Fifth Ward.[101] To a touring journalist, it appeared that "the thunderbolts of Jove" were being cast at the plant. "Innumerable fires could be seen flashing in the interior of the blacksmith shop, while great clouds of smoke twisted around and floated upwards to join the dusky offspring of coal from other Houston industries."[102] In 1891 the shops employed 1,262 persons and paid $76,890 per month in wages, an average of approximately $61 a month per person.[103]

At the same time the H. & T.C. employed 665 people on a $36,690 monthly payroll at its shops. There the railroad did much the same kind of maintenance and repair work but went further to the point of constructing locomotives.[104] John Milsaps, who had labored in the H. & T.C. blacksmith shop as a young man in 1874–1877, later recalled, "Coal smoke and coal dust, hot fires, much noise of hammers, and brawney men, characterized this place. All the helpers excepting two, a German and myself, were negroes; splendid specimens of the human animal they were too." The labor at the forges was all manual and Milsaps worked with three others striking a piece of hot iron with hammers. "But ah me! if I did not pay dearly for appearances. Sometimes I was ready to drop from exhaustion, but my pride would sustain me." About burning sulphur out of coal in order to make coke, a fearful, hot task, he wrote, "Perspiration would stream through the pores of my body like water thro a sieve."[105]

Attracted by such railroad activity, John F. Dickson moved to Houston from Marshall in 1887, borrowed money from a Galveston banker, and established a foundry to manufacture railroad car wheels. Using iron from Texas and Alabama, the Dickson Car Wheel Company prospered and became famous not only for its wheels but also for the production of large centrifugal pumps. The Pullman Company bought the plant in 1927.[106]

Also encouraging to business activity was the ship channel, attracting not only the facilities necessary for commerce, such as wharves, warehouses, and grain elevators, but also enterprises that depended on water transport. A special instance of this occurred during World War I when the Midland Bridge Company of Missouri and the Universal Shipbuilding Company, a local organization, constructed oceangoing wooden transport vessels on the channel. They completed only about a dozen of the ships, which had to be towed to Beaumont for the installation of engines, when the armistice brought a cancellation of contracts. In 1921 three uncompleted hulls and five wooden vessels could be seen rotting where they had been left on the bayou. Most of these later caught fire and burned.[107]

The more significant Houston businesses, however, those concerned with cotton, lumber, and oil, depended usually on the whole of the transportation network. Cotton, of course, had long been important to Houston, with bales moving from the country through Houston to Galveston. Since compressed cotton took less room to ship, various compresses arose, such as the Davis Compress in 1844, Houston Cotton Compress in 1860, Bayou City Compress in 1875, Peoples Compress in 1881, International Compress in 1882, and Inman Compress in 1883.[108] Several seasonal cottonseed-oil factories which produced oil, coke, meal, linters, hulls, and soap stock also operated.[109] In 1910 there existed in Houston six oil mills, seven compresses, twelve cotton warehouses, and forty-seven cotton factors.[110] The city also possessed a long-standing cotton exchange and a "cotton school," begun in 1906 to teach the sons of farmers how to judge the quality of the staple.[111] As a consequence, by 1930 Houston had become one of the leading cotton markets in the nation; symbolic of this is the success of Anderson, Clayton and Company, one of the largest cotton brokerage firms in the world.

Frank E. Anderson, Monroe D. Anderson, and William L. Clayton started the company in 1904 in Oklahoma City. They bought cotton and operated gins and oil mills throughout Texas and Oklahoma but moved their headquarters to Houston in 1916. As Will Clayton explained later: "We moved to Houston because Houston was the little end of the funnel that drained all of Texas and the Oklahoma territory. . . . In other words we were at the back door, and we wanted to be at the front door."[112] Taking advantage of markets disrupted by World War I, Anderson, Clayton set up sales agencies in Europe, Asia, and Central America. Within the United States they established autonomous buying units in Los Angeles, Charlotte, Atlanta, and Memphis; and to assure quick delivery they built warehouses and compresses in Houston and New Orleans. The company, moreover, produced its own bagging material, and in 1924 tested the feasibility of textile manufacture in Houston. During the 1930's Anderson, Clayton established subsidiary companies abroad, and after World War II diversified into food processing, manufacturing, and insurance. Total assets in 1965 amounted to $309,262,000.[113]

When "Bremond's Road" penetrated the east Texas pine forests in 1880, Houston gained the advantage glimpsed by William Brady in 1871: "Houston situated in an intermediate position with the vast timber lands of Texas east of her parallel, and the vast expanse of country where that timber can and will be utilized west of that parallel, must become the great central depot for the lumber trade of Texas. That trade with all others will increase with the progress of our railroads, and for every ten miles further into the interior of the State that the 'iron horse' finds his way, millions of feet of lumber will be required to relieve the necessities he has created."[114]

In 1899 the total volume controlled through the Houston lumber market was 420 million feet, most of which never entered the city but traveled directly over the railroads from the east Texas sawmills to the purchaser. Of the total sold, 254 million feet went to Texas, 100 million feet north of Texas, and 66 million feet to Mexico and Europe.[115] Such men as John Henry Kirby and Jesse H. Jones found their fortunes in this trade. The M. T. Jones Lumber Company, in which Jesse Jones began his career, was formed in 1883 and moved to Houston in 1899. It demonstrated the wide market for Texas lumber with sales not only in the Lone Star State but also in Louisiana, Illinois, Pennsylvania, Iowa, Arkansas, Oklahoma, and New Mexico.[116] In 1923 there were sixty-eight lumber companies in Houston selling 3 billion feet of lumber per year for $75 million.[117]

Petroleum, rather than cotton or lumber, however, ultimately became the most important item moving through Houston's web of transportation facilities. Fortunately, at the time of its discovery and exploitation, the railroads and the ship channel were developed enough to attract the oil industry to the Bayou City. Although there had been discoveries in Texas before 1901, for Houston they held little significance. On January 10, 1901, at 10:30 A.M., however, Allen W. Hamill observed upon a lone, wildcat derrick near Beaumont at a place to be known as Spindletop:

> At about 700 feet or a little over in, why the drilling mud commenced to boil up through the rotary, and it got higher and higher and higher up through the top of the derrick and with such pressure, why, the drill pipe commenced to move up. It moved up and started to going out through the top of the derrick.
>
> . . . .
>
> It didn't last so awful long, but it died down very gradually. Well, we three boys then sneaked back down to the well after it quieted down and surveyed the situation. . . . I walked over and looked down the hole there. I heard—sorta heard some-

thing kinda bubbling just a little bit and looked down there and here this frothy oil was starting up. But it was just breathing like, you know, coming up and sinking back with the gas pressure. And it kept coming up and over the rotary table and each flow a little higher. Finally it got—came up with such momentum that it just shot up clear through the top of the derrick.[118]

The following day on page three the *Houston Daily Post* noted, "Oil Struck Near Beaumont," and shortly the paper was filled with the advertisements of speculative companies as oil fever hit the town.[119] As petroleum argonauts tracked through Houston back and forth to Beaumont, they paid a premium for a cot in the hallway of a crowded hotel and heard stories of instant wealth.[120] For local businessmen, there was other opportunity. Peden and Company, a hardware concern, began to advertise "Oil Well Casing and Pipe, Drilling Cable, Etc.," and Hugh Hamilton of the Houston Ice and Brewing Association journeyed to Beaumont to negotiate for 100,000 barrels of oil for fuel purposes.[121] Local businessmen met at the Business League to investigate the possibility of a pipeline to Spindletop. It was pointed out to these men that in heating power two barrels of oil equaled one cord of wood, and three and a half to four barrels were the equivalent of one ton of coal.[122]

Oil for industry, however, moved to Houston by rail over the next few years. The American Brewing Association, Magnolia Brewery, Houston Electric Street Railway, Southern Pacific, and International and Great Northern, nonetheless, changed to oil for a fuel supply.[123] Pipelines, a highly specialized transportation system, came to Houston with the opening of the Humble field, a few miles north of Houston. There had been exploration in that area since 1902, but only gas had been found. In 1904, however, the Moonshine well struck oil and shortly produced 1,600 barrels daily. Real estate which had sold at $6,400 per acre at Humble shot to $16,000 per acre within a week's time.[124]

In 1905 a plan developed to move oil from Humble via pipeline to Batson and then to Port Arthur, where refineries had been located to process the petroleum of Spindletop. The *Houston Post* feared a diversion of wealth and urged the placement of refineries in Houston.[125] The threat was short-lived because one week later the Texas Company filed in county court for permission to build a line from Humble to Houston.[126] The corporation erected a tank farm at the intersection of the International and Great Northern and the Houston East and West Texas railroads; in April the eight-inch pipe reached

Houston.[127] Gulf Oil Company constructed a mixing plant at Lynchburg on the ship channel in 1915, with a pipeline to Port Arthur, and
to Goose Creek a year later.[128] Houston thus started to become a
focal point for the oil industry in south Texas.

In the early twentieth century the Bayou City found itself with
useful transport potential in the middle of an emerging oil region.
Goose Creek began to produce in 1908, Blue Ridge in 1919, Pierce
Junction in 1921, and in the 1930's Conroe, Eureka Heights, My-
kawa, Tomball, and South Houston.[129] Joseph S. Cullinan, founder of
the Texas Company, listed in 1918 large acreage, fresh water, protection from storms and floods, and deep-water shipping as prerequisite
for oil refineries. To him only Houston, Beaumont, and Orange met
those requirements for the region.[130] Torkild Rieber, a shipmaster for
the Texas Company, explained later that Galveston and Texas City
lost out at this point in development because of devastating storms
in 1900 and 1907.[131] It was consequently inevitable that oil companies located in the convenient, secure, ship-channel area.

The Texas Company moved its offices to the Bayou City in 1908
and bought, twenty years later, the Galena-Signal refinery, which
had been constructed in 1916. Gulf Oil transferred its offices to
Houston in 1916. Harry F. Sinclair completed a refinery in 1918;
Deep Water Refineries established one in 1919; Crown Oil and Refining Company, in 1920; Humble Oil and Refining Company, organized in 1917, in 1920 at Baytown. Shell Oil started construction of
a refinery in 1929 and moved its regional offices to Houston in
1933.[132] By 1930 there were eight refineries along the ship channel.
They possessed a capacity for processing 194,000 barrels a day and
represented a $200 million investment.[133]

The oil industry in Houston in turn inspired several other enterprises. Natural gas became available in 1926 for both domestic and
industrial use, supplied by such firms as Houston Gulf Gas Company, Houston Pipe Line Company, and Houston Gas and Fuel Company.[134] An oil-tool industry also emerged. Howard R. Hughes, a contractor at Spindletop who did not like his drill bit, bought the idea
for a bit from Granville A. Humason, a millwright, one night in a
bar for $150. He then formed a partnership with Walter B. Sharp,
sued a company that was illegally making the bit for $50,000, and
started manufacturing it himself at the Sharp-Hughes Tool Company. Sharp died in 1912 and the firm became Hughes Tool Company, which in 1925, the year after Hughes' death, was worth $2 mil-
lion.[135] This company helped to form the foundation for the wealth
of Howard R. Hughes, Jr., aviator, movie producer, entrepreneur, and
son of the Spindletop contractor. Humason produced another bit,

which was eventually taken up by Clarence E. Reed, who in 1917 established the Reed Roller Bit Company for its manufacture.[136] At the same time James Abercrombie, a driller, supervisor, and contractor, developed a practical device to prevent well blowouts due to high gas pressure. H. S. Cameron, who ran a machine shop and serviced Abercrombie's equipment, started to produce the preventer in 1922. Cameron Iron Works, another large oil-field equipment manufacturer in Houston, thus began operations.[137]

Accompanying the oil companies, especially to the ship channel area, came other business concerns, such as Armour, which in 1914 built a plant to produce twenty thousand tons of fertilizer per year.[138] The Texas Portland Cement Company, attracted by the transportation facilities, began to operate in 1916 with shell from Galveston Bay, clay from Pasadena, and oil brought by barges through the channel.[139] American Maid Flour established facilities in 1922, Carnegie Steel spent $2 million on a warehouse in 1926, and the Texas Chemical Company, a subsidiary of Pacific Bone and Fertilizer Company of San Francisco, produced sulphuric acid in 1920 and fertilizer in 1922.[140] By the end of the 1920's more than fifty businesses had located along the channel.[141]

As might be expected in a period of business growth and transformation, banking activity expanded and labor unrest increased. Strikes occurred periodically, against the Direct Navigation Company in 1880; the streetcar line in 1897, 1898, 1902, 1904; the Southern Pacific in 1906, 1911, 1922; the Citizens' Electric Company in 1899; building contractors in 1900 and 1907; and employees at the docks in 1878 and 1920. Sometimes violence exploded, as during the streetcar strike in 1904 when cars were dynamited and mobs halted the trolleys; or during the railroad trouble in 1911, when several strikebreakers were injured and at least one killed; and in the Southern Pacific conflict in 1922 when a black strikebreaker died in a shower of stones hurled by a mob.[142]

The Houston workingman was somewhat isolated from the rest of the nation except for some influence by the Knights of Labor in the 1880's. Labor was divided by race and sex. Black labor was largely unskilled and unorganized; the bulk of working women and children were black domestic servants. In 1890 average daily wages for industrial workers were $1.82 for a man, $1.05 for a woman, and $.98 for a child. There were no sweatshops, but people worked six days a week for eight to nine hours per day.

In 1889 the Houston Labor Council formed and began to serve as a focal point for union activity. By 1905 Houston was the leading labor city in Texas and in 1914 possessed fifty unions comprising

TABLE 2. *Bank Deposits per Capita in the United States and Houston, 1900, 1910, 1920*

	1900	1910	1920
U.S.	$117	$194	$392
Houston	$118	$370	$617

21.5 percent of the white working force. The unions concentrated in the building trades. By and large, compared to other cities, Houston labor was less violent and workers maintained respect for property rights. They lived scattered throughout the city and were considered friends and neighbors. Even the police sympathized with strikers and refused to move against them during the streetcar strikes of 1898 and 1904. Concern for the community was more significant than union loyalty, even though Labor Day was a popular holiday.[143]

A forward step in local banking occurred in 1890 when the five national banks, burdened with the daily balancing of accounts, established the Houston Clearing House with Emanuel Raphael as manager. Every afternoon the reciprocal accounts of participating banks thus could be balanced without the risk and nuisance of sending large amounts of cash through the streets.[144] More significant for Houston, however, was a remarkable accumulation of wealth between 1900 and 1920 indicated by bank deposits per capita, shown in Table 2.[145] For the city such monetary advance indicates not only the success of local business enterprise but also the increased availability of capital to fund civic development as demonstrated in the case of the Houston Ship Channel bonds in 1911. In Rostow's terminology, this signifies for Houston a point of "take-off."[146]

To its detriment, Houston lost the struggle to win the Federal Reserve District Bank in 1913–1914. Houston, Dallas, Waco, and Austin, among others, competed, but after the hearings, Dallas won the prize. Though there might have been some solace in that Oscar Wells, the first governor of the Dallas bank, was from Houston, the Bayou City nonetheless lost the prestige that the Federal Reserve Bank could command.[147] In 1919 Houston applied to Dallas for a branch, and this request was granted.[148] The city picked up second-place honors in 1917 when it received the Federal Farm Loan Bank and in 1923 the Federal Intermediary Credit Bank. After seven years' operation the Farm Bank had lent $107 million to 37,000 people in the region.[149] The damage which resulted in the loss of the F.R.S. Bank to the north Texas rival, however, was irreparable and Houston

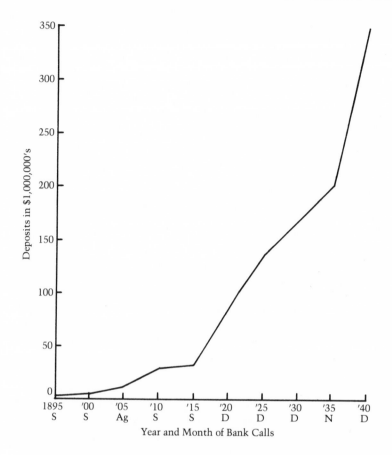

FIGURE 3. Houston bank deposits, 1895–1940. (Data from J. Virgil Scott, "Houston Banks Grow," *Houston* 15 [September 1943]: 6–7.)

has struggled with Dallas for financial supremacy in the state since then. Perhaps, because of its location, Houston was unacceptable, but the loss may also have been due to faulty leadership.

Throughout its history the city has depended for its development not only on geography, technology, and natural resources but also to a certain extent on people willing to promote the community. For the period 1875–1930, Houston found champions in Eber W. Cave, Thomas H. Ball, John Henry Kirby, H. Baldwin Rice, and Jesse H. Jones, as well as various other civic-minded men and organizations. The Board of Trade was one of the outstanding groups, but its effectiveness seemingly faltered in the 1890's when other organizations arose to take on the same tasks of civic promotion. There were formed, for example, the Houston Commercial League, in 1890; the Houston Business League, in 1895; the Houston Manufacturers' Association, in 1900; the Merchants' and Business Men's Association, in 1900; the Industrial Club, in 1906; the Houston Bankers', Jobbers', and Manufacturers' Association, in 1906; the 200,000 Club, in 1908; and the Young Men's Business League, in 1916.[150] The Houston Business League, having 1,200 members and an income of $17,000 in 1911, eventually proved the most viable. The league voted at the end of 1910 to adopt the name "Chamber of Commerce," which resulted in the organization that endures to the present.[151] The Junior Chamber of Commerce emerged in 1927 to assist the senior organization and to promote civic projects.[152]

These associations promoted trade, advertised the city, encouraged the establishment of industry, goaded the municipal government to improve services, offered useful information to members, and tried to attract conventions. The Houston Business League, for example, in its first year of life agitated for a paid fire department, distributed twenty thousand pamphlets, gave out 1 million pieces of advertising matter at the Atlanta Exposition, promoted the Confederate States of America Convention for Houston, investigated sewage and water problems, and protested a railroad tariff on corn from Kansas.[153]

The greatest coup of city boosting came in 1928 when Jesse H. Jones secured for Houston the Democratic National Convention, a feat not since duplicated. Jones had been the financial director of the Davis presidential campaign in 1924, and as such he attended a meeting of the national committee in January 1928 to help pick a site for the forthcoming convention. At the last moment he offered $200,000 plus a 25,000-seat auditorium if the committee would choose Houston over San Francisco, which had bid $250,000. On the fifth ballot, by a vote of 54 to 48, Jesse Jones and Houston won the convention.[154] Texans gratefully selected Jones as a favorite son and seriously mentioned him for the position of vice-president. As the *Houston Post-Dispatch* exclaimed, "If Smith and Jones isn't a democratic combination of names, then what is?"[155] Although Jones refused to run for the vice-presidency, a $100,000 auditorium, open at the sides, was ready when Franklin D. Roosevelt arrived in June 1928 to nominate his friend Al Smith of New York.[156]

As might be expected in a city with such a burgeoning economy, the population increased rapidly. With a population of 292,000 in 1930, Houston placed first in Texas and twenty-sixth in the nation.[157] Blacks, the largest minority group, made up 22 percent of the population compared to 39 percent in 1880.[158] Out of a total labor force of 137,000 in 1929–1930, 16,000 people were involved in manufacturing, 7,000 in wholesale trade, and 17,000 in retailing. The value of manufactured products was $145,050,000, but value added in Houston through manufacturing was only $65,278,000. Total retail sales amounted to $184,680,000, and the wholesale total amounted to $519,913,000.[159] The national ratio between wholesale and retail employees was 1 to 3.6 in 1929.[160] For Houston the ratio was 1 to 2.4, which indicates a relatively greater number of people engaged in wholesale work. Houston thus demonstrated what William Siddall has called "centrality."[161] That is, Houston served as a distribution point for a surrounding hinterland. The national ratio for wholesale-retail to manufacturing workers was 1 to 1.3.[162] Houston's ratio of 1 to 0.7 reveals relatively less emphasis on manufacturing. To a large extent, Houston was still a commercial city. Manufacturing nonetheless had increased in significance between 1875 and 1930 and contributed to the formation of a more diverse economy. Buffalo Bayou, an effective artery of trade, attractive to industry, symbolized this change in Houston's economic life.

5

The Magnolia City, 1875-1930

The period of fifty-five years preceding 1930 was a time of transition in political and social as well as economic life. The municipal government emerged from the depression of the 1870's with an intolerable debt, as revealed by treasurer John Reichman in 1878. His report is shown in Table 3.[1]

The excess of revenue over disbursements, added to the interest paid, amounts to $20,816.35, the total money available to support debt. At a favorable 3 percent interest rate, the city could sustain $693,878.33 of debt, provided that no principal had to be paid. Total debt for Houston in 1878, however, was $1,691,349.03, and the interest rate carried by some of the bonds was as high as 6 percent. It is thus understandable that the town defaulted on bond payments, an action begun in July 1875.[2] The situation was so desperate in 1876 that Judge James Masterson commanded the arrest of Mayor I. C. Lord and the council for nonpayment of $8,957.80, a debt ordered paid by the court.[3] The city fathers considered this affair an "unjustifiable arbitrary and tyrannical exercise of Judicial power, calculated to subvert republican institutions and destroy the dignity and Sovereignty of City Government."[4] This immediate trouble ended when the town officials obtained a writ of habeas corpus from Judge John P. White of the Court of Appeals in Seguin who censured Masterson and held that there could be no imprisonment for debt in the United States.[5]

To meet local needs, the city issued scrip, often worth only thirty cents on the dollar in the market. The paper certificates could be used at full value to pay taxes, and this, of course, made the financial situation worse.[6] To care for the debt problem, the town refunded with new bonds of lower interest, longer life, and less par value.[7] Some bondholders refused to exchange at such unfavorable rates as fifty cents on the dollar and attempted to force payment through court action. Difficulties thus continued through the 1880's. In 1886 there was consideration of repudiation through the Mem-

TABLE 3. *City of Houston, Treasurer's Statement*

Revenue and Disbursements: December 2, 1877, to December 2, 1878	
Revenue:	
Taxes: Back taxes paid	$ 8,077.56
Ad valorem	73,557.55
Bond taxes	10,349.83
Licenses	9,645.70
Rent	232.50
Fines	1,223.36
Total revenue:	$103,086.50
Disbursement:	
General government costs	$ 24,574.19
Interest	11,700.27
Public safety: Police	14,649.26
Fire	12,003.57
Health	7,771.25
Public works: Engineering	271.50
Streets and bridges	23,000.38
Total disbursements:	$ 93,970.42

phis Plan by abandoning the city charter, and in 1887 the mayor reported that even if all taxpayers met their obligation a $21,217 deficit would still exist.[8] The *Houston Daily Post* argued then that the "Shylocks" who had bought the bonds originally at twenty-five to fifty cents per dollar deserved repudiation if they would not exchange. They could "hold their bonds and whistle for their interest."[9] Part of the debt was exchanged, however, and in the 1890's the financial situation brightened.[10]

Although it was still necessary to borrow occasionally to meet current demands, a rise in revenue to $291,300 in 1894 enabled Houston to make payments and even to sell new bonds at a premium.[11] In 1897 treasurer Alexander Szabo reported revenue at $569,136.12, disbursement at $583,533.52, and bonded debt at $2,108,300, with interest ranging from 5 to 8 percent. The city, nonetheless, was paying its obligations and sold a bond issue of $250,000 that year at a premium of $2,420.[12]

While the financial situation fortunately eased, a complex problem involving not only money but also water supply, sewage, fire control, and health arose. Formerly Houstonians obtained water from the bayous and from rain which was stored in cisterns and barrels, but in 1878 the city authorized James M. Loweree of New York to build a waterworks to supply the town from Buffalo Bayou. The twenty-five–year contract required provision of 3 million gallons per day, a 150,000-gallon reservoir, free water for three fountains, and pressure that could throw six streams one hundred feet high through fifty feet of hose, using one–and–one-eighth to two–and–one-half–inch nozzles. Loweree could charge no more than five cents per 100 gallons and had the right to lay pipes under the streets so long as he replaced the pavement. The city agreed to pay $75.00 per year each for fifty hydrants, with a reduction if more were added; and it was privileged to buy the company at its appraised value after twenty-five years.[13]

Loweree installed a dam above the Preston Street bridge, laid water pipes, began operation, and sold out to Houstonians in 1881. However, under the presidency of former mayor T. H. Scanlan, the Houston Water Works Company ran into difficulties. In 1886 the Howard Oil Mills burned while helpless firemen found no water pressure at the hydrants. Scanlan greeted investigators of the matter with "a liberal quantum of profanity, vituperation and personal epithets."[14] In 1891 a fire starting at the Phoenix Lumber Mill in the Fifth Ward swept through twenty acres of urban property and shut out the sun with its smoke. Again the fire fighters could obtain no water at the hydrants, but a messenger sent on horseback to the pumphouse noted 130 pounds pressure on the gauge. Still, it was forty minutes before water would flow out of the hoses, and then the strongest stream reached only twelve feet. It was not until other mains had been cut off that satisfactory pressure was obtained. Too-small pipes in the Fifth Ward, was the Water Company's excuse.[15]

In 1894 pressure during a six-block conflagration in the center of town was insufficient to throw water to the rooftops, and a test afterward revealed that six of the streams could reach only twenty-five to fifty feet in height.[16] Also in 1894, during a $500,000 blaze that killed a nun and a novice and practically destroyed the block Franklin–San Jacinto–Congress–Caroline, firemen had to use a stream so feeble that it turned to spray when it struck the draft of the fire.[17] In 1901 the city hall and market fell prey to flames, and water pressure was so slight streams could not reach the roof. That time, even the fire alarm switchboard was lost.[18] Obviously, the Houston Water Works had failed in the struggle against fire.

The company failed in another important way. It was unable, or perhaps unwilling, to supply pure water to the city. Until 1887 the major source was Buffalo Bayou which at that time yielded, apparently, relatively clean water. The *Houston Post* stated:

A great many people think that the water furnished by the waterworks is unfit for drinking or culinary purposes, but in that
they are greatly mistaken. The supply is obtained from a portion of the bayou which is pregnant with springs, and the
water is free from all impurities and is pure and wholesome to
drink. Of course, after heavy rains the banks of the bayou wash
into the stream and the water is then discolored slightly. But
even then it is good and much better at all seasons than Mississippi river water, especially at St. Louis, where the river is
muddy and dirty.[19]

In 1887 in the Second Ward, however, Henry Thompson, with a
wooden auger attached to a joint of pipe, drilled an artesian well that
produced water free of impurities except for a trace of lime.[20] Shortly
thereafter Gus Warnecke brought up water that was "clear, pure and
soft" through a two-inch pipe sunk 180 feet on his premises at Franklin and LaBranch streets. The cool artesian-well water spurted two
feet above the surface and flowed at a rate of 1,400 gallons per hour.[21]
This incited a rush to tap what later proved to be the nation's third-
greatest artesian reservoir. Houstonians had found a source of pure
water right under their feet.

The Water Works Company began to drill in February 1888, and
by 1891 it operated fourteen wells to supply a seven-square-mile
area through forty miles of pipe.[22] To meet the extraordinary demands of fire fighting, however, the company resorted to its old
source which, of course, placed Buffalo Bayou water in the mains.
Increasing pollution of the stream through the 1890's created a difficulty. In 1893 people complained that tap water was no better than
bayou water; fish died in the bayou as a result of creosote poison-
ing; "tar water" flowed from the pipes.[23] Physicians noted a rise in
"bowel" trouble, and even Scanlan's wife complained about the water. The president of the company promised more wells.[24]

But the difficulty persisted. The Houston Cotton Exchange, referring to the bayou as "an immense cesspool, reeking with filth and
emitting a stench of vilest character," asked the city council to halt
pollution.[25] The city engineer asserted that solids from toilets appeared in the bayou, and a reporter noted a sewer outlet dumping
forty thousand gallons daily from the Houston and Texas Central
shops into the stream—above the Water Works dam.[26] In 1895, when
the Houston District Medical Association warned that the product
of the Water Works was the cause of much illness in town, president
Scanlan retorted that the smell came from tar in new mains, that
Houston tap water was better than Mississippi River water, and that

his company had no obligation to provide pure artesian-well water. The medical group countered with an investigation that revealed about a dozen privies, a smallpox graveyard, a dead cow, an oil mill, and cattle yards as sources of pollution above the dam.[27] Another investigation the same year disclosed cattle from the Southern Oil Mill stockyards stirring the water, more dead cows, in a state of putrefaction, and a drain leading from the mill to the bayou "covered with a light scummy substance," which emitted "an almost unbearable stench." "It is our opinion," the investigators concluded, "that the use of this water is a menace to the lives of the people of this community."[28] Although conditions remained the same, six years later the city council renewed the contract of the water company, allowing the use of bayou water for emergency purposes.[29]

To solve the problem, Houston had to clean up the bayou or it had to restrict the supply to artesian-well water. Cities did not begin to use chlorine for disinfecting purposes until about 1910, and Houston did not try it until 1933.[30] At the turn of the century, therefore, the use of chlorine was not an alternative. The United States government, however, did prompt a move to halt pollution. Major A. M. Miller, while inspecting the potential ship channel in 1895, pointed out to civic leaders that the government had no intention of cleaning Houston's sewage out of the bayou and that the city had better clear up the mess if it desired any federal aid.[31] After confirmation of this threat, the city accepted the plans of Alexander Potter, a consulting engineer, for a $250,000 sewer system and approved a $300,000 bond issue to finance the project.[32]

The sewer system, utilizing advanced concepts then applied only in a few other places in the world, consisted of a series of pipes, varying eighteen to forty-two inches in diameter, which led to a central pumping station in the Fifth Ward. Where necessary, the sewage crossed the bayous through siphons. Centrifugal pumps at the station forced the sewage through a twenty-four–inch iron pipe to filter beds, four and one-half miles away. Heavy matter stayed on the surface of the beds, where it dried. Workmen removed this with rakes, but the rest of the sewage filtered through various layers of broken stone, gravel, coke, and sand. The final effluent flowed into a long canal leading to Buffalo Bayou.[33] At the opening inspection of the system, which finally cost $280,000, Potter bragged about the purity of the effluent. George L. Porter, one of the visitors, jokingly suggested that it should be bottled, but Potter and his assistant demonstrated their conviction by dramatically drinking some of the treated water. Though they declared it quite palatable, no one else could be induced to taste it.[34]

The new system satisfied the army engineers working on the bayou, but unfortunately this bold effort to eliminate pollution was useless. The city abused and neglected the installation. When Mayor H. Baldwin Rice toured the facility in 1905, he found that the filters processed only about half the sewage, that the sand beds were clogged and four to five feet deep in water, and that one of the coke beds was not used at all because it leaked into a keeper's house. Part of the system had become a lake, complete with water birds, snakes, and a family of alligators. At the spot where Potter drank, the mayor noted the malodorous atmosphere and commented, "Well, I do not know how the water looked when Mr. Potter drank it, but I readily relinquish any claim that I may have on any portion of it to Mr. Potter or anyone else who desires the quaff from it."[35]

Although the filtration system continued in use, and new disposal plants were eventually built, pollution in Buffalo Bayou remained. In 1916 Mayor Ben Campbell estimated that 70 to 80 percent of the sewage went directly into the bayou, and the same year the *Houston Post* noticed thirty-five private sewers draining into the stream, a rather sad condition for a town called by its inhabitants the "Magnolia City."[36] As it has turned out, Buffalo Bayou remained polluted from that time to the present day; Houstonians have been unwilling to clear it.

Since its water flowed into the mains, during emergencies, for the citizens of the early twentieth century the bayou was a serious health menace. In 1902 the city council began to consider the purchase of the Water Works which at that time possessed fifty-five wells and sixty-five miles of mains.[37] In 1903 Houston offered $750,000, but Scanlan thought the property worth $1.5 million and refused.[38] Trouble continued. At the women's ward of the police station, a clogged water pipe yielded a three-foot-long eel in a state of dissolution. With sarcasm the chief clerk said, "Now, that eel undoubtedly came from the artesian wells with which the water company is supplying the city."[39]

An experiment with filters failed when A. L. Metz of the Tulane Medical Department found insect wings and fragments of feathers in the filtered bayou water. He claimed a safe bacteria level at 500 per cubic centimeter, but the Houston sample counted 161,606. After this, a meeting of Thomas W. House and J. C. Hutcheson, company representatives, with the city council resulted in a promise of more artesian wells.[40] In 1904 the Water Works possessed sixty-nine wells and pumped, per capita, 170 gallons per day (gpd.). This compared to New Orleans at 35 gpd., Atlanta at 43 gpd., and Dayton, Ohio, at 50 gpd. The next year Houston pumped 207 gpd. and ranked second only to Philadelphia at 236 gpd.[41] Obviously, Houstonians wasted water, the result of a flat charge for water service.

Seth A. Morris, a chemistry professor at the Galveston Medical School, inspected the area around the Water Works dam in January 1906 and classified the water as "rank poison."[42] The following month workmen repairing a main in the Fifth Ward discovered five live catfish in the pipe. "Inasmuch as catfish are not commonly found in artesian water, and in view of the fact that the company claims to be furnishing pure artesian water," commented the *Houston Post*, "the 'catch' is regarded rather remarkable."[43] In May the voters authorized the purchase of the Water Company; they approved a $434,700 bond issue for the project in June; and, subsequently, the city bought the plant for $901,700, a price that included the debt of the company.[44]

The government launched a campaign to stop leakage and began to install meters to check waste. In 1906, when the city assumed control, there were only twenty-four meters in use and total water consumption amounted to almost 11 million gpd. Two years later at least 670 meters existed, and consumption was 9.3 million gpd., despite 595 new connections.[45] By March 1910, there existed 1,641 meters and in September the city pumped 8.7 million gpd., which meant 87.4 gpd. per person.[46] Though there was momentary low pressure at a fire in 1907, eight months later it was entirely sufficient to fight a blaze at the Houston Hotel.[47] Under municipal ownership, consequently, the Water Works became more efficient; it was able to supply pure water and still provide satisfactory supplies for fire control. As Mayor Rice summarized: "In my opinion the purchase of the water works was one of the best investments ever made by the city. The old company made no effort to keep up with the development of the city and as a result there were numerous complaints. Since the city took charge, extensions have been made in all parts of the city and an effort has been put forth by the officials to keep pace with the city's unusual development."[48]

The unraveling of this tangled problem coincided significantly with major changes in city government. When a reform mayor, Orren Thaddeus Holt, took office in 1902, he found the account books so disordered that data for a financial statement on the condition of the city were unavailable. Following a discussion about hiring independent auditors, John Henry Kirby offered to cover the difference if the municipal government did not save, within a year, as a result of the work, enough to pay the auditors. The city, therefore, hired the firm of Haskins and Sells to review records from 1899 to 1902 and to install a new accounting system.[49] At the end of 1902 the accountants reported that the general books were inaccurate, ledgers had not been balanced since January 1, 1900, and a systematic filing system did not exist. In the scattered documents found in the city auditor's office, the market house vault, and the washroom of city hall, they discovered all kinds of errors and irregularities, which showed a total shortage of $54,631.42.[50] Of that amount, $21,612.61 involved school board funds which led to fraud charges against Seth E. Tracy for issuing forged warrants. Although condemned to two years in the penitentiary, Tracy won a reversal from the Court of Criminal Appeals.[51] As reflected in the relatively modern financial statements issued by the city, the accounting system of government became much more efficient after 1902.

At the same moment debate arose concerning a general reform in the structure of government. Charter changes, proposed in 1902, included increasing the number of aldermen to eighteen, creating an office of controller, extending the city limits to four square miles, giving pensions to firemen and policemen, and allowing the city to build hospitals, workhouses, and orphanages.[52] The *Houston Daily Post* suggested a study of the commission form of government at Galveston and its modified version at Dallas.[53] Discussion continued until December 1904, when voters approved, 1,262 to 815, a government to be elected every two years, featuring four aldermen, elected at large, and a mayor who would appoint all other officers with the consent of the aldermen.[54] The newspapers hoped that the new form would be more efficient and less expensive and that it would eliminate politics and fix responsibility.[55]

The Texas legislature, however, received two charters from Houston for approval—one from a citizens' committee supported by the mayor and the other from a group of aldermen. Although dissimilar on many small points, the main difference was that the citizens' committee wanted a full-time mayor and an effective date for the new government forty days after legislative approval. The aldermen's group wanted a part-time mayor and a date for the new government in April 1906, when their own terms would expire.[56] The state accepted the charter of the citizens' committee and, despite obstructions created by the unhappy aldermen, H. Baldwin Rice became mayor on July 5, 1905.[57]

Hailed for its simplicity and efficiency, the new government proceeded to solve the water problem, eliminate the floating debt, and, in time, reduce taxes.[58] Financial statements for 1904 and 1906, when compared, indicate a greater efficiency under the new form. Administrative costs dropped from $154,657.24 to $143,419.25, and expenses for public safety from $175,323.35 to $167,065.85, with no apparent detriment to the city. Revenue rose from $869,778.31 to $1,134,641.18 and, even though expenses in 1906 were greater because of extraordinary school expenditures, the excess of revenue in 1906 amounted to 4.56 percent of total income compared to 3.65 percent in 1904.[59] The *New York Times* suggested that Houston's success might be due to the desire of the participants rather than the structure of the government, but the *Houston Post* pointed out that Rice, as well as two aldermen, had served before without such accomplishment.[60] Of course, the motivation of men can change, but nonetheless the commission government as applied in Houston at the time was, for whatever reason, more efficient than the government it replaced. H. Baldwin Rice, who remained mayor until 1913, was an unusually able man, and the new form may simply have liberated his talents. The commission form of government was no panacea for urban problems, however, and later, especially in the 1920's, there occurred discussion about changing to a city manager plan.[61] Seemingly, in politics, as elsewhere, there was no substitute for honest, conscientious, intelligent leadership.

Among other characteristics, the Rice tenure is noteworthy for its interest in city planning. There had been early attempts to enhance the beauty and order of the town by planting trees and assigning street numbers and names,[62] but, as one Houstonian observed in 1892: "Houston is an overgrown, dirty village, seemingly blundering along without any policy or defined government or management. . . . For many years I lived in Houston and did not leave it. I failed to appreciate the difference in its general appearance and that of other cities until my business took me away to other fields. I am compelled to say that Houston is the most dirty, slovenly, go-as-you-please, vagabond appearing city of which I have knowledge."[63]

Some improvement resulted from the purchase of sixteen acres in downtown Houston for a city park in 1899. Extensively used in its first years, Sam Houston Park, as it came to be called, possessed a zoo and a favorite bronze drinking fountain in the form of a whimsical elf named Brownie.[64] Although this park still exists in the heart of the city, it is practically inaccessible since it is isolated by freeways, Buffalo Bayou, downtown offices, and limited parking space. Empty at almost all times, the park is the preserve of the Harris County Heritage Society which maintains several old houses on the land. Through the generosity of Elizabeth Baldwin Rice, J. J. Settegast, George H. Hermann, and others, the city received additional park land, and in 1924 Houston bought a former National Guard encampment which became Memorial Park.[65] Although Memorial Park was the largest, Hermann Park, located near South Main Street, received a zoo in 1922 and developed into the most important park of the city.[66]

Apparently, around the turn of the century, Houstonians became more sensitive to the appearance and problems of their community. The *Houston Post* noted numerous complaints concerning unnecessary noise—night train whistles, morning factory whistles, boisterous and profane hack drivers, and "strong-lunged" roosters.[67] The profusion of overhead wires also became objectionable. Joining those of the telegraph were the telephone wires. In June 1878, the dispatchers of the Houston and Texas Central experimented with a one-hundred-mile line to Bryan. Although not a success, a group of men listening intently for immortal words from Bryan heard with "tolerable clearness" the question, "Say what kind of a rooster are you down thar, anyhow?"[68] Another experimental wire, less than a week later, demonstrated the usefulness of the instrument for local calls, and in 1879 the Western Union Telegraph Company gave phone service to forty subscribers.[69] Long-distance calls became possible for Houstonians in 1895, hand-cranked telephones disappeared in 1901, and automatic dialing came in 1927.[70] Despite inefficiency and changes of ownership in telephone operation, the town had 2,017 customers in 1900 and 27,000 in 1920.[71]

Contributing to the confusion were the wires of the Houston Electric Light and Power Company, which had received a franchise in 1882.[72] To the cheers of an expectant crowd, in 1884, five 2,000-candlepower arc lights strung twenty-six feet above the ground sputtered to life on Main Street at the intersections of Franklin, Preston, Texas, Rusk, and Lamar. Said the *Houston Post*, "The view from the head of Main street, taking in five lights in a line, is very fine, producing a beautiful effect."[73] This company and its successors, which in 1922 formed the Houston Lighting and Power Company, added to the crisscross overhead.[74] As G. C. Felton of Western Union explained: "The original lines were put up evidently under the belief that they would be the only ones ever strung, hence no preparations were made to have them out of the way of other people. The telegraph lines were first, then came the telephone people, then the electric lights, and lastly the street railways, and as a consequence many of the street crossings were overhead a perfect network of wire."[75]

When broken, the charged wires were not only dangerous but also potentially disruptive to other services. In 1902, however, the Citizens' Telephone Company proceeded to place its wires underground; in 1909 the city announced that it would bury the fire-alarm wires; and in 1911 the electric power company began putting its lines beneath the surface. This movement improved the downtown appearance and made possible the removal of unsightly poles.[76]

Perhaps it was inevitable in a period of economic transition, political experimentation, and a growing consciousness of the urban environment that thoughts about comprehensive city planning should emerge. Reiterating recommendations suggested at a directors' meeting, Edward A. Peden, president of the chamber of commerce, in 1911 urged Houston to take up planning in order to build a desirable community.[77] In the spring of 1912 Arthur C. Comey, a landscape architect from Cambridge, Massachusetts, spent several months in the city and drew up a developmental scheme for the city park commission. His suggestions included an encircling band of parks following the bayous, differentiation of streets according to use, an outer railroad belt to break the "vast spider web" of lines which bound the city, zoning to protect land values, a civic center, and a commission which would prepare and enforce an official plan for Houston.[78]

About the same time Mayor Rice and the city council sponsored a study of European cities by Frank Putnam in order to guide Houston in the future. In his report Putnam commented: "Six years ago, viewing Houston for the first time, and observing that this city had nearly if not quite a hundred excellent churches, but had very few sewers, less than one-half the necessary water service that was needed for people then here, a scant one-eighth of the needed pavement, and only a small percentage of scattering sidewalks, I gained the impression that while people of Houston were admirably equipped for living in Heaven, they were rather poorly equipped for living in Houston."[79]

He acknowledged recent improvements but went on to recommend an extension of the mayor's term to as much as six years; an increase in the mayor's salary from $4,000 to $10,000; lengthening and staggering the terms of aldermen; elimination of aldermen also serving as heads of departments; use of initiative, referendum, and recall; city ownership of gas, lighting, and streetcar utilities, as well as the turning-basin area; public baths and comfort stations; a city slaughter house; and a planning commission that would include women.[80] "It would be nothing less than purblind folly," he concluded, "for the generation now in control of Houston's destiny to neglect to make provision now for a sane, beautiful, healthful, economic plan for city growth—now, while the first foundations of the future great city are being laid."[81]

Although voters approved amendments for initiative, referendum, and recall in 1913, nothing of consequence was done about planning until 1917.[82] Mayor Oscar F. Holcombe decided to create a planning commission in 1922, but he moved in a desultory manner.[83] A commission under Merle E. Tracy, 1924–1926, prepared some studies on zoning, streets, population growth, parks, and a civic center, but no comprehensive design came forward until the reestablishment of the commission under William C. Hogg in 1927.[84] Hogg, son of former governor James S. Hogg and developer of River Oaks, a thoroughly planned upper-class residential subdivision in Houston, was deeply committed to a belief in urban planning. He founded the Forum of Civics, an organization dedicated to the "betterment and beautification of our city and country."[85] The forum published for one year, January 1928–January 1929, *Civics for Houston*, a magazine to promote an awareness of problems: "Drab dirt, disorder and disease are here shown [pictures] to exist right in our midst, almost in our backyards, and those of us who do not like these things have just been blinking our eyes and finally closing them to such sights, rather than recognize that here we have a problem for this city to solve."[86]

In spite of sanguine hopes, the magazine failed, apparently from lack of support. Trouble existed, moreover, for the bold ideas of Will Hogg. In 1927 voters approved $1,400,000 in bonds for purchasing a civic-center site, a plan promoted by Hogg.[87] In 1928 Mayor Holcombe became involved in a dispute over two lots for the civic center. According to the court testimony of Will Hogg, as reported by the *Houston Post-Dispatch*, the mayor, who owned the lots, promised to sell them to the city at a price including carrying charges and cost. Instead, Holcombe sold them to Ben C. Andrews for a $15,000 profit. Andrews then resold them, eleven days later, to Varner Realty, Hogg's company which purchased for the government. Holcombe denied that he possessed prior knowledge, disclaimed any dishonesty, and said that he either should be re-elected in the forthcoming mayoralty race or be sent to jail. His political opponent, Walter E. Monteith, shortly won a sweeping victory, yet Holcombe did not go to jail for misconduct in office.[88]

After two years' labor, Hogg presented to Monteith in 1929 a comprehensive plan to guide the city in the future and to correct past mistakes.[89] Unfortunately, the report appeared at the end of an eight-year construction boom. In 1921 the total value of building permits was $10,398,000; in 1925 it reached a record of $35,041,000; and it set a new mark in 1929 at $35,320,000.[90] The skyline that came into being during this period would remain unchanged until the 1940's.

Reaching completion in 1924 was the sixteen-story Houston

Cotton Exchange Building. The Warwick Hotel, "a rare jewel in a perfect setting," opened on South Main in 1926,[91] the same year the sixteen-story Medical Arts Building, in Gothic style, was completed. The Petroleum Building, a twenty-two–story office building, utilizing a Mayan motif, opened in 1927. Jesse H. Jones finished the impressive thirty-seven–story Gulf Building in 1929, two years after Mellie Esperson completed the nearby Neils Esperson Building, a memorial to her husband, in Italian Renaissance style. The nine-story Humble Building (now Main Building) opened in 1921 and additions were built in 1935 and 1940. The Houston Central Library, in Spanish Renaissance style, began service in 1926, one year before the eight-story Harris County Criminal Courts and Jail Building, designed in Greek classic style.[92]

Jesse H. Jones was a major builder in this period. Starting in the lumber trade and slowly entering real estate operations in the early twentieth century, Jones set the pace in fashion as well as in building promotion. In 1900, while still in his twenties, he was at first refused a seat in the Capitol Hotel dining room because, instead of a coat, he wore one of the new "shirt waists," a colorful garment worn with a tie and without a suit coat. An appeal to the manager gained him a seat, and afterward he triumphantly appeared on the street, to the bemusement of those who beheld him.[93] Jones, who had been impressed by Paris, would have preferred an even skyline with buildings ten stories high, but a friend went to fifteen floors and Jones abandoned the idea. Operating most of the time with borrowed capital, he bought land to the south, drawing the business district along Main Street. By the mid-1920's he had erected about thirty commercial structures, and in 1956 he still controlled the fifty buildings he had put up in Houston, except one, sold in 1951.[94]

The outer edges of town, of course, expanded with the addition of suburbs and subdivisions, such as South Houston, 1890; Pasadena, 1891; Houston Heights, 1891; Deer Park, 1893; Magnolia Park, 1909; Bellaire, 1911; and West University Place, 1919.[95] Coinciding with the downtown building surge was the development of Houston's foremost subdivision, River Oaks. Started in 1923–1924 by Will Hogg, Mike Hogg, and Hugh Potter, River Oaks became the residential area of the city's elite. Architect John F. Staub designed simple, elegant, well-proportioned homes suitable to the quiet wealth of the "best oil money." Its curvilinear streets, deed restrictions, and maintenance fund to aid in the upkeep of the pleasant, uniform neighborhood were doubtless due to the good influence of Will Hogg and Hugh Potter, both of whom were strong advocates of city planning and zoning.[96]

Hogg's 1929 city plan, as presented to Mayor Monteith, though late in coming, nonetheless contained some valuable suggestions. With the thought, "beauty should not be overlooked in any portion of the scheme but should be injected into it as an organic part of the development rather than mere embellishment," Hogg's commission offered a detailed street plan for widening, lengthening, and improving thoroughfares; additional ideas for the civic center development; suggestions for more parks, including the acquisition of squares which would have trees, a few seats, and perhaps a fountain; and a recommendation for zoning to ensure orderly growth. Such zoning would provide specific areas for residences, apartments, business, and light and heavy industry.[97] As Hare and Hare, consultants from New York City, concluded in the report: "Houston's growth has been rapid and promises to increase. It is the purpose of this plan to provide for the welfare, convenience and happiness of present and future citizens. In adopting the provisions of the plan, the people of Houston and their officials will have to decide whether they are building a great city or merely a great population."[98]

For the most part, the 1929 plan was not accepted. Some suggestions, such as those about streets and the civic center, found partial application, but those for parks and zoning did not. Real estate agents and contractors, arguing that such planning was discriminatory, arbitrary, and damaging to small property owners and real estate interests, raised vociferous opposition to zoning.[99] After 350 protestors disrupted a city council meeting and after a conference between the planning committee, the council, and the Houston Property Owners' League, an antizoning group, the government dropped the thought of zoning.[100] Failure for city planning also resulted, at least in part, from the onset of the Great Depression. The municipality then possessed funds only for survival, not for the construction of a great city.

The years from 1875 to 1930 marked not only a transition in government, economy, population, and shape of the city but also in society. The permanent foundations for cultural organizations were laid as the people tried new modes of enlightenment and entertainment. There emerged in the 1890's, for example, a desire to establish a free public library.[101] The city officials allocated $2,400 in 1899 to help the Houston Lyceum support its library and free public reading room, but the greatest boost came when Andrew Carnegie, that same year, offered $50,000 for a building if the city would provide a site and maintain the structure.[102] The women's clubs and the Lyceum rallied to the cause and after some struggle located a site at Travis and McKinney, where in 1904 the free Carnegie Library opened with 14,000 volumes.[103] By 1920 shelf space in the two-story building was inadequate for the 65,000 books, so a new drive began which resulted in 1926 in the central library building at McKinney-Smith-Lamar-Brazos, used as an archives at the present time.[104]

Houstonians always enjoyed music of some variety whether provided by local talent, such as Herb's Light Guard Band, or by visiting artists: Jan Paderewski, John McCormack, Geraldine Farrar, Fritz Kreisler, Sarah Bernhardt, Jascha Heifetz, Alma Gluck, Efrem Zimbalist, and others.[105] Most important, however, was the work of the Symphony Society, formed in 1913. Led by Mrs. Edwin B. Barker and Miss Ima Hogg and supported by such prominent citizens as Jesse H. Jones, Will Hogg, and Joseph S. Cullinan, the society sponsored its first concert in the Majestic Theater in the summer of 1913. From that time forward, at least sporadically, a local symphony orchestra offered classical music. Though the endeavor was disrupted by World War I, the society maintained its enthusiasm and continued its efforts in the years that followed.[106]

There was also sufficient local interest to sponsor the erection of several statues. The memory of Dick Dowling, a hero of the minor battle of Sabine Pass, had been treasured by a local Confederate veterans' organization called Dick Dowling Camp, formed in 1892. They held annual meetings and listened to speeches, music, and poetry. In 1900, for instance, C. C. Beaves sang "Goober Peas" and Ellen Croom read:

Just forty-one men with the Texas yell,
But they scattered those Yankee ships pellmell;
Oh, but they fought right nobly and well,
Those heroes with brave Dick Dowling.[107]

After a long effort to raise money and with the help of a local Irish organization, the Ancient Order of Hibernians, the camp in 1905 put up a statue by Frank Teich in Market Square. The memorial, a statue of Dowling in Confederate uniform on a pedestal, was moved to Sam Houston Park in 1940 and then in 1958 to Hermann Park where it stands today, minus the sword, which has been stolen at least five times.[108]

The Robert E. Lee chapter of the United Daughters of the Confederacy purchased in 1908 the *Spirit of the Confederacy*, a nine-foot-high, bronze, nude angel by Louis Amateis which now stands in a lonely vigil in Sam Houston Park.[109] In 1925, the public financed a bronze equestrian statue of Sam Houston by local sculptor Enrico Cerrachio, placed at the entrance to Hermann Park. Colonel A. J. Houston, son of the hero, tried to stop acceptance of the statue, saying that it was "idealistic" and "fantastic." It bore not a single true characteristic, he contended, and it had "a monkey for a man and a steer for a steed." Nonetheless, with the usual speeches and a band rendition of "Dixie"—ironic, since the old general had opposed secession—officials dedicated the memorial, symbol of the city.[110]

More important perhaps for this aspect of culture was the founding of the Museum of Fine Arts. The Houston Art League, originally formed in 1900 to provide works of art for the public schools, received a triangular plot at Main and Montrose in 1914 from George H. Hermann. There, in a structure with a Greek façade and Ionic columns, designed by Ralph A. Cram of Boston and William W. Watkin of Houston, the league opened a permanent museum in 1924. According to *Time* magazine, an initial crowd of ten thousand people wore the varnish off the floor, but only twenty thousand visited during the rest of the year. It remained the task of James Chillman, the director, to build the collection, expand the facilities, and transform the institution into something more than a one-day novelty. This Chillman succeeded in accomplishing by means of donations, tours, lectures, and art courses.[111]

Related to this cultural development was the establishment of Rice Institute and what later became the University of Houston. In 1891 William Marsh Rice, who had amassed a fortune in Houston and moved to New York City, donated $200,000 in trust for the founding of a library and a school, dedicated to the advancement of art, literature, and science, for the white inhabitants of Houston.[112] A decade later Charles F. Jones, a valet, murdered the old man while he slept by placing a napkin soaked in chloroform over Rice's face. A sensational trial ensued in which Jones confessed and implicated Albert T. Patrick, a lawyer who conspired with him and who attempted to steal the fortune through a forged will. Strangely, Jones went free, since he testified as a witness against Patrick, who was sentenced to death. (Patrick, however, survived through stays of execution, commutation to life imprisonment, and finally a pardon in 1912.)[113]

The will became tangled in litigation but when it was ultimately settled Rice Institute received a fortune which, in 1912, the year instruction began, amounted to $10 million. The endowment was the seventh largest in the nation, ranking behind those of Columbia, the University of Chicago, Cornell, Yale, Harvard, and Stanford.[114] In 1907 a board of trustees had unanimously selected as president Dr. Edgar Odell Lovett of Princeton, who subsequently toured Europe to absorb educational ideas. Cram and Goodhue of Boston designed the new campus, set on the empty prairie near Hermann Park off South Main Street. It featured a projected quadrangle with arched walkways, gardens, and mixed medieval building styles.[115] Central to this architectural mishmash, described by critics John Burchard and Albert Bush-Brown as a "pitiful variation upon Spanish Renaissance," was the administration building, designated in 1947 as Lovett Hall. Though it is a monstrosity with false columns, tiny, useless balconies, a variety of stonework in several colors and textures, and an obstructive hole through the center called the "Sallyport," it nonetheless possesses a certain puckish charm. Oswell Lassig, a Viennese sculptor, placed characters, for instance, in the stonework representing great men of the past and students in various stages of development and activity. Even though Lovett Hall and its neighbor, the Physics Building, were designed to set the pattern for future development, later additions utilized a greatly modified style.[116]

Delayed from 1911 to 1912 because Ralph Cram could not obtain the marble he wanted, the school finally opened to fifty-eight students who came to take the entrance exams. Thirty-five were graduated in the first class in 1916.[117] Meanwhile, Lovett established football at Rice after witnessing a game between Texas A&M and the University of Texas. "I've never regretted it, although I believe I have spent more time on football problems than anything else," said the educator. "The mischief is that you have to win. The week after you win a game everybody is happy and things go well. But when you lose, they are miserable around school and that is bad for studies."[118] Thus, the Rice Owls and the "Harvard of the South" were started.[119]

The University of Houston, even though formally established in the 1930's as a university, originated in the 1920's. The Houston public school system (28,000 students in 1920) moved toward independence and away from municipal control in 1922 as the need for money became critical. The tax limit for the city was $2.50 per $100 valuation and of that in 1922 the schools received 67½¢. Since the tax limit had been reached and costs were rising, an independent district with its own tax limit of $1.00 per $100 valuation would help both the city and the schools. "The children of today must be trained today, or their opportunity is gone," warned the *Houston Post*. "The school system can't wait. It must be rescued or it will drift along to collapse."[120] In 1923 the city voters authorized an elected school board, and in 1924 the schools began to function as an independent system.[121]

Dr. E. E. Oberholtzer, selected as superintendent of schools in 1924, led in the effort to establish Houston Junior College, which started in 1927 with four hundred students.[122] Its purpose was to permit continued education for high school graduates who could not go elsewhere. In its first years the college operated from 4:00 P.M. to 9:00 P.M. at San Jacinto High School, but in 1934 the school board established the University of Houston as a self-supporting municipal school.[123] Considering the presence of tuition-free Rice Institute and the public facilities, Oberholtzer could say in 1931, "It is possible for a Houston child to obtain his complete education, from kindergarten through college, without leaving his home[town], and without the payment of a single penny for tuition."[124]

To provide informal education and entertainment, there were three major newspapers—the *Houston Post* (1880–), *Houston Chronicle* (1901–), and *Houston Press* (1911–1964). Radio station WEV, owned by Hurlburt-Still Electric Company, began broadcasting music and impromptu speeches for three hundred receiving sets in 1922. Other stations, WCAK, WEAY, and WPAN, shortly opened, but the first station to endure was KPRC, operated by the *Houston Post-Dispatch*. It started its first broadcast in 1925 with its call letters and the greeting, "Hello folks, everywhere." Among other programs, it put on the air the World Series of 1925 when Pittsburgh triumphed over Washington; the Tunney-Dempsey rematch, heard by twelve thousand to fifteen thousand listeners at the outdoor theater in Hermann Park; and the 1927 Rice–Southern Methodist University football game, in which the Mustangs defeated the Owls 34 to 6.[125]

Local athletic activities of great variety attracted Houstonians: bicycle riding, horseracing, horse shows, boxing, wrestling, swimming, auto racing, handball, basketball, track, table tennis, military drill, bowling, shooting matches, golf, ice hockey, ice skating, roller skating, motorcycle racing, dog racing, and sailing. Some people, more for novelty than sport, indulged in marathon dancing, and for two glorious days Magdeline Williams, "proportioned like Venus," held the world record at sixty-five hours and twenty-nine minutes.[126] In the 1890's an equally unusual sport, goat racing, was popular, especially among young boys. It all started at the corner of Main and Congress streets when W. R. Sinclair and Nat Floyd, newsmen, induced two boys with goat carts to race down Congress. As wagers came forth and a crowd gathered, Jack White, a policeman, arrived and demanded, "What are you tryin' to do?"

"I've bet this black goat beats the white goat to the court house corner," replied Sinclair.

"I'll bet ye he don't. Clare the streets everybody!" declared White, and the race was on.[127]

In 1891 Sinclair organized races which shortly led to a "Children's Day" sponsored by the *Houston Daily Post*. The contests featured such entrants as Eclipse, Billy the Kid, Dynamite, Sky Rocket, Rapid Transit, McKinley Bill, and Pulletail, but by far the most renowned was Black Bill, "the wonderfully fast goat," which won the local events in 1892–1895 and became "world champion" in 1895 by defeating a Pittsburgh challenger in an intercity race. The mayor and a brass band met him and his driver, Durward "Skinny" Bailey, upon his triumphal return to the Bayou City. As they came down Main Street, several policemen had to hold back the enthusiastic crowd trying to shake Skinny's hand and pet Black Bill, the "great champion racing goat of Houston."[128]

One of the earliest football games, a sport of more enduring interest, occurred in 1886 when a group of young men chose sides, threw off coats, vests, cravats, and collars, and proceeded without a rule book to play a sandlot game. After much running, kicking, and yelling the players finally reclined on the grass where they tried "with considerable difficulty" to collect enough breath to fill the ball again.[129] In the 1890's several amateur teams periodically formed to play a few games; in 1901 the high school began to play on a fairly consistent basis, and in 1912 Rice took up the sport.[130] Throughout the period amateur clubs also played baseball, and sporadically after 1888, when the Texas League was first formed, Houston fielded a professional team. Known variously as the Lambs, Red Stockings, and Buffaloes, the professionals offered games on a fairly constant basis from the early twentieth century. In 1928 a $400,000 park, Buffalo Stadium, was opened for the pleasure of the players and the fans.[131]

For low-priced entertainment moving pictures became popular in the first decade of the century. The *Houston Post* noted in 1907 a number of small theaters scattered about which charged only five cents admission.[132] Larger theaters soon presented movies, and when the New Majestic opened in 1910, it provided both a variety show and motion pictures.[133] The popularity of movies invoked an ordinance requiring the enclosure of the projection machine in a metal booth for fire security and another ordinance creating a board of censors.[134]

Charged to protect morals in places of public amusement, the three-member board of censors could, if unheeded, levy a possible fine of from $25 to $200 and could even cancel a license to operate.[135] Although the censors sometimes reviewed stage productions, their main target was the movie industry. Sometimes, of course, decisions were disputed, as when Mrs. Thomas H. Eggert, secretary of the board and a most diligent worker, condemned as indecent the sixty feet of film showing a kiss in *Don't Call It Love*. C. A. McFarland, the theater manager, said, on the other hand, that it was merely a "plain, whole-souled smack."[136] After the board had banned twenty-eight movies, in contrast to ten in Chicago, during 1923, an editor, noting the existence also of a national board of censors, said: "Considering this whole question of censorship, The Post is wondering if the idea of a local censor board having unlimited power to pass upon all phases of a film is not impractical and unnecessary. As it is now, it is only a matter of the opinion of one person, or perhaps, a few against the opinion of others, perhaps just as capable of judging. Haven't we about reached the point in practice where we have set up an autocracy, or at least, an oligarchy, to rule in the realm of amusements?"[137]

In 1929 the city government eliminated the position of secretary, which paid $2,000 a year, and replaced the triumvirate with a board of eleven persons, enough members to blunt its effectiveness. Mrs. Eggert then summed up her seven to eight years' experience by revealing that out of 12,000 programs reviewed, 2,600 had been censored in part and 225 rejected completely. She thought Houston standards "second to none in the country" and claimed censorship, especially of movies, to be "vitally necessary."[138] In this instance, however, censorship had proved for Houstonians to be too great a price to pay for liberty.

Condemnation of public activities was not wholly new for the Bayou City. Churches and other groups as well as individual critics had previously protested in an effort to reform offensive conditions. Among the foremost protesters was George C. Rankin, Methodist minister of Shearn Church, 1892–1896. In the fall of 1894, incognito, he toured the fleshpots of town and damned from the pulpit, giving names and places, sin in the Magnolia City. To Sunday evening crowds that packed the church from "vestibule to amen corner," he described open gambling, in violation of city laws, and the "hellish" Variety Theater where gamblers "swilled beer and wine like swine in the gutter" and referred to ministers as "God howlers" and "Bible yelpers." Though he spent only a brief time in most places, Rankin stayed for two evenings at the theater, a "disreputable and low flung manufactory of vice, immorality and crime [where] there are more young men in this city and surrounding country traveling straight to hell than along any other one route now open to the public."[139]

This "sodomic institution" offered music and dances by women dressed in "costumes suited to the taste of the most vulgar and dissolute." With clowns, the women made obscene jests and sang prurient songs. "At this point," said the shocked pastor, "some of the utterances and gyrations of these male and female devils incarnate would thoroughly impoverish the vocabulary of a pure-minded mortal."[140] In regard to the "social evil," he claimed that five hundred prostitutes practiced in Houston, and many resided near the church. Said Rankin, "It is the peril of our boyhood: it is the pollution of our manhood: it is the degradation of our girlhood: it is the debasement of our womanhood and it is the plague spot on the sanctity of wedded life."[141] He castigated and embarrassed church members, policemen, government officials, and society in general, but despite his fulminations, little change occurred.[142]

Experiments with closing laws, suppression of gambling and dance halls, and even a "reservation" for prostitutes failed to suppress vice, especially in notorious places like Vinegar Hill, the Hollow, and Tin Can Alley. Drunkenness remained the most common of crimes, and all-night saloons operated where men could buy cheap liquor and sleep on the floor when nights were cold, reminiscent of places described in Jacob Riis's classic study of New York, *How the Other Half Lives*. Gambling, either open or clandestine, continued, and dope addiction, especially with morphine and cocaine, seemingly became worse at the turn of the century.[143]

A study of Houston in 1911 by Dr. Charles Stelzle of New York, for the "Men and Religion Forward Movement," disclosed 7 motion-picture houses, 4 theaters (only one of which was unfit for ladies), 6 dance halls, good and bad lodging houses, decent residential areas, 311 saloons, 117 churches, and 36 pool rooms.[144] Houston, perhaps, was not completely given over to evil. Indeed, Jerome Vannatta, also of New York, working for the National Association for the Suppression of Commercialized Vice, awarded Houston in 1924 the excellent rating of 86 percent, compared to New York at 41 percent and Chicago at 37 percent. He found a few prostitutes and bootleggers but no pandering in the streets, no cabarets, and only mild road houses. A half-hour after the theaters closed, the streets were practically empty; Houston was an "Eleven o'clock town."[145]

Officials, moreover, attempted to suppress flirting in 1905 by declaring that "any male person in the City of Houston who shall stare at, or make what is commonly called 'goo-goo eyes' at, or in any other manner look at or make remarks to or concerning, or cough or whistle at, or do any other act to attract the attention of any woman or female person" in an attempt to flirt would be guilty of a misdemeanor. The "Goo-Goo Eyes" Ordinance, revised in 1968, induced nationwide laughter. The *Denton County News* said, "Ye gods and little fishes . . . what is to become of the cross-eyed fellow that you could not tell whether he was staring at the nominees or looking at a horse on the opposite side of the street."[146] The *New York Tribune* reacted with this bit of doggerel:

> Just because he made those goo-goo eyes
> The copper pinched a chap about his size;
>   In defense he said a cinder
>   Made him wink his windward winder,
> But the girl he winked at called it goo-goo eyes.

> Just because they make those goo-goo eyes
> Western women stare in mild surprise;
>   Texas law may call it vile
>   But New Yorkers only smile—
> And they keep right on a-making goo-goo eyes.[147]

Since the days of the Texas republic antiliquor sentiment had served to offset unbridled drunkenness and, as in other cities, Houstonians responded to the growing crusade for temperance. The Woman's Christian Temperance Union, the Anti-Saloon League, and even Carry Nation became active.[148] In 1902 Carry Nation visited Houston for a few hours, gave a speech, and made $100 from the sale of souvenir hatchets. She was arrested but was not charged with a crime, and, as she caught a departing train, someone told her of a saloon in the Fifth Ward which carried her name.[149] After due warning the proprietor agreed to change the name, but he sold his lease without keeping his promise and neglected to pass on the threat to the new owner. In 1905 the virago suddenly appeared at the Carrie Nation Saloon and with brickbats held "apron-fashion" in her skirt proceeded to cause $750 worth of damage. She again demanded that the name be changed and threatened to destroy the entire building. Since he gained enough publicity to crowd his bar, the owner did not press charges, but the next day he employed a sign painter to alter the name to "Carnation."[150]

During World War I, for the sake of order at a nearby army base, the city restricted saloons to the business district and later eliminated them entirely with the passage of a state law prohibiting saloons within ten miles of a camp. Therefore, when the Prohibition amendment passed, though narrowly approved in Harris County (6,433 to 6,107), Houston was well accustomed to the situation.[151] As elsewhere in the country, Prohibition failed in the Bayou City. There were sufficient stills and bootleggers to keep the town wet.[152]

Included in the societal changes from 1875 to 1930 was also the increased estrangement of the white and black races. Although there earlier had been separation in schools and churches, segregation deepened throughout this period almost to the point of forming two societies in Houston, connected only by economic necessity. Informal residential division developed. As indicated by the scattering of school children in 1878, the city had not then split into large segregated living areas.[153]

Slaves in southern cities often lived on the premises of their masters, working as domestic servants.[154] Continued arrangements after the Civil War could explain this residential scattering, even though there might occur pockets of black concentration, such as Freedmantown, a slum located on the outer edge of the Fourth Ward.[155] In the Fifth Ward in 1910, John Milsaps, a diarist and Salvation Army editor, noted the presence of numerous blacks and commented: "The Fifth Ward is a slouchy city made up chiefly of cheap shacks with uneven sidewalks and no walks, lots of dust, a maze of railroad tracks running in all directions, intermixed with mills and warehouses planted here and there. It is ugly enough to be at home in the picturesque slums of New Orleans."[156]

Segregation was underway and in the 1929 report on city planning, Will Hogg noted three main black areas—San Felipe near downtown, in the southeast, and in the northeast. Though residential separation apparently had already occurred to a large extent, he nonetheless urged elimination of the remaining pockets, arguing: "These negroes are a necessary and useful element in the population and suitable areas with proper living and recreation facilities should be set aside for them. Because of long established racial prejudices, it is best for both races that living areas be segregated."[157]

Blacks celebrated holidays separately and duplicated white organizations. There were black baseball teams, drill squads, a YMCA, goat races, and a Children's Day.[158] From 1899 to 1915 Houston businessmen promoted No-Tsu-Oh, a week-long festival designed to attract fall buyers to town. Though the *Houston Daily Post* in 1900 commented on the celebration, "The highborn lady and the 'Darktown' brunette touched elbows like soldiers on a battlefield," little black participation is indicated.[159] In 1909 the black minority organized, instead, De-Ro-Loc, a fall carnival much like No-Tsu-Oh but on a smaller scale.[160] The black community possessed its own places of amusement—saloons, a park, a variety theater, and motion-picture houses. When President William McKinley visited in 1901, the blacks gathered on specific streets and gave their own welcome; when the storm of 1900 ruined Galveston, Houston blacks organized a separate relief program.[161] A $15,000 Carnegie Library for the blacks opened in 1913.[162] Houston Colored Junior College, organized

TABLE 4. *White-Black Distribution of School Children by Wards in 1878*

Ward	White School Children	Black School Children
1	54	48
2	208	111
3	165	118
4	269	245
5	95	62

in 1927, became Houston College for Negroes, 1934–1935, then Texas State University for Negroes in 1947,[163] and finally Texas Southern University in 1951. It closely paralleled the development of the University of Houston.

Segregation evolved in insidious fashion. The *Houston Daily Post*, for instance, published a children's page on Sunday called "Happyhammers." When it first appeared all children who read the paper were invited to join the Happyhammer Club. In 1898, however, the editor limited membership to *white* children who read the newspaper.[164] A reporter in 1891 noted black prisoners incarcerated on the first floor of the county jail and white criminals on the second.[165] John T. Brown, a candidate for mayor in 1900, found it necessary to explain at a rally why he permitted black carpenters to build a cottage for him.[166] In 1900 a cartoon by "Dix" entitled "Thanksgiving on the Nile" appeared in the *Houston Daily Post*. It depicted nude blacks swimming in an alligator-infested river with the conversation: "Mr. Alligator: What will you have, dearest? Mrs. Alligator: Some dark meat, without dressing, please."[167] In 1913 the city provided separate drinking fountains in front of City Hall, and the Union Station established divided waiting rooms.[168] In 1921 Dr. F. J. Slataper caused an attack on the school board because he vaccinated white children in the presence of black children; segregation came to the dock workers in 1924; at the Democratic National Convention in 1928 officials fenced off with chicken wire about one hundred seats in the gallery for the black spectators; and in 1933 city authorities rejected the plans for a new Southern Pacific station because blacks and whites would have to use the same ramps to reach the trains.[169] Some, at least, revealed compassion in this movement. President R. S. Lovett of the Houston and Texas Central asserted after receiving and rejecting petitions requesting the replacement of black switchmen with white workmen: "If the policy thus urged upon this company is to be the policy of the South toward the negro; if he is to be allowed to do only such labor as no white man will do, and receive only such wages as no white man wants, what is to become of the negroes? How are they to live? Food and clothes they must have. If not by labor, how are they to get the necessities of life? Hunger must and will be satisfied, prisons and chain-gangs notwithstanding."[170]

The laws also reflected the growing segregation. In 1882–1883 the Houston and Texas Central, entangled in a number of civil rights suits involving unequal treatment of blacks, agreed to a compromise with J. N. Johnson, a black attorney from Austin who served the plaintiffs, by providing "separate, exclusive, equal accommodations for colored patrons."[171] The state followed in 1891 and required separate coaches for all railroads.[172] Despite protests from blacks and the company manager, the city council required separate compartments on streetcars in 1903. A temporary boycott of the trolleys flared as blacks refused to ride, jeered at those who did, and threw stones at them. Policemen assigned to the cars stopped the demonstrations.[173] The code of ordinances in 1922 contained several new laws not included in the 1914 codification. Blacks could use only those parks designated for them, and cohabitation between races was unlawful.[174] For Houston, however, no comprehensive black code to regulate rigidly the behavior of the races existed.

When on occasion racial tension became unbearable, violence broke out. A potentially explosive situation occurred in 1910 when Jack Johnson, the black boxing champion from Galveston, defeated James J. Jeffries in a heavyweight championship bout at Reno, Nevada. Crowds of three thousand to four thousand persons gathered at the newspaper offices to catch the results of the fight. The news of Johnson's fifteenth-round victory brought a long groan from the white people and cheers from the black listeners at the rim of the crowds. One three-hundred-pound black woman cheered during the contest, "Come on, li'l black boy, hit that white man, you nigger" and afterward chuckled, "Oh you Jack Johnson." A middle-aged man landed on and stretched across the pavement an unfortunate black who possessed the temerity to throw his hat and leap. Bystanders halted the incipient riot. Though scattered racial fist fights occurred in the city, there were no riots as in New York, Pittsburgh, New Orleans, Atlanta, St. Louis, and Little Rock.[175] Resentment smoldered over this affair even after Johnson lost to the "White Hope," Jess Willard, in 1915. The local censors in 1921 banned two motion pictures at the Lincoln Theater (black), *The World Rolls On* and *The Black Thunderbolt*, because Johnson played with white actors in the films and because the dodgers advertising the shows were "incendiary and inflammatory." [176]

The worst outbreak of violence came in 1917. When America entered the war, Houston received, through the efforts of the chamber of commerce, congressmen, and other interested persons, two training camps—Ellington Field for bomber cadets and Camp Logan for National Guard units.[177] While Camp Logan, located west of town at the present site of Memorial Park, was under construction, a black unit, originally from Illinois, arrived to guard the property. These northern troopers resented the separate drinking receptacles for workmen at the camp, the epithet "nigger," the segregation in town, and the interference of local police. There had been other recent racial conflicts involving black soldiers in Brownsville, San Antonio, and Del Rio. The infamous East St. Louis massacre occurred in July. To minimize contact with the white community, the white officers invited visitation from the black people of the city. There exist conflicting reports about the decorum of this circumstance—both affirmation and denial of liquor and lewd women—but in totality the conflict between black and white created a combustible situation.[178] The explosion came on August 23, 1917.

That morning Lee Sparks and Rufe Daniels, policemen, raided a dice game at San Felipe and Wilson streets. In the melee they arrested a black woman and a partially drunk private, Alonzo Edwards, who tried to defend her. Both the woman and Edwards, who had been struck four times, were taken to jail. Early that afternoon Corporal Charles Baltimore, a black military policeman, spoke to Sparks and Daniels about the arrest, and although accounts vary, hot words passed between the men. Sparks hit Baltimore; the black ran; Sparks fired some warning shots, pursued Baltimore into a house, and caught him hiding under a bed. The policeman then took the corporal, who had been struck several more times, to jail. Rumors began to spread that a black soldier had been killed by a Houston policeman.[179] The newly assigned commander of the camp, Major Kneeland Snow, secured the release of Baltimore and to prevent any difficulty revoked passes and increased the guard. A black sergeant, Vida Henry, warned Snow in the early evening that there might be trouble on this hot steamy night. The white commander then toured the camp, spotted some men stealing ammunition, and ordered all rifles and ammunition secured.

At this moment a black private shouted, "Get your guns men! The white mob is coming!" Although untrue, the troopers panicked, charged the ammunition tents, armed themselves, and in disarray began milling about the camp firing random shots. Sergeant Henry took charge of the turbulence and gave it direction. He ordered the men to fill their canteens and fall in. Then, at their head he led seventy-five to a hundred men on a raid to punish the Houston police. Not all of the soldiers followed Henry. Some fled to nearby woods and others, apparently, formed their own smaller groups to raid the city.[180]

About 9:00 P.M. the rioters moved circuitously toward the San Felipe district, firing as they marched. Alma Reichart, a young white girl, hit in the stomach by a loose bullet, fell while in a store on Washington. Closer to town, the soldiers cut down two boys who had rushed out to see the excitement—one was killed, the other had an arm shot off. They caught two white men in an automobile on Shepherd's Dam Road in drizzling rain and killed one. The other they forced from the vehicle and shot at him as he lay in a ditch. Leaving him for dead, the soldiers departed, crying, "On to victory, boys, on to victory!" Townspeople later found another car on a San Felipe sidewalk containing a dead policeman, his shoulder shot away, and an army officer, the top of his head blasted off.[181] The total wounded equaled eleven; the total dead reached twenty-five policemen, two white soldiers, four black soldiers (including Vida Henry, who apparently shot himself to avoid capture), one Hispanic, and eight white civilians.[182]

The riot, or mutiny as some called it, continued through the night. Crowds of angry citizens gathered, shouting, "Lynch them" and "Come let's go kill them," but the acting mayor, D. M. Moody, requested martial law. Military order prevented possible retaliation, and the insurrection evaporated as rioters scattered, tried to desert, returned to camp, or submitted to capture.[183] The arrival of 350 coast guard troops from Galveston in the morning, followed later by 602 infantry soldiers from San Antonio, strengthened the hand of the military.[184] Subsequently, in the largest court-martial in American military history, the army executed thirteen soldiers by hanging and sentenced forty-one to life in prison. Two additional trials brought life terms to twelve more and a death sentence to sixteen. President Woodrow Wilson, under pressure from black Americans and despite nationwide protest, commuted ten of the latter sixteen to life in prison. Under Presidents Harding and Coolidge most of the men were set free.[185]

Although major racial conflicts like this were rare for Houston, a Ku Klux Klan movement and one lynching did occur in the period. As elsewhere in Texas, the Klan was active during the period from 1920 to 1924. In October 1920, the KKK participated in the United Confederate Veterans reunion held in Houston and established a local chapter.[186] Though Klansmen conducted parades and initiations, intimidated some people, and indulged in charitable acts, they never were able to dominate the community nor did they ever control the city government.[187] Oscar F. Holcombe joined the organization, attended a single meeting, and then quit. The Klan in 1922 offered not to oppose him if he would fire three Catholics in responsible positions. Holcombe refused, and the KKK tried to smear him with a gambling charge, but a panel of Baptist ministers exonerated the mayor at a stormy seven-hour session.[188] Although there was some penetration of Klan influence into the police department, city leaders, including Holcombe, John Henry Kirby, Marcellus E. Foster, and Joseph S. Cullinan, held the organization in check.[189]

Lynching, or extralegal execution by a mob, was rare, but there were some borderline cases. In 1883 four men maliciously fired bullets through a door, killing the wife of Austin Johnson, a black man the assailants wanted to question about the fatal shooting of a policeman.[190] In 1900 six or seven masked blacks flogged to death for undetermined reasons a forty-five–year–old black man living near Greens Bayou.[191] The only lynching, so considered by contemporaries, occurred in 1928, late in the lynching era. Robert Powell, a twenty-four–year–old black accused of murdering a policeman, had been placed in Jefferson Davis Hospital to recover from injuries supposedly sustained in the fight with the dead policeman. Seven men took Powell at pistol-point from the hospital at night and drove to a rickety bridge over Big Gully on Post Oak Road. They then dropped Powell, bound and gagged, over the edge with a rope around his neck. To view their handiwork, one of the lynchers tossed over a match, and, lo, the black sat upon the ground; the rope was too long. The men then hauled him up, took in slack, and dropped the hapless Powell a second time. The next day the bloody corpse, feet almost touching the ground, was discovered. The city appropriated $10,000 for an investigation; the governor offered a reward of $250; and the county shortly indicted seven men. Apparently, only two of the men came to trial and they gained acquittal, even though they had previously signed a confession.[192]

While racial lines were tightening in Houston through the period, curiously enough, a growing humanitarianism also existed. In 1893 leading women of the town began to support the DePelchin Faith Home which had been started in 1892 to care for the children of working mothers.[193] In 1894 charitable people set up the Friendly Inn which for several months fed the indigent, a sort of work later taken up by the Star of Hope Mission.[194] Sheltering Arms, a home for old women, was opened about 1894; a Florence Crittenden Home for the care of unwed mothers was started in 1897; and the Humane Society to prevent cruelty to animals began its work in 1898.[195] A combined fund drive for charities was started in 1894; the Houston Settlement Association provided a settlement house in 1908; the Houston Anti-Tuberculosis League, supporting a free clinic and nursing service, was begun in 1911; and in 1919 the city and county financed a charity hospital.[196] The question, therefore, arises—why did humanitarianism not override the barriers of racial prejudice? Why did white citizens pay willingly for a black charity case at a hospital but separate the races in places of public meeting? To say the least, it was a humanitarianism, or charity, kept decidedly at arm's length. It was aid extended when there was no threat to personal status or well-being.

As a consequence of racial estrangement, manifested in laws, customs, and outbursts of violence, white men and black men lived almost separate lives with social and intellectual contact kept at a minimum. Such a condition was not wholly a white man's contrivance but was supported, at least in part, by the black community. The publishers of the *Red Book of Houston*, a rather remarkable black directory containing essays and biographical sketches of local black leaders, commented in 1915, "A worthy man in his race, whatever it is, loses that worthiness when he attempts to obliterate social and racial barriers imposed by a beneficent Jehovah. He must stay in his own to prove the worthiness of his life."[197] The dichotomy of the races was greater in 1930 than it had been in 1875. For the black and white citizen alike it had been a period of transition.

6

Space City, U.S.A.

After the time of "take-off," according to Walt W. Rostow, there comes a long interval of sustained progress during which the economy expands into "more refined and technologically often more complex processes."[1] This was essentially the case in Houston, but the onset of the Great Depression temporarily delayed expansion. Business restricted operations, and municipal resources quickly vanished. Mayor Walter Monteith complained: "The Home Worker's association asks us to put more men to work, to build hospitals and to do this and that to provide work. Then the Taxpayers' association comes along and says it will enjoin the collection of taxes unless we reduce the tax rate. Then, to make the job of being mayor just that much nicer, the bankers tell me we must reduce expenditures by half a million dollars or they will quit lending us money."[2]

Building permits dropped to $2.9 million in 1932, and because of tight funds, the city commissary ceased accepting relief applications from Hispanics and blacks except in the most desperate instances.[3] Fortunately, in the latter half of 1932, emergency relief money began to flow from the Reconstruction Finance Corporation.[4] Augmented later by allocations from the National Recovery Administration and the Works Progress Administration (later the Work Projects Administration), federal resources poured in for county roads, slum clearance, park improvements, and public buildings, among them City Hall, the San Jacinto Monument, and Lamar High School. By mid-1935, local agencies had provided $400,000; the state, $1,215,000; and the federal government, $6,648,000.[5] In 1935–1936 the WPA employed twelve thousand persons at peak enrollment and spent $2,179,000 on sixty-nine projects in Harris County.[6] The traditional view that the depression struck Houston a soft blow in comparison to other cities in the nation seems correct although there exist few statistics about unemployment in Houston to verify the point.[7] Be that as it may, no banks failed in Houston, and building permits bounced to $18.5 million in 1936 and to $25 million

in 1938. When several banks threatened to collapse in 1931, Jesse
Jones, who knew such an event would be bad for the town, brought
leading bank men together, formed a pool, and forced a change in the
managements of the weak institutions.[8]

To the good fortune of the Bayou City, Jones received an appointment to the Board of the Reconstruction Finance Corporation in January 1932. From 1933 to 1939 he worked as chairman of that organization, then became the Federal Loan Administrator, and from 1940
to 1945 served concurrently as secretary of commerce. On the occasion of the dual appointment, Senator Robert Taft commented, "I
have no great objection to giving Mr. Jones the additional power to
act also as secretary of commerce, but I think it is an extraordinary
precedent which is justified only by the character of the man."[9]
Houston, therefore, possessed a powerful friend in Washington, D.C.
As columnist George Dixon once heard Jones exclaim in a telephone
conversation about a proposal, "I will not give a nickel more than
two billion dollars for it!"[10]

The extent to which Jones aided Houston during the depression
is unknown, but his concern was obvious. In 1939, for example, he
met with Oscar Holcombe and others and commented, "We must
find some means of providing public improvements to catch up and
keep up with Houston's growth."[11] During the preparation for the
Texas Centennial, though Dallas won the exposition site, Houston
obtained an allotment of $1 million from the U.S. Centennial Com-
mission for improvement of the San Jacinto Battlegrounds. Jones had
been dissatisfied with a previous allocation of $400,000 and had ap-
pealed for the greater amount.[12] As a result the site received the impressive San Jacinto Monument, designed by Alfred C. Finn. It tow-
ered 570 feet 4¼ inches above ground level; by the same measure,
the Washington Monument is 555 feet 5⅛ inches high. To avoid possible criticism, Jones and Finn told people that San Jacinto was five
inches shorter, a measurement of the distance from the top of the
stairs at the base of the shaft to the tip.[13] After Jones helped Houston
get $1,337,000 in federal money to construct Sam Houston Coli-
seum, William N. Blanton, general manager of the chamber of commerce, said: "The people of Houston never will know how much
great work for this city Jesse H. Jones, chairman of the RFC, has
done at Washington. We owe him our deepest gratitude."[14]

Because of Jesse Jones, the strength of local industry, and perhaps the ability of civic leaders to attract federal grants, Houston suffered relatively less than did other cities during the depression.[15] A
few "shantytowns" existed, nonetheless, along Buffalo Bayou and
the railroad yards. Those who did suffer, though fewer in number,

felt their destitution just as keenly as people elsewhere.[16] Certainly sympathy can be extended to the Houston man who commented after his first WPA payday: "You know, it's been a year since I've taken home a pay check. That's a long time to tell your kids there's no money for ice cream."[17]

Despite the depression, during the 1930's and afterward, transportation facilities continued to improve, the most dramatic development coming in respect to air travel. In 1936 Captain Eddie Rickenbacker of Eastern Airlines advised Houstonians to become air-minded. According to the air hero, Houston did not realize the significance of commercial aviation, and Fort Worth and Dallas were far ahead.[18] Several days later Mayor Holcombe announced a study of the deficiency, and in 1937 the city council voted to pay $356,400 for the small airfield established by the Houston Airport Corporation on Telephone Road in 1927.[19] Braniff and Eastern airlines began regular schedules, flying from Houston to New York in eleven and a half hours and from Houston to Chicago in nine hours. Chicago and Southern joined these other companies in 1941 after Houston had expanded and improved facilities in 1940 with the aid of federal funds.[20]

Through the efforts of the city council, of Senator Tom Connally, and of Representative Albert Thomas, the Civil Aeronautics Board in 1946 designated Houston an international terminal and certified Braniff, Southern, and Pan American for flights to Central America, South America, and the Caribbean area. T. E. Braniff said about this, "The Civil Aeronautics Board's decision now establishes Houston as a great aerial gateway as well as an international shipping center."[21] Houston's air routes, however, ran for the most part from north to south, and in 1946 the CAB refused a request by American Airlines to open services nonstop to the West Coast.[22]

Air traffic increased as such new airlines as Trans-Texas and Mid-Continent entered Houston, and in 1950 six major companies, two local ones, and an air-freight line utilized the terminal. They transported 538,000 persons, 45,000 of whom came from abroad. This compared to 85,000 total passengers in 1944.[23] The mounting traffic created pressure for better facilities and in 1949 Mayor Holcombe announced plans for a new airport. After difficulty with designs and financing, construction started in 1951, and finally in 1954 Houston International Airport (renamed the William P. Hobby Airport in 1967) opened.[24] Even after an expenditure of $10 million, the terminal was not altogether satisfactory. Airlines complained about maintenance facilities, catering service, and obsolete luggage chutes. Dining-room windows had to be altered, large cracks appeared in walkways, and the terminal lacked such minor items as shower curtains. As reporter Jim Mathis summarized, "The history of planning and construction of the pink-stone and glass plant is one of back and fill, sputter and go."[25]

The predominantly north-south flow of traffic changed in 1956 when National Airlines began nonstop service to Miami and Tampa; K.L.M. Royal Dutch Airlines directed flights from Mexico City to Amsterdam via Houston in 1957; and the CAB authorized routes to the Pacific coast in 1961.[26] The opening of east-west traffic came primarily through the persistence of the chamber of commerce. It took ten years to obtain permission for the flights to Florida, but the struggle to gain connection with the West Coast was especially difficult.

Dallas petitioned the CAB in 1956 for additional service to California to supplement contracts it already possessed. Houston, which had no such service and had to connect through Dallas, asked the board to consider flights from Houston to the coast when taking up the matter of the Dallas petition. The board steadfastly denied consideration through 1957, in spite of numerous counter-petitions and protests, culminating in the visit of a thirty-three–man delegation to Washington, D.C., in November. Finally, in March 1958, the Civil Aeronautics Board, over objections from Dallas, opened the Southern Transcontinental Case to consider all applications for West Coast service.[27] In the hearings, Houston, led by the chamber of commerce, made its point and obtained the desired routes. Houston thus became a principal station between California and Florida, broke the hegemony of Dallas, and completed an east-west flow of air traffic.

By 1957 the airport was handling about 111,000 people per month. It operated at peak capacity, and K.L.M. had difficulty even finding counter space.[28] In July, moreover, a French airliner touched down and introduced the city to jet travel. Just three years after its opening, the terminal was obsolete. A group of seventeen businessmen, however, had foreseen the possibility and purchased a 3,126-acre site on the northeastern edge of the city for a new jet airport. They held the property and then sold it at cost to the city. In 1960 Mayor Lewis Cutrer gave a $1,980,463 check to Ralph A. Johnston, president of Jetero, Inc., for the land, together with a letter of appreciation to the men for their action. One sour note about this transaction—the new airport was in a location whereby the air pollution of the airplanes would combine with that from the ship channel. "Anyone who has made a study of air pollution in Houston would see it shouldn't be there," said Joseph L. Goldman of the University of St. Thomas Storm Research Institute.[29] At the time of decision about the airport, however, civic awareness about the importance of air pollution had not yet developed.

Work started on the new $100 million Houston Intercontinental Airport in 1962. Plans featured two major runways with a terminal between them. Of radical design, the terminal utilized a concept of facilities stacked vertically, connected by escalators, ramps, and elevators. Passengers thus need not walk long distances. From the cube-shaped units of the terminal stretch "fingers" to the runways for loading purposes. Scheduled to open in 1965, the new airport remained incomplete and unused until June 1969.[30]

The Houston Ship Channel, although exhibiting less dramatic change, nonetheless expanded to meet exigencies. The depression had retarded traffic at the port, with the low point in 1932. Recovery came rapidly, however, in 1933–1934, and in 1935 the amount of tonnage handled set a new record.[31] Value of cargoes, of course influenced by the deflation of the times, did not surpass the 1930 high point until 1939.[32] Recovery came in spite of a series of waterfront

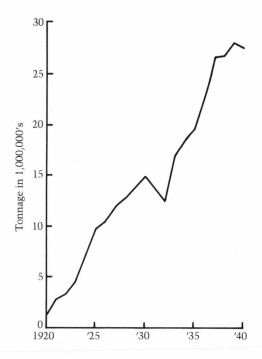

FIGURE 4. Tonnage handled, port of Houston, 1920–1940. (Data from "Comparative Statistics, Port of Houston," *Houston* 20 [May 1949]: 7.)

strikes, the most bitter and bloody in 1935 when a labor boycott lasted seventy days.[33]

The recuperation of the port came in part as a result of continued improvements. In 1932 Colonel Warren T. Hannum informed port authorities that army engineers had approved a depth of thirty-two feet and widths of four hundred feet in Galveston Bay and three hundred feet in Morgan's Cut.[34] As this project neared completion in 1935, the approved depth changed to thirty-four feet and the engineers set the minimum width between Morgan's Point and the turning basin at two hundred feet.[35] The U.S. Lighthouse Department placed thirty-two acetylene lights along the channel between Lynchburg and the Sinclair refinery in 1933, and, with improvements of the range beacons, the waterway could be used at night.[36] Congressmen Albert Thomas and Joseph J. Mansfield requested a resurvey of the channel in 1941 which resulted in approval of a three-hundred-foot width from Fidelity Island to the turning basin.[37] Six years later engineers recommended a depth of thirty-six feet.[38]

During World War II, because of restricted shipping in the Gulf, the port slipped from third to sixth in the nation for tonnage handled. In 1945 it moved to fourth and in 1948 to second, ranking only behind New York.[39] The advance was a result partly of the growth of the region and also of the promotional efforts of the Houston Port and Traffic Bureau, an organization financed by local interests originally to oppose damaging freight rates in the 1930's. In 1947 the bureau established a promotional office in Kansas City to solicit wheat shipments, and in 1948 another office was opened in New York City to attract business and disseminate information.[40]

After ranking second since 1948, the port slipped to fourth in 1955, behind New York, Philadelphia, and New Orleans.[41] Since facilities were fully used, only expansion and modernization could allow the port to regain its former position by attracting more business. Early in 1957, following a year-long discussion by interested persons, voters approved sufficient bonds to allow new sheds, wharves, and railway improvement in the channel district.[42] The same year the port moved into third position, mainly on the strength of oil shipments during the Suez crisis. It retains that rank at the present time, although in 1980 the port led the nation, even New York, in the tonnage of foreign trade. The harbor is important for imports of crude oil, iron ore, chemicals, and iron and steel materials. Significant exports include grains—wheat, corn, and sorghum—chemicals, and oil field equipment.[43] Again, through the urging of Albert Thomas, the engineers in 1958 recommended deepening the watercourse. Consequently, at present, the Houston Ship Channel is forty feet deep and three hundred to four hundred feet wide.[44]

Symbolic of the city's commitment to the port was the opening in 1962 of the twelve-story World Trade Center at Texas and Crawford streets, east of downtown. Christened by Mrs. Howard Tellepsen with water from the seven seas, the $3 million steel, glass, and marble structure provided a focal point for port activity with offices for consuls, exporters, and freight forwarders.[45] Although advertised as the only building devoted exclusively to such purposes in the United States, the idea was not new. During World War II, promoters of New Orleans started an "International House" which occupied a ten-story building in 1945. Beginning with 500 members, the organization numbered 2,400 by 1955. Established specifically to promote foreign trade, the house provided office space, a library, reservations service, multilingual secretaries, and even baby-sitters.[46] With enterprise such as that, it is not surprising that the port of New Orleans bypassed Houston. The World Trade Center thus symbolizes not only Houston's commitment to foreign trade but also its slow response to the challenge of competition.

In 1963, nonetheless, the ship channel represented a $2.55 billion investment which employed about 11 percent of Houston's labor force.[47] In 1979 it had more than one hundred wharves in operation and handled 122.4 million short tons. It was serviced by 6 railroads, 32 trucking lines, and 180 steamship lines. Between 1957 and 1980 the Port Authority spent $140 million on improvements. The United States government spent about $68 million on the project between 1910 and 1965; it received customs taxes of $32.7 million from the port in 1965.[48] As Warren Rose of the University of Houston commented in his study of the economic impact of the channel, "With the exception of basic resources, waterborne commerce probably is stimulating the economy [of Houston] more than any other force."[49] A 1975 study from the University of Houston claimed that one-third of the money generated by the city was port related.[50]

Compared to water and air development, the railroads present an almost static history. In 1911 Adolph Boldt, manager of the chamber of commerce, coined the slogan, "Where seventeen railroads meet the sea" which had to be altered later to include an eighteenth line. By the mid-1930's all but one of the railroads were still in use, but they had been consolidated under six major systems—Southern Pacific; Missouri Pacific; Missouri, Kansas and Texas; Santa Fe; Burlington; and Rock Island.[51] The Southern Pacific constructed a four-story, $3 million depot near downtown Houston in 1933–1934 and opened its $7 million Englewood switching yards in 1956.[52] The Missouri Pacific began using its new $3 million Settegast railroad yards in 1950, and the Santa Fe established a six-hundred-acre industrial park for heavy industry in 1963.[53]

Passenger traffic, strong through the World War II period, declined in the 1950's and 1960's to a point where extensive service was both unnecessary and unprofitable.[54] The editor of the *Houston Post* in 1967 called the old Union Station, which had opened in 1910, a "civic eyesore" and complained: "It is dirty, it smells, the walls are grimy, the paint is peeling off the ceiling, people lie stretched out on the benches Skid Row–fashion, and it is hotter than the hell Dante visualized."[55] Such comment was unneeded, for in a few months the Houston Belt and Terminal, which operates the depot, lowered the forty-five–foot ceiling to ten feet, installed air conditioning, and reduced the space and facilities of the waiting room. A few years before, the number of passenger trains in and out had numbered thirty-six; now, there were only three. The Union Station closed completely in 1974. At the Southern Pacific depot there was only a single train in and out per day. For railroad passenger service, an era had closed, and as Martin Dreyer concluded in a sentimental article: "So it's a new day, and most of the passenger trains are gone. And the blast of a locomotive whistle is a lonely note in the distance."[56]

The decline in railroad passengers, of course, paralleled improvements in air travel and highway facilities. Following the Federal Road Act in 1916 and the creation of the Texas Highway Department in 1917, slow changes began to come.[57] Before 1930, most roads forty miles out of the city were impassable when wet, but the depression proved a boon to the highway traveler. Ten paved roadways were opened between 1930 and 1938, with connections to San Antonio, Beaumont, Alvin, Angleton, West Columbia, Lufkin, Texarkana, Dallas, and Waco. More than fifty thousand vehicles traversed these roads daily in 1938.[58] These included not only automobiles but also trucks and buses which offered services not possible for the railroads. Bayshore Bus Lines, incorporated in 1923, started routes around Galveston Bay; Missouri Pacific Transportation Company, another bus company, began to operate between Houston and Freeport in 1928; Kerrville Bus Lines opened service from Houston to Austin in 1930. By 1950 nine lines connected with the Bayou City, carrying 15,000 people per day.[59] In 1929 there were 13,000 commercial trucks in Harris County; in 1961 there were 76,000. Included in the 270 various trucking companies listed for Houston in 1967 were

Red Arrow Freight Lines and Herrin Transportation Company, both successful Houston-based carriers.[60]

The construction of streets and the rationalization or planning of traffic flow within the city were also of great significance for transportation. The city planning commission reported in 1929 that the transit system had increased its passenger numbers 10 percent in the preceding five years, but that the population had increased 60 percent.[61] It was, therefore, in the 1920's that Houston committed itself to mass transportation by automobile with all of its expensive ramifications. By emphasizing traffic control—signal lights, one-way streets, freeways, and so on—the city encouraged the use of private motorcars. As people found them convenient, more cars came into use, which in turn forced further provision for auto traffic. By the 1960's the city had so spread out that public transit was both unprofitable and inconvenient. For Houstonians the automobile was almost a necessity of life. The fact that there exists a practical limit to the number of automobiles that can travel to a central point at the same moment, and that a vehicle of public transport, such as a bus, can move more people and occupy less room, has just been recognized in city policy. In terms of health, land usage, and city finance, this commitment to the motorcar appears expensive beyond calculation.

A Works Progress Administration survey in 1939 revealed that almost 80 percent of the vehicles entering the central business district, bounded by Caroline, Polk, Milam, and Franklin, were automobiles. They transported 72 percent of the people entering the area. In contrast, buses and streetcars counted a little over 2 percent of the vehicles but carried 15 percent of the people. The WPA suggested a thoroughfare plan, no left turns or U-turns, various street-widening projects, painted lane stripes, and bypass routes to avoid downtown.[62] In 1941 the planning commission began work on a major street design which emphasized thoroughfares and a loop system for defense purposes.[63] Following the war, the city completed designs for a freeway to Galveston down the abandoned right-of-way of the Interurban and tunnels under the ship channel.[64] Thomas E. Willier, city director of traffic and transportation, gained temporary relief for congestion downtown by wide use of one-way streets, restriction of trucking during business hours, elimination of parking on Main Street, banning turns at strategic spots, retiming traffic lights, and encouraging shoppers' buses to move people to and from just outside the business area.[65]

In 1950 a tunnel, named after a long-time county auditor, Harry

Washburn, was opened between Pasadena and the north side of the ship channel. Constructed by sinking prefabricated tunnel sections into a prepared trench, the $9 million, four-lane Washburn Tunnel eased traffic[66] and allowed elimination of an inadequate ferry boat. Two years later, the four-lane expressway to Galveston, the Gulf Freeway, was complete. It had cost $28 million, but the state and federal governments paid 86 percent of the total, under the first nationwide program to improve urban roadways. Construction expense averaged $573,000 per mile in most places but amounted to $1.6 million a mile in Houston where costs were greater. W. J. Van London, an expert from the Texas Highway Department, estimated a "comfortable capacity" at 125,000 vehicles per day. In 1952 it carried 75,000 per day; in 1960, 100,000; and in 1969, 140,000.[67]

Also in 1952 a state survey revealed that all major Houston highways should be four lanes wide, and the next year Van London disclosed plans for a $2.5 million freeway interchange that would be part of a $100 million system to encircle downtown Houston.[68] The federal highway provisions in 1956 made $453 million available for Texas roads, and from that Houston received a $243 million allotment.[69] By 1957, $60 million had been expended on 85 miles of a 237-mile system projected for the future.[70] That same year, residential promoters led by Frank W. Sharp gave ten miles of a 300-foot right-of-way for the construction of the Southwest Freeway. Their only desire, in return, was to hurry the project, and work began in 1958.[71] These people obviously benefited from increased property values and access to their housing projects. Land adjacent to the Gulf Freeway, for example, rose in price 200 to 300 percent in the years 1945–1949. Some property which had sold for six cents per square foot in 1945 commanded sixty cents in 1949.[72]

Meanwhile, the rationalization of traffic flow on downtown streets had progressed about as far as possible, and as Eugene Maier, the city traffic engineer, commented in 1954, "There is absolutely nothing more that can be done to speed up downtown traffic except to further curtail curb parking or push the buildings back and widen the streets.[73] A test run in 1955 of one mile at 5:30 P.M. in the downtown rush-hour traffic took seven minutes and forty seconds (almost eight miles per hour).[74] In 1960, with thirty minutes of effort in rush-hour traffic, a driver reached the Katy Freeway west of Voss Road from downtown. In 1969 a driver moved ten miles farther, but in 1976 a commuter got only to Gessner Road—farther than in 1960 but less than in 1969. In 1979 there existed 368 miles of expressways in Harris County, but the roads were gaining 600 vehicles per day.[75] In 1940 there were 170,000 registered automobiles in Harris County;

in 1950, 322,000; in 1964, 587,000; in 1979, 1,295,000.[76] Most people, 87 percent, used an automobile to get to work and only 14 percent of these used a car pool in the early 1970's. This was similar to
situations in other Texas cities.[77]

The traditional answer for the increasing traffic was to build
more freeways, which intensified the problem. The largest bridge in
Texas, 150 feet high and 500 feet in a horizontal span, for example,
was completed over the ship channel in 1973.[78] The new freeways,
however, encouraged more people to use private automobiles, and as
could be expected, there were frustrations and tragedies. In 1971 on
the hottest day of the year the roadway on the Post Oak overpass
buckled and stranded thousands of motorists. Workers had to cut
the pavement with jackhammers.[79] In the same area in 1976 a tank
truck carrying anhydrous ammonia failed to make a curve, punched
through the guardrail, fell twenty-four feet, and exploded. The deadly
gas spread like fog over the freeway. One trapped motorist abandoned his car and ran as the gas overtook him. He collapsed and
died. Altogether, the accident involved twenty vehicles, killed 5 people, and injured 197.[80]

Traffic jams were inevitable and have become an expected part
of commuting life. On one occasion when a stalled mobile home
halted the flow, the wife of a *Houston Post* columnist was stuck behind a white Lincoln Continental containing men wearing large
cowboy hats. Apparently they had a telephone in the car, for soon a
helicopter dropped from the sky to the grass beside the Lincoln. One
of the men left the car, boarded the helicopter, and whirled away.[81]
That was certainly one way to beat the traffic.

Then there existed the nightmares of the gasoline shortages in
1973–1974 and in 1979. Forty percent of the stations ran out of fuel.
Stations closed over the weekends and served customers only on an
odd-even license plate basis. Traffic jams declined because people
were waiting in lines to obtain gasoline. At their worst, delays at the
pump lasted over an hour.[82] In this automotive town the rumor
spread that the situation caused half the population to become neu-
rotic. At least one positive outcome was the demand for better public transportation, even though, earlier, only 8 percent of the commuters said they would give up their cars.[83]

As might be expected with such long-standing dedication to the
motorcar, public transit over the years encountered hardship. Buses
replaced the streetcars in 1941; but after 1947 the number of passengers declined, and in 1951 revenue began to drop. Annual per capita bus rides declined from 214 in 1947 to 97 in 1953; buses traveled
23 million miles in 1947, but only 15.2 million in 1957, as unprofit-

able routes and schedules were abandoned.[84] As the number of cars increased, buses had to move more slowly, becoming even less efficient and attractive to passengers. Newsman Jim Mathis once wrote about this, "A kindly elephant hemmed in by a flood of aggressive mice could feel no more helpless than a bus driver in downtown traffic."[85] Despite the efforts of Bernard E. Calkins of Wichita, Kansas, who tried to revitalize the system with better scheduling and air-conditioned buses, public transit in Houston remained in poor condition. After a squabble between Calkins and the city council, the company fell into receivership, and in 1966 the National City Lines of Florida took over and maintained service.[86]

The bus system remained in ill condition while experts, officials, and commuters expressed growing concern over the traffic problem. In 1973 voters were asked to approve a rapid transit authority which would have the power to tax vehicle emissions. "Through providing an alternative transportation system," said Mayor Louie Welch, "we will make our community a better place in which to live. We must take this approach if we are to avoid strangulation. . . . We cannot afford to wait another year, or two, or five."[87] The electorate, nevertheless, rejected the plan by a three to one margin. It was a defeat of the solution, however, not a denial of the problem.

The bus company could no longer sustain its steady losses. The city, consequently, took over the ailing system shortly following the election of Mayor Fred Hofheinz. The new mayor was able to obtain federal support to purchase one hundred new buses, but meanwhile two long strikes by the Transport Workers Union crippled the system.[88] Despite that, Hofheinz pushed the city toward the use of buses. "Anyone in Houston who still harbors dreams of sleek new mass transit systems featuring expensive gadgetry like monorails or subways is not living in the real world," the mayor stated. "We cannot afford to build or operate such fanciful systems."[89] The logic was there. Houston was too spread out for any arrangement other than buses which were flexible and could operate over existing facilities. The city committed itself, at least for the short run, to buses.

The first "park and ride" service began in 1977 on the Gulf Freeway; commuters could park their cars free of charge and ride a bus downtown for sixty cents. The same year the city applied for state and local funds to finance a "contraflow" experiment.[90] The idea was to run buses on reserved lanes against the flow of traffic. In the mornings the buses and also, incidentally, any vans used for carpools would use one of the outgoing lanes of a freeway to move commuters to the inner city. In the evenings the arrangement was reversed. This experiment was based on the assumption that the rush hour clogged half the freeway and left the other half comparatively open.

In 1978 voters approved the establishment of the Metropolitan Transit Authority with the power to collect a one-cent sales tax. About the same time the contraflow operation began and the Transport Workers Union agreed to a no-strike clause in their contract. The city led the nation in the use of van pools—company-owned vans used to carpool employees to work—with about five hundred of them moving five thousand people. Between buses and van pools, the ten-mile experimental contraflow system on the North Freeway carried four thousand people per rush hour. It was considered a success.[91]

The bus company, too, was overhauled. When the new operations manager, Dick Drake, arrived from Denver to take over in 1978, he found 115 late runs and 65 cut routes. The Polk Street garage had no doors, no heaters, no spare parts, and thirty-five stripped vehicles. The other main garage on Milby Street had doors, but they did not work. Its heaters were inadequate and the roof leaked. It had spare parts but no inventory system. Drake resigned in fifteen months, exhausted, but before he left in January there were no late or missed runs.[92] Obviously, for the system to work it had to operate on time and had to travel where people wanted to go. The mechanical failure of new equipment, however, reversed Drake's success.

In general the transportation network with its various components served both as a necessary adjunct to commerce and as a magnet to attract manufacturers. Houston, even in the modern period, was to a large extent a commercial city. The national ratio of wholesale to retail employees in 1972 was 1 to 2.8. For the Houston standard metropolitan statistical area the ratio was 1 to 2.0, which underscores Houston's role as a distribution point. There has been little change in the past decade. Retail sales amounted to $5.291 billion, wholesale reached $12.805 billion, and value added by manufacture was $4.179 billion in 1972 for the metropolitan area. Compared to national percentages the Houston SMSA had about 12 percent fewer workers involved in manufacturing. It thus trails the nation, but Houston still reflects a general increase in manufacturing activity since 1929.[93]

Demonstrating the attraction of commercial facilities to manufacturing was the conversion of the Houston Ship Channel to an industrial watercourse. In 1935, 24 percent of the known Texas oil reserves existed within one hundred miles of the city, and 40 percent of all Texas petroleum moved out through the channel.[94] Also in close proximity were vast deposits of natural gas, salt, and sulphur. In 1930, 57 percent of the world's supply of sulphur came from Brazoria, Matagorda, and Wharton counties.[95] In addition, Houston offered a secure harbor, fresh water, and favorable weather. In 1940 the fourteen refineries along the ship channel held 11 percent of the nation's capacity to produce gasoline, and the oil companies around Houston employed fifty thousand people.[96] The area therefore possessed the resources, facilities, and personnel necessary to respond to the stimulus of war.

In 1940, Humble Oil and Refining Company, a firm that manufactured more than a billion gallons of aviation fuel during World War II, received a $12 million contract from the War Department to produce toluene, an ingredient of high explosives, from petroleum.[97] Shell Oil, however, at its Deer Park Plant, processed the country's first barrel of such toluene in December, after working around the clock to erect a plant in four months. Through expansion of facilities, Shell's capacity shortly increased from two million to ten million gallons of toluene yearly.[98] In 1943 the Defense Plant Corporation of the federal government opened a plant at Baytown, operated by General Tire and Rubber Company. Utilizing butadiene made from petroleum at the nearby Humble plant and styrene manufactured by Monsanto Chemical Company at Texas City from ethylene and benzol from petroleum and coke-oven gases, the new plant produced Buna-S rubber. At the time experts estimated that 50 percent of the nation's synthetic rubber would come from Texas, though the material would be transformed into tires, lifeboats, and balloons at Akron, Ohio.[99]

At Baytown the same year, Sinclair Oil erected a $24 million butadiene plant and Goodyear a $12 million Buna-S factory, supplied with styrene from Monsanto at Texas City and Dow at Velasco. The proximity of the plants to raw materials and to each other reduced shipping and storage costs.[100] This marked the beginning of a chemical complex with a chief characteristic of interdependence.

Investment in the local chemical installations amounted to about $600 million during World War II and $300 million immediately thereafter. This generated a regional boom in the petrochemical industry which encompassed a "golden triangle" from Houston to Freeport to Port Arthur–Orange. From such basic materials as salt, sulphur, natural gas, and petroleum came sulphuric acid, methane, ethane, propane, butane, toluol, and xylol. Through interconnecting pipelines flowed such items as butylene, hydrogen, hydrogen chloride, ethylene, butadiene, sodium chloride, acetylene, acetone, chlorine, and ammonia.[101] The *Houston* magazine observed in 1957, "If an air-to-ground X-ray were made of Harris County, these interlaced pipelines would show up like a nerve system around the backbone—the Houston Ship Channel—of an industrial giant."[102] This complex attracted chemical companies wishing to utilize various feed stocks: so much so that the list of companies involved reads like a roll call of the chemical industry—Shell, DuPont, Humble, Gulf, Texaco, Monsanto, Union Carbide, Dow, Celanese, Ethyl, Phillips, Diamond Alkali, and Amoco.[103]

Chemical sales in the area increased six times between 1940 and 1966. With 639 plants, Texas became one of the largest chemical-producing states, second only to New Jersey. In the Houston region total investment reached $4 billion to $5 billion by 1966, which ranked it first as a point of capital expenditure for the preceding decade. The industry employed 47,000 people, manufactured 415 items at 187 installations, and produced more than 50 percent of the materials for plastics and synthetic rubber in the United States.[104] For Houston a major fault was that the various plants processed only through an intermediate stage. Final production, such as tires from synthetic rubber, occurred elsewhere. To reach a condition of full maturity in this field, Houston seemingly needed manufacturers of finished products.

World War II served as a catalyst not only for the chemical industry but for others as well. Even though some natural gas was used locally and piped elsewhere, before 1943 it was nonetheless so plentiful that it was almost valueless. Companies removed the hydrocarbons and then pumped the dry gas into the ground for storage or burned it. The exigencies of war, however, created a demand for natural gas along the eastern seaboard. Tennessee Gas Transmission Company, a Houston company known after 1966 as Tenneco, was formed in 1944 and within eleven months operated a 1,265-mile pipeline to West Virginia. By 1957 this firm, the first transcontinental company to tap the Gulf Coast fields, possessed 9,811 miles of lines and $1,006,562,000 in assets. In 1966 Tenneco claimed over one billion dollars in annual revenue.[105] Texas Eastern Transmission Company followed the lead of Tennessee Gas and bought the Big Inch and Little Inch for $143,127,000 in 1947. These lines, reaching from Texas to the East Coast, had been constructed during the war.[106] In 1966 ten major natural gas companies maintained headquarters—and four others had operating divisions—in Houston. Altogether they controlled 83,000 miles of pipeline. The most important were Tenneco, Natural Gas Pipeline Company of America, Texas Eastern Transmission, Transcontinental Gas Pipeline, and United Gas Pipe Line.[107]

Early in 1941 Sheffield Steel Corporation, a subsidiary of American Rolling Mill Company, began plans for a steel plant on the ship channel with the help of $12 million from the Reconstruction Finance Corporation. George M. Verity, the seventy-seven–year–old chairman of Armco, broke ground for the mill on the same day in May that President Franklin D. Roosevelt declared an unlimited national emergency.[108] Although Sheffield officials had thought to use scrap iron, shortages due to prior shipments to the Japanese and the demands of wartime forced them to utilize raw ores from Texas and Mexico. Contracts from the Defense Plant Corporation made possible the necessary alterations.[109] Following the war Sheffield proceeded to become the only integrated (raw material to finished pieces) steel producer in mid-continent.[110] Though Jones and Laughlin in 1956 and U.S. Steel in 1966 bought sites on the channel, so far the area has failed to attract other major steel producers. This is probably because of heavy investment elsewhere and the lack of nearby raw materials.[111]

As could be expected, shipbuilding flourished once again with the commencement of war. In order to provide merchant vessels, the U.S. Maritime Commission contracted with Houston Shipbuilding Corporation, a subsidiary of Todd Shipyard Corporation, to build vessels of 7,500 tons each. The company established a $5 million yard at Irish Bend on the channel near Deer Park and laid the first keels in July 1940.[112] It took 254 days to launch the first Liberty Ship, but the company soon cut that time to 53 days.[113] With further contracts, Houston Shipbuilding expanded at an enormous rate. In March 1942 it had six thousand employees; in May, twelve thousand; in June, eighteen thousand; and in July, almost twenty thousand. Though only 3 percent of the personnel had prior shipbuilding experience, they worked forty-eight to fifty-six hours a week and kept the yards in continual operation. Using assembly-line techniques and specialized teams, the firm turned out 208 cargo vessels and 14 tankers during the war and won an "M" award for merit.[114] In 1959–1960, Todd Shipyards, using a different site bought in 1947, constructed in part the $1 million *Atomic Servant*, a tender for the nuclear-powered *N.S. Savannah*.[115]

War contracts also went to Platzer Shipbuilding and Dry Dock Company, San Jacinto Shipbuilding Corporation, and Brown Shipbuilding Company. This industry, shortly of great importance to Houston, employed forty thousand people and had a $2 million weekly payroll.[116] Houston Shipbuilding was the largest company, but Brown Shipbuilding was second. Located on Greens Bayou, the Brown yards produced over three hundred subchasers, destroyer escorts, and landing craft by April 1945. Also utilizing assembly-line techniques, Brown launched the welded-steel ships broadside into the bayou with a tremendous splash. The company, started by local engineers George and Herman Brown, won an Army-Navy "E" award for efficiency in 1942.[117]

Somewhat less meritorious was the service of San Jacinto Shipbuilding Corporation, which received in 1941 a contract to build twenty-two large concrete barges. In April 1943 the Truman Commission condemned the project, directed by the McCloskey Corporation of Philadelphia, because of "rapacity, greed, fraud, and negligence." The estimated cost of the initial five barges had increased from $2,921,220 to $7,229,797; the site was so ill-chosen that the barges would be unable to pass under a bridge between it and the ship channel; the deed to the land was such that the original owner, who had donated the site, would get it back with free improvements; subcontracts had gone to friends at inflated prices; an inexperienced twenty-five-year-old member of the McCloskey family was in charge; and, worst of all, the company had produced no barges. In August 1943 the Maritime Commission restricted its order to the four vessels already on the ways, despite the denial of charges by M. H. McCloskey III.[118]

The war stimulated not only business along the ship channel but also Houston industry everywhere. Though the federal government at first hesitated to award contracts to places close to a coastline because of the defense difficulties, such reluctance was soon overcome by Houston's chamber of commerce and by Albert Thomas.[119] The McEvoy Company, an oil-field equipment firm, received the first prime (direct from the government) contract, to make machine-gun tripods.[120] Cameron Iron Works manufactured depth charges for the navy and won an "E" award.[121] The Texas Washer and Texas Specialty companies worked together to make fins for mortar shells. They also won an "E" award—and argued over who should fly the coveted pennant. The difficulty evaporated, however, when each received a flag.[122] Reed Roller Bit and Hughes Tool Company manufactured airplane parts, and by April 1943 forty-five companies held prime contracts and the federal government had spent about $265 million in Houston.[123]

As population increased by 54 percent and bank deposits by 282 percent between 1940 and 1950, a boom began that has endured into the 1980's.[124] In 1945–1948 Harris County ranked first in the nation for value of industrial construction and, with building permits of $266,802,075 for the county and $100,160,322 for the city, in 1948 Houston rated as the fastest-growing city per capita in the country.[125]

Oveta Culp Hobby, wartime leader of the Women's Army Corps and a director of the *Houston Post,* may have expressed the feelings of all citizens experiencing the rapid expansion when she commented, "I think I'll like Houston if they ever get it finished."[126]

Leading the building boom were the department stores. In 1945 George S. Cohen sold for $3.5 million the long-time Houston establishment Foley Brothers Dry Goods Company to Federated Department Stores, led by Fred Lazarus, Jr. At the time of sale the store grossed $8 million per year, but by 1947 it earned $17 million and occupied new quarters. Perhaps influenced by the Sears building on South Main Street, erected in 1939, Kenneth Franzheim designed for Foley's an almost windowless, six-story, $9 million structure. Foley's immediately became Houston's chief department store.[127] Ben Wolfman, owner of The Fashion, specializing in women's and children's apparel, spent $2.5 million for remodeling in 1947; Wolfman sold the store to Neiman-Marcus of Dallas in 1955.[128] Joske's, a department store, and Sakowitz and Battelstein's, dry goods stores, were also enlarged and remodeled in the same period.[129] Somewhat sensational, at least for Houston, was the payment in 1946 of $2,000 per front inch for the land on Main Street to be occupied by a new Woolworth store.[130] Federated Department Stores had acquired an option to buy this nearby site for $1.25 million when it bought Foley's. Lazarus exercised the option and then resold it for $3,050,000 in a telephone conversation which, according to *Fortune,* went like this:

> "How much do you want for that Houston site?"
> "Still $3 million."
> "Dammit, Mr. Lazarus, that's robbery."
> "I know it is."
> "We won't pay it."
> "Then what did you call me for?"
> "Well . . ."
> "Now look here, we've created the value on that piece of property. We've made it a good merchandising site. We're not going to sell it and let somebody else cash in on it."
> "All right, the hell with it. We'll take it."[131]

Following the downtown development, which undoubtedly aided Houston in achieving the number-one ranking for percentage gain in retail sales from 1939 to 1949 for cities of over 500,000 population, the major stores began to expand to suburban sites.[132] Sears had previously located outside the downtown area, and Battelstein's, with a branch store on Shepherd at the edge of River Oaks, was next, in 1953.[133] In 1955 Sakowitz announced two suburban stores, one at the corner of Post Oak and Westheimer and the other at Gulfgate, a $20 million shopping mall on the Gulf Freeway, developed by Theodore W. Berenson of Boston.[134] Gulfgate opened in 1956, but the $5 million Sakowitz store on Westheimer, which (questionably) used a colonial design to "fit architecturally into its environment," did not begin to operate until 1959.[135] Foley's made its suburban debut at the seventy-acre, air-conditioned Sharpstown Mall along with another Battelstein's in 1961.[136] In 1963 Joske's, with a store already at Gulfgate, opened another across from Sakowitz at Post Oak and Westheimer; Sakowitz in turn opened an additional store on Memorial Drive in 1967; Foley's in 1966–1967 added two more, one on Almeda-Genoa Road in the southeast and the other near the Hempstead Highway and the North Loop in the northeast; and in 1969 Neiman-Marcus, closing its downtown store, opened a new one at Post Oak and Westheimer.[137] As a result of outlying stores such as these, the share of total retail sales for downtown dropped from 51 percent in 1948 to 28 percent in 1958, even though the dollar amount of sales remained much the same.[138]

The exodus of downtown retail business continued in successive years. Houston in 1980 possessed over two hundred outlying shopping centers, seventeen of which were over 750,000 square feet.[139] Robert Sakowitz noted about this shift that the downtown stores still service professional people and visitors, but that there is sufficient reason to question the future of retailing in an area where there is no life on the weekends or after 5:00 P.M.[140]

An array of new office buildings also appeared downtown to help alter the skyline of the city. Much of the construction was on the southern edge of the business district, stretching away from the bayou along Main, Fannin, Travis, Milam, and Louisiana streets, thus giving the district an unusual, elongated configuration. Since most of the postwar office towers utilized the straight-lined, right-angled, boxlike configuration of contemporary architecture, they contributed a bold, striking, new appearance to the southern side of the business area.

First came the City National Bank in 1947; then a new county courthouse in 1953; and then the Texas National Bank, with a weather ball, fifteen feet in diameter, on top, in 1955.[141] In 1956 the aluminum-faced Bank of the Southwest and in 1959 the five-story Gibraltar Savings and Loan Association building with bold, gray-tinted, solar-glass curtain walls appeared.[142] The First City National Building was opened in 1961, a thirty-two–story glass-and-marble "monument to high finance" with exterior supporting columns completely around it.[143] During 1962 the square, functional, eleven-story Federal Office and Court Building opened, west of the downtown area in the Civic Center. Its small, square windows, out of place with the extensive glass windows of the other new structures, engendered unflattering epithets: "prison," "fort," "pigeon house," and "monstrosity."[144]

Ten edifices came into use in 1963, increasing office space by 41 percent. The most important were the $32 million, forty-four–story Humble Building; the dark-gray aluminum, thirty-three–story Tennessee Building; the twenty-one–story Southwest Tower; and the twenty-one–story 500 Jefferson Building in the Cullen Center, a projected cluster of office, apartment, and hotel buildings near the Humble Building.[145] During 1967 the twenty-eight–story Houston Natural Gas Building, utilizing gas as the sole source of power for the office structure, opened, while the planned fifty-story One Shell Plaza, to be the tallest west of the Mississippi River, was in preparation. Shell executives had taken over a year to decide where to locate their headquarters. The choice of Houston, among thirty others, reinforced the Bayou City's influence in the petroleum industry. The building opened in 1970.[146]

In the same year Texas Eastern Transmission Corporation, with the largest real estate transaction in the city's history, bought thirty-two blocks of downtown Houston to construct a city of the future. The master planner for the project, William L. Pereira of Los Angeles, commented, "A city is like a living organism that grows and decays and depends upon its heart for survival."[147] It was a bold commitment to the central business area. In nine years, however, Texas Eastern completed only two office buildings and a garage. It then sold 50 percent of the project to Cadillac-Fairview Corporation, a real estate development firm from Toronto. The Canadian company expected to continue the original plan and construct some downtown residential buildings.[148]

In 1972 the Hyatt-Regency opened a thirty-four–story hotel and Gerald D. Hines announced the beginning of Pennzoil Place, a black, twin-trapezoid tower designed by Philip Johnson of New York. In 1977 Hines began the First International Bank Building, fifty-five stories, which opened in 1980. In 1978 he announced the seventy-story, 998-foot high Texas Commerce Plaza designed by I. M. Pei, which will be a five-sided shaft of pale gray granite, a retreat from glass-sided structures. Rivaling this in height will be the Allied Bank Building constructed by Kenneth L. Schnitzer and designed by Skidmore, Owings, and Merrill. The Federal Aviation Administration placed a 1,000-foot limit on the skyline. The Allied Building, described as a "slipped tube," or a semi-circular tube sliced lengthwise into two parts, will reach 970 feet. Its blue-green exterior will contrast with the white, tan, and black coloration of the cityscape. As the decade closed, there were six other downtown buildings in the forty- to sixty-story range being planned and built.[149]

The transformation of the central business district during the 1970's was spectacular. Admired by architects for its drama, energy, and variety, it has been also criticized for inconsistency, absence of parks, and lack of life after the workday. Architect Jack McGinty commented: "I guess that it's pretty humbling from an architect's viewpoint, but Houston proves that architecture in itself doesn't make a city. You can walk down Travis Street for blocks and pass some of the finest highrise buildings in the world. And it's a boring walk. In Washington [D.C.] you would be able to walk the same amount of blocks and see all kinds of interesting spaces. There are good things scattered all over the city [Houston]. But the sense of the city itself is fragmented, uncoordinated."[150]

At the same time this heavy construction occurred downtown, there appeared a number of buildings in the outlying sections, seemingly repelled by the same magnet that drew other structures to the core of the city. Shell Oil started a new $1 million research laboratory on Bellaire Boulevard in 1945 and added to it in 1956.[151] Humble Oil, in turn, placed a $3 million research center on Buffalo Speedway in 1951–1954.[152] In 1945 the Hermann Hospital Estate Board began work on the $1.5 million Hermann Professional Building on Fannin Street near Rice Institute, while the Veterans Administration planned a $970,000 office on LaBranch.[153] Most significant of the new buildings, however, was the Shamrock Hotel.

In order to serve the transient trade, the major hotels of Houston had located in the downtown area; only a few apartment hotels, such as the Warwick, were in outlying places.[154] Glenn McCarthy, oil millionaire, land speculator, and promoter in general, apparently had different ideas about the hotel business. In 1944 he bought fifteen acres at the intersection of South Main Street and Bellaire Boulevard (now Holcombe Boulevard) for $175,000.[155] The following year McCarthy announced preliminary plans for the site which included seven apartment hotels, a department store, movie theater, grocery store, drug store, haberdashery, ice-skating rink, swimming pool, and an eighteen-story hotel. In 1946 he broke ground for McCarthy Center and the Shamrock Hotel, located five miles from downtown.[156] On St. Patrick's Day 1949, the Shamrock opened. An estimated 50,000 people turned out to see the 175 movie stars brought in for the occasion, to witness the broadcast of the Dorothy Lamour radio show, and to consume at $42.00 each a dinner including pineapple surprise, supreme of pompano Normandie, stuffed artichoke hearts, blue ribbon steak à la Shamrock, and frozen pistachio mousse.[157]

It was chaos. The crowd was so dense in the lobby that it required thirty minutes to get through; Jesse Jones got stuck at the entrance, and Mayor Holcombe remained outside for two hours. For the scheduled radio performance the doors closed and the liquor service stopped, but "the tide of people and bourbon seemed endless." The actors had to shout their lines above the din of the crowd; unidentified people cut in, and some seized the microphone and hooted into it. NBC cut off the broadcast and the star of the show went to her room to weep. The meal, calculated at $1.00 per bite, was like "trying to eat dinner in the Notre Dame backfield," according to writer Erskine Johnson, and one disappointed woman was heard to remark about the supreme of pompano Normandie, "Why, it's only fish." Southwestern Bell Telephone supposedly ranked the opening, from its viewpoint, with the Galveston flood and the Texas City disaster.[158] Without doubt, it was the wildest such affair in the history of Houston.

The $21 million hotel itself, eighteen stories high, resplendent in sixty-three shades of green, offered accommodations from $6 to $45 per night or penthouses at $2,100 per month. It had a refrigeration room for garbage, a one-thousand-car garage, a fifty-meter, fan-shaped swimming pool, decor described as "international modern," and in the lobby a large portrait of McCarthy with folded arms, tousled hair, mustache, and an austere gaze, said to soften slightly when McCarthy himself confronted it.[159] The architecture, however, was so prosaic that Frank Lloyd Wright, in town to accept a gold medal from the American Institute of Architects, reportedly offered a one-word appraisal, "Why?" After a tour of the hotel, the grand master said, "I always wondered what the inside of a juke box looked like."[160] Critics, moreover, estimated a necessary occupancy rate of 80 percent to 82 percent to permit the Shamrock to survive.[161]

Rumors began to circulate in 1950 as McCarthy apparently faced a financial crisis caused by a decrease in Texas oil prorations.[162] Large-scale borrowing which had begun in 1946 caught up, and in 1951 Warner H. Mendel, a controller placed in the McCarthy organization by the Equitable Life Assurance Society, estimated indebtedness of $55 million and indicated that the oilman would need to strike a whole new field.[163] No new oil field came, however, and the Irish luck failed. Though the Shamrock was profitable, other McCarthy properties were not, and Equitable acquired the hotel after a defaulted payment on a $34 million loan to McCarthy Oil and Gas Corporation. Hilton Hotels assumed control of the Shamrock in 1954 from the insurance company and took over complete ownership in 1955 when McCarthy sold his redemptive right for $625,000. At that moment the name of the proud hotel was changed to "Shamrock Hilton," and presently the portrait of Glenn McCarthy in the lobby yielded its place to a picture of Conrad Hilton.[164]

The Shamrock, despite troubles, reinforced the southerly expansion of downtown Houston and served as a focal point for the development of a group of buildings in uptown Houston. Carroll M. Shanks, president of the Prudential Insurance Company, announced the location in 1950 of a regional office near the Shamrock. Motivated by a decentralization program and Houston's growth potential, company officials placed the office in the Bayou City to be close to the scene of its regional investments.[165] The nineteen-story building designed by Kenneth Franzheim, with a swimming pool, tennis courts, fountain, and the Prudential trademark at the top, opened in 1952.[166] This event not only added to uptown Houston, which was further developed with the construction of the nineteen-story Fannin National Bank in 1963 and the eleven-story Siteman Building in 1964, but also marked an advance of insurance enterprise in the city.[167] In 1965 insurance companies employed 12,000 people in Houston. In that year American General Life Insurance constructed a twenty-five–story office several miles west of the downtown area on Allen Parkway.[168]

Accentuating the flight from downtown was the construction of small offices, usually two to twenty stories high, in outlying areas, such as along Richmond Avenue west of Greenbriar; at the "Magic Circle," encompassing the land around the intersection of Westheimer and Post Oak—this is the location of the world-famous shopping mall Galleria—and, most recently, in the areas around the Astrodome and the Intercontinental Airport. Builder-investors, among them Kenneth L. Schnitzer and Gerald D. Hines, promoted such suburban ventures.[169] The phenomenon of office proliferation over the countryside suggests that the downtown section is losing cohesiveness and that at least certain businesses do not require the proximity which is the magnetic power that forms a central business district.

A survey of twelve major office buildings downtown in 1967 revealed a concentration of banks, oil companies, oil-related enterprises, law firms, and some insurance, airline, and investment companies. Doctors, architects, engineers, those concerned with electronics, and real estate agents were in noticeably small numbers.[170] In 1940, 70 percent of the doctors, 76 percent of the engineers, and 30 percent of the architects worked in Houston's central business district. In 1963 there remained only 14 percent of the doctors, 24 percent of the engineers, and 10 percent of the architects.[171] A separation has thus occurred in the downtown community, the dynamics of which are unclear. Certain people and businesses seem to require daily personal contact despite modern communications, whereas others do not. Paradoxically, both Humble and Shell maintain research laboratories in the suburbs and vast offices downtown. Shell, when seeking a site for its new fifty-story headquarters, required a location close to the financial district and the civic center, the seat of local government.[172] As Gerald D. Hines, who has constructed buildings both downtown and in outlying areas, explained: "Oil companies such as Shell give a considerable amount of their business to oil brokers and other oil men and contact with these people is very important to their operation; therefore, their proximity is an essential consideration in the location of the oil company's main offices. . . . Other firms such as stock brokerage houses, financial institutions and oil operations also intercommunicate and this applies to attorneys and accountants as well. Houston will always have a central core area surrounding financial institutions."[173]

The scattering of offices across the landscape, of course, allows businesses to locate near executive housing and to avoid expensive sites. If so placed, they can yield helpful taxes to an incorporated suburb and they can divert some traffic that otherwise might contribute to downtown congestion. On the other hand, decentralization subtracts from the variety of activity which Jane Jacobs, in *The Death and Life of Great American Cities*, notes is vital to a city.[174] Although the scattered offices may add some vitality to their particular neighborhoods, for better or worse they contribute to the spread of the city—to what has been called urban sprawl.

Generous amounts of space exist in downtown Houston to allow vast parking lots and office buildings with ample setbacks, such as the Humble Building, which occupies an entire block. Land developers have leap-frogged, leaving unoccupied property between occupied properties. Somehow city services must span the unused land to reach people in these developments. Eventually, the gaps may be filled, but for Houston there exist no natural barriers to halt the spread and force concentration. As French journalist Pierre Voisin said in 1962: "There is no plan. I am horrified. Everyone is doing just as he pleases, building here and building there . . . Houston is spreading like a spilled bucket of water. If something isn't done about it quickly, it will be horrible, horrible."[175]

For the city, sprawl poses a dilemma. The town must either expand its limits to encompass the growth, and pay the expensive consequences for extension of services across empty spaces, or allow itself to be ringed by incorporated suburbs which may block future expansion. The Houston city council, thus far, has chosen to extend the boundaries, with the result that the Bayou City claimed 72 square miles in 1930 and a little more than 556 square miles in 1980.[176] This expansion, although perhaps necessary for the future, provided some ludicrous but serious annexation fights.

Until 1948–1949 Houston, covering seventy-six square miles at that time, had not exercised its power of annexation in any dramatic manner. Hearing rumors about secret annexation meetings in the independent suburbs of Galena Park and Pasadena, the city council passed an ordinance in late 1948 that doubled the size of Houston and encircled the suburbs of West University, South Side Place, Bellaire, Galena Park, Jacinto City, South Houston, and a part of Pasadena. Most of the communities voiced no great objection, but the mayors of Galena Park and Pasadena protested, and Mayor B. F. Meador of South Houston called it "not a neighborly act."[177] Although Warren S. Bellows, president of the Houston Chamber of Commerce, said the step was taken only after "long study" and "careful consideration," the police, public utilities, and health departments were taken by surprise.[178]

After a failure of compromise between Mayor Oscar Holcombe of Houston and Mayor Sam Hoover of Pasadena, Houston annexed a strip of land around Pasadena in 1949. Meanwhile, LaPorte, southeast of Houston on Galveston Bay, took in land all the way to the Pasadena border. Adding to the confusion, Sinclair Oil sued both Houston and Pasadena to prevent annexation, arguing that its facilities were self-contained and would not benefit from payment of taxes.[179] With the difficulty between Houston and Pasadena at a simmer, the Bayou City again doubled in 1956, but it had to pay a penalty of $31 million.

Out-of-town subdivisions often formed "water districts" in order to finance service at low cost. Water district bonds, since they were somewhat risky, however, ran for long periods at high interest rates. In the annexation of 1956 Houston had to absorb more than twenty-seven districts which carried a bonded debt of $31 million. Six of these did not exist when Houston began annexation proceedings. To ensure service, fifteen of them sold $18 million in bonds

FIGURE 5. Houston, 1980.

while the city delayed and pondered the expansion. Quick accession might prevent this, but the city has discovered it cannot immediately afford to construct the necessary facilities. Somewhat with council approval, therefore, seventy-four districts existed on the urban perimeter in 1967. In that year seven water districts voted $16.9 million in bonds with a total of only fifty-six votes cast.[180] Such debt, at high interest, created by a few people, would eventually have to be assumed by the expanding metropolis.

In 1960, while Houston moved to absorb fifty square miles around the Intercontinental Airport to offset a threat by the town of Humble, its neighbors held clandestine meetings in Dallas to avoid detection. When all was set, four city councils moved precisely at the same time. LaPorte, Lomax, and Deer Park transferred enough land to Pasadena to permit flanking Houston's 1949 strip, which had reached to the LaPorte limits. Pasadena then grabbed seventy-two square miles; LaPorte, twenty; Deer Park, seven; and Lomax, two. All told, these incorporated towns controlled about 25 percent of Harris County.[181] The stunned Houston city council tried to negotiate with the conspirators but failed. With Baytown and Texas City also on the move, the council voted favorably on the first of three necessary readings of an ordinance to annex all unincorporated land in Harris County. "Annexing the entire county is preposterous," exclaimed Mayor Lewis W. Cutrer, who opposed this action that would expand the city to 1,560 square miles.[182] As the first reading gave Houston prior claim, the land war came to a halt; Houston had to go no further to carry out the threat. A compromise in 1962 allowed the Bayou City to claim the Clear Lake region to the southeast, while Pasadena absorbed some land relinquished by Houston.[183] Although smoke from the annexation battles still obscures some points of the issue, in 1967 the First Court of Civil Appeals upheld Houston's authority in the southeastern portion of the county.[184]

Trouble, however, continued. In 1969 the Texas Supreme Court invalidated Houston's earlier attempt to contain Pasadena. A four-year dispute ensued which was settled again by allowing Pasadena to take Bayport while Houston maintained an option to take land around Clear Lake City and the Manned Spacecraft Center.[185] Houston, meanwhile, took in fifty square miles along the western border of the city.[186]

At stake in all of this, of course, was control not only over future growth but also over lucrative tax properties. Pasadena, Deer Park, LaPorte, and Baytown were all interested in nearby industry, some of the communities actually extracting payments "in lieu of taxes" under a threat of annexation and taxation.[187] A case demonstrating the interplay of business, government, city expansion, and land development is that of the Manned Spacecraft Center of the National Aeronautics and Space Administration. In 1938 the Humble Oil and Refining Company bought the 30,000-acre West Ranch southeast of Houston for purposes of oil exploitation. While contemplating new uses for the ship channel, the chamber of commerce thought of dredging a deep-water channel westward across Galveston Bay to the Humble property. Marvin Hurley of the chamber suggested this possibility to Humble in 1955, but the company was not interested.[188] Urging a balanced establishment of industrial, commercial, and residential facilities, the civic organization nonetheless continued to promote the idea. The oil company began to study the project in 1960, and in 1961, according to Hurley, prepared to announce a development program, but annexation difficulties forestalled the move.[189]

In June 1961, however, Albert Thomas confirmed that NASA was preparing to select a site for the Manned Spacecraft Center, and Thomas, chairman of the House appropriations subcommittee which controlled NASA funds, insisted upon consideration of Houston. He was determined that the Bayou City, forgotten in the first round of installations, should not be missed again.[190] Apparently, through the work of Albert Thomas, Morgan J. Davis, who was president of Humble, and George R. Brown, who was both a principal in Brown and Root and chairman of the Board of Trustees at Rice University, the oil company gave to Rice a 1,000-acre tract worth $3.5 million in the midst of the West Ranch. In August a NASA inspection team visited Houston. The members talked with local government officials, with Kenneth S. Pitzer, president of Rice, and others. In September, after meeting with Albert Thomas and Vice-President Lyndon B. Johnson, who was chairman of the National Space Committee, James E. Webb of NASA announced the location of the new $60 million center. It was to be twenty-two miles southeast of Houston, on land donated by Rice University—the same land recently transferred from Humble.[191]

In addition to obvious political leverage, Houston offered transportation advantages, industry, science and research installations, skilled workers, a mild climate, and satisfactory cultural-recreational facilities.[192] Brown and Root became the major architectural and engineering contractor for the project, estimated to cost $125 million in 1962. While Texas A&M and the University of Houston received grants of $84,800 and $71,250, respectively, for research programs on space problems, Rice got $192,000. In 1963 Rice established the Department of Space Science, the first in the nation.[193]

Humble announced in 1962 a 15,000-acre industrial commercial-residential development around the spacecraft center and in 1964 revealed a master plan for Bayport, a projected channel, port, and industrial complex which over twenty years might attract a $900 million investment and create 25,000 jobs.[194]

Land values boomed two to ten times in the vicinity, the subdivisions of Clear Lake City and Nassau Bay emerged, and Houston in its annexation moves prepared to absorb the area.[195] After five years the Manned Spacecraft Center possessed an authorized personnel strength of 4,854 with a payroll of $50 million. It was estimated, moreover, that MSC inspired 65 jobs on the outside for every 100 it created, and that 125 companies had established offices in Houston to deal with the center.[196] In triumph for the nation and the city as American astronauts landed for the first time on the moon, Neil Armstrong radioed to Earth, "Houston . . . Tranquility Base here. The *Eagle* has landed!"[197] Such accomplishment, illustrative of the expansive nature of Houston and the interplay of institutional forces, lent deep meaning to the chamber of commerce sobriquet of the 1960's, "Space City, U.S.A."

Since the halcyon days of the Apollo program the budget of the Manned Spacecraft Center (renamed in honor of President Lyndon B. Johnson in 1973) has been cut by 30 percent. It has meant the loss of one hundred jobs, an abbreviated program, and cutbacks in the maintenance of the facility. The grass at the Clear Lake installation grows long before being cut, library hours are less, offices are cleaned only half as often—it is a form of "tarnish" on a once-glittering program.[198]

For Houston the 1970's brought a new sobriquet—the "International City." The spirit of the new nickname was reflected not only in the activities of the port but also in business and finance. With the energy crisis, Houston, due to its petrochemical complex, became a focal point—an energy capital—for the nation and for the world. Because of low real estate prices—prime land in Houston cost $125 per square foot; New York, $500; London, $2,000; Tokyo, $3,000—the Bayou City became a favorite investment site for British, Canadian, German, and Saudi Arabian money. The Friedrich Flick family of West Germany, for instance, sold Daimler-Benz stock and bought the thirty-five–story Entex Building in downtown Houston. Deutsche Bank of West Germany, moreover, bought 80 percent of the Pennzoil Building and resold it in shares to German investors.

There is no accounting of the amount of foreign money in Houston, but an estimate in 1976 was $200 million. The city has become a comfortable place for conservative money because of the businesslike attitudes of the people and the aggressive annexation policies which have preserved the urban tax base. In 1968–1969 Harris County bank deposits passed those of Dallas County.[199] There are 47 consular and 230 foreign business representatives in Houston. In turn, the city has 275 firms with offices abroad and 8 local banks with international departments.

The new international flare of the Bayou City was demonstrated by Colette Grinstead, an administrative assistant to the mayor. While visiting a relative in Paris she was asked if she wished to go shopping. Looking at the clothes she bought in Houston she said, "What for? I'm wearing French hose, Italian shoes, a Chinese blouse, a Swiss sweater, and an American skirt."[200]

7

Conservatism and Culture

Through Houston's modern civic and social history seeps a pervasive conservatism, reflected to varying degrees in politics, public schools, and reactions to urban problems. It is the conservatism of a nineteenth-century robber baron—exploitative, laissez-faire, and at times generous in philanthropy. Its roots lie in the Southern heritage of the town, the expansive, opportunistic nature of the area, and the strong business orientation of the economy. It gives to the people a certain bold, reckless, stubborn, independent, and sometimes lawless attitude, which means that the conservatism both helps and hinders the development of the city.

Perhaps, as Willie Morris, former editor of *Harper's Magazine*, once argued, the conservatism is, in part, a product of rapid growth.[1] In 1930 the city population was 292,000, in 1960 it reached 938,000, and in 1980 it was 1,573,847.[2] In 1954 the metropolitan population (Harris County) passed 1,000,000, and the city celebrated by giving gifts to "Mr. Million," a new resident, and to "Mr. Million-and-one," a newborn baby.[3] Citizens also sported bumper stickers bragging, "I'm One in a Million—Houston" and used a postage-meter message, "Houston's A Million Strong July 3, 1954."[4] By 1961 the city population numbered 1,000,000, and in 1965 the Bureau of the Census, after agitation by the chamber of commerce and Congressman Albert Thomas, redefined the metropolitan area to include not only Harris County but also Brazoria, Fort Bend, Liberty, and Montgomery counties.[5] In 1980 the metropolitan population was 2,891,146.[6] This accretion, of course, with the expansion of business, intensified old troubles and helped to create new urban problems.

In problems pertaining to water supply and flood control, Houston achieved partial success. With a vast artesian reservoir and nearby rivers, Houston's difficulty was not so much in finding water, but in deciding which source to tap. Of course, at times, with four river basins within seventy-five miles, there was too much water, as during the floods of 1929 and 1935. During the catastrophe in

1935, seven persons died, fifteen blocks south of Buffalo Bayou were flooded, and two-thirds of the county was under water. The inundation caused $2.5 million in damage, compared to $1.4 million in 1929, and so silted the ship channel that vessels had to back into the turning basin to avoid going aground. It required eight months to clear the waterway. In 1937 the state legislature created the Harris County Flood Control District, but because of antipathy of some taxpayers, confusion about the means of control, and piecemeal programs, the city was not secure from danger until army engineers completed two earth-filled dams west of the urban center in 1945–1946.[7]

Sporadic storm flooding has continued. In 1976, for example, a ten-inch downpour knocked out the power at the Texas Medical Center and flooded the Sims Bayou area.[8] In July 1979 tropical storm Claudette dumped twenty inches of rain and inundated the southeastern segment of the city. It blocked major roads, shut off 48,000 telephones, caused sewage plants to spill raw sewage, and damaged 15,000 homes.[9] Continued urban development with more land covered by hard surfaces has increased the flood potential by forcing a quicker runoff. This has raised a fear that a major hurricane would cause such extensive flooding that people would be trapped and unable to escape. Hurricane Allen in August 1980 bypassed Houston but provided a "dry run in dry weather." Harris County has no detailed hurricane evacuation plan, but under the threat of Allen people were able to move from the coastal area in time. There remained some uneasiness, however. An editorial in the *Houston Post* commented: "If because of Allen we ignore future warnings, then Allen might well become, indirectly and in the long run, the most deadly storm of all."[10]

As early as 1934 there was some thought of obtaining drinking and industrial water from the San Jacinto River—an idea endorsed in 1938 by Alvord, Burdick, and Howson, a Chicago engineering firm hired to survey the water supply system.[11] During World War II the Federal Works Agency built two open canals to serve ship channel industry with untreated water from the San Jacinto.[12] In 1944, with proceeds from a $14 million bond issue, the city bought the western canal and planned to utilize the remaining money to erect a filtration plant, improve distribution facilities, and dam the San Jacinto. The construction of the dam, however, had to await the additional funds from a $24 million bond issue before work could start in 1950. Water began flowing from the new reservoir four years later.[13] Meanwhile, Houston planned to tap the Trinity River, which also lies northeast of the city. This resulted in a fight between Houston and the combined forces of Dallas, Fort Worth, and the Trinity River Authority. After a long struggle, Mayor Lewis W. Cutrer hammered out an agreement, only to see it defeated at home by taxpayers who objected to the increased water rates which resulted. Mayor Louie Welch, however, signed a successful contract with the river authority in 1964 which won approval of voters and secured Houston's future supply.[14] Although water from this source began to flow for the use of ship channel industries in 1976, shortages forced water rationing in 1966–1969, in 1978, and during the heat wave of 1980.[15]

Increasing amounts of Houston water for the future must of necessity and safety come from surface sources. Houston has drawn its water in the twentieth century primarily from artesian wells, now numbering over two hundred scattered across the metropolitan area. Consumption has been at such a rate that the ground level has sunk. Subsidence around the "epicenter" of the San Jacinto Monument amounted to six feet from 1900 to 1964. High tides now wash into the area and 30 percent of the park land has been lost for use. Subsidence not only presents potential damage to structures because of the cracks and slippage of the earth but also increases the danger of flooding. In 1975 the Texas legislature created a subsidence district to regulate withdrawal of subsurface water. Through the use of surface water and decreased pumping, the rate of subsidence has slowed to several inches per year and the water level in wells has risen by fifteen feet.[16]

The metropolis, however, has never solved the problem of water pollution in the bayous. Though officials established sewage-treatment plants and made some move to clean the streams and prevent pollution, the efforts were halfhearted, so that, especially after 1940, the bayous became seriously contaminated. In 1945, after complaints by residents and a poliomyelitis scare, the U.S. Public Health Service inspected the malodorous Brays Bayou and found flowing into the small stream enough raw sewage to equal that produced by a town of 54,000 people.[17] Further work by Frank J. Metyko, an investigator hired by the county, revealed similar pollution in the other watercourses, with the worst concentration in Buffalo Bayou, into which they all poured.[18] Here was raw sewage from sewers and overloaded pumping stations, partly treated sewage from treatment plants, and all sorts of industrial wastes, such as grease, oil, chemicals, blood, and manure. Buffalo Bayou water was 80 percent sewage.[19] Only four companies responded to Metyko's suggestions for improvement, and the investigator found himself maligned as having a personal interest in chlorine sales, since he recommended the disinfection of sewage.[20]

Dr. Walter A. Quebedeaux, Harris County pollution-control officer, reported in 1964 that most of Houston's sixty-four sewage-treatment plants worked poorly, twenty-two operated at near capacity or beyond, and twenty-one emitted noxious odors.[21] The same year, the Texas Water Pollution Control Board claimed that most of the water in some tributary bayous came from treatment plants, and that 90 million gallons of sewage effluent flowed daily into Buffalo Bayou.[22] If well processed, sewage and industrial wastes need not be dangerous, as San Antonio has shown, but for Houston this fact held little meaning until recently. In 1966, fire, feeding upon flammable material floating on the water, swept across the channel and burned a shipyard worker to death.[23] In 1967 and since, Dr. Joseph L. Melnick of Baylor Medical School, an expert in virology and epidemiology, discovered in Buffalo Bayou water a whole array of bacteria and viruses, including those which cause common colds, rash, diarrhea, encephalitis, and meningitis. At Main Street the bayou carried enough viruses to infect 77 million people every hour. Said Melnick, "It's just plain sewer water. You shouldn't bathe in this water. You shouldn't even get it on your skin. You shouldn't have anything to do with it. It should be put in a closed pipe and carried out to sea."[24]

If that was not sufficient, in the same year James M. Quigley, a commissioner of the Federal Water Control Administration, commented, after inspection: "The Houston Ship Channel, in all frankness, is one of the worst polluted bodies of water in the nation. In fact, on almost any day this channel may be the most badly polluted body of water in the entire world. Most days it would top the list." The *Houston Post* editor laconically concluded about that statement, "another first for Houston."[25] One of the disturbing factors to the President's Water Pollution Control Advisory Board, stated in a report shortly afterward, was the "apparent indifference" of city and county officials who seemed to possess an attitude that pollution was so bad there was no need to worry about further contamination.[26]

The pollution also damaged the channel. Mal Kallus of the Federal Water Quality Administration commented in 1970: "I doubt you could name a chemical you couldn't find in the channel, including heavy metals of all descriptions. Certainly it is one of the most polluted bodies of water in the nation."[27] The grease, debris, and chemicals created "dead" water which silted the bottom with as much as four feet of disease-laden putrid sludge every year. There was no oxygen in the water between the San Jacinto Monument and the turning basin. Heavy rains periodically flushed the channel, causing downstream fish kills in Galveston Bay. A group of students from San Jacinto College even went so far as to hold a funeral service for the watercourse.[28]

But, changes did occur. Friendswood Development Company, the Humble Oil subsidiary in charge of Bayport, placed antipollution restrictions in the deeds sold to industry. The Houston Chamber of Commerce, recognizing the parallel between the quality of air and water with the quality of life, declared active support for the improvement of the environment in 1969. The next year the Gulf Coast Waste Disposal Authority came into existence to aid industry to eliminate industrial refuse in the channel. Over the next decade the authority issued $500 million in bonds.[29]

Both industrial and municipal pollution came under attack in the early 1970's. Under pressure from the Texas Water Quality Board the city adopted a plan to spend $200 million to upgrade the sewage system over a five-year period from 1974 to 1979. In 1971 the U.S. District Court ordered Armco to cleanse its discharges, which were killing small fish within minutes of contact. The company responded and two years later seagulls at the outfall revealed the presence of healthy shrimp in the water. Armco officials triumphantly ordered the shrimp dipped out and served at the company cafeteria.[30]

County vigilance continued and became more effective through the work of Walter A. Quebedeaux, Jr. The intrepid investigator once had garbage dumped on his head from the stern of an Italian tanker while he was out in a rowboat searching for an oil leak.[31] Samples of biological life in the channel in 1972 revealed eighteen species; in 1975 there were thirty-four species. In 1980 fish were seen in the turning basin.[32] The problem had not been completely solved, but there was obvious improvement.

The problem of air pollution was similarly difficult. Arthur Comey, who studied Houston in 1913, found no problem of air pollution, but complaints emerged in the 1940's, such as the one by "V. Doran" who wrote in a letter to the *Houston Post,* "I don't know whether you could call the unpleasant odor here a smog or not, but anyway it stinks and I believe something should be done about it."[33] In 1953 the county created a pollution-control section of their health department which over the next eight years worked on 435 cases. Though only 6 percent of the cases involved dangerous pollution, the businessmen in these instances evinced no desire to change unless forced by the courts. The county relied on complaints from residents and a common-nuisance law to bring the exploiters of the air to terms, but effective action against them became practically impossible after the early 1960's when Texas courts released corporations from criminal liability in such cases.[34]

In the meantime, the chamber of commerce hired the Southwest Research Institute of San Antonio to study Houston's air problem in order to determine the nature of the trouble, to help prevent future pollution, and to provide a bench mark with which to gauge future air contamination. After two years' work and 10,900 samples, SRI concluded in 1958: Houston weather localized problems downwind, rather than community-wide; pollution was worst when the rare east or northeast wind swept up the ship channel and concentrated industrial discharges in the eastern, southern, and southeastern portions of the city; sulphur dioxide, a common culprit elsewhere, existed in Houston as it did in those coal-burning towns that had had to take corrective measures; sulphur compounds were low most of the time but occasionally high enough to blacken lead-based paints and damage foliage in the channel area; hydrocarbons, dust, and carbon monoxide were about the same as in comparable cities, and there existed no evidence of pollutants interacting to form new compounds in the air. Although the research organization admitted that safe levels had been exceeded occasionally in Houston and that information concerning the permanent effect of the pollutants on human beings was "sorely lacking," its report optimistically concluded, "It seems safe to say that if any community-wide health hazard does exist in Houston due to air pollution, then an equal or greater hazard exists in many other cities in the country."[35] This statement is reminiscent of those at the turn of the century, comparing Buffalo Bayou water to that of the Mississippi at St. Louis, in order to justify pumping the befouled liquid into Houston homes.

The problem remained. By 1958 commercial pilots could observe a mile-wide plume of industrial haze from Houston streaking inland to Austin, San Antonio, and at times even to Dallas.[36] In 1962 several hundred people in southeast Houston complained about a pollutant from an unknown source that smelled like rotten eggs, brought headache and nausea, and caused discoloration of paint both outside and inside homes.[37] That same year a pocket of mercaptan gas, held by a low air ceiling, wafted back and forth across the city, causing more than a dozen cases of nausea.[38] Several years later the chamber of commerce again employed Southwest Research Institute to measure air pollution in the Bayou City.

The report of 1966 revealed no major changes but did show increased amounts of dust and a few ozone (smog) readings which neared the level of eye irritation. This oxidizing smog, or photo-chemical smog, which first appeared in Los Angeles in the 1940's, resulted from compounds formed by nitrogen dioxide and certain hydrocarbons in the presence of sunlight. These compounds, not observed in the earlier study by SRI, could cause eye irritation, vegetation damage, and haze. The research institute blamed the greater number of automobiles for the ozone condition and reiterated the opinion that pollution was worst when the winds swept from east to west up the channel into the city rather than from south and south-east to north and northwest across the channel, as was normal. When compared to other cities, again SRI found Houston in a favorable position.[39]

Although, as before, the investigators stressed the local rather than the community-wide nature of the problem, they should have noted that downtown Houston, a place of concentrated population, lies in the path of air pollution when it is at its worst. As large numbers of people in their work patterns move into or through a contaminated zone, air pollution becomes a community-wide problem. The mobility of people should be counted in such analysis. Walter Quebedeaux, the embattled pollution-control officer for the county, claimed that the 1966 report was a "whitewash" for industry since there was no evidence against the automobile and because the number of samples and their location were not revealed. "The people are being sold a bill of goods," said the officer.[40]

State and local officials did not precisely ignore this growing problem in the air. In 1966 the Houston city council passed a pollution ordinance, thus eliminating the need for Quebedeaux, a county employee. The gadfly had to move his office to Pasadena where, according to councilman Bill Elliott, he would not be in the center of activity and could not make embarrassing statements.[41] In 1961 the Texas legislature created the Texas Water Pollution Control Board (which incidentally relieved Quebedeaux of water-control duties), and in 1965–1966 established the Texas Air Control Board.[42] John T. Files, president of the Merichem Company, became one of the three Houston members of the six-man board. In April 1966, Quebedeaux designated Merichem as "polluter of the month," at the head of a "dishonor roll" based upon the number of complaints received. Files denied the charges, but his company topped the list again the following month.[43] In October 1967, Quebedeaux received authority from the county, based on new state laws, to enter and inspect suspected plants. If he found a violation, a suit could be brought through the county or a complaint could go to the state board.[44]

Quebedeaux developed measuring devices so sensitive that he could track a polluter from ten miles away. In the 1970's the city, county, and federal agencies cracked down on air pollution and became more sophisticated about the problem.[45] Reports in 1969 indicate that a number of plants were exceeding their emission levels, and the city began to have periodic air stagnation alerts.[46] By the mid-1970's most companies were in compliance with standards and the Council on Municipal Performance of New York counted Houston above average for clean air.[47] The air problem, however, proved intractable. It still looked bad and the Environmental Protection Agency reported that Houston had one of the worst ozone levels in the nation.

Quebedeaux explained that large particulate matter had been filtered out, but there was still light, fine material in the air which made it look bad.[48] Interestingly, the automobile was not to blame. Ozone levels did not decline on weekends when automobile usage was lighter. According to Quebedeaux, if one took 500,000 automobiles using four gallons of gasoline per hour and collected all the emissions, not enough sulphur compounds could be found to equal 10 percent of a single sulphuric acid smokestack.[49] Although a chamber of commerce study revealed that Houston smog presented little health hazard, skepticism remained. Ozone levels, especially along the ship channel, still periodically exceeded federal standards of health.[50]

A related problem of waste control involves garbage disposal. The city produced 2 million tons of garbage per year in the 1970's and found that the sanitary landfill was the cheapest method of elimination. Open burning, which contributed to air pollution, stopped in 1969. Attempts at incineration failed because of expense; it turned out that no one wanted compost; and the one small recycling experiment required over twice the cost of a simple landfill. Despite efforts to open new dump sites, the city possessed only one authorized area. As Mayor Louie Welch commented, "You know, when it comes to garbage, people want us to pick it up, but they don't want us to put it down again, especially if it is near their house."[51]

Another common urban difficulty shared by all large cities is that of crime. In Houston, there are several unusual features—no proven organized crime activities, a high murder rate, and, at least until the 1970's, an understaffed police force. In 1934, an editor, noting that Houston neared the top of the list for per capita murders, above even Chicago, blamed the juries which failed to convict. A person who murdered had a 1-in-5 chance of escaping punishment entirely, a 1-in-3 chance for a suspended sentence, and an even chance to draw less than a five-year sentence. Life was cheap, but juries were not so lenient when property was involved.[52] The police department in 1937 numbered 340 men. The men received one uniform a year, no ammunition with which to practice shooting, and no instruction about the law they enforced. The quality of the force was illustrated by a popular story of the time concerning the patrolman who found a dead mule in the street. As he began to write his report, "Found dead mule at Commerce and . . ." he faltered over the spelling of "San Jacinto," the cross street. So, he seized the beast by the tail, dragged it to Commerce and Caroline, and completed his record.[53]

Houston maintained a top-ranking murder rate and a low number of policemen through the 1940's, 1950's, and 1960's.[54] In 1947, for example, the Federal Bureau of Investigation recommended 2.23 patrolmen for every 1,000 people; with 540 patrolmen, Houston had a ratio of 0.93 per 1,000 persons.[55] *Time*, in 1958, noting Houston's murder rate of 15 per 100,000 population, stated that in 1957, with 136 killings, only 27 suspects went to trial. Of those, most received prison terms, but only one drew the death penalty.[56] Still, this was the period when the police department became a professional organization. In 1948 in a state referendum voters gave aggrieved police officers immediate access to the courts which, in turn, gave them protection from arbitrary demotion. Despite tenure protection since 1897 and a civil service commission created during the reforms of 1913 to 1914, the police department remained subject to political machinations. Roy Edward Floyd, for example, who began as a chauffeur for Mayor Oscar Holcombe in 1935, became a detective of police in 1936 while remaining the driver for the mayor. He was demoted to patrolman in 1937 when his benefactor went out of office, but he became an inspector of police in 1939 when Holcombe returned. Floyd again returned to the ranks after Pickett became mayor in 1942 but became director of the civil service in 1947, again after an election victory by Holcombe.

Policemen were expected to choose political sides, but they suffered as a consequence. One officer was promoted and demoted ten times in eleven years. A transformation occurred, however, through the work of the Houston Police Officers Association, the return of World War II veterans who looked upon police work as a career, the start of a police science course at the University of Houston in 1945, the new civil service laws, and the successful reestablishment of a police academy for training new officers. The police department, except for its head officer, escaped political control and became a professional organization. "Do right" officers, for example, were able to enforce gambling laws without reprisals in 1950.[57]

In 1963, nonetheless, the editor of the *Houston Post* claimed that the town had half the number of policemen, twice the number of murders, and one-third more major crimes than other leading cities.[58] The International Association of Chiefs of Police in 1966 suggested 2,600 policemen for a community the size of Houston, yet at the time the Bayou City possessed only 1,342.[59] In 1967 the city ranked fourth in the nation in the per capita murder rate, behind Cleveland, Dallas, and New Orleans, and major crimes had risen 7 percent over the preceding year.[60] The Bureau of the Census reported that Houston, which was spending more of its budget on police and fire protection than other Texas cities, had the least increase in crime among major Texas cities in 1970 to 1975. In 1979, however, the *Houston Post* reported that crime was increasing at three times the rate of other comparable places in the nation. Houston was similar to New York and Los Angeles but not as bad as Dallas, Detroit, Denver, St. Louis, or Atlanta. Of all the locations in the city, the *Post* revealed, the deadliest was the near northside ghetto.[61] A writer for *Texas Monthly* reported about that region: "After my three month stay, I felt that Fifth Ward's most haunting quality was the frequency of lurking disaster that awaited all men and women there, the certainty that no life, no matter how virtuous, would escape the pain, misery, and degradation caused by poverty, racism, and prejudice. And until the politicians and financiers sitting two miles away in downtown Houston smell self-interest in the winds blowing from Fifth Ward, this will not change."[62]

Houston, like other major cities, in addition, had its share of sensational crimes—a socialite doctor accused of murdering his wife, a wealthy real estate developer indicted for bank fraud, a homosexual mass killer of twenty-seven youths, and a man who put cyanide in his children's Halloween candy in order to collect insurance.[63] In the 1970's, however, there was particular public concern about the excesses of the police. There were investigations about a police shootout in 1970 with a radical black political group, People's Party II; a case in which policemen planted a gun on a suspect; and an incident of extortion involving an assistant police chief.[64]

The most important case, however, involved Joe Campos Torres, Jr., a twenty-three–year–old Hispanic. In the spring of 1977, late at night, six police officers subdued Torres at a bar where he was drunk and abusive. They beat him up and took him to jail, but the jailer refused to accept him and told the officers to take him to the hospital for treatment of his injuries. Instead, the policemen took Torres to an embankment overlooking Buffalo Bayou. Thinking to scare him and turn him loose, one of the officers asked him if he could swim. Then, Torres either fell, jumped, or was pushed seventeen feet into the murky water. The policemen threw his wallet to him as he treaded water. After that Torres disappeared behind a tree and they thought he had swum away.

Some of the policemen worried enough to come back later to look for the young man, but the rest returned to work. Unfortunately, Torres drowned. The officers were interrogated, dismissed from duty, and indicted. At a state trial in Huntsville two officers were convicted of a misdemeanor and given a probated sentence. Two hundred Hispanics promptly marched in protest on City Hall chanting, "We want justice" and "Stop killer cops." At a second trial in federal court over violation of Torres' civil rights, five policemen were sentenced to a year in prison; one was given probation.[65] Sometime later, police chief Harry Caldwell retired after twenty-six years of service. He had taken over as chief at the time of the Torres case and he sadly commented after the turmoil of his tenure, "All my life I had perceived my administration as the one that opened the police college, established the academic and professional skills of police officers, and made us the Athens of the police profession."[66] It was not to be.

Henry Allen Bullock, a professor at Texas Southern University, in a thorough study of Houston's crime problem in 1961 noticed a close relationship between homicide and geography and stated, "Generally, murder is a Southern problem and Houston's high murder rate helps keep this Southern tradition alive." Murder encouraged general lawlessness, according to Bullock, and reflected a communal lack of control over other criminal behavior.[67] Illustrative of Houston's rather casual approach to law enforcement was the case of the West brothers, oil millionaires. Wesley West in the late 1940's regularly parked his bright green Cadillac in a bus zone next to his downtown office. Just as regularly he paid his daily $5.00 fine, but his car was not hauled away.[68] Jim West, noted for his penchant to give silver dollars as tips, liked to cruise the streets with officers in his Cadillac while playing the role of amateur policeman.[69] After an incident in which West shot at a burglar and reportedly hit his police companion in the foot, Hubert Mewhinney of the *Houston Post* offered this bit of doggerel to be sung to the tune of "I'm an Old Cowhand":

I'm an old John Law
With a lightning draw
And the mostest guns
That you ever saw.

I'm a cop that prowls in a Cadillac
While them other cops drive a run-down hack,
I've got all that stuff that the others lack—
Yippy-yi-yo-ki-yah! Yippy-yi-yo-ki-yah!

I get lots of fun
When I pack a gun;
If you ain't seen me,
Then you ain't seen none—

Oh I shot at a burglar and hit my pard
But I did not shoot him so very hard
And I hope next time that he watches his guard!
Yippy-yi-yo-ki-yah! Yippy-yi-yo-ki-yah! [70]

In regard to Houston killings, however, as Bullock revealed, 62 percent of the assailants were black, 61 percent of the victims were black, and 60 percent of the crimes occurred on Friday, Saturday, and Sunday. Homicide was a weekend activity. The causes, to Bullock, were uncontrolled, rapid expansion, segregation, drunkenness, and lenient juries.[71] Perhaps callousness toward murder resulted because it affected largely a politically impotent minority and because the conservative temperament of society insisted on low taxes and a frontiersman's reliance upon himself for survival. Be that as it may, Bullock suggested, as possible actions to reduce crime, a destruction of areal crime pockets, urban renewal, and housing desegregation.[72] In 1962 the Houston Crime Commission, noting three thousand scattered taverns and lounges, which are difficult to patrol, suggested zoning for purposes of crime prevention.[73] Houstonians, however, have never accepted on a grand scale either zoning or urban-renewal plans.

In 1936 Hugh Potter, former president of the chamber of commerce and president of the River Oaks Corporation, began to agitate for the utilization of the zoning plan worked out in 1929 by his associate, Will Hogg.[74] The *Houston Post, Houston Chronicle,* and *Houston* magazine supported the idea, but the proposal aborted.[75] Antizoning groups and individuals attacked Potter's suggested ordinance even before it was fully presented. Led by real estate interests, these people packed the city council chambers and testified that zoning would throttle city growth and would interfere with the constitutional right to hold property. It was proposed, they said, because the planning committee led by Potter just wanted to continue receiving $1,000 per month. As a result of the pressure, the council halted the funds, and the eight-member board resigned without comment. S. A. Starkey, the city commissioner who proposed the elimination of the allocation, said lamely, "We would like to have heard the other side of the question, but those who favor zoning did not give us the opportunity."[76]

Potter, however, did not give up and in 1943, as chairman of a chamber of commerce postwar planning committee, suggested the formation of a master plan of development which would include the idea of zoning.[77] A city planning committee, led by Jesse Andrews, meanwhile, hired S. Herbert Hare of Kansas City, as had been done in 1938, to work as a consultant, and proceeded to propose a $31 million comprehensive improvement program for the city.[78] In 1946, under Andrews, neighborhood meetings took place to rally support for a proposed ordinance to zone the city into ten categories of land use.[79] Those in favor argued that it would protect property owners, prevent tenements, and allow long-range planning; and those in opposition countered that zoning would limit business, fail to protect homeowners, and create a "dangerous club in the hands of any dictatorial administration."[80] Support came from new residential areas and various civic groups, including the chamber of commerce and the League of Women Voters. Opposition arose from property owners in old residential areas where business was moving in, from real estate interests, and from those who disliked being told what to do.[81]

As time neared for the straw vote which would guide council action, J. G. Miller, one of the leaders in the 1938 defeat, stated at an antizoning rally, "A zoning ordinance is an exercise of the police power of government. . . . Houston was built by men of vision, not by slide-rule experts armed with an omniscient egotism and a pocket full of silly statistics." Vernon Elledge, an attorney at the meeting who thought no one possessed the wisdom to figure out zoning, said, "It just goes back to the idea of Joe Stalin, that one man can figure out everything—the whole plan."[82] Hugh Roy Cullen, benefactor of the University of Houston, fearing nuisance industry across from the campus, commented during the controversy, "We are doing too well to try this un-American, German plan."[83] Though zoning elsewhere has been supported by conservatives, Houstonians went to the polls and defeated zoning by a ratio of 2 to 1, and thus preserved their town's status as the only major unzoned city in the United States.[84]

The idea that cogitative power might be applied to urban life, as it was elsewhere, did not die easily. In 1950 M. Emmett Walter, of the Houston City Planning Commission, stated in a speech to the Kiwanis Club:

> The shame of the cities of today to my mind is not that many of them have corrupt and inefficient administration. The real shame is that they lack in great plans and dreams. Our shame is mediocrity in planning for the future. Our shame is toleration for filth and slums and traffic snarls.
>
> We have an opportunity in Houston to develop a magnificent city; a city that will be adequate to the economic demands and also provide facilities needed to make it a satisfactory place in which to live.
>
> Such a city can be built, if a little attention is given to planning, and it will cost less in the long run than a haphazard development.
>
> Surely a program that will be economically profitable and at the same time satisfy every man's craving for the beautiful should receive the support of all citizens.[85]

In 1957 and 1958 Ralph Ellifrit, the city planning director, advocated a master plan for the city, and once more the zoning issue came to life.[86] A commission on zoning held hearings, investigations, and meetings through 1959, but because of various delays, work was not completed until 1962. Then the planners presented for public approval a design to zone the city into eleven categories of residential, apartment, commercial, and manufacturing usage.[87] Despite the efforts of Citizens for Zoning and the chamber of commerce, the proposal again met defeat as 57 percent of those participating decided against the measure in a straw vote. The issue met approval in the upper-class residential areas of River Oaks and Tanglewood but drew heavy negative response in the lower-class black sections.[88] Since 1962 zoning has not again come up for serious consideration.

The consequences of Houston's rejection of zoning are debatable. The absence of restriction has allowed the scattering of offices and businesses in disarray over the landscape, for better or worse, depending upon the neighborhood and type of business; it has created a burden of law enforcement with taverns located willy-nilly through the city; it has prevented comprehensive directing of city expansion; and it has disallowed participation by Houston in federal urban-renewal programs. On the other hand, lack of zoning has given freedom of action to promoters and land developers of all sorts; it has averted possible political corruption that might result from such an ordinance; and it has prevented the growth of a city bureau with all the concomitant expense.

Though the absence of zoning apparently has not influenced to a measurable extent Houston's growth, it would be an error to attribute the city's achievements to it. Fourteen other places in the United States, all zoned, enjoyed a much faster rate of expansion between 1920 and 1960.[89] The lack of a general zoning ordinance, moreover, does not denote a complete absence of planning, or even of zoning in specific areas. Since 1940 a full-time city planning department has exercised some control over the platting of new streets and in the design of subdivisions by regulating lot size, streets, and setback lines.[90] Planning can also be seen in traffic control, the Civic Center, and building ordinances. Business, especially heavy manufacturing, has to a large extent zoned itself by concentrating along the ship channel. Almost no industry exists in the downtown district, except small, scattered shops north of McKinney and east of Crawford.[91]

Developers, moreover, have often zoned their subdivisions with long-term, renewable deed restrictions. In River Oaks, for example, the River Oaks Corporation restricted the land to allow only one resident or family per lot, no hospitals, no duplexes, no apartments, only white ownership, no livestock, no dumping, and no signs. It regulated the placement, type, and value of houses, required the periodic cutting of grass, and made allowance for the corporation to enter the property to correct violations. Filed in 1926, these restrictions ran until 1955, but they could be renewed with a majority vote of landowners for successive ten-year intervals without limitation. Though sometimes there occurs difficulty securing votes necessary for continuation of restrictions, River Oaks residents voted approval of renewals in 1949 and 1960.[92] The older incorporated bedroom suburbs, such as Bellaire, West University, and Southside Place, possess their own zoning laws, and recently a series of small incorporated townships along Memorial Drive, an upper-class residential area, have emerged, not to avoid city taxation but to zone out the gas stations, shopping centers, and other such enterprises that might detract from the beauty of the drive.[93]

In Houston, where the lack of a general zoning ordinance prevents participation in federal urban renewal programs, there has been, nonetheless, partial success in combating the blight that has come with age and the shift of the business district.[94] The most impressive achievement has been the Civic Center, an area immediately west of the downtown office district and containing in 1967 the Public Library, City Hall, Federal Office Building, Jones Hall, the Coliseum, the Music Hall, and the Convention and Exhibit Center. The original plan for the center, of course, had come from Will Hogg in the 1920's, but Stanford Research Institute had designed a master plan in 1962. The institute outlined a development program which involved an expenditure of $45 million to $50 million by 1980 on a 147-acre site. The philosophy was, "The Civic Center is only one element in the economic and social structure of Houston, but in its ability to serve as a physical base for civic and cultural activities, it may have a catalytic effect on the downtown area and on the city in general."[95]

Though it is still too soon to measure the impact of the center as a vitalizing force for downtown, it may prove a disappointment. For viability, Jane Jacobs stressed the need for conditions that will bring people into an area at different times for different purposes. Such conditions are necessary to avoid periods of stagnation and to stimulate secondary economic activity. "This is why projects such as cultural or civic centers, besides being woefully unbalanced themselves as a rule, are tragic in their effects on their cities," she states. "They isolate uses—and too often intensive night uses too—from the parts of cities that must have them or sicken."[96]

Much less grandiose but more in line with this thought was the building of Old Market Square and Allen's Landing. Interest in reviving the older segments of downtown arose immediately after World War II. In 1946 local businessmen formed the Central Houston Improvement Association, which over three years' time obtained better police protection, shoppers' buses, and a $10,418,000 investment in remodeling, new construction, and public improvements. It functioned at least until 1951.[97] In 1954 the Rehabilitation Committee of Downtown Houston was formed, led by John L. Andrew, a vice-president of the First National Bank. This organization focused on the section between Buffalo Bayou and Texas Avenue characterized by Andrew as a "cancerous blight on the largest city of the South."[98]

Andrew, who was chairman of Mayor Lewis W. Cutrer's urban-renewal committee in 1961, clashed with C. Cabanne Smith, a vice-president of the Bank of the Southwest, over the fate of the old city hall square at Travis-Prairie-Milam-Preston. The city had rented the old city hall in 1939 for a bus depot, but the structure burned in 1960 and the city proposed to sell the block. Andrew wanted it sold for use by a large enterprise, such as a motel, but Smith desired a park with shops around it. Mayor Cutrer supported Andrew, but the Harris County Heritage Society and thousands of citizens backed Smith. After some verbal pyrotechnics, the city council agreed in July 1961 that the land should be a park; Old Market Square, a tree-lined parking lot, thus came into existence.[99]

As work on the square reached completion, John T. Crooker, Jr., chairman of the chamber of commerce civic affairs committee, began to promote a park at the foot of Main Street as a project to beautify the bayou area. The Southern Pacific gave the land and through private donations Allen's Landing Park developed in 1966–1967.[100] Though somewhat misnamed, since early Houstonians referred to the place simply as the "landing" or the "wharf," the park, along with Old Market Square, a new post office, and some motels brought a semblance of renewal to the section. Specialty shops, night spots, hippies, and an excursion boat on the bayou supply local color to both the Square and Allen's Landing.

As with the Civic Center, the permanent benefit of such efforts must await future evaluation, but it is of some interest that the attempt has featured two parks. Houston has at most times lacked sufficient park land, at least according to national standards, and the city has moved with notorious slowness in respect to recreation facilities.[101] In 1954, for example, the city had an opportunity to purchase the old but well-kept 177-acre Houston Country Club at $125,000 less than its appraised value. Because of bureaucratic procrastination, however, Gus Wortham, a local insurance leader, bought the property for use as a commercial country club. An opportunity for six acres of wooded land in the inner city, the Parker estate, was lost in 1980. The main park additions in recent times were 850 acres on the far east side, a gift of the Brown Foundation, and the remodeled one-block area across from City Hall, renamed Tranquility Park in honor of the moon walk.[102] The absence of great concern about parks may stem from both the conservative nature of local society and the presence of nearby recreational areas on Galveston Bay and the Gulf coast.

Since the city government has supported urban renewal on a large scale only in the Civic Center and has evinced little interest in parks, housing projects, and slum clearance elsewhere, it seems doubtful that funds would be so used even if available.[103] According to Ralph Ellifrit, city planning director in 1960, Houston is one of the last strongholds of rugged individualism.[104] The first major low-cost housing project came in 1940 after a survey revealed 25,680 families living in substandard housing. With federal funds of $585,000, the city built San Felipe Courts, a 1,000-unit apartment complex located on a thirty-acre site near Jefferson Davis Hospital on Buffalo Drive (now Allen Parkway).[105] In 1948, with 20 percent of the residences inadequate, the city ran only four housing projects—Cuney Homes and Kelley Court for blacks, and San Felipe Courts and Irvington Courts for whites.[106]

During 1950 Mayor Oscar F. Holcombe and Will Clayton stirred some interest in housing by visiting slums and making speeches. The "Council for Free Enterprise" and the "Houston Home Protection Committee" offered resistance, and in a vote to test public sentiment a proposal for public housing met defeat.[107] Through the generosity of Will and Susan V. Clayton, who gave a $290,000 site, the city in 1952 opened its first housing project since World War II, a $2.6 million, 348-unit undertaking, mainly for use by Hispanics.[108] Though Houstonians chose to ignore it, the problem of a lack of low-cost housing continued to exist. The Houston–Harris County Economic Opportunity Organization, in a detailed study of the Settegast area in northeast Houston, revealed open sewage ditches, 30 percent of the houses in disrepair, unpaved streets, no city water, rats that outnumbered inhabitants three-fold, 25 percent of the homes using outhouses, one-third of the wells polluted, and fifty-two households drawing water at a fee of $4.00 per month from a polluted communal well owned by a Houston law firm. The area involved 1,545 homes and 7,000 people, 99.9 percent black.[109]

Attempts to qualify for federal housing funds by revising building codes failed in 1969–1970. Federal aid was therefore restricted to social welfare projects. In that realm Houston's record was poor. Despite the expenditure of $100 million over a ten-year span, about one-fifth of the population remained on the poverty rolls.[110] In 1967 the Houston Housing Authority operated only 2,500 units while 21,000 families lived in substandard housing. There was little change over the next decade. When discussing the housing problem, Clovis Heimsath, a member of the Governor's Committee on Mental Health Planning, pointed to the lack of planning and zoning desired by "the Establishment" as a hindrance. "Houston has a very difficult problem with itself," he said.[111]

Such an establishment, however, rules by consent of the people. The municipal government, for the most part, has been responsive to public wishes. There is no evidence of a "machine" in Houston's political history, although Oscar F. Holcombe, the "Old Gray Fox," may have possessed an informal, personal machine based on job assignments, favors, and friendship. Conditions for such development have been poor. There have been limited material rewards, only one public utility, no zoning, and little opposition to policies. Politicians have run on the basis of personality and local issues, making almost no use of party labels. Liberals, labor unions, and minority groups, being weak, have, for the most part, focused on state or national issues. Every two years city officials must stand for election, and bond issues must have the approval of the electorate. Therefore, if government officers have been conservative, cautious, and business oriented, it is because they reflect community attitudes, not because a machine or establishment intimidates an unwilling majority.[112]

During most of the time from 1930 to the present, Houston utilized a strong-mayor government, although there was some difficulty involved. In 1933, under the impact of the depression, changes in the charter reduced the council to an approval body without administrative authority and concentrated the power in the mayor.[113] Under the ensuing administration of Mayor Oscar F. Holcombe, the councilmen balked at yielding their positions as department heads and thus engendered a long-running struggle for authority.[114] In 1935, after special difficulty over the creation of a water bureau, an arbitration board of five lawyers agreed with Holcombe that councilmen had no right to head specific departments unless appointed by the mayor.[115] The power struggle nonetheless continued, with friction usually minimized by the mayor's appointing councilmen to head the departments they desired. The trouble ended in 1942 when Houston established a city-manager form of government with eight council members and a part-time mayor paid $2,000 a year.[116]

John North Edy, former city manager of Dallas, served Houston in the same capacity, but in 1946 Holcombe won reelection on a platform advocating a strong-mayor government. In 1947, consequently, Houston reverted to a strong mayor, eliminated the city manager, and raised the salary of the full-time mayor to $20,000.[117] In 1955 trouble again arose when pertinacious Mayor Roy M. Hofheinz bickered with his entire council about charter changes and some minor scandals. The affair featured a mock trial and an attempted impeachment of the mayor, but the people wisely settled the issue this time by voting against all nineteen proposed charter amendments except the one requiring a new election within a few months.[118] A change of personnel rather than a change in structure was in order.

In 1979, however, Houstonians voted to expand the city council from eight to fourteen members and end the "at large" election method with nine members selected from districts. The idea had arisen earlier, but the Justice Department forced the issue by holding that recent annexations violated the Voting Rights Act of 1975. There was no great resistance about the change, and, subsequently, in November 1979 the people elected an expanded council. Although a black man, Judson Robinson, Jr., had been elected in 1971, this was the first time for a Hispanic and for women. There were now three blacks, one Hispanic, and two women on the council.[119]

One problem the council did not have in the 1970's was insufficient money. Due to revenue generated by a 1 percent sales tax, the city government was able to provide raises for employees, cut the property tax by 10 percent, and run budget surpluses in 1969, 1970, 1975, and 1976. At the same time in 1970 and 1976 voters approved obligation bonds for general improvements and received the highest rating from Moody's Investment Service. Under such circumstances Mayor Hofheinz found it somewhat difficult to defend Houston's need to take federal revenue-sharing funds.[120] Critics pointed out, however, that the city underpaid its employees and neglected cemeteries, streets, flood control, parks, subsidence, planning, and garbage dumps.[121]

Although municipal politics have not demonstrated a liberal-conservative dichotomy, a split of that nature has been obvious within the board of the Houston Independent School District, where a virulent strain of conservatism has flourished. In 1948–1949, with 81,000 students in 126 schools, the system experienced its first major outburst of extreme conservatism, sparked by a proposal to use federal aid for lunches.[122] Early in 1949, Ewing Werlein, chairman of the school board, who once characterized himself as a "conservative conservative," in a speech before school supervisors, attacked federal aid to schools, claiming that it would end initiative and individuality and cause federal inspection, regulation, and uniformity. It was a "pork barrel," a "creator of decayed societies," while advocates of such aid were mistaken, biased, and ignorant of history.[123]

That fall the board decided to collect private funds for lunches through a special drive and, led by Werlein, banned Frank Magruder's text *American Government*, which had been used for the preceding sixteen years and had the approval of 90 percent of the teachers. Though it is considered by many persons to be a conservative book, the board cast it out because of a single comment—that the United States was a capitalist country with some strong socialist, even communist tendencies.[124] Commented Hubert Mewhinney of the *Houston Post*, "If so shrewd and experienced a man as Ewing Werlein took 10 years to catch on to the meaning of that paragraph, the guileless little high school students never caught on at all."[125]

Resistance to federal aid for lunches remained steadfast until 1967–1968, when a conservative board finally gave way; textbook attacks occurred sporadically and, in the early 1950's, a new facet of conservatism appeared.[126] At a school board meeting in 1953, John P. Rogge, an attorney, accused George W. Ebey, deputy school superintendent, of communist affiliation through the California American Veterans Committee, of which Ebey had been chairman in 1947.[127] Despite an FBI report which revealed Ebey "clean as a whistle" and a 348-page report by the General Research Company which showed no communist connections, the board voted 4 to 3 against a renewal of his contract. James Dellmar, chairman of the school board, claimed that Ebey had been fired because he could not do the job adequately, but it was apparent that the innuendo of disloyalty had played a role in the dismissal.[128]

The event so shook the school system that the Houston Teachers Association through the Texas State Teachers Association invited an investigation of the Houston schools by the National Education Association.[129] After a thorough study, opposed by the school board, the NEA judged that the Ebey case was a culmination of past troubles and that the board had acted "precipitately" in the affair. An NEA poll of 1,918 persons in the system disclosed that 258 had been pressured to support a political candidate or to slant courses to a certain political belief, 259 had been asked not to support the Houston Teachers Association, and 44 percent feared reprisal by loss of employment because of social or political beliefs and actions. To the credit of the teachers, the NEA found evidence of good instruction in spite of "sharp division, deep-seated suspicion, animosity and fear" within the professional staff.[130]

Most of the pressure on the teachers from outside the system, according to the NEA, came from a militant group called the Minute Women. Using the slogan "Guarding the Land We Love," the local branch of this nationwide body was started in 1951 for the purpose of fighting communism in all forms and rooting out such activities in the government and schools. Within its own structure the Minute Women allowed no parliamentary procedure, no motions from the floor, and no elections. The group was able to prevent the appearance of scheduled speakers at a Texas State Teachers Association meeting, the chamber of commerce, and the University of Houston. In addition they provided enough additional agitation to force the resignation of the president of the University of Houston, Walter W. Kemmerer.[131] The Minute Women reached a high point of one thousand members in 1952 and maintained a close watch over the school board. With others they attacked Ebey, sitting en masse on the front row at one hearing. In 1952 Mrs. Frank G. Dyer, a member of that group, won a seat on the school board by using an anti-UNESCO platform.[132] However, in 1953, Ralph O'Leary, a *Houston Post* journalist, drained the venom of the Minute Women in an outstanding series of articles, replete with facts, dates, and names.[133] Although the Minute Women and their friends charged the newspaper with "smearing" patriotic housewives and suppressing freedom of speech, the award-winning series seemingly brought the group into relative abeyance.[134] Nina Cullinan, perhaps expressing the thought of many people, wrote in a letter to the *Houston Post*: "There has been a sense of relief on the part of many Houstonians, that, at last, this atmosphere of fear and suppression has been relieved. . . . From now on, citizens should feel free to discuss openly any and all subjects pertaining to the public interest without the ugly prospect of being labeled 'suspect.'"[135]

For a two-year span after the NEA investigation the conservatives lost control of the school board, but in 1956 they regained their position on the issue of segregation.[136] During the 1950's, in Houston as elsewhere in the South, the walls of segregation began to crack, generating social stress and anxiety. Five blacks filed suit to use the municipal golf course in 1950; the Public Library integrated facilities without publicity in 1953; the National Association for the Advancement of Colored People protested segregation in the cafeteria of the new county courthouse in 1953; segregation on city buses ended in 1954; and in 1955 a biracial school committee suggested desegregation immediately, "if the superintendent finds it possible, under existing circumstances."[137] The school board, momentarily controlled by liberals, started discussion of the racial problem in February 1956. After disruption by segregationists who yelled, heckled, carried placards, and sang "Dixie," the board ordered integration of the administration but postponed desegregation of students until the impact could be reduced by the construction of new buildings.[138] A few blacks tried unsuccessfully to register at white schools in the fall, and in December, Dolores Ross and Beneva Williams, sponsored by the NAACP, filed suit to break the segregation policy.[139]

Back in power, the conservatives of the school board selected Mrs. Dyer chairman, refused to go on record in support of the Supreme Court's desegregation rulings, refused funds for a representative to attend a conference of the National Council for Social Studies because two speakers had had some connection with communists in World War II, and attacked the geography texts because they contained "United Nations propaganda" and ideas about "one worldism."[140] To avoid criticism during the impending lawsuits over segregation, the board adopted a vague policy of no desegregation before completion of the current building program and no desegregation before 1960.[141] Federal District Court Judge Ben C. Connally, however, ordered desegregation with all "deliberate speed," but he set no definite dates.[142]

After a summer disturbed by a minor scandal concerning irregularities in the school business office, Mrs. Charles E. White, a black, won a place on the school board in 1958. She brought to the board an unusual amount of common sense and an ability to ask incisive and sometimes embarrassing questions. She had been educated at Prairie View Agricultural and Mechanical College and she was deeply disturbed by segregation. She found it impossible to explain, for example, to her six-year-old son, that because he was a black, he could not go on the pony rides. But she tended to meet adversity with equanimity and disarming candor. After supposed teenage pranksters burned a cross in her yard, she remarked: "I regret that anyone would desecrate a cross. Clearly those who did it were ashamed of their work, since they took pains not to be discovered."[143] After a bitter, disreputable campaign, in which her opponents used half-truths and rumors, Ed Franklin, a conservative, defeated Mrs. White when she ran for reelection in 1967.[144]

Meanwhile, in May 1959, the NAACP filed a petition in the Federal District Court charging that no action had been taken on school desegregation. Judge Connally asked for a report from the school board. The superintendent replied in a 373-page paper begging for more time and revealing that no plan had been adopted. The judge then ordered the board to submit a plan by June 1, 1960.[145] Ignoring a vote of 58,000 to 29,000 against desegregation in the school district, Connally reviewed the plan of the board to integrate in 1961 one elementary, one junior high, and one high school, which would work as a unit to serve the same students as they were promoted. The judge, calling the plan "a palpable sham and subterfuge designed only to accomplish further evasion and delay," ordered desegregation to commence in all first grades in September 1960 and to proceed at one grade per year thereafter.[146]

Entreaties to the U.S. Fifth Circuit Court of Appeals, the U.S. Supreme Court, and Governor Price Daniel to interpose the sovereignty of the state against "unwarranted acts on the part of the federal government" all failed, and in September the schools quietly desegregated. Of course, under the qualifications—six years of age, in the first grade, a health certificate, a transfer slip if having attended a black kindergarten, and no older brother or sister attending an all-black school—only twelve black pupils, in a system containing

177,000 students, met the requirements to attend a white school.[147] Demonstrating further ill-grace, the board voted to eliminate pools in new schools, thereby preventing swimming under desegregated conditions. This served to ruin competitive swimming at the interscholastic level, a sport of growing popularity in the area.[148] In 1962 the Federal Appeals Court in New Orleans overturned Houston's brother-sister rule, and under an accelerated program the schools completed desegregation in 1966–1967.[149]

In the next decade the Houston schools suffered a series of changes which resulted in a decline of the system. There was, first of all, a decrease in the number of white students. This meant that students with greater economic and educational advantages were lost. In 1968 the system contained 29 percent blacks with the rest white. Hispanics were not counted separately then. In 1974 the school population was 42 percent black, 39 percent white, and 19 percent Hispanic. By 1980 the numbers were 45 percent black with whites and Hispanics about equal at 27.5 percent each. Totals, too, declined from 234,000 students in 1968 to 190,000 in 1980. Low birth rates were blamed for this change.[150] The shift meant that the Houston Independent School District became a black majority system. In an unexpected manner segregation thus continued despite court orders, desegregation of faculties, interchange of students in paired schools, and the use of "magnet schools" which presented special academic programs for the entire district.[151]

Concurrently, the HISD faltered in its ability to educate. Students scored below national averages throughout the 1970's with the exception of the third grade in 1977. Tests revealed in 1980 that the ninth grade was below the state average and that one-third of the students failed the requirement of minimum basic skills. The tenth and eleventh grades at minority schools (black and Hispanic) scored only at eighth-grade level. Only students in the elite magnet school tested above the national average.[152] There is no available analysis of this problem, but the difficulty would seem to lie with teaching methods, quality of students, and racial tension.[153]

Through the period, moreover, the HISD had to fight off an attempt by a part of the district to break away. The proposed Westheimer Independent School District would have taken away twenty-three square miles and eight thousand students, most of them white. This secession would have injured the tax base and attempts to achieve desegregation, but after eight years of litigation the U.S. Circuit Court ruled in favor of the Houston school system.[154]

One other problem plagued the beleaguered schools—the education of illegal aliens. In 1975 the Texas legislature restricted free

public education to citizens and legal aliens. Mexicans who had illegally crossed the border flooded Houston. They provided cheap labor and wanted their children to go to school. The U.S. Immigration
Service made little move to deport them, so the HISD charged $162
tuition each month for enrollment. After a group of parents chal-
lenged the tuition, U.S. District Judge Woodrow Seals ruled free education for the seven thousand to nine thousand illegal aliens who
lived in the area. He based his opinion on the concept of equal protection of the laws and the idea that lack of education would only
create a dependent underclass of people. "Children are the basic
resource of our society," he said. The decision was turned over on
appeal but reinstated by decision of a Supreme Court judge.[155] The
issue raised a multidimensional conflict between the need of a de-
mocracy for an educated electorate, the desire for cheap labor, and
the thought that no one should be allowed to make use of public facilities without paying taxes to support them.

Though the school board remained basically conservative—
resisting federal aid, requiring history and economics teachers to attend lectures on the evils of communism and socialism, allowing
harassment of a teacher, Kenneth Parker, by Minute Women who accused him of being atheistic and communistic because he reacted
negatively to criticism of Dwight Eisenhower and Franklin D. Roo-
sevelt, and refusing to rent space in Pershing Junior High School to
the American Civil Liberties Union because the board did not want
public facilities used by those whose "feelings are not in keeping
with the thinking of the people of Houston"—the walls of segregation, inexorably, continued to crumble.[156] In the spring of 1960, black
students from Texas Southern University, in the first action of this
nature in Texas, began a series of sit-ins to force equal service at lunch
counters for their race, which comprised 19.5 percent of Houston's
metropolitan population. They first struck at Weingarten's grocery
at 4100 Almeda, where a demonstrator argued, "We buy our food
here and spend our money here and think we should be able to eat
here." Weingarten executives closed the lunch counter.[157] As the agitation spread in succeeding days, the students moved on to Wal-
green's at 3200 Main Street, Woolworth's and Grant's downtown,
and the City Hall cafeteria. Small groups of bemused employees
gathered to watch at City Hall as twenty-five students bought soft
drinks and cheese crackers. Though the cafeteria a few days later refused service to blacks, it was a temporary victory. Said one of the
participants, "This was our first home run."[158]

Foley's led the way in department store food service integration.
Max Levine, the store's chief executive, talked to other Houston

store owners, persuaded the press to keep quiet, talked to employees and offered them the opportunity to transfer elsewhere in the store, and requested the presence of plain-clothes policemen. The black organizations agreed to infiltrate quietly with well-groomed individuals. Integration was thus accomplished with no problem and no fanfare.[159]

In 1961 the City Hall cafeteria began to serve city employees of both races; the next year U.S. Judge Joe Ingraham ordered desegregation of Sylvan Beach, a county park, and Mayor Lewis Cutrer ended discrimination in all city-owned buildings; in 1963 Cutrer ordered city swimming pools open to everyone.[160] Through the 1960's blacks burst the bonds of the old Third Ward in search of better housing. As blacks spread southward into Riverside Terrace and across Brays Bayou, white residents, trying to maintain property values and prevent panic-selling, placed signs on their lawns, "This is our home. It is not for sale."[161]

Walls apparently do not crash without, at least, some violence and in November 1965, 400 students at T.S.U. on Wheeler Avenue rioted after a pep rally and hurled rocks, beer cans, and vegetables at police. After authorities sealed off the area, the tumult stopped with four arrests and a black policeman injured.[162] At the same place, in May 1967, rioting of a more serious nature erupted. After much gunfire, the turbulence ceased, but a police officer, Louis Kuba, died, a number were wounded, and 488 students were arrested. The cause of this convulsion, the extent of police brutality, and the repercussions are still undetermined. The facts of the affair may never be known because of the wide variance in eyewitness accounts and the ingrained animosity between the students and police.[163]

Shortly thereafter, in that same year, an annual job fair began to provide summer jobs for ghetto youngsters and by 1968, with segregation officially gone from the public schools and buildings and with blacks moving into better residential areas, it was evident that conditions of racial separation, a city characteristic in 1930, had been irrevocably altered.[164]

Discrimination in the 1970's was much more likely to be based upon economics than race. Middle-class people, ironically, can no longer afford the central city and must move to the suburbs. According to a report from Barton Smith, an economics professor at the University of Houston, in 1977 people paid $1,000 per mile for comparable-sized houses closer to town. Homes, moreover, are likely to be more expensive in a white area and thus there exists little incentive to integrate. "It's not that blacks can't move," said Smith, "but that it is terribly expensive."[165] The problem now is not so much discrimination in housing as it is discrimination in jobs and level of education. There exists also the factor that people, even if they could afford it, do not necessarily choose to move. The Black Power advocates, for example, have encouraged people to stay in the old neighborhoods.[166] The rate of black movement to the suburbs, 20 percent, has remained unchanged since 1955. Dallas, in comparison, possessed the same rate in 1970, but jumped to 30 percent in 1974.[167]

The city has a fair housing ordinance which prohibits discrimination in the sale or rental of houses. There were 1,200 complaints in 1979, mostly from renters. Even so, segregation in housing predominates—75 percent of the blacks live in areas that are 70 percent black. Only 9 percent of the black population lives in the suburbs; most live in a belt stretching from the south central to the north and northeast portions of the city.

The black unemployment rate is about half that of the rest of the nation, but median income is $4,000 less than for whites.[168] Still, there have been breakthroughs. In 1963 Ollie B. Harris became the first black administrator in the Houston Independent School District. The following year Carolyn White became the first black ever employed in a clerical job at City Hall. Valerie Johnson, in 1969, became the first black president of the Houston Teachers Association.[169] Blacks began to successfully move into politics, but the shift in acceptance can best be illustrated with the story of attorney Francis Williams. He began to practice law in 1951 when there were separate drinking fountains and restrooms in the courthouse and he was not allowed to join the bar association. White lawyers treated him as a curiosity or as if he were invisible. There were no threats, but some would move away if he sat near them in court. By 1974 this had all disappeared. There was no longer a shadow of discrimination in the courtroom; the situation had become one of competition between professionals.[170]

Although Hispanics are Houston's second-largest minority, they rarely figured in the city's history and were seldom mentioned in the sources. They infrequently clashed with the white majority, and as a Roman Catholic priest explained, "The Negro's problem is the white man. But the Latin's problem is the Latin."[171] In the 1970's the Hispanic became much more apparent, mainly because of political activity. Of the estimated 300,000 Hispanics in the city, half live in the barrios located in the near north side, Second Ward, Denver Harbor, and Magnolia Park where they moved while working on the ship channel. It is thought that half are illegal aliens, which makes it difficult for political organizers. The Moody Park riot of 1978 and the Torres Case served as unifying causes for PASO (Political Association of Spanish-Speaking Organizations), MAYO (Mexican-American Youth Organization), LULAC (League of United Latin American Citizens), and La Raza Unida. The groups differ in style and method and, in general, are unable to unite enough to defeat better-organized black candidates. As Daniel Bustamente of La Raza commented: "We're all coming from the same place and headed toward the same destination. It's the methods and tactics to get there that we differ on. And here's where we lose our unity."[172]

The Hispanics have often found themselves in political and economic competition with black people. There has been little cooperation or social mixture between the groups.[173] The Hispanic, in fact, just began to gain visibility in the past decade. A prime illustration is the achievement of definitional distinction in the school system. MAYO in 1970 began to agitate for separation from the white classification used in the district. This was a problem because the system was pairing white and black schools for desegregation through the transfer of students. As it worked, Hispanic children who were being counted as white were often paired with black students. The Hispanic community wanted to halt such pairing and also win recognition as a separate group for staffing, special projects, and federal funding.

At one point a group of Hispanics, angered because they could not get placed on the agenda, interrupted a school board meeting, leaped upon the tables, and kicked off the papers and glasses. They screamed, "Police brutality!" as officers hauled eighteen of them off to jail. A boycott of the schools in 1970 and 1971 brought results, however, and the definitional changes were made.[174] Hispanics made other gains by electing a representative, Ben Reyes, to the reformed city council in 1979 and seeing one of their members, Ephrine F. Leija selected as a police captain in 1980.[175]

A third group also seeking recognition, and sometimes defined as a minority, were women. The women's movement, which operated mainly in the economic and political realms, was primarily an effort to gain equality. It emerged from the activities of the National Organization of Women (NOW) which started in Houston in 1970 and the Harris County Women's Political Caucus which began with three hundred members in 1972. The feminist movement attracted people like Betty Barnes, an officer of NOW who was told when eight years old that she could not play clarinet because she was a girl, who disliked playing dumb to be popular with boys, who was asked while in graduate school at the University of Houston why she was not content to stay at home, and who found discrimination even at Rice University.[176]

Inspired by a meeting of the National Women's Political Caucus which met at the Rice Hotel in 1973, women began to examine their positions. They discovered that females made up 18 percent of the city employees, but that over 40 percent were in the lowest-paid bracket. "I don't think we are discriminating because we haven't had any complaints," explained Sidney Lanier, the head of the city civil service department.[177] This led to the appointment of a women's advocate during the mayoralty of Fred Hofheinz. Fulfilling a campaign promise, he selected Poppy Northcutt, a political leader. She resigned after nineteen months and Nikki R. Van Hightower, a Ph.D. from New York, took her place. "Her job," according to Hofheinz, "will be to keep pressure on the bureaucracy for the rights of women who are employed by the city."[178]

Van Hightower did her job too well. She was outspoken and irritated an increasing number of people. She complained about a work force reduction of nine people, eight of whom were women. She objected to a statue of Confucius in the City Hall Annex because of an inscription which said, in part, "men have their respective occupations and women have their homes." Van Hightower quipped, "Confucius was the sexist of his time." The city council voted to eliminate her job despite feminist protests and an all-night candlelight vigil at the City Hall reflecting pool. Hofheinz, however, took the position that the council could not fire anyone and transferred her to a vacant post of "specialist." After becoming mayor following Hofheinz, Jim McConn fired her and abolished the position. In spite of some minor gains in the fire and police departments, unfortunately, the pattern of sex discrimination remained much as Poppy Northcutt described: "Resembling a parfait, white males float like whipped cream at the top. Underneath are minority males. They are followed by white females, and at the very bottom are minority females."[179]

The women's movement nevertheless continued. In 1977 the National Women's Conference met in Houston to advocate the Equal Rights Amendment. First Ladies Rosalynn Carter, Betty Ford, and Lady Bird Johnson attended, and a series of two thousand runners carried a torch from Seneca Falls, New York, the nineteenth-century birthplace of women's rights. A counter-convention of twenty thousand, however, met at the Astrodome to hear Phyllis Schlafly speak against the Equal Rights Amendment. A sign at that rally proclaimed, "God is a family man."[180]

The two major institutions of higher learning, the University of Houston and Rice University, generally escaped the disruptions of minority groups. Rice obtained a new president, William V. Houston (pronounced House-ton), in 1946 and another, Kenneth S. Pitzer, in

1961. It got a $1 million library in 1946 through the philanthropy of
Ella A. Fondren and a handsome, 70,000-seat football stadium in
1950 which Brown and Root constructed at cost in about ten months'
time. It was here that the first Bluebonnet Bowl game was played, in
1959. Rice had also received as a gift from the Atomic Energy Commission in 1951 a Van de Graaff accelerator; its name was changed
from Rice Institute to Rice University in 1960; and, strangely enough,
it became owner of the Yankee Stadium, in 1962, through the generosity of a former student, John W. Cox.[181] Though the university
benefited from the gifts of prominent Houstonians, such as W. W.
Fondren, J. Newton Rayzor, Jesse H. Jones, Harry C. Wiess, J. S. Abercrombie, and George R. Brown, as well as from various federal
grants, by the 1960's Rice had begun to feel some financial stress.[182]

To meet future demands, it became obvious that the school
would have to start charging tuition and garner more government
grants. Federal agencies indicated, however, that Rice's policy of racial discrimination was a barrier. In 1963 the trustees, therefore,
filed suit to reinterpret the trust instrument drawn by the founder,
who had indicated a desire to make free facilities available to white
inhabitants of Houston. The trustees based their case on the premise
that a trust may be altered if the primary purpose of the founder cannot be accomplished without the change. The primary purpose was
to establish an "Institute for the Advancement of Literature, Science, Art, Philosophy and Letters," which implied a school of the
first class. The other provisions were secondary. During the proceed-
ings President Pitzer testified that unless the racial bar was broken it
would be the "beginning of the end of Rice as an important institution." Rice was perhaps at the top of the "minor league," he added,
but certainly not a "major league" school.[183] Such an admission
must have been painful to those who looked upon the university as
the "Harvard of the South."

The courts agreed with the trustees' argument, and they won
their case in 1964.[184] Shortly thereafter NASA granted $1.6 million for
a space technology laboratory and the school announced tuition of
$1,200 a year for undergraduates and $1,500 for graduate students.[185]
The court action, however, proved to be no panacea. In 1966–1967
Rice counted a $950,000 budgetary deficit, and even though it was in
no "imminent danger," it was being restricted by lack of funds. The
president admitted spending almost 50 percent of his time raising
money and Rice advanced the tuition to $1,500 for undergraduates
and $1,700 for graduates.[186] In spite of these difficulties Rice was able
to complete its inner quadrangle with a $4.3 million classroom
building; acquire a new president, Norman Hackerman from the

University of Texas; and maintain a faculty-student ratio of about one to ten. In 1979 and 1980, its operating income exceeded its expenses.[187]

The University of Houston also experienced monetary stringency. In 1935 the school, utilizing temporary buildings behind San Jacinto High School, had 1,355 students. In 1936, however, Ben Taub gave thirty-five acres and Julius Settegast donated seventy-five acres for a campus southeast of downtown. The WPA offered to landscape the site.[188] During 1937–1938 E. E. Oberholtzer, the head of the institution, launched a $1 million building-fund drive with Hugh Roy Cullen, oil millionaire, as chairman. Because the school stressed self-help and treated rich and poor equally, Cullen donated $260,000 for the construction of the Roy Gustav Cullen Memorial Building in memory of his son, a former Rice student who had died in an oil-field accident in 1936.[189] The university moved to the new campus in 1939, the same year the WPA granted $553,284 for a heating plant and other improvements.[190] Operating on tuition charges, the school expanded through gifts, especially from Hugh Roy Cullen.

He gave $4.6 million in oil royalties in 1945, part of which was later used to construct the Ezekiel Cullen Building, and in 1946, with the M. D. Anderson Foundation, he presented enough land to double the size of the campus.[191] At this point the university was preparing for the return of veterans, offering remedial and refresher courses, starting additional night classes, and even aiding the returned soldiers to find living quarters. In contrast, President Houston of Rice announced that their 1946–1947 student group would probably be "the most rigorously selected in the history of the Institute."[192] This underscored a basic difference between the two schools—the community concern of the University of Houston.

In 1949 the M. D. Anderson Foundation provided $1.5 million for a library and Cullen gave $550,000 to U.H., "just so they would have a little extra."[193] In 1952 Walter W. Kemmerer replaced Oberholtzer as president, and in the same year the university received jointly with the Houston Independent School District the old facilities of KPRC-TV, a gift from the Hobby family. Channel 8, KUHT-TV, the world's first educational television station, began operation in May 1953. This was an accomplishment not only for the university but also for Frieda Hannock of the Federal Communications Commission, who had led a three-and-a-half-year fight for educational television channels.[194] The school district, which had not bothered much with the station, gave U.H. full control in 1959.[195] Kemmerer resigned in 1953, and after Charles F. McElhinney had served as acting president, Lieutenant General A. D. Bruce became president in 1954. Under Bruce, U.H. attained full accreditation with the Southern Association of Colleges and Secondary Schools.[196] In 1956 Bruce became chancellor and chief executive, and Clanton W. Williams, president.[197] Williams resigned in May 1961, and in August 1961 Philip G. Hoffman replaced Bruce.[198]

In spite of various gifts—$2,250,000 from Cullen, inspired supposedly by Houston's victory over Baylor in football; $1 million from the Jones Foundation; $5 million from the M. D. Anderson Foundation—the school sank into a financial mire.[199] The university's greatest benefactor, Cullen, announced in 1955, two years before his death, that because of limited funds, his aid to U.H. would perforce remain modest in the future.[200] In 1959, 72 percent of the budget came from tuition and fees, and despite the $600 tuition charge, the school had sustained operating deficits since 1954–1955. The enrollment had declined by 1,500 students in 1959–1960 because of the high charges. The university was failing and, consequently, in 1959 the board of governors voted to request full state support.[201] Through the work of Criss Cole, Robert W. Baker, A. R. Schwartz, and others, the legislature approved such action, effective in September 1963 in exchange for the campus and facilities valued at $33,456,000.[202] The University of Houston thus avoided disaster and went on to become one of the state's leading institutions, with an enrollment of nearly thirty thousand in 1977.

The university joined the Southwest Conference in 1971 and avoided any major confrontations over the Vietnam War. State auditors, however, warned school officials about financial irregularities in 1977. This eventually led to the indictment and conviction of a financial analyst and several others connected with the university. In other cases the university television station protected its right to control its programming without outside censorship or coercion.[203]

Hugh Roy Cullen, who so helped the university that there were suggestions to alter the name in his honor, was a prime example of a philanthropic conservative. His attitude toward wealth was the same as that of Andrew Carnegie, a parallel not recognized by Cullen or his biographers. In his early years he worked as a cotton buyer in Oklahoma, but he moved to Houston in 1911 because he saw the products of the trans-Mississippi west funneling through the city. At a friend's suggestion he became an oil contractor and in time pioneered in deep drilling and the penetration of the heaving shale that had baffled oilmen in the Humble field.[204] He accumulated a fortune of $250 million. In 1936 he received an honorary degree from the University of Pittsburgh.[205] As he began his ventures in philanthropy in the late 1930's, he commented: "I consider it the first duty of financially successful men to provide for their dependents. When this duty has been performed, the further problem presents itself. What shall I do with my surplus earnings?"[206]

Though conservative on many matters, such as politics, foreign policy, and even music, he gave away money with admirable aplomb. He donated funds to the University of Houston, Houston College for Negroes, and local hospitals.[207] Within one week in 1945 Cullen gave $1 million each to Hermann, Memorial, Methodist, and St. Luke's hospitals. "It's just as easy to give away $2,000,000 as two bits," he said after the initial gift to Hermann and Memorial.[208] He gave money also to Baylor Medical School and for the Cullen Nurses Building in the Texas Medical Center. He aided, in addition, St. Joseph's Hospital and the Gonzales Warm Springs Foundation.[209] In 1955 Cullen announced that, after providing for his family, he had given away 93 percent of his wealth.[210] Andrew Carnegie would have admired Hugh Roy Cullen.

As illustrated by the generosity of this oilman, philanthropy greatly enhanced medical services in Houston. Through such benevolence the Texas Medical Center succeeded. Monroe D. Anderson, one of the founders of Anderson, Clayton and Company, established in 1936 the M. D. Anderson Foundation, a trust to benefit the public, advance knowledge, and alleviate human suffering. At his death in 1939, the trust received the bulk of Anderson's estate, about $20 million. Though the trustees gave money to Rice and to the University of Houston, their major project was the Texas Medical Center.[211] At a meeting in the mayor's office in 1942 of the city council, Homer T. Rainey, president of the University of Texas; Roy Hofheinz, county judge; Mayor Oscar Holcombe; and the Anderson trustees, W. B. Bates, H. M. Wilkins, and John H. Freeman, it was arranged for the foundation to buy 134 acres from the city next to Hermann Hospital and there to provide a site for a state cancer hospital to be operated by the University of Texas.[212] Soon thereafter, Rainey announced that the Texas Dental School would move into the area, and in 1943 Baylor Medical School, unhappy in Dallas, agreed to relocate there. Baylor had been tempted with a twenty-acre site, a $1 million building, and $100,000 a year for ten years, to come from the Anderson Foundation and the chamber of commerce.[213]

In time, the center would include such institutions as the Arabia Temple Crippled Children's Clinic, New Hermann Hospital, Methodist Hospital, Texas Children's Hospital, St. Luke's Episcopal Hospital, Jesse H. Jones Medical Library, Ben Taub Hospital, Baylor Medical School, M. D. Anderson Hospital and Tumor Institute, Texas Dental School, and University of Houston College of Nursing.

In 1979 the Texas Medical Center covered two hundred acres, represented a $632 million investment, and required a $552 million annual operating budget. The center gained international fame through the work of Dr. Michael DeBakey and Dr. Denton Cooley in the late 1960's. In a well-publicized incident Cooley sustained life in a forty-seven–year–old man, Haskell Karp, for five days by using a mechanical heart and a heart transplant. It was surgery of the last resort— Karp was near death—but Cooley had violated federal research guidelines and used DeBakey's ideas without authorization. Heart transplants declined after this, although some experimentation with mechanical devices continues.[214]

Several medical office buildings appeared close by, and in 1945–1946 the U.S. Navy, encouraged by Albert Thomas and the chamber of commerce, placed an $11 million complex of hospital buildings on Holcombe Boulevard near the center. The Veterans Administration received the facilities from the navy in 1949. Recently, the University of Texas, which began a medical school in the center in 1969, acquired one hundred acres nearby for expansion beyond the original site of the medical complex.[215]

Impressive as this development was, it did not guarantee good health to Houston inhabitants. Tuberculosis remained a constant problem; poliomyelitis took its toll in deaths and crippled bodies, especially in the 1940's and 1950's before the Salk vaccine became freely available in 1955; encephalitis struck in 1964, leaving thirty-two dead; and venereal disease had spread at an alarming rate.[216] In 1962 Houston ranked sixth in the nation for venereal diseases, and in 1964 second. In 1952 the "epidemic" level was defined for polio as 20 cases per 100,000 population. In 1967 Houston recorded 515 cases of gonorrhea and 25.3 of syphilis per 100,000 population. In 1969 Houston suffered almost twice the national rate, but in 1973 the rate decreased for syphilis and the city no longer led the nation in venereal diseases. Apparently, the establishment and utilization of VD clinics had had an effect.[217]

More disturbing, perhaps, was the episode concerning the construction and operation of Ben Taub Hospital, a city-county charity institution. Overcrowding at the old Jefferson Davis Hospital in the 1920's necessitated new facilities, and officials selected a ten-acre site on Buffalo Drive in 1930.[218] The depression halted progress, however, and the situation became critical. Journalist H. R. Grobe reported in 1935, "There is probably no thoroughfare in Houston so congested and so heavily traveled as the hallway through the emergency department of the Jefferson Davis Hospital." After noting the noise, confusion, and bloody floor, Grobe concluded, "The man with a job and an income can daily thank his God that he does not have to face the prospect of sometime having to go to the Jefferson Davis emergency room for treatment."[219] Built with federal funds, the new $2.23 million Jefferson Davis Hospital opened in 1937, and County Judge Roy Hofheinz commented, "The poor folks are really going to be lucky."[220]

The number of hospital beds, however, was inadequate by 1940 and a new charity hospital was needed by the end of the decade.[221] Dr. Basil P. McLean, an administrator brought to Jefferson Davis by Ben Taub, chairman of the hospital board, suggested to Hugh Roy Cullen at a dinner the idea of building a new hospital and converting Jefferson Davis into a tuberculosis sanatorium. Cullen offered $1.5 million for the project, which was first estimated to cost $5 million, and then $7.5 million.[222] Harris County voted $1.5 million in bonds, the Anderson Foundation volunteered $1.5 million, and the city planned to use $1.75 million in bonds already approved.[223] The undertaking was, therefore, well launched, but it got caught in a two-dimensional fight involving a squabble between the city and the county over operating costs and a petty controversy between the Harris County Medical Society and Baylor Medical School over control of the staff. Coloring the whole affair, moreover, was the pervading conservatism of the electorate. The poor folks turned out to be not so lucky after all.

Initial delay came in 1952–1953 when the estimated cost jumped to $16 million, and when Mayor Roy Hofheinz objected to the "red tape" involved with the federal aid necessary for the new hospital.[224] Hospital administrators in El Paso and Dallas at the time claimed that the federal "red tape" was neither a nuisance nor unreasonable.[225] More serious, however, was the split between city and county. In 1958 the county paid 30 percent and the city 70 percent of Jefferson Davis costs, but since Houston contributed 75 percent of Harris County taxes, the metropolis, in reality, supplied 92.5 percent of the hospital funds. Since only 81 percent of the patients were residents of the city, Houston wanted an adjustment of expenses.[226] County resistance created an impasse.

To complicate matters, the Harris County Medical Society wanted to break the control of Baylor, which staffed Jefferson Davis for teaching purposes. The society objected to the placement of the new hospital in the Texas Medical Center where it would be convenient to the medical school. The medical board of the society wanted more facilities at the location on Buffalo Drive and suggested that Baylor build its own hospital.[227] The doctors of the society favored split control of Jefferson Davis.[228] Shortly before a crucial referendum election on the location in 1958, Dr. Stanley J. Oliver, chairman of the Medical Jurisprudence and Public Relations Board of the society, blundered when he said: "Once and for all the public will decide whether or not the sick who use Jefferson Davis Hospital want to go there to be cured or want to go to the Medical Center to be experimented upon. We don't think the people will vote to become human guinea pigs."[229] The Harris County group repudiated the statement, but the damage had been done. The people voted in favor of location in the Texas Medical Center, which spelled ultimate defeat for the society.[230]

Baylor, however, had little to celebrate because it caught the criticism for the situation at Jefferson Davis. Late in 1957, babies began to die at the hospital under unusual circumstances. Staphylococcus infection (resulting in boils, abscesses, bloodstream ailments, pneumonia, meningitis, and death) caused apparently by unsanitary and overcrowded conditions, increased. In the week of February 12–18, 1958, staphylococcus struck twenty-one babies and thirteen mothers; four infants died that week. By March, sixteen babies had expired, and tests for staph carriers commenced. In the same month three new nurseries opened, but the contagion remained. In April the state health department labeled the infant facilities "extremely hazardous in every respect," and in May a joint committee of the American College of Physicians, American College of Surgeons, American Hospital Association, and American Medical Association withdrew the hospital's accreditation.[231]

By this time, although it could not prevent the loss of accreditation, the death rate had sharply declined through the use of novobiocin and of a new Japanese antibiotic, kanamycin. The number of cases was nonetheless alarming. In November–December 1957, there had been 38 cases and 7 deaths; in 1958 there were 279 cases and 17 deaths; and in 1959 there were 33 cases and no deaths.[232] The first staph-free day for the beleaguered hospital came on September 10, 1959, as the last case checked out; but the institution did not regain accreditation until 1961.[233]

Although the new Ben Taub General Hospital for city-county charity patients opened in 1963, criticism of the public hospitals did not cease. In 1964 Jan de Hartog, writer and teacher and a Quaker who worked for religious motives as a volunteer orderly, exposed the filth, penury, and "conservatism" found in Jefferson Davis and Ben Taub hospitals.

Someone had brought up some coffee and I was offered a cup by Dr. Miller as I came past the nurses' station. I joined them;

of course, they were talking about the budget cut. I was not really listening; I was thinking about a patient I had found lying on a full bedpan. He must have lain on it a long time, and I could have sworn that I saw cockroaches scurry away as I uncovered him. But it probably had been my imagination; the light was very bad. Miss Lucas [a nurse] called me out of my brown study by asking, "And what is our humanist thinking about?"

"Cockroaches," I said.

"Ah!" she replied with mock conversational interest. "A fascinating subject. If you'd care to stay through the night, the cockroaches will become even more fascinating. Or have you already seen them attack the patients?"

"Pardon?"

"Didn't you know?" she asked, with a taut smile. "When the wards get really quiet at dead of night, they come out in search of food. That's when the cursing and thrashing starts. Patients who can't defend themselves start to scream; the cockroaches try to get underneath their bandages; they go for the blood, you see."

"Come, come, Lucas," the young surgeon said. "You're mixing this place up with the Late Horror Show."

"Don't tell me it isn't true!" Miss Lucas exploded, with sudden, alarming violence. "How dare you sit there and joke about it! How dare you!" and her eyes filled with tears.[234]

Daniel C. Arnold, chairman of the board of Ben Taub Hospital, said that the book was excessively "theatrical," and that de Hartog was unqualified to observe.[235] Dr. Stanley W. Olson, chief of the hospital staff for Baylor, took refuge in the hospital's accreditation, claimed that de Hartog was emotional, and gagged the staff by requiring that public statements be cleared through the board of managers.[236] Hospital personnel, however, confirmed the low salaries, immense workload, abysmal morale, filth, and the accuracy of de Hartog.[237] Even councilman Bill Elliott, who roamed Ben Taub unnoticed in an orderly's gown, corroborated the description of conditions. Daniel Arnold asserted that Elliott had observed at a bad time, after a run of emergencies when the housekeeping staff was lightest.[238]

The central problem at the charity hospitals was lack of money, but in 1954 Texas law had provided a solution, a hospital district with the power to tax. Previous elections to create such a district had failed mainly because of opposition by the Harris County Medical Society, but in 1965, after the publication of *The Hospital*, the society chose to take no official stand.[239] Once more the people voted, but once again the proposal met defeat with a negative response from the industrial suburbs and from the northern and eastern sections of the town, generally low-income areas. De Hartog responded bitterly, "Today's defeat means to me personally that I have been mistaken when I assumed for two and a half years that Houston would do something about the scandalous conditions . . . if only it could be made aware of them."[240]

All was not lost, however. Late in the year Leon Jaworski, a prominent local attorney who once considered becoming a physician, presented to the city council a supporting list of sixty leading Houstonians and asked for another election to establish a hospital district. Although rural areas and the industrial suburbs opposed, in November 1965 the electorate sanctioned the district which had missed approval four times before.[241] This action resolved, at least for the moment, the charity-hospital problem. The blame for the unnecessary suffering and death in Jefferson Davis and Ben Taub between 1949 and 1965 belongs not only to Baylor Medical School but also to the city council, the county commissioners, the Harris County Medical Society, and the people of the city and county. All share the inhumanity involved. Ironically, in 1980 the same problem of overcrowding surfaced again and further expansion became necessary.[242]

If Houstonians found it difficult to support public hospitals, they did find it easier to expend money for the fine arts and for entertainment. Under conductor Ernst Hoffmann, who led the Houston Symphony from 1936 to 1947, the orchestra progressed from ten to forty concerts a season. It offered, also, free summer-evening programs in Hermann Park, performed weekly for the Cities Service program, and once played for the "Voice of Firestone."[243] It was not an easy achievement. Hoffmann had to deal with poor instruments and eccentric musicians. He had a cigar-smoking tympanist, for example, who took breaks in the middle of performances but somehow never missed a beat. He also had a bassoonist who played with his shoes off. Hoffmann had his own odd habits. He always conducted in the same pair of shoes, which he kept between performances in a felt-lined case, and he refused to lead the final movement of Tchai-kovsky's Pathétique Symphony. He thought it evil because he had received news of his father's death after its presentation.

Under successive conductors, Efrem Kurtz, Ferenc Fricsay, Sir Thomas Beecham, Leopold Stokowski, Sir John Barbirolli, André Previn, and Lawrence Foster, the orchestra improved, increased its earnings, and once recorded Dmitri Shostakovich's Eleventh Symphony for Capitol Records.[244] Perhaps the greatest accolade for the orchestra came in 1964 while on tour under the direction of Sir John Barbirolli. At a performance in Philharmonic Hall in New York City, an audience of 2,500 called Sir John back for applause four times at intermission and six times at the conclusion of the performance. With ninety-two musicians sharing the praise, enthusiastic listeners shouted "Bravo!" stood in their seats, and gathered at the stage to applaud. Though he had some reservations, critic Harold C. Schonberg of the *New York Times* concluded: "But it is a superior organization nevertheless; and in Sir John it has a conductor who is an honest and efficient music maker. Naturally he has put his impress on the orchestra." Alan Rich of the *New York Herald Tribune* said, "Clearly the state of Texas, and specifically the city of Houston, deserves inclusion among the [cultural] centers."[245]

Sir John was one of the most beloved of the conductors. Upon his return from the New York triumph he commented: "I must say that I feel very proud, privileged, and honored to have returned with my troops and our mission accomplished. I cannot say I'm surprised, knowing the troops I had under my command." Mayor Louie Welch presented him a gold key to the city.[246]

The tenure of André Previn, in contrast, was stormy and disturbing. In his second season he brought Mia Farrow with him, and to the delight of gossips they paraded around the Bayou City in blue jeans and sandals. They were unmarried at the time and later she bore him twins.[247] More importantly, Previn wanted international tours and visits by other orchestras which the Symphony Society could not afford. Subscriptions fell off and Previn left. He made a worthwhile point, though: "What I have to make clear here is that this orchestra is light years beyond being a provincial orchestra and cannot be considered as such. But it's much trickier to recognize the difference between good and excellent than between good and bad." To reach excellence he thought it necessary for Houston to compete at a higher level—an international level, with the very best.[248] It was a worthy, although perhaps impractical ambition.

The city possessed, therefore, a first-rate symphony orchestra to match its resplendent Jesse H. Jones Hall for the Performing Arts.

Jesse Jones had once commented to his nephew, John T. Jones, Jr., "Remember, John, we still need a better opera house." In 1962, therefore, the nephew, president of Houston Endowment, Incorporated, a philanthropic foundation started by Jesse Jones, offered to build on the downtown site of the outdated city auditorium a $6 million replacement.[249] In October 1966, the $7.4 million Jones Hall, replete with cherry-red carpets, teak walls, a sculpture by Richard Lippold, and a chrome fireplug outside, opened during a city-wide arts festival. With the orchestra playing the first strains of the national anthem, as music critic Carl Cunningham phrased it, "music burst forth like a sparkling bubble of champagne."[250] Since acoustical engineering is not too precise, the construction of any such facility is a gamble. Apparently, Jones Hall succeeded; at least Howard Taubman of the *New York Times* found the sound "live and full" and thought it had a good chance of "making the acoustical grade."[251]

Diagonally across the street, completed two years later, is the Alley Theatre, the home of Houston's most significant theatrical enterprise. Even though such places as Houston Little Theatre, Playhouse, Theatre, Inc., and Houston Music Theatre have all made a contribution to Houston life, the Alley has been most impressive. It started in the summer of 1947 when a small group decided to form an "intimate theater." Bob and Vivian Altfeld donated a studio at 3617 Main Street that had a long brick corridor from which the group took its name. Nina Vance, a tall, calm speech teacher who had studied drama at Texas Christian University and who had had some experience, agreed to become the director. Operating with volunteer help, donations, and box-office receipts, the undertaking inspired infectious participation.[252]

Membership soared from six to more than five hundred in a year's time, but in 1948–1949 the group had to abandon their studio-playhouse upon orders of the fire marshal. An S.O.S. went out to members to bring a "buck and a brick," and "like a flock of magpies bearing morsels of brick, board, and baling wire," the members moved the theater to 709 Berry, where a converted fan factory became home.[253] The Ford Foundation recognized the accomplishment of the Alley by granting $10,000 in 1959 to pay salaries for more actors, for study, and for better communication between Nina Vance and other directors. In 1960 the Ford Foundation gave $156,000 to help test the idea of a repertory theater using professional actors under three-year contracts, and in 1962 it offered $2.1 million in matching funds for building and development.[254] Also in 1962, Houston Endowment donated land near Jones Hall as a site and in late

1968 the new theater, with floodlights sweeping the skies, opened with a presentation of Bertolt Brecht's *Galileo*.[255]

Sharing this growth in fine arts was the Houston Art Museum. From Miss Ima and Thomas E. Hogg in 1942 the museum received sixty-five paintings by Frederic Remington, the famous western artist, a sculpture, and several other items; it opened the Robert Lee Blaffer Memorial Wing in 1953; and it began to use Cullinan Hall, another wing, in 1958.[256] Though the modern design of the Cullinan addition contrasted strongly with the other architecture of the museum, the hall placed first as a favorite in an informal poll of Houston architects. In 1974 the Brown Pavilion, the last design of architect Mies van der Rohe, opened as another addition to the museum. It was a gift of the Brown Foundation and it doubled the size of the facility.[257] Also from Miss Hogg, the museum received in 1966 a collection of early American furniture, porcelain, brass, silver, and art, along with her River Oaks mansion, Bayou Bend.[258]

Although the Art Museum and the Contemporary Arts Association, organized in 1948, encouraged interest in art, life for an artist in Houston was none too profitable. A panel discussion among a painter, actor, musician, poet, and writer in 1964 brought out that painters found it difficult to obtain exhibits, and when they did, the art was often poorly displayed. Art reviews were mostly brief, superficial, and irrelevant; thus artists left Houston for more appreciative places.[259] This suggests that Houston was not the cultural center it would have liked to be. Until the construction of the Burke Baker Planetarium and a small connecting building in 1964 the Houston Museum of Natural History was a "public disgrace" and "an orphan of twenty years of neglect and obscurity."[260] The Public Library has never come near the American Library standard of $1.50 per person a year, with the result that its collections are relatively poor and the central facilities antiquated. In 1966, Houston, serving a population of 1,091,800, possessed 859,836 volumes, had a circulation of 2,503,310, and received taxes of $1.27 per capita. In contrast, Dallas served a population of 810,000, possessed 879,696 volumes, had a circulation of 3,286,959, and received taxes of $2.79 per capita. In 1975 Dallas possessed 1,700,000 volumes and served 844,000 people; Houston had almost the same number of books, but served 1,233,000 population.[261] Houstonians have attempted to disprove their supposed lack of culture by counting theaters, churches, cultural institutions, and so forth.[262] In just the past fourteen years there has been an interesting cultural shift reflected in the statistics. In 1963 Dallas, long assumed as the cultural center of Texas, outpaced

Houston in the per capita sales of books and music. In 1977 the situation reversed. Houston led Dallas.[263]

In regard to mass entertainment Houston also compares favorably. Radio stations and movie houses have flourished; and in 1949 Houstonians began to suffer the mixed blessings of television. It began with two thousand receiving sets in town and the first broadcast of KLEE-TV, a station owned by W. Albert Lee, a rancher, laundry owner, and hotel man.[264] The station changed to KPRC-TV after purchase by the *Houston Post* in 1950.[265] Coaxial cables reached the Bayou City in 1952 and a year later KGUL-TV, a Galveston station, began broadcasts. After moving to Houston in 1959, this station changed to KHOU-TV.[266] KNUZ-TV operated briefly on an ultra-high-frequency channel in 1953–1954; at the same time KLEE-TV signals, gone from the air for more than three years, eerily appeared on London TV screens.[267] In 1954 KTRK-TV started, and that same year KPRC-TV made its first color broadcasts.[268] The addition of KUHT-TV, the University of Houston station, in 1953 and KHTV, an ultrahigh frequency station, in 1967 completed Houston's television picture up to the present time.[269]

Professional athletics have also added a dimension to mass entertainment. Such sports as wrestling, baseball, ice hockey, horseracing (in the 1930's), basketball, and rodeo contests at the Houston Fat Stock Show have been promoted.[270] The livestock show and rodeo, an annual affair organized in 1932 to inspire better husbandry and encourage local meat-packing, possesses some unique significance. Although the first show took place in the vast, open-sided hall left over from the Democratic Convention while a blue norther forced cowboys to huddle around a bonfire in the center, the show survived and became one of Houston's most popular events.[271] With some help from the University of Houston's Frontier Fiesta in the 1940's and 1950's, the Fat Stock Show has probably done more than anything else to convince Houstonians that they possess a western, cowboy heritage. There exists little in Houston's past, however, to support such a belief.

Major league activity started when Glenn McCarthy and others brought professional football teams to Houston in 1949, 1951, and 1952 for the Shamrock Bowl charity games. McCarthy made a brief, abortive effort to buy a team in 1950.[272] K. S. "Bud" Adams successfully established the Houston Oilers, a member of the American Football League, in 1959–1960.[273] In 1979 the Oilers reached a high point when they played the Pittsburgh Steelers for the division championship. The team lost thirty-four to five on the icy, wet field in Pittsburgh, and Coach "Bum" Phillips moaned, "The behinder we got, the worser it got." Houston fans, nonetheless, celebrated the fine season of their team with the slogan "Luv ya, Blue" and cheered the bruising rushes of popular rookie running back Earl Campbell.[274] Other professional sports got their start: golf, when the Champions Golf Club hosted the U.S. Open in 1969; basketball, with the establishment of the Houston Rockets in 1971; and ice hockey with the Aeros in 1972. A new arena for the hockey and basketball teams, the Summit in Greenway Plaza financed by $18 million in city bonds, opened in 1975. It is a junior-size Astrodome operated by a private association.[275]

The financial pattern followed by the owners of the Summit was formed in 1960 when the National League allowed the Houston Sports Association to acquire a baseball franchise. Led by Roy Hofheinz and R. E. "Bob" Smith, the H.S.A. acquired the Houston Buffaloes for an "undisclosed amount" and launched the first season of the Colt .45's in 1962. Hofheinz, experiencing difficulty with the name, changed it abruptly to the Astros in 1964 and promised the fans, "The name will grow on you." The following year he took steps to acquire a controlling interest in the sports association.[276]

The Houston Sports Association needed an arena and this led to the construction of the Harris County Domed Stadium, or, as Roy Hofheinz called it, the "Astrodome." Though the idea of a covered stadium was not new—Glenn McCarthy considered it in 1950, and Hofheinz claimed to be inspired by the ancient Romans who had covered their coliseum with an awning in bad weather—the thought of an enclosed, air-conditioned arena was nonetheless awesome.[277] Such a plan had figured in the granting of the baseball franchise in 1960 and, fortunately for the H.S.A., it was able to fulfill the requirement with the help of Harris County. In 1958 county voters approved a $20 million bond issue for a combined football-baseball park and an air-conditioned coliseum.[278] The H.S.A. offered to lease the proposed facility at a rent sufficient to pay off the bonds. The sports group would maintain and control the installation, and the county would build according to the wishes of the H.S.A. It was necessary, however, to gain approval of a new bond issue of $22 million and to cancel the 1958 issue, which had not been sold. The remaining contribution for the projected $28 million stadium would come from various government agencies and from private landowners who would donate rights-of-way. Of course, if the H.S.A. failed, the county tax-payers would be left with the bonds and, at the time, the county had already reached its tax limit.[279]

Various groups, such as the Houston Farm and Ranch Club, Houston Home Builders, Houston Fat Stock Show, Houston Restaurant Association, Harris County Park Board, and AFL-CIO Council, endorsed the project, and at a public rally in the Rice Hotel, Hofheinz intoned, "This stadium will take its place alongside the Eiffel Tower and the great wonders of the world in construction."[280] There were a few voices raised in opposition, such as that of former councilman Gail Reeves who argued that a public debt for a private corporation set a bad precedent, but the county voters approved the bond issue. Reeves commented: "It's hard to stop a panzer division with a cap pistol, but we tried. It's hard to fight dollars with sense." Hofheinz said: "Dirt will fly on South Main immediately."[281]

With construction under way at the site seven miles southwest of downtown and with a contract signed giving H.S.A. a forty-year lease with two ten-year renewal options at a maximum $750,000 annual rent, reports came forth that more building funds would be necessary.[282] In December 1962, voters approved another $9.6 million in bonds.[283] At completion the domed stadium cost $45.35 million, the expense distributed: $31.6 million from the county; $3.75 million from city and state; $4 million from property owners for rights-of-way; and $6 million from the H.S.A. for such items as a restaurant, skyboxes, and a $2 million scoreboard. The air-conditioned arena is 710 feet in diameter, reaches 218 feet high, and can seat 45,000 fans for baseball and 52,000 for football. It possesses a 642-foot clear span and a roof of 4,596 Lucite skylights that could resist a wind of 130 mph or gusts of 165 mph.[284] Of course, if it is calculated that the H.S.A. received a $39.35 million investment ($45.35 million minus H.S.A.'s $6 million) for $750,000 a year (1.9 percent), it may seem somewhat unfair to the taxpayer.[285] But at the opening in April 1965, celebrated by an exhibition game between the New York Yankees and the Astros, it somehow seemed to be worthwhile.

On that "giddy, spectacular night," wrote sports writer Mickey Herskowitz, "baseball moved this side of paradise."[286] Governor John Connally threw out the first ball; President Lyndon B. Johnson slipped in on a special pass from Hofheinz; the crowd of 47,900 roared as Mickey Mantle lofted a home run to right center field while the four-story-high scoreboard flashed "Tilt"; and Houston won 2 to 1 in twelve innings. As Herskowitz recorded, "Fantasy met reality, and the New York Yankees lost. It was, in short, Domesday."[287]

There was, however, some trouble in paradise. Before the opening game, at the daytime workout, fielders experienced trouble tracking the ball against the maze of girders and skylights. Sunglasses did not help. The H.S.A. received more than a thousand suggestions for remedying the matter, including a layer of foam on top, a smoke screen, and fifty thousand helium-filled balloons, but instead the association simply coated the skylights with an off-white acrylic paint which filtered out part of the light.[288] The grass, moreover, fared poorly and Hofheinz had to paint it green.[289] He replaced it the next year with AstroTurf, an emerald-green imitation surface manufactured by Chemstrand. It cost $2.00 per square yard and zipped together in fourteen-foot strips.[290] Also, Bud Adams and Roy Hofheinz did not agree on the terms for Oiler games in the Astrodome until 1968; meanwhile, the team played in Rice Stadium.[291] Despite annoyances, H.S.A. did not suffer much. John K. Easter, the association controller, testified in a court case that H.S.A. had made a $3 million net profit on $11 million gross for the twelve months ending January 31, 1966.[292] Moreover, on land near the Astrodome in 1968 Hofheinz opened an amusement park called Astroworld.[293] It is certainly understandable why Dene Hofheinz Mann, in a speech introducing her laudatory biography of her father, said, "I don't know about everyone else, but I sleep just a little bit better each night knowing that Roy Hofheinz is running that Astrodome."[294]

It turned out that there was some difficulty. Because of heavy debt Hofheinz lost control of the complex in 1975–1976. Eventually a syndicate led by John J. McMullen bought the Houston Sports Association. The association pays the county $750,000 yearly, which is sufficient to retire the initial $15 million bond issue; the county pays $450,000 each year to retire the additional $10 million indebtedness. It is a subsidy, but it is much less than the taxpayers give in New Orleans for the Superdome or in Seattle for the Kingdome. The Astrocomplex, moreover, became a focal point for conventions. The National Association of Home Builders, for example, brought 50,000 people to the Astrohall in 1969 and 1970 and planned to return in the early 1980's. In 1979 Houston hosted 465 conventions involving 667,000 visitors.[295] It was good business for the city.

The account of the Harris County Domed Stadium illustrates not only the driving entrepreneurial spirit of Roy Hofheinz—who, above any others, deserves credit for the project—but also the nature of a community which supports such freewheeling promotion, for better or for worse. Modern Houston, with its nineteenth-century business attitude, is a product of its heritage. It started as a real estate venture at a fortuitous location. It grew by exploiting natural resources, by developing transportation facilities to serve a growing population in south Texas, and by inspiring investment of private and public capital. Certainly the influx of federal money during the world wars and the depression, as well as the application of such funds for airports, freeways, the ship channel, the Veterans Administration Hospital, and the Manned Spacecraft Center have been of major significance for the advancement of the city. Most important, however, Houston attracted men of enterprise—men willing to promote Houston for their own benefit. It was a businessman's town. Such a past, which shaped current culture, will form the future of the Bayou City.

8

Epilogue: Houston and
an Urban Renaissance

Once in a while in the history of a civilization, nation, or city there occurs a moment when all of the dynamic forces of existence flow together to produce extraordinary greatness. Such times are rare, but when they happen the meaning of humanity acquires an expanded dimension. The renaissance of Western civilization, for example, ended the dark ages, revived interest in the ancient world, shifted thought to mundane affairs, and opened the door to modern life. England in the late sixteenth and early seventeenth centuries with a burst of national energy became the leading sea power on earth, provided a stage for Shakespeare, developed the foremost Protestant church in Europe, and started the industrial revolution.

In the United States in the 1890's the city of Chicago, as another example, experienced its own renaissance. At that time Jane Addams worked to relieve the misery of poverty with a social innovation called Hull House, the Chicago newspapers developed a school of literary criticism, Louis Sullivan taught Frank Lloyd Wright the secrets of modern architecture, and the city demonstrated for the rest of the country the excitement of urban life at the dazzling "White City" of the 1893 World's Fair.

For Chicago, renaissance dynamics consisted of a strong business base, a vast railroad network, a legion of wealthy, concerned people, optimism, and enormous growth. Chicago possessed power and energy; the whole nation looked to the Windy City for leadership.

Houston, in 1980, already stands within the border of its own urban renaissance. Some of the greatness is apparent.

In high-rise architecture the accomplishment of the past decade is stunning. The great architectural minds of the world—I. M. Pei, Philip Johnson, Ludwig Mies van der Rohe—have provided examples of their genius. The wealth of the city, low real estate costs, and open acceptance of architectural ideas have made it possible. Johnson commented: "I like Houston, you know. It's the last great nineteenth-century city . . . what I mean is that Houston has a spirit about it that is truly American. An optimism, if you will. People there aren't afraid to try something new."[1] If everything halted right now, at the least Houston would provide a showcase for the best of modern architecture in the 1970's—an entire skyline dedicated to the form of art most symbolic of urban life, the skyscraper.

There are a few detractions from this accomplishment. It has created a certain isolation. The isolation is there, in one sense, because such monumental art can be appreciated only from a distance—say, from the area of Jefferson Davis Hospital along Allen Parkway. Viewed from downtown, at ground level, it is beyond sight and comprehension. You are in the midst of it, too close to see it. Office workers avoiding the heat move through tunnels and walk hurriedly from one island of air conditioning to another. At night the whole area, lacking downtown apartments, empties. It is isolated again and left to bands of nightriders on rollerskates—the "Urban Animals" and the "Bastards from Hell"—who use the color and flash of lights to provide a surrealistic effect on their senses as they whirl through the deserted thoroughfares.[2]

Air conditioning in buildings, homes, and automobiles also forces isolation. It is certainly more comfortable to live with air conditioning, and it is understandable why Houstonians spend $250 million per year for cool air.[3] There is nothing closer to hell in modern America than to be caught after a rain in a Houston jam at midday in an unair-conditioned car. It is possible, at that moment, to appreciate the plight of a steamed clam, and the situation does nothing to improve human temperament. In a way air conditioning represents a triumph over nature, but the price is separation not only from nature but also to an extent from other people. Human contact, throughout history, has been one of the great purposes of urban life.

There is, perhaps, no better way for Houston. Nature is oppressive in the Bayou City and not especially attractive. Houston lacks such natural vistas as the mountains of Denver, or the bay of San Francisco. This may explain why there is no effort to preserve open space or reserve land for parks. The sights worth looking at were all constructed by humans. As such they fall apart, age, and people are willing to replace them. As George Luhn, an architect, noted: "There is really no sense of history felt in the city. So everything is bright and shiny and new."[4]

If there is little concern about nature, there is care about the beauty of the constructed environment. A popular columnist, Lynn Ashby, described the scruffy face Houston offered to visitors traveling from the airport to downtown along Interstate Highway 45. The route was marred by intrusive billboards, trash, and poor maintenance. Returning home from a trip on which he had bragged about his home city, he said, "Now I am back in town to be made a liar. . . . My trees are telephone poles, my flowers are castaway tires, my limitless growth is eye-gouging greed. Where did we go wrong?"[5]

But, even in the phenomenon of countless billboards, large as boxcars and hoisted three stories high on steel pylons, there was a seed of hope. The city council passed a sign ordinance to limit size, height, and location.[6] The seed of hope may turn into a plant of growing urban consciousness.

An urban renaissance, however, is more than a billboard ordinance and imposing skyscrapers. It is also prominence in literature, music, art, and technology. Although Larry McMurtry once taught at Rice and the debut of Paul Zindel's Pulitzer Prize play, *Effect of Gamma Rays on Man-in-the-Moon Marigolds*, took place at the Alley Theatre, there is little evidence of a literary movement in Houston. Preeminence, moreover, still eludes a very fine symphony orchestra. It is obviously among the best in the nation, but it has yet to push beyond competence into the untracked realm of greatness. André Previn, for all his faults, may have been right. Houston needs to hear other orchestras and needs to send her own on tour in order to experience the level of competition from which unquestioned excellence may emerge.

Accomplishment in music, incidentally, is not confined to that from an orchestra. There are other levels of excellence—for example, jazz from New Orleans or outlaw country-western music from Austin. Important is a tolerant urban environment which allows experimentation with all kinds. Johnny Lee, a country-western singer, set up his own western dance club after the success of Gilley's in Pasadena. Lee commented about his club: "It's like Gilley's, but a different atmosphere. Gilley's is like a barn. Johnny Lee's is a class club. I'm gonna get armadillos and Texas flags and keep it a class place."[7] Various definitions of "class" deserve understanding.

In the realm of art, Houston has a small claim on renaissance greatness. It possesses museums and galleries of traditional and contemporary painting and sculpture. It has the second-best market, next to New York, for the sale of art and is starting to attract some top professionals, such as Dick Wray, Earl Staley, Phil Renteria, and Jack Boynton.[8] There is room for newcomers. James Surls, a sculptor who teaches at the University of Houston, started an alternative art gallery in a warehouse near the Gulf Freeway. To avoid undue bureaucratic interference he used no committee to rule on the quality of potential shows. The quality was thus uneven, but he gave opportunity to pioneering work. As Surls explained: "We need some place to take chances. The museums can't do it. The fine arts museums are historical and the contemporary museum in Houston has a 10-year range of art, showing basically safe art with some controversy, but not much. It's all art that has gone through the filtering process, and that's all right. But we need some place for grass roots art, so it can rise, too."[9]

It is this sort of activity that will create a Houston "school" of art. But there is more. In 1971 John and Dominique de Menil opened the Rothko Chapel on the campus of the University of St. Thomas. The campus, designed by Philip Johnson, is located in an older segment of the city and the ecumenical chapel is unimposing and somewhat obscure. Yet, it is sought by pilgrims from around the world. The small building contains no symbolic imagery, but rather fourteen large, dark, abstract paintings by Mark Rothko. Meditation is the main use of the structure. In front of the chapel in a small pool stands Barnett Newman's sculpture *The Broken Obelisk*, a truncated steel shaft balanced on a pyramidal point. William Agee, the director of the Houston Museum of Fine Arts, characterized it as "probably the greatest sculpture of the late 20th century."[10]

John de Menil was former chairman of the board of Schlumberger, a manufacturer of oil tools in Houston, and Dominique inherited the Schlumberger fortune. They were from France, both patrons of art and concerned about the welfare of their adopted city. They had wanted to give *The Broken Obelisk* to the city and place it in front of City Hall, but the council rejected the offer, not because of the nature of the art but because it was inscribed, "Forgive them for they know not what they do." Instead, the twenty-six–foot piece, dedicated to Martin Luther King, became a part of the chapel.

Houston can also claim greatness in technological achievement. The Texas Medical Center has gained world renown with its work on cancer and heart disease. The researchers have probed deeply into the frontiers of medicine. In addition, Houston supported as an urban host the single greatest technical achievement of the twentieth-century—the voyage to the moon.

Perhaps because of its overwhelming expansion—Houston in 1979 was the first United States city to ever issue more than $1 billion in building permits—there is also an overwhelming optimism and self-confidence.[11] Charles Herald, principal of Wheatly High School, a long-time, low-income black institution, said: "There are two things to remember about the ghetto. One, evil often triumphs over good. Two, in spite of that most of its residents retain a goodness that proves indestructible. No matter how ill the world treats them, they remain good in the deepest sense—charitable, honest, forgiving, compassionate—not gloomy and full of foreboding like Job, but buoyant and full of hope, like the astonishing products of Wheatly High School." [12]

You might expect Herald to say something more pessimistic. In another situation the confidence of the leaders was demonstrated. The *Chicago Tribune* published a scathing article about American cities. They ranked Houston worst in public transportation, parks, planning, weather, and energy conservation. Also, it was the city which was worst for pedestrians, had the worst new skyscraper, and possessed the most dismal future. At a breakfast seminar of the Houston Business Forum, Jonathan Day, a former Houston attorney, answered the criticism. "We are creating something unique," he said. "We are trying to be Houston and we are trying to make the best of it." [13]

And so it must be. A renaissance by its nature cannot be an imitation. The Houston renaissance will be unique, a combination of elements that flow together only once. Houston has reached out and touched greatness in architecture and technology. There can be more. The power and energy are present. Houston has the opportunity, perhaps even the obligation, to extend the human spirit and immortalize its name in the history of the world.

APPENDIX A
The Name "Buffalo Bayou"

Andrew Forest Muir in "The Destiny of Buffalo Bayou" and in "The Municipality of Harrisburg, 1835–1836" claims that the name of the bayou came from the buffalo fish which teemed in the clear water. He denies the existence of bison in the area and uses as his authority his grandmother, Mrs. Mary Hayes Ewing Charwane, who was born in Houston in 1857. In "Four Historical Talks," A. C. Gray, a man with roots in Houston's past, also argues in favor of the buffalo fish.

Julia Jones, however, in *Houston: 1836–1940*, pages 33–34, relying on an Indian legend related by the mother of her black washerwoman, argues that the name came from bison, not fish. According to the story, the natives called the stream "Buffalo River" because bison lived in the area and drank from the bayou. The legend goes on to say that the indigenous magnolia tree, with its large white flowers, was called "buffalo tree" after a white hunter killed a sacred white buffalo. Following the death of the buffalo, supposedly, the magnolia tree appeared, embodying the spirit of this animal.

Although the origin of the name of the bayou may never be fully determined, it seems significant that Stephen F. Austin, on his 1822 map of Texas, labels a stream, located approximately in the position of Buffalo Bayou, with the name "Cibolo," a Spanish-Indian word which, according to dictionaries and the *Handbook of Texas*, can mean "buffalo." A copy of Austin's map is on pages 52–53 of Eugene C. Barker's *The Life of Stephen F. Austin*. Alan R. Duke, director of the Houston Archeological Society, commented in a letter September 23, 1967: "I have found bison bone in just about every site I have excavated in the Houston area. These sites are located on all sides of Houston and represent a pretty fair cross section of the archeology of Houston and Harris County so I think we can say, without fear of contradiction, that bison did abound in this area."

The weight of evidence seems in favor of bison, but this does not deny the existence of the fish or their possible role in the name of Buffalo Bayou.

APPENDIX B
Mayors of Houston

1837	James S. Holman	1880–85	William R. Baker
1838	Francis Moore, Jr.	1886–89	Daniel C. Smith
1839	George W. Lively	1890–91	Henry Scherffius
1840	Charles Bigelow	1892–96	John T. Browne
1841–42	James D. Andrews	1896–98	H. Baldwin Rice
1843	Francis Moore, Jr.	1898–00	Samuel H. Brashear
1844	Horace Baldwin	1900–02	John D. Woolford
1845	W. W. Swain	1902–04	O. T. Holt
1846	James Bailey	1904–05	Andrew L. Jackson
1847–48	B. P. Buckner	1905–13	H. Baldwin Rice
1849–52	Francis Moore, Jr.	1913–17	Ben Campbell
1853–54	Nathan Fuller	1917	J. J. Pastoriza
1855–56	James H. Stevens	1917–18	J. C. Hutcheson, Jr.
1857	Cornelius Ennis	1918–21	A. Earl Amerman
1858	Alexander McGowen	1921–29	Oscar F. Holcombe
1859	William H. King	1929–33	Walter E. Monteith
1860	Thomas W. Whitmarsh	1933–37	Oscar F. Holcombe
1861	William J. Hutchins	1937–39	R. H. Fonville
1862	Thomas W. House	1939–41	Oscar F. Holcombe
1863–65	William Anders	1941–43	Neal Cornelius Pickett
1866	Horace D. Taylor	1943–47	Otis Massey
1867	Alexander McGowen	1947–53	Oscar F. Holcombe
1868–69	Joseph R. Morris	1953–55	Roy M. Hofheinz
1870–73	T. H. Scanlan	1956–57	Oscar F. Holcombe
1874	James T. D. Wilson	1958–64	Lewis W. Cutrer
1875–76	I. C. Lord	1964–74	Louie Welch
1877–78	James T. D. Wilson	1974–78	Fred Hofheinz
1879	Andrew J. Burke	1978–	Jim McConn

Note: Information from "Mayors Book," Texas History Room, Houston Public Library.

NOTES

INTRODUCTION

1. *Tri-Weekly Telegraph*, March 31, 1858. For a description of the Academy Building, see ibid., July 9, 1858.
2. An architectural description of the older buildings can be found in Writers' Program, *Houston: A History and Guide*, pp. 230–342. Information on the Gulf "lollipop" from "Action Line," *Houston Post*, May 11, 1966.
3. David E. Williams, ed., *Houston Eight Million*, unpaged.
4. *Texas Almanac and State Industrial Guide, 1966–1967*, p. 268.
5. *Houston Post*, January 29, 1961.
6. Ashbel Smith (in Houston) to Copes, June 25, 1838, Ashbel Smith Papers, letter book, May 1, 1838–December 29, 1838.
7. *Morning Star*, September 23, 1839. A norther is a winter cold front which strikes from the north, causing a rapid drop in temperature.
8. *Houston Post*, June 17, 1964.
9. Ibid., May 25, July 4, August 2, 24, 1980.
10. Ibid., June 2, 1969.
11. August Lösch, *The Economics of Location*, pp. 68–84. See also Edgar M. Hoover, "The Economic Functions and Structure of the Metropolitan Region," in *Planning and the Urban Community*, ed. Harvey S. Perloff, p. 4.
12. H. V. Geib, *Soil Survey of Harris County, Texas*, pp. 1903, 1952; *Texas Almanac, 1966–1967*, p. 268.
13. *Houston Post*, June 13, 19, 20, 1969, November 1, 1975, December 9, 1979, April 4, 1980.
14. Ibid., May 18, December 13, 21, 1980; *Texas Almanac and State Industrial Guide, 1978–1979*, p. 304; U.S. Bureau of the Census, *County and City Data Book, 1977*, p. 800, and *Preliminary Reports, 1980 Census of Population and Housing, Texas*, pp. 45-20, 25; "50 Biggest Metropolitan Areas," *U.S. News and World Report*, March 16, 1981, p. 73.
15. W. W. Rostow, *The Stages of Economic Growth*, p. 59.
16. Roy Lubove, "Urbanization, Technology and the Historian," a paper delivered at the Fifty-ninth Annual Meeting of the Organization of American Historians, April 29, 1966.

1. THE TOWN OF HOUSTON

1. *Telegraph and Texas Register* [Columbia], August 30, 1836.
2. Ibid.
3. Writers' Program, *Houston*, p. 36; Sam Houston, *The Writings of Sam Houston, 1813–1863*, ed. Amelia W. Williams and Eugene C. Barker, 2:180–183; John Henry Brown, *Indian Wars and Pioneers of Texas*, pp. 354–359; *History of Texas, Together with a Biographical History of the Cities of Houston and Galveston . . .*, pp. 257–261; Francis R. Lubbock, *Six Decades in Texas*, ed. C. W. Rains, p. 45; Walter Prescott Webb, ed., *The Handbook of Texas*, 1:29; *Houston Post*, May 22, 1884.
4. Ashbel Smith (in Houston) to Charles Fisher, July 5, 1837, Ashbel Smith Papers. The Allens also possessed some interest in the importation of slaves to Texas (A. Briscoe to A. C. and J. K. Allen, January 24, 1834, Briscoe-Harris-Looscan Papers).
5. Deed Records of Harris County, A, 157–158; Writers' Program, *Houston*, p. 37.
6. Andrew Forest Muir, "The Destiny of Buffalo Bayou," *Southwestern Historical Quarterly* 47 (October 1943): 93, 97. See also Appendix A.
7. Nan Thompson Ledbetter, "The Muddy Brazos in Early Texas," *Southwestern Historical Quarterly* 63 (October 1959): 238.
8. Muir, "The Destiny of Buffalo Bayou," p. 97.
9. Eugene C. Barker, *The Life of Stephen F. Austin*, p. 180.
10. Andrew Forest Muir, ed., *Texas in 1837*, p. 8.
11. Marilyn McAdams Sibley, *The Port of Houston*, pp. 31–33.
12. Charles H. Cooley, *The Theory of Transportation*, pp. 91–93.
13. *Houston Daily Post*, July 14, 1895; "Last of the Allens," Augustus C. Allen Papers.
14. Writers' Program, *Houston*, p. 38; W. A. Leonard, comp., *Houston City Directory for 1867–'8*, pp. 130–131; *Houston Post*, December 31, 1935 (interview with O. F. Allen).
15. Joe B. Frantz, ed., "Moses Lapham: His Life and Some Selected Correspondence," *Southwestern Historical Quarterly* 54 (January 1951): 327, 54 (April 1951): 468–469.
16. Richard C. Wade, *The Urban Frontier*, pp. 27–29.
17. Writers' Program, *Houston*, pp. xi–xii.
18. *Journal of the House of Representatives, Republic of Texas, First Congress, First Session*, p. 213.
19. The word *city* replaced *town* on October 25, 1836, with "The Present Seat of Government of the Republic of Texas" being added to the advertisement in the *Telegraph and Texas Register* on December 27, 1836. No other comparable advertisements appeared in this newspaper at the time. The Allens, perhaps, recognized the value of such action.
20. Lubbock, *Six Decades*, p. 46. There exists debate about the precise date of arrival of the *Laura* in Houston. The *Telegraph and Texas Register*, January 27, 1837, states that the ship arrived "some few days since," and Sibley, *Port of Houston*, mentions (p. 38) that Lubbock bought land in Houston on January 21, 1837. Abe Lincoln Weinberger, in "The His-

tory and Development of the Houston Ship Channel and the Port of Houston," reviews this problem (p. 22 n. 54).
21. Lubbock, *Six Decades*, p. 46.
22. Sam Houston to Robert A. Irion, April 28, 1837, *Writings*, 4:29.

2. THE COMMERCIAL EMPORIUM, 1836–1875

1. *Telegraph and Texas Register* [Houston], October 14, 1837.
2. Kelsey H. Douglass to wife, "Houston 27, 1837," and December 10, 1837, Kelsey H. Douglass Papers.
3. H. P. N. Gammel, comp., *The Laws of Texas, 1822–1897*, 2:161–165; *Morning Star*, April 15, 1839.
4. *Morning Star*, April 17, 30, July 18, 1839.
5. Ibid., August 13, 1839.
6. Ibid., September 25, 1839.
7. *Telegraph and Texas Register*, April 28, 1841.
8. Ibid., July 6, 1842.
9. Ibid., November 30, 1842, February 22, 1843.
10. Ibid., September 20, 1843.
11. Ibid., May 24, 1843, April 24, May 22, 1844, April 12, 1847, February 24, 1848; *Morning Star*, April 20, 1844.
12. *Democratic Telegraph and Texas Register*, September 25, 1850; *Tri-Weekly Telegraph*, March 6, 1860.
13. *Weekly Telegraph*, February 19, 1862; Writers' Program, *Houston*, p. 242.
14. *Weekly Telegraph*, September 29, 1870.
15. *Daily Houston Telegraph*, January 21, 1871.
16. Ibid., January 26, 1871.
17. U.S. Bureau of the Census, *Eighth Census, Manufactures of the United States in 1860*, pp. 584–585; idem, *Ninth Census, The Statistics of the Wealth and Industry of the United States . . .*, 3:572. In 1880 the census office noted that manufacturing data, 1850–1870, had been collected by the family enumerators and limited to firms with over $500 annual products. In 1880 special agents began to collect the data. It would therefore seem that information about 1870 would be more reliable (idem, *Report on the Manufactures of the United States at the Tenth Census*, p. viii).
18. *Tri-Weekly Telegraph*, September 1, 1860.
19. Wade, *The Urban Frontier*, p. 66.
20. *Telegraph and Texas Register*, June 16, 1838, February 3, 1841, December 28, 1846; *Morning Star*, April 9, 1839, April 25, 1840; *Tri-Weekly Telegraph*, April 7, 1860; *Galveston Daily News*, March 18, April 4, 30, May 21, 1865.
21. Robert Greenhalgh Albion and Jennie Barnes Pope state that auctioneers attracted buyers to New York from the South and West and that the institution was a major factor in that port's prominence as an import center (*The Rise of New York Port, 1815–1860*, pp. 66, 280).
22. *Morning Star*, May 11, 1839.

23. Ibid., September 28, 1839.
24. Ibid., October 15, 1839.
25. Ashbel Smith to Mirabeau B. Lamar, December 31, 1839, *The Papers of Mirabeau Buonaparte Lamar*, ed. Charles Adams Gulick, Jr., 3:220–221.
26. *Morning Star*, April 11, 1840.
27. *Telegraph and Texas Register*, May 5, 1838, October 21, 1847; *Weekly Telegraph*, May 7, 1856 (letter to editor), April 20, 1871.
28. *Tri-Weekly Telegraph*, October 16, 1857. For early labor union development, see James V. Reese, "The Early History of Labor Organizations in Texas, 1838–1876," *Southwestern Historical Quarterly* 72 (July 1968): 1–20.
29. L. W. Kemp, "Early Days in Milam County, Reminiscences of Susan Turham McCown," *Southwestern Historical Quarterly* 50 (January 1947): 370–371.
30. Pearl Hendricks, "Builders of Old Houston," *Houston* 12 (July 1941): 2; Henry C. Grover, "The Dissolution of T. W. House and Company," pp. 1–9.
31. Thomas P. Collins to T. W. House, May 7, 1849, Thomas W. House Papers.
32. E. N. Clarke to T. W. House, March 7, 1855, ibid.
33. E. Zwilchenbark to T. W. House, October 29, 1838, February 25, April 21, 1859, ibid.
34. F. Huth Co. to T. W. House, February 1, 1865, ibid.; Grover, "The Dissolution of T. W. House and Company," pp. 4–9.
35. Andrew Forest Muir, "William Marsh Rice, Houstonian," *East Texas Historical Journal* 2 (February 1964): 32–33; Hendricks, "Builders of Old Houston," pp. 2–3.
36. *Morning Star*, August 3, 1841, August 9, 1842; *Telegraph and Texas Register*, August 3, 10, 1842; Groce Family Records.
37. *Telegraph and Texas Register*, June 25, 1845. The weight of a bale could vary. The *Telegraph and Texas Register* on November 7, 1851, reported, for example, a wagon pulled by six yoke of oxen with fifteen bales weighing 493 pounds each and another wagon with sixteen bales at 475 pounds each, both sent to Houston by General W. Willborn from the Brazos River, thirty miles away. On June 8, 1842, the newspaper noted a number of bales four feet eight inches long and twenty-two inches thick, weighing over 500 pounds, which had been compressed by a planter using a screw and a yoke of oxen.
38. W. A. Leonard, comp., *Houston City Directory for 1866*, pp. 90–100.
39. *Weekly Telegraph*, February 4, 1863. For a general discussion of the impact of the war on Southern agriculture, see Paul W. Gates, *Agriculture and the Civil War*, pp. 3–27.
40. *Galveston Daily News*, September 21, 1865.
41. *Telegraph and Texas Register*, December 23, 1847.
42. Frederick Law Olmsted, *Journey through Texas*, ed. James Howard, pp. 227–230.

43. Abbé E. H. D. Domenech, *Missionary Adventures in Texas and Mexico*, pp. 25–26.
44. Ibid., pp. 26–31.
45. Ferdinand Roemer, *Texas*, trans. Oswald Mueller, p. 71.
46. Jonnie Lockhart Wallis and Laurance L. Hill, *Sixty Years on the Brazos*, p. 198.
47. Ibid.
48. Roemer, *Texas*, p. 72.
49. *Morning Star*, July 31, 1839.
50. *Houston Post*, March 31, 1907.
51. *Morning Star*, August 7, 1839.
52. *Telegraph and Texas Register*, April 21, 1841, March 29, 1843.
53. Ibid., November 5, 1845, March 1, 1847, January 20, 1848.
54. Ibid., November 19, 1845; Doswell, Adams and Company Papers, account book, April 24, 1838–January 1, 1839, p. 9.
55. *Morning Star*, June 8, 1839; *Telegraph and Texas Register*, January 26, 1842; *Tri-Weekly Telegraph*, December 19, 1856.
56. *Telegraph and Texas Register*, January 1, 1840.
57. *Morning Star*, December 3, 1842.
58. *Telegraph and Texas Register*, January 11, 1843, July 29, 1846.
59. *Democratic Telegraph and Texas Register*, January 31, 1859.
60. Roemer, *Texas*, p. 75.
61. *Telegraph and Texas Register*, September 22, 1841.
62. *Democratic Telegraph and Texas Register*, July 8, 29, 1846.
63. Ibid., September 13, 27, October 4, 1849.
64. Ibid., September 27, 1849.
65. Ibid., April 25, May 16, 1850.
66. Ibid., September 11, 1859; Dermot H. Hardy and Ingham S. Roberts, *Historical Review of South-East Texas*, 1:240.
67. *Weekly Telegraph*, February 1, 1872.
68. C. H. Brooks to Oscar M. Addison, March 10, 1856, Oscar M. Addison Papers.
69. *Tri-Weekly Telegraph*, January 11, 1858.
70. Ibid., February 9, 1857.
71. Ibid., February 17, April 7, July 21, 1858.
72. Ibid., September 24, 1858.
73. Ibid., May 25, 1859.
74. *Telegraph and Texas Register*, November 14, 1838; Notes, Pearl Hendricks Papers.
75. *Morning Star*, August 23, 1839; *Tri-Weekly Telegraph*, July 2, 1858.
76. *Weekly Houston Telegraph*, May 2, 1874.
77. *Telegraph and Texas Register*, May 2, 26, 1837; Eugene O. Porter, "Railroad Enterprises in the Republic of Texas," *Southwestern Historical Quarterly* 59 (January 1956): 364–367; S. G. Reed, *A History of Texas Railroads*, pp. 10, 18.
78. *Morning Star*, March 18, 20, 1840; Porter, "Railroad Enterprises," pp. 369–370.

79. *Morning Star,* July 28, 1840; Porter, "Railroad Enterprises," pp. 370–371.
80. *Telegraph and Texas Register,* March 2, 1848.
81. Andrew Forest Muir, "Railroads Come to Houston, 1857–1861," *Southwestern Historical Quarterly* 64 (July 1960): 47–48; idem, "Railroad Enterprise in Texas, 1836–1841," ibid. 47 (October 1943): 370; Sibley, *Port of Houston,* p. 73. See also Harry D. Holmes, "Boston Investment in the Buffalo Bayou, Brazos and Colorado Railway: A Study in Entrepreneurial Decision-Making."
82. *Telegraph and Texas Register,* May 9, 1851; Reed, *Texas Railroads,* pp. 57–58.
83. *Telegraph and Texas Register,* June 25, July 16, 30, October 8, 1852; Wallis and Hill, *Sixty Years on the Brazos,* p. 200.
84. *Telegraph and Texas Register,* October 15, 1852.
85. *Weekly Telegraph,* February 20, 1856.
86. *Tri-Weekly Telegraph,* February 27, April 9, 1856.
87. *Weekly Telegraph,* April 30, 1856; *Tri-Weekly Telegraph,* October 24, 1856. According to Andrew Forest Muir (interview, January 3, 1968), the junction was named after Thomas W. Peirce, but it is usually spelled as in the text; see, for example, Webb, *Handbook of Texas,* 2:376.
88. *Tri-Weekly Telegraph,* May 28, June 2, 1858, February 22, May 27, 1859; Reed, *Texas Railroads,* p. 82.
89. *Weekly Telegraph,* August 8, 1872 (a reprinted letter from Paul Bremond to the *Dallas Herald*).
90. *Tri-Weekly Telegraph,* February 6, 1857.
91. Ibid., July 21, 1858.
92. Ibid., July 28, 30, 1858, November 23, 1859; Reed, *Texas Railroads,* pp. 75–76.
93. *Tri-Weekly Telegraph,* February 3, 6, 1860.
94. Ibid., May 15, 1860.
95. Ibid., June 7, 1860.
96. Ibid., August 28, 1857, April 12, 1858; Muir, "Railroads Come to Houston," p. 51; Reed, *Texas Railroads,* pp. 84–85.
97. Earl Wesley Fornell, *The Galveston Era,* pp. 159–179.
98. *Weekly Telegraph,* September 4, 1861; Muir, "Railroads Come to Houston," p. 52.
99. Reed, *Texas Railroads,* p. 317.
100. *Weekly Telegraph,* October 7, 1869; Webb, *Handbook of Texas,* 1:851–852.
101. *Weekly Telegraph,* January 27, 1870; Webb, *Handbook of Texas,* 1:240.
102. *Weekly Telegraph,* January 7, 1869, June 26, 1873.
103. *Houston Daily Post,* August 31, 1880; James P. Baughman, *Charles Morgan and the Development of Southern Transportation,* p. 224.
104. *Galveston Daily News,* August 27, November 12, 1865.
105. *Weekly Telegraph,* June 25, 1868, September 5, 1872; *Galveston Daily News,* March 25, 1873.

106. The national connection brought an unexpected difficulty with tramps who rode the trains to Houston to spend the winter months. The drifters created a problem not only of law enforcement but also of health when they slipped past quarantine limits. See *Houston Daily Telegraph*, November 24, 1876, January 10, 1877; *Houston Daily Telegram*, September 24, November 27, December 3, 1878, January 25, 1879.
107. *Weekly Telegraph*, March 31, 1870.
108. *Galveston Daily News*, September 25, 28, 1873; Reed, *Texas Railroads*, p. 311.
109. *Weekly Telegraph*, April 25, August 1, 8, 1872.
110. *Weekly Houston Telegraph*, February 26, July 9, October 15, 1875.
111. Reed, *Texas Railroads*, p. 479. Often called Patterson, the name originally seems to have been Pattison, named for George M. Pattison who gave the land for the townsite (see Webb, *Handbook of Texas*, 2 : 346).
112. Writers' Program, *Houston*, p. 144.
113. *Weekly Houston Telegraph*, July 3, August 28, 1874.
114. *Weekly Telegraph*, October 1, 1856.
115. *Tri-Weekly Telegraph*, June 25, 30, November 10, 1858. Because of the large crowd, the toasts which had been prepared were not read.
116. Wallis and Hill, *Sixty Years on the Brazos*, p. 202.
117. Sibley, *Port of Houston*, pp. 36–37.
118. *Telegraph and Texas Register*, January 27, 1837. The story exists also that John K. Allen paid $1,000 cash to induce a large steamboat called the *Constitution*, 150 feet in length, to come to Houston in the summer of 1837. The ship made it, but had to back down the bayou to a place one mile above Harrisburg before it could turn around. This place became known, thereafter, as Constitution Bend. See Sibley, *Port of Houston*, p. 39; "J. K. Allen First Booster for Houston," *Houston* 11 (April 1940) : 28; *Galveston Daily News*, March 13, 1874 (location of Constitution Bend).
119. Domenech, *Missionary Adventures*, p. 24. See also, for a description, Gustav Dresel, *Houston Journal*, trans. Max Freund, p. 30.
120. Millie Richards Gray, *The Diary of Millie Gray, 1832–1840*, pp. 150–151.
121. Matilda Charlotte Houstoun, *Texas and the Gulf of Mexico; or Yachting in the New World*, 2 : 208–209.
122. Ibid., p. 179.
123. *Telegraph and Texas Register*, May 2, 1837.
124. Sibley, *Port of Houston*, p. 49.
125. Ibid.; *Morning Star*, April 19, 1839; Thomas M. League Papers, League-Andrews Receipt Book, March 4, 1839.
126. *Morning Star*, February 13, April 14, 1840, March 6, 1841; Sibley, *Port of Houston*, p. 50. Sibley refers to the ship as the *General Houston*, but the newspapers call it the *Sam Houston*. There may have been several vessels named for Houston.
127. Sibley, *Port of Houston*, pp. 50–51; Gammel, *Laws of Texas*, 2 : 753–754; *Morning Star*, June 10, 1841.

128. Sibley, *Port of Houston*, p. 69; *Morning Star*, January 30, 1840; *Tri-Weekly Telegraph*, September 1, 1856, April 13, 1857, April 1, 1859.
129. *Galveston Daily News*, November 22, 1865.
130. Sibley, *Port of Houston*, pp. 77–78.
131. Ibid., p. 87.
132. Ibid., pp. 87–88; *Weekly Telegraph*, October 28, 1869; *Daily Telegraph*, March 31, 1871.
133. Minutes of the City Council of Houston, B (February 1, 1865–July 1, 1869), 312–313, 329, 342–344, 346.
134. *Weekly Telegraph*, November 5, 1867.
135. Sibley, *Port of Houston*, pp. 92–93.
136. Ibid., p. 94; *Weekly Telegraph*, July 21, 1870.
137. The Ship Channel Company wanted a twelve-foot channel and the *Weekly Telegraph* (March 28, 1873) argued that a six-foot watercourse would be inadequate for competition with Galveston.
138. Sibley, *Port of Houston*, pp. 94–96; *Weekly Telegraph*, January 23, 1873.
139. L. Tuffly Ellis, "The Revolutionizing of the Texas Cotton Trade, 1865–1885," *Southwestern Historical Quarterly* 73 (April 1970): 496–497 n. 60.
140. *Weekly Telegraph*, April 10, 1873.
141. Sibley, *Port of Houston*, p. 99.
142. Ibid., pp. 100–101.
143. *Houston Daily Telegraph*, April 23, 25, 28, 1876.
144. *Houston Daily Telegram*, September 28, 1878.
145. "Life and Adventures of Henry Woodland of Texas, Veteran and Mier Prisoner," Louis W. Kemp Collection, unpaged (handwritten).
146. *Telegraph and Texas Register*, December 29, 1838.
147. Charles H. Dillon, "The Arrival of the Telegraph in Texas," *Southwestern Historical Quarterly* 64 (October 1960): 200–211; idem, "A Story of the Telegraph and the Western Union and How They Reached the Southwest," pp. 91–100, 131, 160–164 (typescript); *Tri-Weekly Telegraph*, January 25, 1860.
148. *Telegraph and Texas Register*, January 6, 1838.
149. *Morning Star*, October 16, 1841.
150. *Weekly Telegraph*, September 18, 1867; *Houston Chronicle*, May 26, 1929 ("Ingham S. Roberts Pays Tribute to Benj. A. Shepherd"). The Texas constitutions of 1845, 1861, 1866, and 1876 prohibited incorporation of state banks.
151. Grover, "Dissolution of T. W. House," p. 20.
152. R. Henderson Shuffler, "Decimus et Ultimus Barziza," *Southwestern Historical Quarterly* 66 (April 1963): 501–512.
153. For a survey of banking, see Avery L. Carlson, "Laying the Foundations of Modern Banking in Texas: 1861–1893," *Texas Monthly* 4 (December 1929): 617–637.
154. *Weekly Houston Telegraph*, May 16, 1874.

155. *Democratic Telegraph and Texas Register*, August 28, September 18, 1850.
156. *Weekly Telegraph*, July 9, 1856; *Tri-Weekly Telegraph*, March 12, 1858; Carlson, "Foundations of Modern Banking in Texas," p. 620.
157. *Morning Star*, April 6, 1840; Gammel, *Laws of Texas*, 2:448; Pearl Hendricks, "Chamber 98 Years Old," *Houston 9* (December 1938): 50.
158. *Morning Star*, October 3, 1840; *Telegraph and Texas Register*, October 13, 1841.
159. *Weekly Telegraph*, September 2, 30, 1869.
160. *Houston Daily Telegraph*, May 17, 1874.
161. Ibid., May 13, 16, 1874; *Weekly Houston Telegraph*, May 16, 1874.
162. *Houston Daily Telegraph*, June 12–14, 16, 20–21, 28, July 2, 1874.

3. A FRONTIER SOCIETY, 1836–1875

1. These data were gathered from a count of birthplaces of the population noted in the *Seventh Census of the United States, 1850, Harris County, Texas, City of Houston, free schedule*; and the *Ninth Census of the United States, 1870, Harris County, Texas, Houston schedule*. The term "South" is defined here to include only those states which were (or had been) a part of the Confederate States of America. The slave schedules for 1850 do not give birthplaces. A demographic study by Susan Jackson, "Movin' On: Mobility through Houston in the 1850s," *Southwestern Historical Quarterly 81* (January 1968): 251–282, reveals a large turnover of population. Only one-third of the free residents listed in 1850 remained on the census rolls of 1860 even though the population doubled during the decade.
2. Wade, *Urban Frontier*, pp. 102, 108.
3. *Telegraph and Texas Register*, May 16, 1837.
4. *Tri-Weekly Telegraph*, March 12, 1858.
5. Wade, *Urban Frontier*, pp. 103–104.
6. *Telegraph and Texas Register*, June 9, 16, 1838.
7. *Morning Star*, June 6, 1844 (ventriloquist); *Telegraph and Texas Register*, July 9, 1845 (phrenologist), July 23, 1845 (comedian), August 20, 1845 (minstrel); *Tri-Weekly Telegraph*, February 10, 1858, February 15, 1858, February 17, 1858 (trained animals), March 24, 1860 (bell ringers), March 29, 1860 (singer); *Weekly Telegraph*, November 6, 1860 (play), April 16, 1862 (amateurs), April 11, 1872 (play); *Galveston Daily News*, March 4, 1865 (play), May 4, 1865 (play). For a chronological presentation of theatrical productions in Houston and Galveston, see Joseph Gallegly, *Footlights on the Border*.
8. *Telegraph and Texas Register*, August 25, 1838.
9. Ibid., May 9, 1837, June 2, 1841.
10. Mattie Austin Hatcher, *Letters of an Early American Traveller*, p. 70.
11. *Morning Star*, August 19, 1839; *Telegraph and Texas Register*, January 27, December 8, 1838; *Tri-Weekly Telegraph*, April 6, 1857; *Weekly Telegraph*, March 12, 1856.

12. *Weekly Telegraph*, September 22, 1870; *Daily Telegraph*, November 11, 1871.
13. Moritz Tiling, *History of the German Element in Texas*, pp. 49, 163; *Weekly Houston Telegraph*, November 29, 1874.
14. *Telegraph and Texas Register*, January 13, 1838; Ashbel Smith to Muller, December 6, 1837, letter book, July 5–December 18, 1837, Ashbel Smith Papers.
15. *Morning Star*, August 5, 14, 1839; *Telegraph and Texas Register*, October 11, 1837.
16. Orin Walker Hatch, *Lyceum to Library*, pp. 1–3.
17. *Morning Star*, June 18, July 1, 1839; *Telegraph and Texas Register*, November 6, 1844; Hatch, *Lyceum to Library*, pp. 3–5.
18. For a review of library activity, see Hatch, *Lyceum to Library*, pp. 1–49.
19. *Texas Newspapers, 1813–1939*, pp. 107–119.
20. *Morning Star*, December 11, 1839.
21. *Telegraph and Texas Register*, September 8, 1838, October 2, 1844; *Weekly Telegraph*, September 4, 1861; *Weekly Houston Telegraph*, April 25, 1874.
22. *Morning Star*, July 18, 1839.
23. Wade, *Urban Frontier*, pp. 130–131.
24. *Morning Star*, May 22, 1841, January 15, 1842; *Telegraph and Texas Register*, May 4, 1842, April 3, 1844.
25. *Tri-Weekly Telegraph*, November 14, 1856.
26. *Weekly Telegraph*, February 27, 1856.
27. *Tri-Weekly Telegraph*, February 4, 27, 1857, December 6, 1858.
28. Ibid., December 8, 1858, January 3, 1859.
29. Ibid., April 15, 1859.
30. *Weekly Telegraph*, April 9, 1862; *Daily Houston Telegraph*, February 3, 1871; Leonard, *Houston City Directory for 1866*, p. 114.
31. *Galveston Daily News*, October 1, 1865.
32. Ibid., November 12, 1865.
33. *Weekly Telegraph*, March 31, 1870.
34. Ibid., February 17, 1870.
35. Ibid., April 24, 1873.
36. *Weekly Houston Telegraph*, October 23, 1874; *Houston Daily Telegraph*, March 3, 1876.
37. *Weekly Houston Telegraph*, October 23, 1874.
38. Minutes of the City Council, D (June 12, 1875–May 31, 1877), 378, 447–551; Helen Katherine Keller, "A History of Public Education in Houston, Texas," pp. 40–43.
39. *Telegraph and Texas Register*, January 2, 1852; *Tri-Weekly Telegraph*, April 15, 1857, December 24, 1858, March 6, 1860; *Weekly Houston Telegraph*, October 23, 1874.
40. *Morning Star*, July 6, 1841.
41. *Weekly Telegraph*, July 8, 1869.
42. *Daily Telegraph*, December 27, 1871.

43. *Telegraph and Texas Register,* May 28, 1845.
44. *Tri-Weekly Telegraph,* February 24, 1858.
45. Ibid., May 9, 1856, January 9, August 17, 1857, February 23, 1860; *Weekly Telegraph,* March 26, 1861; *Weekly Houston Telegraph,* October 2, 1874.
46. *Morning Star,* September 25, 1839; *Telegraph and Texas Register,* October 27, 1838, July 26, 1847.
47. *Weekly Telegraph,* April 22, 1869.
48. Ibid., April 16, 1861; *Daily Telegraph,* June 14, 1871.
49. *Houston Daily Telegraph,* October 24, 1875.
50. *Telegraph and Texas Register,* December 14, 1842.
51. *Weekly Telegraph,* June 20, 1872.
52. *Houston Daily Telegraph,* May 6, 1874.
53. *Weekly Telegraph,* March 24, 31, May 5, June 2, 1870, May 16, 1872.
54. Ibid., May 16, 1872.
55. *Houston Daily Telegram,* November 23, 24, 1878.
56. Dora Fowler Arthur, ed., "Jottings from the Old Journal of Littleton Fowler," *Southwestern Historical Quarterly* 2 (July 1898): 79–80.
57. Ibid., p. 82. A typescript letter from Fowler to Mrs. M. M. Porter (Littleton Fowler Papers), dated May 14, 1838, records much the same story except that Fowler compares the travelers to lunatics and adds, "I was afraid God Almighty would send a clap of thunder from even a clear sky and shiver the Boat to atoms."
58. *Morning Star,* November 15, 1839.
59. Muir, *Texas in 1837,* p. 34.
60. James Harper Starr, memo book, 1839–1840 to February 23, 1841, James Harper Starr Papers, pp. 5–6 (typescript).
61. *Morning Star,* September 18, 1839.
62. S. W. Geiser, "Naturalists of the Frontier," *Southwest Review* 16 (Autumn 1930): 126; Andrew Forest Muir, ed., "Diary of a Young Man in Houston, 1838," *Southwestern Historical Quarterly* 53 (January 1950): 284.
63. Lubbock, *Six Decades,* pp. 55–56.
64. *Weekly Telegraph,* June 11, 1856.
65. Ibid., March 5, 1856.
66. *Tri-Weekly Telegraph,* January 30, April 28, 1860; *Weekly Telegraph,* January 29, 1861; *Galveston Daily News,* July 7, 1865; *Houston Chronicle,* May 26, 1929.
67. *Morning Star,* April 18, 1839, October 1, 1840; *Telegraph and Texas Register,* December 8, 1838, June 23, 1841, March 5, 1852; *Democratic Telegraph and Texas Register,* June 28, 1846; *Galveston Daily News,* September 13, 1865.
68. *Morning Star,* April 20, 1839.
69. Ibid., September 9, 10, 1839.
70. Ibid., March 6, July 1, 1841.
71. William Ransom Hogan, "Pamelia Mann, Texas Frontierswoman,"

Southwest Review 20 (Summer 1935): 360–370; Ellen Garwood, "Early Texas Inns: A Study in Social Relationships," *Southwestern Historical Quarterly* 60 (October 1956): 232–233.

72. *Telegraph and Texas Register*, May 30, 1837.
73. Unsigned letter to M. M. Noah, June 27, 1837, Ashbel Smith Papers; *Telegraph and Texas Register*, July 1, 1837; William Ransom Hogan, "Rampant Individualism in the Republic of Texas," *Southwestern Historical Quarterly* 46 (April 1941): 466–468.
74. Chauncy Goodrich to Ashbel Smith, June 30, 1837, Ashbel Smith Papers.
75. *Telegraph and Texas Register*, July 1, 1837.
76. Ibid., September 16, 1837; Ashbel Smith to Dr. Lewis, October 31, 1837, Ashbel Smith Papers; Hogan, "Rampant Individualism," p. 468.
77. *Telegraph and Texas Register*, June 18, 24, 1840, February 9, 1842.
78. Ibid., February 24, 1838.
79. Hogan, "Rampant Individualism," pp. 471–473, 479–480.
80. Minutes of the 11th District Court, C (January 1, 1841–May 24, 1842), 152–153.
81. *Telegraph and Texas Register*, September 7, 1842.
82. *Morning Star*, January 6, 1844.
83. *Telegraph and Texas Register*, December 1, 1838.
84. *Tri-Weekly Telegraph*, August 16, 1860.
85. Ibid., May 31, 1860.
86. *Telegraph and Texas Register*, April 21, 1838; *Morning Star*, June 22, 1839.
87. *Tri-Weekly Telegraph*, September 10, 1858.
88. Minutes of the 11th District Court, B (December 3, 1838–January 7, 1841), 170–171 (jail conditions); *Morning Star*, January 20, April 6, 1840 (escape); *Tri-Weekly Telegraph*, September 9, 1857 (guards), May 17, June 2, 1858 (escape); *Weekly Telegraph*, August 29, 1872 (food).
89. Muir, "Diary of a Young Man," pp. 299–300.
90. *Tri-Weekly Telegraph*, June 27, 1859.
91. Arthur, "Jottings from the Journal of Littleton Fowler," p. 79.
92. Louis Howard Grimes, *Cloud of Witnesses*, pp. 12–13; Samuel C. Red, *A Brief History of First Presbyterian Church, Houston, Texas, 1839–1939*, pp. 10–12; William S. Red, ed., "Allen's Reminiscences of Texas, 1838–1842," *Southwestern Historical Quarterly* 17 (January 1913): 289.
93. Red, "Allen's Reminiscences," pp. 292, 295; *National Intelligencer*, April 18, 1839.
94. *Morning Star*, June 18, 1839.
95. Ibid., October 14, 1839.
96. Red, "Allen's Reminiscences," p. 292; Grimes, *Cloud of Witnesses*, p. 31; Marguerite Johnston, *A Happy Worldly Abode*, p. 59; Jesse Guy Smith, *Heroes of the Saddle Bags*, p. 160; Sister Mary Brendan O'Donnell, "Annunciation Church—Catholic Motherchurch of Houston," pp. 34–36.

97. *Morning Star*, September 16, 1839.
98. *Telegraph and Texas Register*, August 5, 1837; Gammel, *Laws of Texas*, 1:1298–1299.
99. Record of Board of Commissioners and Election Returns, January 30, 1837, to January 25, 1866, pp. 6–9. Houston became the county seat of Harrisburg County in 1836; Harrisburg County became Harris County in 1839. Appendix B lists Houston's mayors.
100. Gammel, *Laws of Texas*, 2:94–98, 411–413.
101. Ibid., p. 677.
102. *Tri-Weekly Telegraph*, January 18, 1858.
103. Ibid., December 10, 1858, May 19, 1860; Sibley, *Port of Houston*, p. 76.
104. *Morning Star*, August 27, 1839, January 10, 1840, December 20, 1841; *Telegraph and Texas Register*, June 20, 1848, February 21, 1851; *Tri-Weekly Telegraph*, January 18, 1858; Minutes of the City Council, B (February 1, 1865–July 1, 1869), 107, C (March 2, 1872–June 5, 1875), 403–413.
105. Minutes of the City Council, B, 376–378.
106. *Weekly Telegraph*, November 13–14, 20, 27, 1860, January 8, March 5, 1861.
107. Ibid., April 23, 1862.
108. Ibid., June 12, August 7, 1861.
109. Ibid., August 28, 1861.
110. Ibid., August 21, 1861, November 5, 1862, January 7, 1863; John Milsaps, Diary, 1:47–49.
111. *Weekly Telegraph*, August 21, 1861.
112. Ibid., December 11, 1861.
113. Ibid., August 7, October 9, 1861.
114. Ibid., October 23, 30, 1861.
115. Ibid., October 23, November 6, 1861.
116. Ibid., November 6, 1861.
117. Ibid., October 16, 1861, January 8, 1862, March 11, 1863.
118. Ibid., January 15, 1861, June 25, 1862, January 28, May 5, 1863.
119. Eliza McHatton Ripley, *From Flag to Flag*, pp. 74–75.
120. *Galveston Daily News*, April 23, 1865.
121. Ibid., April 22, May 6, 1865.
122. Ibid., May 21, 1865.
123. William Job Hale to Sue, May 21, 1865, William Job Hale Papers (typescript).
124. *Galveston Daily News*, May 26, June 1, 1865.
125. Ibid., June 3, 1865.
126. Ibid., May 26, June 20, 1865.
127. Ibid., June 4, 1865.
128. E. N. Gray, *Memories of Old Houston*, unpaged.
129. *Galveston Daily News*, June 21, 1865.
130. Ibid.; Gray, *Memories*, unpaged.
131. *Galveston Daily News*, August 16, 1865.
132. Ibid., November 22, 1865.

133. Marion Merseburger, "A Political History of Houston, Texas, during the Reconstruction Period as Recorded by the Press: 1868–1873," pp. 1–3.
134. Minutes of the City Council, B, 409. There is some controversy over Scanlan's first name since the city directories starting in 1882 often list him as "Timothy." The newspapers and the minutes of the city council during the period when he was mayor consistently refer to him as "Thomas." John Brown, ninety-three years old when interviewed by the *Houston Post*, March 23, 1938, referred to "Tim Scanlan." Perhaps he changed his name or was nicknamed "Tim." According to the evidence, it seems probable that his legal name was "Thomas."
135. Merseburger, "Political History of Houston," p. 101.
136. Ibid., pp. 101–102, 108, 127–128; *Houston Daily Union*, May 29, 1872.
137. B. H. Carroll, Jr., *Standard History of Houston, Texas*, p. 457; Writers' Program, *Houston*, pp. 86–87; Merseburger, "Political History of Houston," pp. 127, 185–188.
138. Minutes of the City Council, C, 403–404.
139. *Daily Telegraph*, March 14, 1871; *Weekly Telegraph*, February 1, 1872; *Houston Daily Telegraph*, January 1, December 20, 31, 1876.
140. Minutes of the City Council, C, 403–404, 406, 407, 411.
141. Ibid., B, 166–167.
142. *Daily Telegraph*, September 10, 1871.
143. *Houston Daily Telegraph*, July 9, 1876; Minutes of the City Council, C, 406–407.
144. *Houston Daily Telegraph*, July 9, 1876. Volunteers handled fire fighting at this time. These social organizations purchased much of their own equipment and fought fires for adventure. They used hand and steam pumps, buckets, hooks, and ladders. Water came from the bayou, from cisterns at major street corners in 1859–1879, after 1879 from water mains. A fire department consisting of the various volunteer companies was formed in 1859 but had to be reorganized in 1867 and 1874. The town established fire limits at least as early as 1859 and afterward attempted to control building material, construction, and use in order to prevent conflagrations. See *Tri-Weekly Telegraph*, March 7, 1859; *Houston Post-Dispatch*, June 30, 1929; Leonard, *Houston City Directory*, pp. 91–92; Minutes of the City Council, B, 292–298, C, 398–400; Charles D. Green, *Fire Fighters of Houston, 1838–1915*.
145. *Houston Daily Telegraph*, August 15, 1876; Minutes of the City Council, D, 298.
146. *Houston Daily Telegraph*, December 20, 1876.
147. Ibid., January 1, December 20, 1876.
148. Charles N. Glaab and A. Theodore Brown, *A History of Urban America*, p. 181.
149. Minutes of the City Council, B, 107, D, 398. See also Howard L. Pratt, "Urban Public Services and Private Enterprise: Aspects of the Legal and Economic History of Houston, Texas, 1865–1905," pp. 5–10.

150. *Weekly Houston Telegraph,* August 14, 1874.
151. *Weekly Telegraph,* September 25, 1873; *Galveston Daily News,* October 7, 9, 1873.
152. *Weekly Telegraph,* November 14, 1872; Merseburger, "Political History of Houston," p. 157.
153. *Weekly Telegraph,* November 21, 1872.
154. From a count in *Ninth Census,* Houston population schedules.
155. *Weekly Telegraph,* November 21, 1872.
156. *Morning Star,* August 13, 1839.
157. *Eighth Census of the United States, Population,* p. 486.
158. Andrew Forest Muir, "The Free Negro in Harris County, Texas," *Southwestern Historical Quarterly* 46 (January 1943): 214–215; *Morning Star,* April 10, August 13, 1839.
159. Minutes of the 11th District Court, B, 173.
160. Muir, "Free Negro in Harris County," p. 238.
161. *Morning Star,* April 12, September 19, 1839, March 4, 6, 1841.
162. *Tri-Weekly Telegraph,* April 7, 1856.
163. League-Andrews Receipt Book, December 19, 1838, Thomas M. League Papers; Gustave Gerson Receipt Book, 1856–1870, October 21, 1856, Gustave Gerson Papers.
164. F. R. Lubbock to "My Dear Friend," May 18, 1855, Briscoe-Harris-Looscan Papers.
165. See advertisements, *Morning Star,* April 22, 1839; *Telegraph and Texas Register,* June 1, November 16, 1842, February 1, 8, 1843; *Tri-Weekly Telegraph,* November 4, 16, 1857. The Thomas M. League Receipt Book, December 20, 1838, notes a $750 receipt for the sale of a black man at auction.
166. Olmsted, *Journey through Texas,* p. 227.
167. *Tri-Weekly Telegraph,* July 9, 1858.
168. *Galveston Daily News,* June 24, 27, 1865.
169. Gray, *Memories,* unpaged.
170. *Galveston Daily News,* June 27, July 6, 18, 1865.
171. *Weekly Telegraph,* October 1, 1868.
172. Ibid., August 11, 1870.
173. Ibid., May 6, 1871, March 21, 1872; *Houston Daily Post,* August 23, 1897.
174. *Weekly Telegraph,* July 17, 1873.
175. *Weekly Houston Telegraph,* August 7, 1874.
176. Ibid., June 20, 1874; *Daily Telegraph,* June 20, 1871.
177. *Galveston Daily News,* March 22, 1874 (Vinegar Hill).
178. *Democratic Telegraph and Texas Register,* March 28, 1850; *Telegraph and Texas Register,* April 18, 1851; Gilbert J. Jordan (ed. and trans.), "W. Steinert's View of Texas in 1849," *Southwestern Historical Quarterly* 80 (April 1977): 411–415.
179. C. C. Cox, "Reminiscences of C. C. Cox," *Southwestern Historical Quarterly* 6 (October 1902): 118.

180. Ashbel Smith to Lee and Butler, July 5, 1837, letter book, July 5–
     December 18, 1837; Ashbel Smith to "Sister," January 27, 1838, letter
     book, December 22, 1837–April 18, 1838, Ashbel Smith Papers.
181. *Morning Star*, July 20, 1839; *Telegraph and Texas Register*, November
     17, 1838, August 24, 1842; *Tri-Weekly Telegraph*, November 25, 1859.
182. *Telegraph and Texas Register*, April 26, July 19, 1843.
183. *Morning Star*, July 23, 1839; *Telegraph and Texas Register*, July 1,
     1840, August 27, 1845, July 18, 1851; *Daily Telegraph*, May 13, 1871;
     Weekly Telegraph, July 10, 1873; *The Charter of the City of Houston
     Together with the Revised Code of Ordinances*, p. 72.
184. *Morning Star*, September 16, 1839 (market), April 20, 1840 (milk), May
     21, 1839, and May 7, 1840 (board of health), March 23, 1840 (scav-
     enger), June 17, 1841 (board of health); *Telegraph and Texas Register*,
     July 31, 1844 (board of health), December 26, 1851 (isolation); *Tri-
     Weekly Telegraph*, July 22, 1857 (board of health); *Weekly Telegraph*,
     August 1, November 21, 1872 (hospital); *Weekly Houston Telegraph*,
     October 2, 1874 (hospital).
185. *Tri-Weekly Telegraph*, October 27, 1858, November 9, 1859; *Weekly
     Telegraph*, October 15, 1862, September 3, 1867.
186. Gray, *Diary of Millie Gray*, p. 134.
187. *Telegraph and Texas Register*, February 5, 1840.
188. William McCraven, "On the Yellow Fever of Houston, Texas, in 1847,"
     New Orleans Medical & Surgical Journal 5 (1848–1849): 229; *Tri-
     Weekly Telegraph*, October 22, 1858.
189. McCraven, "Yellow Fever of Houston," p. 227; *Tri-Weekly Telegraph*,
     October 22, 1858, September 18, 1867.
190. *Democratic Telegraph and Texas Register*, October 19, 1848. The Brit-
     ish consul in Galveston reported in 1867 that yellow fever had spread
     inland from that point causing panic and flight at the interior towns;
     see William Barnes, Annual Reports of the British Consulate, Gal-
     veston, 1843–1879, p. 158.
191. *Tri-Weekly Telegraph*, November 14, 1859.
192. *Morning Star*, August 15, 1839.
193. *Weekly Telegraph*, September 22, 1870.
194. Ibid.
195. *Houston Daily Telegram*, August 1, 1878.
196. Ibid., September 20, 1878.
197. *Houston Daily Post*, May 10, 1887.
198. *Houston Post*, August 14, 1887.

4. THE BAYOU CITY, 1875–1930

  1. Sibley, *Port of Houston*, pp. 105–106.
  2. Ibid., pp. 106–110; Mary Lasswell, *John Henry Kirby, Prince of the
     Pines*, pp. 54–58; *Houston Daily Post*, February 5, 1881, December 3,
     1891, April 1, 1892, May 5, 1892.
  3. Thomas H. Ball, *The Port of Houston*, flyleaf; Palmer Hutcheson, "Ear-

liest Effort to Secure 25 Foot Channel Described," *Houston* 8 (November 1937): 3; Sibley, *Port of Houston*, pp. 111–112.

4. Sibley, *Port of Houston*, p. 114.
5. Ibid., pp. 114–115; Hutcheson, "Earliest Effort," pp. 3–4.
6. Hutcheson, "Earliest Effort," p. 4; Ball, *Port of Houston*, pp. 6–8; Sibley, *Port of Houston*, pp. 115–120.
7. *Houston Daily Post*, March 14, 1901; Sibley, *Port of Houston*, pp. 124–125.
8. *Houston Post*, December 18, 1904; Sibley, *Port of Houston*, pp. 126, 129.
9. Sibley, *Port of Houston*, p. 129; Muir, "Destiny of Buffalo Bayou," p. 106.
10. *Houston Post*, August 10, 1908.
11. Ibid., September 9, 1908.
12. Sibley, *Port of Houston*, p. 131.
13. *Houston Post*, January 19, 1909.
14. Ball, *Port of Houston*, p. 32; Sibley, *Port of Houston*, pp. 133–134.
15. *Houston Post*, February 1, June 7, July 3, 1910; Ball, *Port of Houston*, pp. 33–34; Sibley, *Port of Houston*, pp. 136–137.
16. *Houston Post*, November 5, 1911; Ball, *Port of Houston*, p. 34; Sibley, *Port of Houston*, pp. 137–138.
17. *Houston Post*, June 18, September 19, October 1, 1922; Sibley, *Port of Houston*, pp. 139, 157–158.
18. *Houston Post*, November 11, 1914; Sibley, *Port of Houston*, pp. 141–145. Mrs. George E. Woods (née Sue Campbell) recalled irreverently about the ceremony, "It broke my heart to throw those lovely roses in that greasy, dirty water. They were such beautiful flowers. The channel was really only a stream then and there was a lot of oil on the water from the oil barges and it seemed such a shame to drop those gorgeous white petals into that dirty stream" (*Houston Post*, November 9, 1964).
19. *Houston Post*, September 1, 1914.
20. Ibid., January 18, 1915; Sibley, *Port of Houston*, p. 147.
21. *Houston Post*, August 23, 1914.
22. Ibid., April 14, 1915.
23. Ibid., July 3, 1915; Sibley, *Port of Houston*, pp. 147–149; Harvey C. Miller, "First Houston S.S. Line Began in August," *Houston* 3 (August 1932): 13.
24. *Houston Post*, March 25, August 13, September 23, 1917, March 19, 1919.
25. *Houston Post-Dispatch*, July 22, 1925; Sibley, *Port of Houston*, pp. 153, 158–160.
26. *Houston Post-Dispatch*, August 15, 1929; Sibley, *Port of Houston*, p. 161. See also U.S. Engineering Department, *Houston Ship Channel, Texas*, p. 2.
27. John S. Spratt, *The Road to Spindletop*, p. 32.
28. *Weekly Houston Telegraph*, April 9, 1875; Robert S. Maxwell, *Whistle in the Piney Woods*, p. 4.

29. *Houston Daily Telegram,* October 27, 1878; Maxwell, *Whistle in the Piney Woods,* p. 11.
30. Maxwell, *Whistle in the Piney Woods,* pp. 17, 67–68.
31. *Houston Daily Post,* June 10, 1881.
32. Maxwell, *Whistle in the Piney Woods,* pp. 20, 21, 26, 30, 42, 43, 46.
33. *Houston Daily Telegraph,* July 29, August 1, 1876.
34. Ibid., November 8, 1876.
35. *Houston Daily Telegram,* April 10, 1879; *Daily Post,* February 27, 1883.
36. *Houston Daily Post,* February 25, 1900.
37. *Houston Post,* September 1, 1904.
38. *The Standard Blue Book of Texas: Who's Who,* pp. 51–54.
39. S. G. Reed, "A Romance of the Rails," *Houston* 8 (January 1938): 35.
40. *Houston Post,* September 1, 1910.
41. Joseph Nimmo, Jr., *Report on the Internal Commerce of the United States* (1879), *House Executive Documents,* 45th Congress, 3rd Session (Serial No. 1857), Document No. 32, part 3, pp. 122–125.
42. Hardy and Roberts, *Historical Review of South-East Texas,* 1:260.
43. Ibid., p. 262. For a discussion of the differential, see also Sibley, *Port of Houston,* pp. 164–168; Louis Tuffly Ellis, "The Texas Cotton Compress Industry: A History," pp. 169–170.
44. *Houston Daily Post,* September 13, 1891, July 10, 1892, August 12, September 2, November 9, December 2, 1894; *Houston Post,* March 25, April 26, 1905, January 5, August 26, 1909; *Houston Post-Dispatch,* August 28, 1925, December 21, 1927, August 31, 1928, December 14, 1930.
45. Sibley, *Port of Houston,* pp. 166–168, 180.
46. *Houston Daily Telegram,* January 19, 1879.
47. Ibid., January 26, February 21, March 6, 1879.
48. *Houston Daily Post,* January 18, February 17, March 17, 1882.
49. *Daily Post,* June 13, 1882; *Morrison and Fourmy's General Directory of the City of Houston, 1882–1883,* pp. 16–17.
50. *Daily Post,* February 8, June 20, 1883.
51. *Houston Daily Post,* May 10, September 10, 1887, June 26, September 14, November 30, 1888.
52. Ibid., January 14, 1903.
53. Ibid., March 23, May 7, 1903; *Houston Post,* October 8, November 1, 1905.
54. *Houston Post,* February 16, 1912.
55. Minutes of the City Council, R (February 9, 1914–September 14, 1915), 56.
56. *Houston Post,* March 17, 1915, June 18, 1922; *Houston Post-Dispatch,* March 17, December 29, 1926.
57. *Houston Daily Post,* November 27, 1892.
58. *Houston Post,* February 15, 1890; *Houston Daily Post,* May 20, 1897.
59. *Houston Daily Post,* April 14, 1901; *Houston Post,* November 12,

1905, May 26, 1912. On March 16, 1897, the *Houston Daily Post* reported the appearance of an electric car with solid rubber tires used as an advertising novelty by Montgomery Ward and Company. It weighed 2,000 pounds, cost $3,000, and used twenty-eight batteries connected to two 2-hp motors.

60. *Texas Almanac and State Industrial Guide, 1911*, p. 127; *Texas Almanac and State Industrial Guide, 1925*, p. 192; *Texas Almanac and State Industrial Guide, 1931*, p. 198.
61. *Houston Post*, March 5, 1908.
62. Ibid., June 16, 1905.
63. Ibid., August 10, 1905.
64. Ibid., October 23, 1908.
65. Ibid., May 26, 1912.
66. Ibid., September 29, October 3, 1909.
67. Ibid., May 7, 1907.
68. Ibid., February 8, April 2, 1914.
69. Ibid., January 4, 1920, July 17, 1921; *Houston Chronicle*, July 15, 1921.
70. *Houston Post*, May 19, 1922.
71. *Houston Post-Dispatch*, July 13, August 24, 1926.
72. Ibid., April 12, November 9, 1927, October 3, 9, 24, 1929.
73. *Houston Post*, May 16, 1920; Burt Rule, "Motor Truck Supplants Horse Power in Houston," *Houston* (Young Men's Business League) 2 (February 1920): 20. See also, for general information, Merrill J. Roberts, "The Motor Transportation Revolution," *Business History Review* 30 (March 1956): 57–95.
74. *Houston Post-Dispatch*, January 20, 1928; "Cotton Greatest Contribution to Port Houston Growth," *Houston* 2 (May 1931): 26.
75. *Houston Post-Dispatch*, August 1, 1931.
76. "When Houston Was Young," *Tangent* 3 (February 1913): 9–11.
77. *Houston Daily Post*, April 30, 1890.
78. *Houston Post*, June 30, 1912.
79. *Houston Daily Post*, November 22, 1903; *Houston Daily Telegraph*, January 11, 1876.
80. *Houston Post*, September 19, 1886.
81. Ibid., March 19, 1889.
82. Ibid., November 9, 1889, March 2, 1890.
83. *Houston Daily Post*, September 18, 1890.
84. Ibid., June 13, 1891; "When Houston Was Young," p. 17.
85. *Houston Daily Post*, October 2, 1901, November 22, 1903, September 1, 1910, October 9, 1913.
86. Ibid., January 12, 1915, April 3, 1919.
87. Ibid., July 15, 1920.
88. Ibid., February 20, September 6, October 17, 1922, April 3, 1923; *Houston Post-Dispatch*, December 1, 1924.
89. *Houston Post-Dispatch*, March 1, 1927.
90. Ibid., April 17, 1927.

91. *Houston Post,* November 29, December 6, 1911, November 2, 1936; *Houston Post-Dispatch,* December 29, 1926; *Houston Chronicle,* November 2, 1936; "An Engineering Masterpiece," *Tangent* 1 (December 1911): 9–20; "Galveston-Houston Electric Railway," *Pan American Magazine* 36 (October 1923): 181–182.

92. *Houston Post,* February 12, 19, 20, 1910; *Houston Chronicle,* February 19, 1920.

93. *Houston Post,* December 11, 1910.

94. Ibid., January 28–30, February 1, 1911, May 12, 1912, October 18, 1921, February 19, 1924; *Houston Post-Dispatch,* September 16, 1925.

95. *Houston Post-Dispatch,* May 6, November 15, 17, 1926.

96. Ibid., January 16, May 20, June 25, 1927, March 3, 1928; *Houston Chronicle,* March 3, 1928; Writers' Program, *Houston,* pp. 148–149.

97. *Houston Post,* May 26, 1912.

98. Ibid., September 26, 1920, December 1, 1922, September 20, 1924.

99. Ibid., February 13, 1921, April 23, 1944.

100. Ibid., April 6, 13, 1919, November 16, 1920.

101. *Daily Post,* March 25, 1882; *Houston Daily Post,* April 15, 1892.

102. *Houston Daily Post,* November 13, 1887.

103. Ibid., September 25, 1891.

104. Ibid., *Houston Daily Telegraph,* September 2, 1876.

105. John Milsaps, Diary, 1:118–136.

106. *Houston Post,* January 22, 1905; *Houston Post-Dispatch,* April 4, 1927.

107. *Houston Post,* May 13, 15, August 5, 1917, April 6, 7, 28, October 31, 1918, April 27, 1919, September 11, 1921, June 27, 1943.

108. *Telegraph and Texas Register,* March 6, 13, 1844; *Weekly Telegraph,* March 26, 1861; *Daily Post,* July 1, 1883; *Houston Post,* August 11, 1883. See also Ellis, "Texas Cotton Compress Industry."

109. *Houston Post,* September 1, 1904.

110. Ibid., September 1, 1910.

111. Ibid., August 8, 1915.

112. Ibid., June 7, 1950.

113. Lamar Fleming, Jr., *Growth of the Business of Anderson, Clayton & Co.,* ed. James A. Tinsley, pp. 1–21, 25–26, 40–42 (financial statement follows page 32).

114. William Brady, *Glimpses of Texas, Its Divisions, Resources, Development, and Prospects,* p. 51.

115. *Houston Daily Post,* April 8, 1900.

116. M. T. Jones Lumber Company Papers, Minutes of the Board of Directors, 1883–1914, July 28, 1883; invoice book, September 1899–December 1899.

117. *This Week in Houston,* September 2–8, 1923, p. 26.

118. Allen W. Hamill, "Spindletop, the Lucus Gusher," Oral History of the Oil Industry, Tape No. 84, September 2, 1952, pp. 18–19 (typescript, carbon copy). The quotation is slightly different in the multilithed copy.

119. *Houston Daily Post,* January 11, 1901.

120. Ibid., April 23, 24, 1901.

121. Ibid., January 15, 17, 1901.

122. Ibid., January 27, 29, 1901.

123. Ibid., March 20, April 9, 26, May 19, August 1, October 4, 1901.

124. Ibid., September 13, 1903; *Houston Post,* September 1, November 7, 11, 1904; *Houston Chronicle,* November 7, 8, 10, 1904.

125. *Houston Post,* January 15, 1905.

126. Ibid., January 22, 1905.

127. Ibid., March 20, April 7, 1905.

128. Ibid., July 11, 1915, September 24, 1916.

129. Ibid., June 6, 1908, May 11, 1919, July 3, 1921; Writers' Program, *Houston,* pp. 164–165; C. A. Warner, *Texas Oil and Gas since 1543,* pp. 185–220.

130. Sibley, *Port of Houston,* p. 152.

131. Torkild Rieber, "Pioneers in Texas Oil," Oral History of the Oil Industry, Tape No. 146D, January 25, 1954, p. 1 (multilithed).

132. *Houston Post,* July 1, 1916, October 28, 1917, February 2, August 27, 1919, January 1, 1933; Ball, *Port of Houston,* pp. 80–81.

133. J. Kent Ridley, "Petroleum Refining," *Houston* 1 (June 1930): 18.

134. *Houston Post-Dispatch,* December 29, 1926. The Houston Oil Company owned the Houston Pipe Line Company which served industrial users of natural gas. John Henry Kirby had formed the Houston Oil Company and the Kirby Lumber Company with eastern capital to exploit both timber and oil on the same East Texas land. Success depended on lumbering, but this failed and litigation commenced in 1904. The oil company emerged in 1908 without Kirby and continued until 1956 when it was liquidated. See John O. King, *The Early History of the Houston Oil Company of Texas, 1901–1908,* pp. 2–3, 10, 15–31, 66, 87, 90; Lasswell, *John Henry Kirby,* pp. 77–114, 123–139.

135. *Houston Post,* January 15, 1924; *Houston Post-Dispatch,* August 16, 1925; Granville A. Humason, "Interview," Oral History of the Oil Industry, Tape No. 102, July 7, 1953, pp. 6–7 (multilithed).

136. Humason, "Interview," pp. 7–8, 12.

137. *Houston Post,* December 14, 1952.

138. Ibid., July 19, September 1, 1914.

139. Ibid., June 25, 1916.

140. Ibid., June 6, 1920; *Houston Post-Dispatch,* February 9, 1926; Ball, *Port of Houston,* pp. 78–82.

141. Chamber of Commerce, *Houston,* unpaged.

142. *Houston Daily Telegram,* December 12, 1878; *Houston Daily Post,* October 5, 1880, July 5, 1897, March 16, 1898, June 18, 1899, April 10, 1900, December 3, 1902, June 2, 4, 13, 1904; *Houston Post,* December 21, 1906, April 2, 1907, October 3, 1911, May 26, 1920, July 9, 1922.

143. *Houston Daily Post,* September 3, 1889, September 4, 1900; *Houston Post,* November 22, 1903; Ruth Allen, *Chapters in the History of*

Organized Labor in Texas, pp. 221–227; Robert E. Zeigler, "The Workingman in Houston, Texas, 1865–1914," pp. 41, 43–44, 47–48, 53, 73–74, 78, 139, 145–149, 153, 232–233; Louis J. Marchiafava, "Institutional and Legal Aspects of the Growth of Professional Urban Police Service: The Houston Experience, 1878–1948," pp. 65–74.

144. *Houston Daily Post,* October 1, 1890, April 8, 1900.
145. The figures were derived by dividing total population into total bank deposits. Data came from *The Statistical History of the United States from Colonial Times to the Present,* pp. 7, 625; *Texas Almanac, 1966–1967,* p. 135; and J. Virgil Scott, "Houston Banks Grow," *Houston* 15 (September 1943): 6–7.
146. Rostow, *Stages of Economic Growth,* pp. 7–8, 39.
147. *Houston Post,* December 28, 1913, April 16, 1914; Avery L. Carlson, "The Expansion of Texas Banking: 1894–1929," *Texas Monthly* 5 (January 1930): 93. For the story of Dallas' success, see Ernest A. Sharpe, *G. B. Dealey of the Dallas News,* pp. 172–174.
148. *Houston Post,* February 1, March 15, August 4, 1919.
149. Ibid., January 14, 1917; *Houston Post-Dispatch,* October 3, 1924.
150. *Houston Daily Post,* April 18, 1890, December 27, 1895, December 8, 1900; *Houston Post,* February 13, September 2, 1906, May 24, 1908, August 4, 1916, November 16, 1920.
151. *Houston Post,* January 1, 1911. The present chamber of commerce celebrated its 125th anniversary in 1965. There is no evidence, however, of direct linkage to the chamber that existed in 1840. At most, the present chamber can claim the Houston Business League as its predecessor and thus reach back to 1895.
152. *Houston Post-Dispatch,* November 10, 1927.
153. *Houston Daily Post,* February 27, 1896.
154. Bascom N. Timmons, *Jesse H. Jones,* pp. 136–145.
155. *Houston Post-Dispatch,* January 29, 1928.
156. Ibid., January 30, February 12, June 24, 28, 1928; Timmons, *Jones,* p. 147.
157. U.S. Bureau of the Census, *Fifteenth Census of the United States: 1930, Population,* 1:18–19.
158. Ibid., 2:69; U.S. Bureau of the Census, *Tenth Census of the United States: 1880, Statistics of the Population of the United States,* p. 424.
159. *Fifteenth Census, Population,* 4:1561; *Manufacturers: 1929,* 3:509; *Distributions: 1930,* 1:1083 (retail), 2:13 (wholesale). The most important items in wholesale trade were farm products (mainly cotton), groceries, machinery, and lumber. In retail trade the important items were automobiles, food, and clothing.
160. Data for calculation from *Statistical History of the United States,* pp. 520, 524.
161. William R. Siddall, "Wholesale-Retail Trade Ratios as Indices of Urban Centrality," *Economic Geography* 37 (April 1961): 124–130.
162. Data for calculation from *Statistical History of the United States,* pp. 409, 520, 524.

5. THE MAGNOLIA CITY, 1875–1930

1. *Houston Daily Telegram*, December 14, 1878. The form of the original report has been altered for clarity.
2. Ibid.
3. *Houston Daily Telegraph*, December 8, 1876.
4. Minutes of the City Council of Houston, D (June 12, 1875–May 31, 1877), 371.
5. *Houston Daily Telegraph*, December 23, 1876; *Houston Post*, December 11, 1904.
6. *Houston Daily Telegram*, March 9, 1879.
7. Minutes of the City Council, E (June 7, 1878–February 24, 1882), 413–415, 564–566; *Daily Post*, June 2, 25, 1882.
8. *Houston Daily Post*, December 21–22, 29, 1886, August 11, 23, 1887.
9. Ibid., September 22, 1887.
10. Minutes of the City Council, G (January 9, 1888–October 29, 1891), 56–61; *Houston Daily Post*, March 22, 27, April 11, 1888; Pratt, "Urban Public Services and Private Enterprise," pp. 20–29.
11. Minutes of the City Council, H (November 9, 1891–December 30, 1895), 438–439, 570; *Houston Daily Post*, June 26, 1891, July 4, 1895.
12. *Houston Daily Post*, January 25, 1898.
13. Minutes of the City Council, E, 90–95; *Houston Daily Telegram*, December 1, 1878.
14. *Houston Post*, August 31, October 5, 1886.
15. Ibid., May 21–22, 1891.
16. *Houston Daily Post*, September 29, October 9, 1894.
17. Ibid., October 17, 1894. Volunteer firemen prevented the inauguration of a paid fire department in 1882, but in 1895 after insurance companies raised rates, in part because of the nonprofessional status of the department, the proud amateurs gave up. See *Houston Daily Post*, January 22, 1882, March 2, October 24, December 15, 1894, April 6, May 21, June 1, 1895, July 8, 1897.
18. *Houston Daily Post*, June 22, 1901.
19. *Houston Post*, September 19, 1886.
20. *Houston Daily Post*, July 20, 1887.
21. Ibid., October 8–9, 1887.
22. Ibid., February 14, 1888, January 2, 1891.
23. Ibid., March 24, May 13–14, 1893.
24. Ibid., May 14, 1893.
25. Ibid., September 6, 1893.
26. Ibid., September 6, 1893, September 25, 1893.
27. Ibid., June 11–12, June 15, 1895.
28. Ibid., November 12, 1895.
29. Ibid., July 16–19, 1901.
30. *Houston Post*, October 6, 1933; Nelson Manfred Blake, *Water for the Cities*, p. 263.
31. *Houston Daily Post*, May 3, 1895.
32. Ibid., July 10–12, November 10, 1899; Minutes of the City Council, J

(January 1, 1896–June 19, 1899), 631–632, 685–686.
33. *Houston Daily Post*, July 11, 1899, March 13, 1902.
34. Ibid., March 14, 1902. The experience apparently caused no lasting harm, since Potter was still alive in 1906 when he won an appeal case to force the city to pay $1,200 still owed to him for the system (*Houston Post*, January 19, 1906).
35. *Houston Post*, July 19, 1905.
36. Ibid., April 30, October 19, 1916.
37. *Houston Daily Post*, September 11, 16, 1902.
38. Ibid., June 13, 23, 1903.
39. *Houston Post*, December 22, 1903.
40. Ibid., December 28, 1903, January 27, 31, 1904.
41. Ibid., October 2, 1904, September 24, 1905.
42. Ibid., January 28, 1906.
43. Ibid., February 11, 1906.
44. Minutes of the City Council, P (May 14, 1906–December 18, 1911), 65; *Houston Post*, June 22, 1906; *Houston Chronicle*, June 21, 1906.
45. *Houston Post*, November 22, 1908, November 6, 1921.
46. Ibid., September 1, 1910.
47. Ibid., September 6, 1907, May 7, 1908.
48. Ibid., December 22, 1909.
49. Minutes of the City Council, M (May 19, 1902–July 1, 1903), 356–357; *Houston Daily Post*, May 13, 1902.
50. *Houston Daily Post*, January 6, 1903.
51. Ibid., September 12, December 10, 1902, August 2, 1903; *Houston Post*, June 11, 1904, December 7, 1905.
52. *Houston Daily Post*, October 22, 1902.
53. Ibid., November 5, 1902.
54. *Houston Post*, December 4, 11, 1904; *Houston Chronicle*, December 11, 1904.
55. *Houston Post*, December 4, 7, 1904; *Houston Chronicle*, December 4, 1904.
56. *Houston Post*, February 12, 1905; *Houston Chronicle*, February 12, 1905.
57. Minutes of the City Council, O (July 18, 1904–May 7, 1906), 438–442; *Houston Post*, March 19, 23, April 2–3, 16, May 7, June 28, July 6, 1905.
58. *Houston Post*, December 17, 1906; H. J. Haskell, "City Government by a Board of Directors," *Outlook*, April 13, 1907, pp. 839–843.
59. Annual Report of the City Controller for the Year Ending December 31, 1904, varied paging (in a bound volume); Annual Report of the City Controller for the Year Ending February 28, 1907, varied paging (in a bound volume).
60. *Houston Post*, July 3, 1906.
61. Ibid., March 1, 1917; *Houston Post-Dispatch*, September 30, 1927, December 5, 1928, October 2, 1929.
62. Minutes of the City Council, A (June 8, 1840–January 11, 1847), 203;

Tri-Weekly Telegraph, February 25, 1857; *Houston Daily Post*, October 24, 1891.

63. *Houston Daily Post*, January 14, 1892 (letter to the editor).
64. Ibid., June 25, 1899, August 3, 1902; *Houston Post*, July 5, 1907, December 14, 1966. In 1968 Brownie, after years spent in storage, found an honored place in the Children's Zoo of Hermann Park.
65. *Houston Post*, May 21, 1905, July 20, 1907, June 15, 1912, February 21, June 7, 1914, May 15, 1924.
66. Ibid., April 30, 1922.
67. Ibid., December 7, 1907.
68. *Houston Daily Telegram*, June 12, 1878.
69. Ibid., June 18, 1878; *Daily Post*, July 1, 1883.
70. *Houston Daily Post*, July 12, 1895, April 28, 1901; *Houston Post-Dispatch*, September 28, 1927.
71. *Houston Post*, November 16, 1920.
72. *Daily Post*, June 7, 1882.
73. *Houston Post*, June 20, 1884, March 7, 1915.
74. For a review of the electric utility in Houston, see *Origins and History of Houston Lighting and Power Company*.
75. *Houston Daily Post*, September 21, 1892.
76. Ibid., August 20, 1902; *Houston Post*, October 15, 1909, August 20, 1911.
77. *Houston Post*, July 26–27, 1911.
78. Arthur C. Comey, *Houston*, pp. 1–83.
79. Frank Putnam, *City Government in Europe*, p. 14.
80. Ibid., pp. 15–18.
81. Ibid., p. 17.
82. *Houston Post*, October 17, 1913.
83. Ibid., June 29, September 11, October 30, 1922.
84. *Houston Post-Dispatch*, April 13, 17, June 26, July 1, 1927; Houston City Planning Commission, *Comprehensive Plan—Houston Urban Area*, 1a:31.
85. *Houston Post-Dispatch*, July 1, 1927.
86. "The Drab Side of Houston," *Civics for Houston* 1 (September 1928): 5.
87. *Houston Post-Dispatch*, April 13, 1927.
88. Ibid., November 23–25, 27, December 2, 1928; *Houston Chronicle*, November 23, 1928.
89. *Houston Post-Dispatch*, October 31, 1929.
90. Ibid., January 27, 1925, January 2, 1929.
91. Ibid., March 2, 1926.
92. Writers' Program, *Houston*, pp. 258–284.
93. *Houston Daily Post*, August 31, 1900.
94. Timmons, *Jones*, pp. 11, 50, 64–67, 73, 77, 79, 81, 83, 119.
95. *Houston Daily Post*, October 1, 1890, September 17, October 17, November 18, 1893, March 18, 1894, March 30, 1909, February 25, 1910, April 2, 1911; *Houston Post-Dispatch*, January 16, 1927, December 8, 1929.

96. Don Riddle, *River Oaks; Living in River Oaks;* Howard Barnstone, *The Architecture of John F. Staub,* p. 12.
97. *Report of the City Planning Commission,* pp. 31–127.
98. Ibid., p. 122.
99. *Houston Post-Dispatch,* December 14, 29, 1929, January 1, 1930.
100. Ibid., January 8, 1930; *Houston Chronicle,* January 7, 1930.
101. *Houston Daily Post,* December 4, 1891, October 9, 1892.
102. Ibid., September 19, 1897, November 17, 1899; Hatch, *Lyceum to Library,* pp. 43–44.
103. *Houston Post,* March 3, 1904; Hatch, *Lyceum to Library,* pp. 45–49.
104. *Houston Post,* September 4, 1920.
105. Ibid., August 4, 1886, January 31, 1896, November 22, 1903, March 31, 1906, January 16, February 20, December 5, 1915, February 22, 1919, March 21, 1922, February 2, 1923; *Houston Daily Post,* March 1–2, 1900.
106. *Houston Chronicle,* June 22, 1913; *Houston Post,* December 14, 1913; *Houston Post-Dispatch,* December 31, 1931; "Symphony Society," *Houston* 22 (February 1948): 12–13.
107. *Houston Daily Post,* December 6, 1900.
108. *Houston Post,* March 17–18, 1905, August 23, 1958.
109. Ibid., December 19, 1907, January 19, 1908.
110. Ibid., January 14, 1917, September 30, 1923; *Houston Post-Dispatch,* June 2, 14, August 17–18, 1925.
111. *Houston Post,* July 2, 1907, October 21, 1914, May 3, 1915, August 20, 1916, February 19, 1922, February 23, 1923; "Harvest in Houston," *Time,* March 30, 1953, p. 68; Writers' Program, *Houston,* pp. 306–310.
112. *Houston Daily Post,* May 19, 1891.
113. Ibid., September 25, October 5, 1900, April 3–4, 1901, March 27, April 8, 1902, July 24, 1903; *Houston Post,* August 28, 1905, January 28, December 21, 1906, November 28, 1912.
114. *Houston Post,* September 1, 1912.
115. Ibid., December 29, 1907, May 9, 16, August 29, 1909, September 1, 1910, September 1, 1911, April 13, 1953; Writers' Program, *Houston,* p. 319. Lovett, who was thirty-seven years old and a vigorous man when chosen president, supposedly walked daily to and from his residence in the Rice Hotel and the campus. On September 15, 1967, I duplicated this walk, one way. At a moderately fast pace, with some waiting at traffic lights, it took sixty-five minutes to reach the campus from downtown.
116. *Houston Post,* September 1, 1911, October 13, 1912, October 1, 1951; John Burchard and Albert Bush-Brown, *The Architecture of America,* p. 315.
117. *Houston Post,* June 14, 1916, January 13, 1946; "The Rice Institute," *Tangent* 2 (October 1912): 5.
118. *Houston Post,* April 13, 1953.
119. The *Houston Post* referred to Rice as the "Harvard of the South" as

early as June 26, 1928. The appellation has remained to the present time. The Rice team was known as the "Grays" for the first few years (ibid., November 18, 1913).

120. Ibid., November 16, 1920, October 21, 1922.

121. Ibid., May 8, June 11, 1923; *Rules and Regulations*, see Foreword by William E. Moreland; Keller, "A History of Public Education in Houston, Texas," p. 65.

122. *Houston Post-Dispatch*, February 9, 1927; Board of Education, *High Spots in Houston Public Schools*, unpaged.

123. *Houston Post*, December 31, 1932, May 1, 1934.

124. E. E. Oberholtzer, "Houston . . . Passes Rigid School Test," *Houston* 2 (September 1931): 4.

125. *Houston Post*, May 19, 21, June 10, September 3, 1922; *Houston Post-Dispatch*, May 10, October 12, 1925, May 9, 1926, September 23, October 14, 1927, December 29, 1929; Writers' Program, *Houston*, pp. 209–210; Eroll R. Bogy, *Houston in Brief*, p. 58.

126. *Houston Post*, April 16, 1923.

127. Ibid., July 21, 1912; *Houston Daily Post*, July 14, 1894.

128. *Houston Daily Post*, September 5–6, 1891, July 26, 31, August 24–25, 1895, August 26, 1897.

129. Ibid., November 30, 1886.

130. Ibid., December 30, 1891, November 15, 1896, November 7, 1897, October 8, 1902.

131. *Houston Post*, May 26, 1904, April 19, 1908, December 21, 1913, March 8, 1914, March 18, 1922, April 21, 1934; *Houston Post-Dispatch*, April 12, 1928. According to Harry M. Johnston, a long-time fan, the term "Texas Leaguer" originated in Houston when a young man named Pickering arrived in a box car and so impressed the local coach that he played the same afternoon. He hit seven for seven, each a pop ball just over the infielders and out of reach of the outfielders. Pickering, supposedly, went on to play for the Philadelphia Athletics (*Houston Post*, July 10, 1904).

132. *Houston Post*, May 8, 1907.

133. Ibid., February 22, 1910.

134. Ibid., December 13, 1910, September 19, 1911.

135. Ibid., December 13, 1910.

136. Ibid., February 20, 1924.

137. Ibid., March 26, 1924.

138. *Houston Post-Dispatch*, April 12, 1929. In 1969 ministers and religiously oriented people picketed the Heights Theatre which was showing the movie *I Am Curious-Yellow*. There were incidents involving a stink bomb, Ku Klux Klan literature, a bomb scare, and a three-alarm fire which destroyed the theater (see *Houston Post*, May 25, June 7, 1969). Years later after a jury failed to reach a verdict about the movie *Deep Throat*, the police, by and large, limited themselves to pornography involving animals or children (see *Houston Post*, March 26, 1977).

139. *Houston Daily Post,* October 22, 29, November 12, 1894.
140. Ibid., November 19, 1894.
141. Ibid., November 26, 1894.
142. G. C. Rankin, *The Story of My Life,* p. 327.
143. *Houston Daily Post,* February 2, 1896, September 5, November 24, 1897; *Houston Post,* January 1, 1890, October 31, 1905, August 31, 1907, March 19, 1911, December 8, 1912, July 30, August 1, December 2, 1919, January 12, 14, 1923; Jacob Riis, *How the Other Half Lives.*
144. *Houston Post,* December 7, 9–10, 1911.
145. *Houston Post-Dispatch,* November 1, 1924.
146. *Houston Daily Post,* September 17, 1905; *Houston Post,* May 8, 1968; Ordinances of the City of Houston, 2 (August 7, 1903–October 27, 1910), 237.
147. *Houston Daily Post,* October 9, 1905. In 1912 Oliver Cash, a black, was fined $34.45 in Corporation Court under this ordinance for flirting with a white girl. Cash proclaimed innocence, but the girl and a friend testified to the contrary (*Houston Post,* March 30, 1912).
148. *Houston Daily Post,* March 20, 1892, May 10, 1900, February 18, March 7, September 8, 15, 1901.
149. *Houston Chronicle,* October 21, 1902.
150. *Houston Post,* December 31, 1905, January 1, 1906, September 20, 1966 (see Leon Hale's column); Andrew Forest Muir, "The Night Carry Nation Smashed a Houston Saloon," *Texas Tempo Sunday Magazine, Houston Post,* January 7, 1968, pp. 16–17.
151. *Houston Post,* December 5, 1917, February 7, February 22, April 14, 1918, May 25, 1919.
152. Ibid., March 27, 1920, September 9, November 29, 1921, March 30, November 24, 1923, February 29, 1924; *Houston Post-Dispatch,* September 20, 1925, March 27, 1926, July 1, 3, December 29, 1927.
153. Minutes of the City Council, E, 98.
154. Richard C. Wade, *Slavery in the Cities,* p. 75.
155. *Houston Daily Telegraph,* July 1, 1876.
156. Charles Orson Cook, "John Milsaps' Houston: 1910," *Houston Review* 1 (Spring 1979): 41.
157. *Report of the City Planning Commission,* p. 25.
158. *Houston Daily Telegraph,* June 20, 1876; *Houston Daily Post,* October 26, 1880, November 12, 1887, May 5, 1888, September 19, 1891, July 26, 1896.
159. *Houston Daily Post,* December 12, 1900.
160. *Houston Post,* December 10, 1910, November 15, 1914.
161. *Houston Daily Post,* September 12, 1900, April 27, May 4, 1901.
162. *Houston Post,* April 12, 1913.
163. Webb, *Handbook of Texas,* 2:764–765.
164. *Houston Daily Post,* November 18, 1894, August 14, 1898.
165. Ibid., March 14, 1891.
166. Ibid., February 27, 1900.

167. Ibid., November 25, 1900.
168. *Houston Post,* July 13, August 30, 1913.
169. Ibid., June 2, 1921, June 4, 1933; "Correspondence—Cooped," *Nation,* July 13, 1928, p. 63; Charles J. Hill, *A Brief History of ILA Local 872,* p. 10.
170. *Houston Post,* June 28, 1909.
171. Ibid., April 18, 1882, September 21, 1883.
172. *Houston Daily Post,* July 31, 1891.
173. Minutes of the City Council, N (July 6, 1903–July 11, 1904), 70, 91, 130; Ordinances of the City of Houston, 2:25–27; *Houston Daily Post,* September 1, 1903; *Houston Post,* November 1–2, 1903.
174. J. G. Hautier, comp., *Revised Code of Ordinances of the City of Houston of 1922,* p. 730, sec. 1583b; p. 1435, sec. 1434.
175. *Houston Post,* July 5, 1910; *Houston Chronicle,* July 7, 1910.
176. *Houston Post,* April 6, 1915, October 22, 1921.
177. Ibid., June 12, August 22, September 20, 1917, October 31, 1918.
178. Ibid., August 29–30, 1917; C. D. Waide, "When Psychology Failed," *Houston Gargoyle,* May 15, 1928, pp. 5–6; Robert V. Haynes, "The Houston Mutiny and Riot of 1917," *Southwestern Historical Quarterly* 76 (April 1973): 424–425.
179. *Houston Post,* August 30, 1917; Waide, "When Psychology Failed," May 15, 1928, p. 6.
180. Haynes, "The Houston Mutiny and Riot," pp. 428–430.
181. *Houston Post,* August 24, 26, 1917, February 28, 1918.
182. Ibid., August 25, 1917; Robert V. Haynes, *A Night of Violence,* pp. 167–169.
183. *Houston Post,* August 24, 1917.
184. Ibid., August 25, 1917.
185. Haynes, *A Night of Violence,* pp. 322–323; Waide, "When Psychology Failed," June 12, 1928, p. 10.
186. Charles C. Alexander, *Crusade for Conformity,* pp. 4–5.
187. *Houston Post,* November 28, 1920, February 7, March 13, 19, June 29, September 4, December 11, 1921; *Houston Post-Dispatch,* March 19, 1925; interview with Richard T. Fleming, July 30, 1968.
188. *Houston Post,* December 27–28, 1922; *Houston Post-Dispatch,* March 26, 1925; Frank M. Stewart, "Mayor Oscar F. Holcombe of Houston," *National Municipal Review* 17 (June 1928): 317–321.
189. Alexander, *Crusade for Conformity,* pp. 10–12, 17; interview with Richard T. Fleming, July 30, 1968; Linda Elaine Kilgore, "The Ku Klux Klan and the Press in Texas, 1920–1927," p. 40. In 1915, an estimated 18,000 people saw, in thirteen performances, D. W. Griffith's *The Birth of a Nation,* a film which glorified the Ku Klux Klan (*Houston Post,* October 19, 24, 1915).
190. *Daily Post,* March 20, 1883.
191. *Houston Daily Post,* July 10, 1900.
192. *Houston Post-Dispatch,* June 18, 21–22, October 8, 1928, December

22, March 24, 1929; *Houston Chronicle,* December 22, 1929.

193. *Houston Daily Post,* January 14, 1892, January 26, September 4, 1893, July 22, 1894.

194. Ibid., March 4, 1894; *Houston Post,* November 29, 1910, February 4, 1912.

195. *Houston Daily Post,* November 7, 1896, August 29, 1897, January 28, 1900, October 14, 1901.

196. *Houston Post,* March 8, 1908, September 1, 1910, April 5, 1914, October 3, 1919.

197. *The Red Book of Houston,* p. 3. This directory lists black professional people, shopkeepers, merchants, artisans, contractors, and so on, which indicates a self-sufficient community.

6. SPACE CITY, U.S.A.

1. Rostow, *Stages of Economic Growth,* p. 9.

2. *Houston Post-Dispatch,* November 24, 1931. For a discussion of city administrative problems, see William Edward Montgomery, "The Depression in Houston during the Hoover Era, 1929–1932."

3. Franklin O. Thompson, "Houston Makes Giant Strides," *Houston* 7 (January 1937): 9; Marsha Guant Berryman, "Houston and the Early Depression: 1929–1932," p. 66.

4. *Houston Post,* August 13, 23, October 15, 1932; Montgomery, "Depression in Houston," p. 153.

5. Crawford Williams, "Here's a Houston Firm You Should Know," *Houston* 6 (June 1935): 27.

6. "WPA Aids Deserving, $4,245,000 Spent in Houston Area," *Houston* 7 (October 1936): 8–9.

7. Writers' Program, *Houston,* p. 119; Berryman, "Houston and the Early Depression," pp. 19–23; Montgomery, "Depression in Houston," p. 137.

8. *Houston Post,* December 30, 1939; Thomson, "Houston Makes Giant Strides," p. 9; Timmons, *Jones,* pp. 156–159.

9. "Jesse Holman Jones," *Houston* 11 (October 1940): 2.

10. "A Washington Columnist Pays Jesse H. Jones a Real Tribute," *Houston* 16 (June 1944): 26.

11. *Houston Post,* November 28, 1939.

12. Ibid., September 18, 1934, August 18, 1935. The lack of historical sites around Dallas prompted a Houston book store to market a booklet, *Historic Landmarks in and around Dallas and Vicinity: A Descriptive Guide for the Visitors to the Texas Centennial.* Inside were thirty blank pages.

13. *Houston Post,* June 2, 1956.

14. Ibid., December 12, 1935, March 12, 1936.

15. The *Houston Post* (July 22, 1936) reported loans and grants to Houston totaling $3,878,162. This led the state, with Fort Worth second at $1,148,977.

16. Berryman, "Houston and the Early Depression," p. 84.
17. *Houston Post*, November 26, 1933.
18. Ibid., June 14, 1936.
19. Ibid., June 19, 1936, May 12, 1937; Writers' Program, *Houston*, pp. 148–149.
20. *Houston Post*, September 28, 1940; "Additional Air Service," *Houston* 7 (September 1936): 18; "A Great Airport Completed," *Houston* 11 (June 1940): 13–14; "Houston's Municipal Airport Formally Dedicated," *Houston* 11 (October 1940): 25.
21. *Houston Post*, May 23, 1946; "International Air Gateway," *Houston* 18 (June 1946): 6.
22. *Houston Post*, November 30, 1946.
23. A. W. Snyder, "Twenty Years of Aviation Progress," *Houston* 21 (November 1947): 20–22; Claude B. Barrett, "Houston—Growing Air Center," *Houston* 22 (November 1951): 12; "A Growing Industry—in the Air," *Houston* 37 (August 1966): 63.
24. *Houston Post*, October 30, 1954, March 13, 1955, June 1, 1967.
25. Ibid., March 13, 1955.
26. Ibid., November 21, 1956, March 16, 1961; "Houston Goes Dutch," *Houston* 28 (May 1957): 59–60; "Victory in Air Power," *Houston* 32 (April 1961): 52–53.
27. "What We Need—And Why," *Houston* 30 (April 1959): 84, 86–87, 89–90, 92; *Southern Transcontinental Service Case, Exhibits before the U.S. Civil Aeronautics Board, Docket No. 7984 et al.*, varied paging.
28. "Reach for the Sky," *Houston* 28 (November 1957): 81–82.
29. "Jetero Site Landed," *Houston* 31 (August 1960): 50; *Houston Post*, June 13, 1969.
30. "Jetero Groundbreaking," *Houston* 33 (September 1962): 76–77; "A Growing Industry—in the Air," pp. 62–63; *Houston Post*, April 30, 1964, June 2, 8, July 20, 1969.
31. "Comparative Statistics, Port of Houston," *Houston* 20 (May 1949): 7.
32. Sibley, *Port of Houston*, p. 175.
33. *Houston Post-Dispatch*, November 3, 1930, October 1, 1931; *Houston Post*, May 12, June 1, 1934, October 14, December 13, 1935, November 23, December 30, 1936; Sibley, *Port of Houston*, pp. 176–178; Hill, *A Brief History of ILA Local 872*, pp. 13–14.
34. "Extensive Port Improvements Planned for 1932," *Houston* 3 (February 1932): 27; Sibley, *Port of Houston*, p. 184.
35. "New Channel Improvement Assures Added Business," *Houston* 6 (July 1935): 26–27; "Usable Depth 34 Feet Assured Ship Channel," *Houston* 6 (September 1935): 25.
36. Sibley, *Port of Houston*, p. 184.
37. Ibid., p. 191.
38. Ibid., p. 196.
39. *Houston Post*, October 26, 1946; *The World Almanac and Book of Facts, 1945*, ed. E. Eastman Irvine, p. 384; "Port Houston Second in U.S.," *Houston* 20 (January 1950): 24.

40. George K. Reeder, "The Port's Salesman," *Houston* 22 (May 1951): 13, 57; Sibley, *Port of Houston*, p. 181.
41. *Houston Post*, April 10, 1955; "Clearing Decks for Action," *Houston* 27 (November 1956): 88, 91.
42. *Houston Chronicle*, February 1, 1957; Sibley, *Port of Houston*, pp. 202–204.
43. "A Port Fights Back," *Houston* 29 (June 1958): 69; *Texas Almanac, 1978–1979*, pp. 304, 552; *Houston Post*, August 30, 1980.
44. Sibley, *Port of Houston*, pp. 4, 204.
45. *Houston Post*, January 29–30, 1962; "World Trade Center," *Houston* 33 (February 1962): 64.
46. *Houston Post*, April 11, 1955, July 16, 1960.
47. Warren Rose, *The Economic Impact of the Port of Houston, 1958–1963*, pp. 1–3.
48. Houston Chamber of Commerce, *Houston Facts '80*, p. 3; "Where Houston's Ships Come In," *Houston* 37 (August 1966): 22–23.
49. Rose, *Economic Impact of Port*, p. 5.
50. *Houston Post*, January 27, 1975.
51. "18 Railroads Which Meet the Sea," *Houston* 22 (November 1951): 8–9; Reed, "A Romance of the Rails," pp. 12, 35.
52. *Houston Post*, June 4, 1933, September 2, 1934, February 16, 1956; "So-Pac Pulls 'Switch,'" *Houston* 27 (February 1956): 95–97.
53. *Houston Post*, June 1, 1950; "Central Industrial Park," *Houston* 34 (August 1963): 58; "Clear the Tracks," *Houston* 34 (January 1964): 22–23.
54. *Texas Almanac, 1966–1967*, p. 499.
55. *Houston Post*, July 7, 1967.
56. Martin Dreyer, "An Era Ends for Old Union Station," *Texas Tempo Sunday Magazine, Houston Post*, September 24, 1967, p. 5; *Houston Post*, August 1, 1974.
57. "Trucking Transport," *Houston* 33 (January 1963): 19–20.
58. Dorothy Jewett, "Highways De Luxe," *Houston* 9 (November 1938): 62–64.
59. "Passenger Buses of Today," *Houston* 21 (November 1947): 33, 35, 37; "Nine Modern Bus Lines Serve City," *Houston* 21 (January 1951): 19, 57, 59, 60 (volume numbers were revised January–February 1949).
60. *Houston Post*, June 30, 1933; "Setting the Pace," *Houston* 28 (July 1957): 80–81; "Trucking Transport," pp. 19–21.
61. *Report of the City Planning Commission* (1929), p. 61.
62. Earl J. Reader, *Houston Traffic Survey, City of Houston, 1939*, pp. 67–68.
63. *Houston Post*, February 20, 1941.
64. Ibid., March 29, 1940, April 9, 1941, November 22, 1945; "Nine Surveys Made to Locate Tunnels," *Houston* 17 (February 1945): 27.
65. *Houston Post*, February 24, May 16, November 28, 1948.
66. Ibid., May 28, 1950; "New Highway Tunnel Is South's Largest: Washburn Tunnel," *American City* 65 (July 1950): 72.
67. W. J. Van London, "Modern Expressways Under Way in Houston,"

Houston 21 (November 1947): 19; "100-mph Zone Ahead," *Houston* 31 (November 1960): 44, 47; *Houston Post*, August 2, 1952, March 16, 1969.

68. *Houston Post*, November 23, 30, 1952, April 14, 1953.
69. Ibid., June 30, July 8, 1956.
70. "Where Do We Stand," *Houston* 28 (July 1957): 68–71.
71. "Freeway Give-Away," *Houston* 28 (November 1957): 67.
72. Department of Traffic and Transportation, *Economic Evaluation of the Gulf Freeway*, p. 19.
73. *Houston Post*, July 11, 1954.
74. Ibid., August 14, 1955.
75. Richard Stanley, "Three Decades of Freeways, and Still Pouring," *Houston* 50 (May 1979): 14.
76. *Texas Almanac and State Industrial Guide, 1941–1942*, p. 271; *Texas Almanac and State Industrial Guide, 1951–1952*, p. 276; *Texas Almanac, 1966–1967*, p. 268; Houston Chamber of Commerce, *Houston Facts '80*, p. 1.
77. *Houston Post*, December 12, 1973.
78. Ibid., March 3, 1973.
79. Ibid., July 8, 1971.
80. Ibid., May 12, 13, July 21, 1976.
81. Ibid., June 20, 1980.
82. Ibid., December 2, 1973, January 31, February 22, 1974, March 20, June 20, 23, July 3, 1979.
83. Ibid., March 22, 1973, June 24, 1979.
84. Ibid., April 2, 1953, August 1, September 26, 1954, January 26, 1958.
85. Ibid., August 2, 1954.
86. Ibid., February 10, 1961, May 18, July 7, October 15, 1965, February 10, 1966; "Buses on the Move," *Houston* 33 (April 1962): 58–59.
87. *Houston Post*, October 5, 1973.
88. Ibid., October 10, 1973, December 21, 1974, March 13, 1975, November 24, 1976, January 19, 1977.
89. Ibid., October 8, 1975.
90. Ibid., March 1, August 11, 1977.
91. Ibid., August 13, October 1, December 19, 1978, August 27, September 10, 1979, June 21, 1980.
92. Ibid., March 2, 1980.
93. U.S. Bureau of the Census, *County and City Data Book, 1967*, pp. 3, 6, 441, 444, 446, 447, 555, 557, 558, 560; idem, *County and City Data Book, 1977*, pp. 565–567; idem, *Statistical Abstract of the United States, 1979*, pp. 804, 830, 838, 841.
94. John R. Suman, "Amazing Facts about Texas Oil Industry," *Houston* 6 (May 1935): 19.
95. *Houston Post-Dispatch*, December 1, 1930.
96. John R. Suman, "Importance of Oil and Gas Industry to Houston," *Houston* 11 (April 1940): 50–52.
97. *Houston Post*, September 19, October 22, 25, 1940; "Thousands Attend

as Humble Celebrates," *Houston* 16 (January 1945): 24.

98. *Houston Post,* May 8, 1941; "$265,000,000 for Gulf Coast," *Houston* 12 (February 1941): 6–7.

99. "Now Comes Rubber," *Houston* 14 (June 1943): 26–27; James C. Kiper, "Monsanto Supplies Styrene," *Houston* 14 (July 1943): 28–29.

100. *Houston Post,* June 28, 1943; "Sinclair's $24,000,000 Butadiene Plant," *Houston* 14 (July 1943): 46–47; "Goodyear Rubber Plant Opens November 17," *Houston* 15 (December 1943): 32.

101. Lewis B. Reynolds, "Big Chemical Companies Spending $300 Million on the Gulf Coast," *Houston* 19 (April 1947): 53–54; "The Unusual Development of Chemicals on the Gulf Coast of Texas," *Houston* 22 (June 1948): 6–8, 10.

102. "Plastics: Will They Boost the Boom?" *Houston* 28 (April 1957): 17.

103. "Money in the Spaghetti Bowl," *Houston* 29 (April 1958): 16–17.

104. *Houston Post,* February 13, 1966; "Test Tube Riches," *Houston* 37 (February 1966): 26–27.

105. *Houston Post,* March 4, 1957; Brown Booth, "Texas Gas Goes East," *Houston* 22 (October 1948): 13; "Houston Billionaire," *Houston* 37 (September 1966): 42.

106. "Big and Little Inch Pipe Lines Purchased," *Houston* 20 (March 1947): 37; "Texas Gas Now in the Chips," *Houston* 21 (October 1950): 40.

107. "Down the Long Lines," *Houston* 37 (December 1966): 90–92.

108. *Houston Post,* May 28, 1941; "$17,000,000 Steel Mill for Houston," *Houston* 12 (February 1941): 2.

109. J. C. Shepherd, "Houston and Steel," *Houston* 14 (April 1944): 6.

110. "Steel: Strip-mine to Strip-mill," *Houston* 27 (July 1956): 68, 70–72.

111. "Tough & Growing," *Houston* 37 (February 1966): 23–25.

112. *Houston Post,* January 14, July 19, 1940.

113. "No. 1 Industry," *Houston* 14 (April 1943): 7.

114. *Houston Post,* May 5, 1947; Anthony Gibbon, "Creator of Cargo Ships," *Houston* 14 (June 1943): 10–11, 46–47.

115. *Houston Post,* May 5, 1947, February 3, June 9, 1960; "Todd Shipbuilding Corp. Returns," *Houston* 20 (May 1949): 35.

116. "No. 1 Industry," p. 7.

117. Ibid., pp. 7, 9; "Brown Builds Ships for the Navy," *Houston* 14 (June 1943): 6–7; "300th Warship Built by Brown Launched," *Houston* 17 (April 1945): 27.

118. *Houston Post,* April 22, August 6, 1943.

119. Ibid., December 8, 1940.

120. "McEvoy Makes Tripods," *Houston* 12 (June 1941): 13.

121. "Cameron Iron Works Honored," *Houston* 12 (August 1941): 22.

122. "Double Feature in Houston," *Time,* February 15, 1943, p. 80.

123. *Houston Post,* February 7, June 14, 1941; "114,000 Employed in Houston's Busy Industrial Plants," *Houston* 14 (April 1943): 4.

124. *Texas Almanac, 1966–1967,* p. 135; Scott, "Houston Banks Grow," p. 6; "Houston: Southwest Money Market," *Houston* 35 (October 1964): 63.

125. "Houston 'Tops' Industrially," *Houston* 20 (April 1949): 24; "Houston

Leads Nation in Per Capita Building," *Houston* 20 (April 1949): 8.

126. "Booming Houston," *Life*, October 21, 1946, p. 108.

127. *Houston Post*, February 17, 1946, October 21, 1947; "$6,000,000 Foley Bros. Home," *Houston* 18 (June 1945): 17; "Federated Foley's," *Newsweek*, November 3, 1947, pp. 60–62; "Mr. Fred of the Lazari," *Fortune* 37 (March 1948): 108–115ff (reprinted courtesy of *Fortune* magazine and Mr. Lazarus); "Sears $1,000,000 Store Opens Soon," *Houston* 10 (November 1939): 10.

128. *Houston Post*, September 18, 1947, June 17, 1955; "An Enlarged and Modernized Fashion Greets Public," *Houston* 21 (September 1947): 31.

129. "Now It's Joske's," *Houston* 22 (September 1948): 26–27; "$8,000,000 New Home Underway for Sakowitz," *Houston* 20 (September 1949): 29, 76; "The New Battelstein's Formally Opens in March," *Houston* 21 (March 1950): 10–11, 36.

130. "Woolworth Store Opens," *Houston* 20 (November 1949): 14–16, 50.

131. "Mr. Fred of the Lazari," p. 174.

132. "Metropolitan America: How It's Changed since '39," *Sales Management*, November 10, 1950, pp. 164–172.

133. *Houston Post*, August 23, 1953; "Battelstein's Opens River Oaks Store," *Houston* 24 (August 1953): 20–22.

134. *Houston Post*, April 10, 1955, September 16, 1956; "$12,000,000 Gulfgate to Soon Get Underway," *Houston* 24 (June 1953): 36. The Gulfgate Corporation announced the development of Northline, an eighty-acre center in the northern part of town in 1955 (*Houston Chronicle*, March 27, 1955).

135. *Houston Post*, March 24, 1959; "Booming Gulf Surf," *Houston* 27 (November 1956): 40.

136. *Houston Post*, September 14, 1961. Frank Wesley Sharp, a prominent Houston homebuilder, started Sharpstown in 1954, which, at the time, with a projected 25,000 homes in a $400 million planned community, was the largest subdivision in the United States. Covering 6,500 acres west of Bellaire, Sharpstown consisted mainly of three-bedroom brick houses valued in 1956 at an average price of $14,500. See *Houston Post*, August 6, 1954, January 1, 1956; "Blooming Prairie; Sharpstown," *Newsweek*, March 21, 1955, pp. 88–90.

137. *Houston Post*, August 1, July 21, 1963, July 30, November 12, 1967, January 26, 28, 1969.

138. *CBD Today*, p. 18.

139. Houston Chamber of Commerce, *Houston Facts '80*, p. 2.

140. *Houston Post*, February 14, 1980.

141. Ibid., October 12, 1947, July 6, 1953, October 18, 1955.

142. Ibid., June 14, 1956, June 29, 1959.

143. Ibid., February 5, 1961; "Monument to Money," *Houston* 32 (March 1961): 40–41.

144. *Houston Post*, July 4, 1962; "Togetherness for Federal Offices," *Houston* 30 (December 1959): 35.

145. *Houston Post*, December 6, 1959, March 1, 1963, July 26, 1959, March

31, December 22, 1963; "Opening: Cullen Center," *Houston* 34 (March 1963): 38; "Southwest's Tallest Skyscraper," *Houston* 34 (April 1963): 34; "Open: The New Tennessee Building," *Houston* 34 (June 1963): 75; "Office Space Race," *Houston* 34 (December 1963): 23–25.

146. *Houston Post*, August 1, 1965, April 12, 1966, August 15, 1969. The most prominent architects of the city before the 1970's were Kenneth Franzheim (1890–1959), who designed the Bank of the Southwest, Texas National Bank, Police Administration Building, Woolworth's downtown, Foley's, Prudential Building, Hermann Professional Building, and the Blaffer Wing of the Fine Arts Museum; and Alfred C. Finn (1884–1964), who worked on the Gulf Building, Rice Hotel, National Bank of Commerce, Ezekiel Cullen Building, Sam Houston Coliseum, Music Hall, San Jacinto Monument, and Crippled Children's Hospital (*Houston Post*, March 17, 1959, June 27, 1964). Jean Gottmann offers a general explanation for the existence of large office buildings in "Why the Skyscraper?" *Geographical Review* 56 (April 1966): 190–212.

147. *Houston Post*, April 26, October 11, 1970.

148. "Better Luck This Time," *Forbes*, August 6, 1979, p. 78.

149. *Houston Post*, June 18, December 5, 1972, November 13, 1977, July 23, 1978, June 4, 10, August 31, 1980.

150. Gay McFarland, "The Good, the Bad and the Ugly," *Houston* 46 (August 1975): 12.

151. *Houston Post*, May 6, 1956; "Million Dollar Laboratory Being Built Here by Shell," *Houston* 17 (November 1945): 10.

152. *Houston Post*, January 27, 1951; "Humble Oil Research Center to Open Jan. 1st," *Houston* 24 (November 1953): 66.

153. *Houston Post*, May 13, 1945, February 19, 1948.

154. John W. Mecom, oilman, bought the Warwick in 1962 for $1.4 million at public auction. He spent $11 million remodeling, filled the hotel with art treasures, placed a glass elevator on the side, and reopened for permanent and transient guests in 1964. To enhance the beauty of the environment, Mecom donated a three-tiered fountain to the city for the intersection of Main and Montrose streets (*Houston Post*, February 20, May 17, 1962, September 11, 1963; "Objet d'Art," *Houston* 35 [November 1964]: 36).

155. *Houston Post*, October 24, 1944.

156. Ibid., March 22, 1946; "$16,000,000 Community Center to be Built," *Houston* 17 (June 1945): 26.

157. *Houston Post*, March 17–18, 1949; program and menu, Glenn McCarthy Biography File; "Shamrock Opens," *Houston* 20 (February 1949): 6 ff.

158. *Houston Post*, March 18, 1949; "$21 Million Hotel Opens: Shamrock," *Life*, March 28, 1949, pp. 27–31; "Big Time in Houston: Opening of the Shamrock Hotel," *Fortune* 39 (May 1949): 80–82; "Shamrock Opens with a Bang," *Newsweek*, March 28, 1949, pp. 64–66.

159. "Shamrock Opens with a Bang," p. 66; "$21 Million Hotel Opens,"

p. 28; "Big Time in Houston," p. 80; "Texas: King of the Wildcatters," *Time*, February 13, 1950, p. 18.

160. *Houston Post*, October 23, 1953; George Fuermann, *Houston: Land of the Big Rich*, p. 70.

161. "Shamrock Opens with a Bang," p. 66; "$21 Million Hotel Opens," p. 27; "Big Time in Houston," p. 80.

162. *Houston Post*, May 15, 18, 1950.

163. Ibid., November 1–2, 1951.

164. Ibid., August 3, November 13, 1954, May 3, 15, 1955, October 6, 1956; "Hilton Rides Again," *Time*, April 9, 1954, p. 71. In 1965 Associated Brands, Inc., McCarthy chairman, marketed Wildcatter, a ninety-proof bourbon, and in 1967 McCarthy, with his son, Glenn, Jr., hit his first wildcat well in over a decade (*Houston Post*, March 5, 1965, July 2, 1967).

165. *Houston Post*, March 31, 1950; "Prudential to Build $6,000,000 Home," *Houston* 21 (April 1950): 6, 27, 96.

166. *Houston Post*, July 28, 29, 1952; "Southwest's Prudential," *Houston* 23 (July 1952): 28.

167. "Fannin Bank: A 'Texas-Size Annex,'" *Houston* 34 (April 1963): 50; "Ten on Eleven," *Houston* 35 (November 1964): 34.

168. *Houston Post*, February 21, March 7, 14, 1965; "Insured for Growth," *Houston* 36 (September 1965): 21–23. In the 1950's and 1960's scattered high-rise apartments began to appear: the Park Towers, Mayfair, Inwood Manor, Parc IV, Parc V, Houston House, Alabama House, and Conquistador, a condominium. Townhouses became popular in 1964–1965.

169. *Houston Post*, May 9, August 8, 1965, June 10, 1970, March 8, November 9, 1980.

170. Personal survey, October 9, 1967.

171. *CBD Today*, p. 15.

172. *Houston Post*, April 12, 1966.

173. Letter, September 28, 1967.

174. Jane Jacobs, *The Death and Life of Great American Cities*.

175. *Houston Post*, May 4, 1962.

176. See Houston City Planning Commission, *Comprehensive Plan*, 1C: 106, for a list of annexations and dates.

177. *Houston Post*, January 1–2, 1949.

178. Ibid., January 2, 1949; "City Triples Size, Adds Population by Annexation of Outlying Areas," *Houston* 22 (January 1949): 85.

179. *Houston Post*, August 17–18, 1949, January 19, 1950.

180. Ibid., February 2, December 30, 1956, May 4, 1957, June 10, 1958, July 30, August 15, 1967. For a discussion of water districts, see the series by Tom Olmstead and Harold Scarlett (ibid., October 5, 7–9, 1958).

181. Ibid., May 21, June 7–8, 1960.

182. Ibid., June 7, 22–23, 1960; "Houston's Texas-size Land Grab," *Business Week*, July 23, 1960, pp. 54, 56.

183. *Houston Post*, June 14, 1962.
184. Ibid., November 10, 1967.
185. Ibid., February 27, December 31, 1969, July 30, 1977.
186. Ibid., August 17, 1972.
187. Ibid., June 15, July 13, 1961.
188. Marvin Hurley, *Decisive Years for Houston*, pp. 177–178.
189. Ibid., pp. 206–207; "Bayport Expands Industrial Complex," *Houston* 35 (March 1964): 23.
190. *Houston Post*, June 13, 1961.
191. Ibid., August 25–26, September 20, 1961; Hurley, *Decisive Years*, p. 207.
192. Stephen B. Oates, "NASA's Manned Spacecraft Center at Houston, Texas," *Southwestern Historical Quarterly* 67 (January 1964): 354–355.
193. *Houston Post*, January 5, 1963; "Space-Age Impact on Houston," *Houston* 33 (September 1962): 29, 33–34.
194. "Chemicals and Petrochemicals," *Houston* 33 (March 1962): 46–49; "Bayport Expands Industrial Complex," pp. 22–24.
195. *Houston Post*, June 21, 1962, February 2, 10, 1963.
196. "From Cow Pasture to Moon," *Houston* 37 (September 1966): 22–23.
197. *Houston Post*, July 21, 1969.
198. Ibid., October 3, 1980.
199. Ibid., May 6, July 4, 1969.
200. "Nobody Here But Us Texans . . . ," *Forbes*, February 1, 1977, pp. 52–53; Jennifer Lawrence, "The City in Worldly Perspective," *Houston* 50 (February 1979): 49–50, 52.

7. CONSERVATISM AND CULTURE

1. Willie Morris, "Houston's Superpatriots," *Harper's Magazine* 223 (October 1961): 50–52.
2. *Texas Almanac, 1966–1967*, p. 135; *Houston Post*, May 18, December 13, 21, 1980; Bureau of the Census, *Preliminary Reports, 1980*, p. 45-20.
3. *Houston Post*, July 4, 1954.
4. "Million Day," *Houston* 25 (July 1954): 18–19.
5. "One Million Plus," *Houston* 32 (January 1962): 62; "SMSA Promises More Prosperity," *Houston* 36 (May 1965): 34–35.
6. "50 Biggest Metropolitan Areas," *U.S. News and World Report*, March 16, 1981, p. 73; Bureau of the Census, *Preliminary Reports, 1980*, p. 45-25.
7. *Houston Post*, December 8–11, 1935, February 25, 1939, November 3, December 20, 29, 1939; Harry L. Washburn, "Flood Control and Protection for Texas' Greatest Port," *Houston* 9 (February 1938): 12, 25–26; "New Dams to Bring Profit and Safety," *Houston* 22 (September 1948): 38, 103.
8. *Houston Post*, June 16, 17, 1976.
9. Ibid., July 27, 28, 1979.

10. Ibid., March 2, 3, August 13, 1980.
11. Ibid., January 3, 1934, March 22, 1938.
12. Ibid., October 18, 1942.
13. Ibid., September 7, 1948 (see article by Hubert Mewhinney); "City's Water Supply to be Increased 18,000,000 Gallons," *Houston* 17 (April 1945): 43, 73; "Houston's Greater Water Supply Near," *Houston* 23 (August 1952): 8–11; "Utilities: Water," *Houston* 27 (March 1956): 9; "What Is . . . Houston's *Real* Water Picture?" *Houston* 28 (April 1957): 24–25.
14. *Houston Post*, April 15, 1955, January 26, September 10, 1959, March 28, 1960, December 5, 1963, January 19, 30, May 31, June 28, 1964.
15. Ibid., July 5, 1969, February 22, 1970, July 1, 1973, February 27, 1976, August 31, 1978, July 4, 1980.
16. Ibid., October 20, 1968, July 13, December 17, 1972, May 16, 1976, March 30, 1978; Ed Wagoner, "Subsidence: Can It Be Stopped," *Houston* 47 (November 1976): 27, 60, 62; Barbara Stokes, "The Next Hurricane," *Houston* 50 (July 1979): 20.
17. *Houston Post*, November 14, December 6, 1945.
18. Ibid., April 2, October 15, 1946, July 30, 1947.
19. Ibid., July 30, 1947.
20. Ibid., August 10, 1947.
21. Ibid., January 25, 1964.
22. Ibid., June 18, 1964.
23. Ibid., September 29, 1966.
24. Ibid., January 8, 1967, November 18, 1979.
25. Ibid., July 1, 1967.
26. Ibid., September 13, 1967.
27. Ibid., October 11, 1970.
28. Ibid.
29. Ibid., August 24, 1969, February 16, 1980; "Air and Water: A Trust," *Houston* 40 (November 1969): 17.
30. *Houston Post*, August 20, September 18, 1971, December 6, 1973, April 24, 1974.
31. Ibid., June 10, 1969.
32. Ibid., September 26, 1976, February 16, 1980.
33. Ibid., November 22, 1948; Comey, *Houston*, p. 9.
34. *Houston Post*, March 9, 1962; Harris County Health Department, "Progress Report, Stream and Air Pollution, December 1953 through December 1961," pp. 2–5, 9, 15 (mimeographed).
35. "Taking a Scientific Sniff," *Houston* 27 (June 1956): 56, 58; Southwest Research Institute, "Air Pollution Survey of the Houston Area, Technical Report No. 5, Summary Report, Phase II, Project No. 566-1; for the Houston Chamber of Commerce," pp. ii–x.
36. *Houston Post*, January 26, 1958 (see article by Brian Spinks).
37. Ibid., September 14, 1962.
38. Ibid., December 11, 1962.

39. Herbert C. McKee, "Air Pollution Survey of the Houston Area, 1964–1966, Final Report, Project No. 21-1587," pp. 4–6, 13–22, 29, 32, 44–46.
40. *Houston Post*, October 20, 1966.
41. Ibid., October 25, 1966, March 9, 1967 (editorial reply to a letter).
42. Ibid., March 29, 1967 (editorial reply to a letter).
43. Ibid., February 25, March 6, May 6, June 9, 1966. Quebedeaux maintained his dishonor roll only for the year 1966.
44. Ibid., October 17, 1967.
45. Ibid., December 20, 1969, January 14, 1970, January 16, 1975, March 11, 1977, August 9, 1977; Louis Marchiafava and J. Mauer, "Walter A. Quebedeaux," Oral History Interview, April 15, 1975.
46. *Houston Post*, December 20, 1969, October 8, 1971, September 12, 1972.
47. Ibid., February 24, 1975, September 28, 1976.
48. Ibid., March 28, 1973, September 28, 1976, July 27, 1978.
49. Ibid., April 11, 1973, February 15, 1980; Marchiafava and Mauer, "Quebedeaux."
50. *Houston Post*, September 30, 1979, May 18, 1980.
51. Ibid., December 4, 1969, May 21, November 17, 1970, March 16, 1973, January 9, 1974, December 5, 1976, September 21, 1980.
52. Ibid., September 25, 1934.
53. Ibid., January 8, 1937.
54. Ibid., March 26, 1948, March 16, 1949, September 18, 1953, September 15, 1967.
55. Ibid., September 23, 1947.
56. "Murdertown, USA," *Time*, February 3, 1958, p. 17.
57. Marchiafava, "Growth of Professional Urban Police Service," pp. 104–115, 128, 166–173, 190–200.
58. *Houston Post*, June 9, 1963.
59. Ibid., November 10, 1966.
60. Ibid., September 15, 1967.
61. U.S. Bureau of the Census, *County and City Data Book, 1977*, pp. 762; *Houston Post*, October 7, 8, 1979.
62. Richard West, "Only the Strong Survive," *Texas Monthly* 7 (February 1979): 181.
63. *Houston Post*, August 12, 1969, January 19, June 15, 1971, August 9, 10, 11, 14, 1973, August 9, November 2, 3, 12, 1974.
64. Ibid., July 28, August 26, 1970, April 28, December 15, 1978, April 5, July 26, 1979, February 9, October 16, 1980.
65. Ibid., May 10, 11, June 3, September 14, 15, 16, 21, 23, 27, October 8, 9, 21, 1977, February 9, April 3, 1978, October 5, 31, 1979, April 4, 22, 1980.
66. Ibid., February 14, 1980.
67. Henry Allen Bullock, *The Houston Murder Problem*, pp. 7–8.
68. *Houston Post*, December 2, 1948.
69. Ibid., November 1, 1950, April 23, 1953, December 19, 1957, May 29,

1958; James Aswell, "How to Have Fun with 100 Million Dollars," *Collier's*, May 2, 1953, pp. 50–53.

70. *Houston Post*, February 5, 1952.
71. Bullock, *Houston Murder Problem*, pp. 23, 41–42, 55.
72. Ibid., pp. 90–97.
73. *Houston Post*, December 19, 1962.
74. Ibid., February 19, 1937; "City Planning Needed," *Houston* 7 (October 1936): 14–15.
75. *Houston Post*, July 3, 30, 1937; *Houston Chronicle*, July 5, 14, 1937; Charles E. Gilbert, "City Planning," *Houston* 8 (September 1937): 25.
76. *Houston Post*, April 17, May 22, 27, June 1, 1938; *Houston Chronicle*, May 26, 1938.
77. *Houston Post*, June 6, July 10, 1943; "Hugh Potter Tells of City's Post War Needs," *Houston* 16 (June 1943): 36.
78. *Houston Post*, July 23, 1943; "City's Postwar Planning Group Makes Its Report," *Houston* 16 (June 1944): 20–21, 58–62.
79. *Houston Post*, February 8, August 24, 1946.
80. Ibid., October 16, 1946, January 21, 24, 1948.
81. Ibid., January 26, 1948.
82. Ibid., January 28, 1948.
83. Ibid., January 28, 31, 1948. It was during this zoning fight that Cullen clashed strongly with Jesse H. Jones, who favored zoning. Cullen threatened to sever all civic connections because of the issue (*Houston Chronicle*, January 29, 1948); "Houston Millionaire Beats Jones on Zoning," *Business Week*, February 14, 1948, p. 48.
84. *Houston Post*, February 1, 1948; Richard F. Babcock, *The Zoning Game*, p. 20.
85. M. Emmett Walter, "City Planning Progress," *Houston* 21 (June 1950): 49.
86. *Houston Post*, April 27, 1957, September 11, 1958; Planning Commission, *Comprehensive Plan*, vols. 1a, 1b, 1c.
87. *Houston Post*, December 18, 1959, June 18, 1961, January 2–10, 1962, (see series by Ralph O'Leary).
88. Ibid., February 14, October 10, November 7, 1962.
89. Ibid., November 5, 1962 (see Marguerite Johnston's column).
90. Ibid., January 5, 1962 (see Ralph O'Leary), March 2, 1980; Planning Commission, *Comprehensive Plan*, vols. 1a, 1c.
91. *CBD Today*, p. 22.
92. Deed Records of Harris County, 668:613–627, 2011:416–419, 4508:74.
93. *Houston Post*, September 4, 1958, August 9, 1962, August 10, 1970.
94. Federal aid for urban renewal dates from the Housing Act of 1949 and housing investigations in 1954. The national government provides loans to cover full costs of projects and grants to pay two-thirds of costs. The requirements for participation laid down by the Eisenhower administration include local housing and health codes, a master plan for development, analysis of the area subject to renewal, an agency to

carry out the program, and community support. It has been the attitude of Houston officials that the city fails, more or less, on all of these counts and that zoning would be necessary (*Houston Post,* January 26, 1958).

95. Robert A. Sigafoos and Gerald A. Fox, "The Need for Governmental and Cultural-Convention Facilities in the Houston Civic Center to 1980," pp. 8, 27.

96. Jacobs, *Great American Cities,* pp. 168–169.

97. Central Houston Improvement Association, "Report on Bayou Utilization"; "The Old Makes Way for the New," *Houston* 20 (July 1949): 6–7.

98. *Houston Post,* September 21, 1954.

99. Ibid., May 2, June 10, July 11, 17, 20, 21, 23, 26, 1961.

100. Ibid., March 8, 1964; Gail Whitcomb, "Allen's Landing Park . . . Another C of C Project," *Houston* 37 (June 1966): 96; "Visitors to Landing," *Houston* 37 (October 1966): 79.

101. *Houston Post,* May 29 (editorial), July 5, 1968 (editorial), January 19, 1979; "Where the City Plays," *Houston* 29 (September 1958): 16–17; Lawrence Gillingham, "An Appraisal of Municipal Recreation in Houston, Texas," p. 132.

102. *Houston Post,* January 17, 1954, April 23, 1955, May 22, 1980, September 30, 1979; "Tranquility Park," *Houston* 50 (August 1979): 21–22.

103. Kenneth E. Gray, *A Report on the Politics of Houston,* 1:22, 6:26.

104. Ibid., 1:23–24.

105. "War Needs . . . Houston," *Architectural Record* 91 (April 1942): 47–50; Writers' Program, *Houston,* pp. 122–123.

106. *Houston Post,* February 27, 1948.

107. Ibid., January 15, February 4, 9, June 15, 20, July 19, 23, 1950.

108. Ibid., January 4, 1950, March 23, 1952; "Modern Apartments Replace Schrimpf Alley Slum Area," *Houston* 23 (April 1952): 38.

109. Houston-Harris County Economic Opportunity Organization, the Settegast Report.

110. *Houston Post,* January 7, October 28, 1969, June 24, November 9, 1970, January 11, 1971, March 24, 1974, January 3, 1976, February 19, 1978, July 30, 1980.

111. Ibid., September 7, 1967; Barbara R. Phillips, "Housing for the Poor in Houston: Dynamic Factors," pp. 3–4, 8–9 (mimeographed).

112. Gray, *Report on Politics of Houston,* 2:3, 13, 17–20, 26, 5:10, 19–20, 35–38.

113. *Houston Post,* April 19, 1933.

114. Ibid., May 10, 23, 25, 1933, October 30, 1934.

115. Ibid., April 4, 11, 24, May 11, June 6, 1935.

116. Ibid., March 14, April 19, September 24, December 31, 1936, June 2, July 8, 1937, August 16, 1942; Larry Jewell, "The City-Manager Plan," *Houston* 13 (September 1942): 13.

117. *Houston Post,* December 16, 1942, November 2, 6, 1946, July 26, 27, 1947; "Full Time Mayor Succeeds City-Manager Form Here," *Houston* 21 (August 1947): 68.

118. *Houston Post,* July 3, 13, 16–20, 22, 24, 29, August 9–11, 16–17, 1955.
119. Ibid., January 31, 1973, August 12, November 21, December 27, 30, 1979; *Denver Post,* March 3, 1980.
120. *Houston Post,* June 26, December 29, 1969, February 24, March 1, 19, 1970, July 9, 1974, July 7, 1975, April 4, November 9, 1976.
121. Ibid., August 10, 1975, March 11, 1980; *Denver Post,* March 3, April 21, 1980.
122. *Houston Post,* September 21, 28, 1948; *Houston Chronicle,* September 20, 1948.
123. *Houston Post,* January 26, 1949, January 22, 1954.
124. Ibid., September 27, October 25–26, 1949.
125. Ibid., October 28, 1949.
126. Ibid., January 18–19, 1968.
127. Ibid., May 13, 1953.
128. Ibid., July 14, 16, 21, 29, 1953; *Houston Chronicle,* July 14–16, 1953.
129. *Houston Post,* October 4, November 26, 1953.
130. Ibid., December 15, 1953, January 7, 27–28, 30–31, 1954; National Education Association of the United States, *Houston, Texas,* pp. 12–13, 15, 22–29, 31, 33; John W. Letson, "Controversy in Houston," *National Education Association Journal* 44 (January 1955): 45–46.
131. Don E. Carleton, "A Crisis of Rapid Change: The Red Scare in Houston, 1949–1955," pp. 127–141, 204–205.
132. *Houston Post,* July 8, 1951, October 11, 14, 20–21, 1953.
133. Ibid., October 11–21, 1953.
134. Ibid., October 23, 31, November 18, December 3, 1953, February 14, March 12, April 1, 1954.
135. Ibid., October 21, 1953.
136. Ibid., November 7, 1956.
137. Ibid., January 25, 1950, July 24, 1953, July 13, 28, 1955, April 24, 1956; *Houston Chronicle,* July 28, 1955; Fayrene Neuman Mays, "A History of Public Library Service to Negroes in Houston, Texas, 1907–1962," pp. 45–46.
138. *Houston Post,* February 19, 28, May 1, 1956.
139. Ibid., September 8, 11, December 27, 1956, September 10, 1967.
140. Ibid., November 14, December 9, 11, 1956, January 3, March 24, 1957.
141. Ibid., May 19, 1957.
142. Ibid., October 16, 1957.
143. Ibid., May 13, June 1, July 16, September 30, November 5, 1958, February 24, 1959; "Houston's Quiet Victory," *Negro History Bulletin* 23 (January 1960): 75–77.
144. *Houston Post,* October 18 (see editorial), November 19, 1967.
145. Ibid., May 21, July 2, August 18, 1959, April 12, 1960.
146. Ibid., August 5, 1960.
147. Ibid., September 9, 1960, September 1, 1961.
148. Ibid., August 31, 1960, September 24, 1967.
149. Ibid., December 29, 1962, November 11, 1966. Early in 1969 the U.S. Department of Justice filed a motion stating that separation of the races

still existed and asking the court to order a new desegregation plan (ibid., February 12, 1969).

150. Ibid., May 6, 1970, October 22, 1974, September 25, 1978, September 10, 1980.

151. Ibid., March 11, 1975, September 1, 1978.

152. Ibid., August 25, 1976, June 2, September 14, 1977, June 24, 1978, July 12, August 13, September 20, 1980.

153. Ibid., September 26, 1970, February 6, 14, March 25, 1971.

154. Ibid., August 31, September 14, 1976, May 18, 1977, November 7, 1978, July 4, 1980.

155. Ibid., November 17, 1977, July 22, 25, August 13, September 5, 1980; "A Costly Break for Illegal Aliens," *Newsweek*, August 4, 1980, p. 60.

156. *Houston Post*, February 16, 1960, February 14, April 6, 9, 11–12, 15, 22, May 9, 11, 16, 1961. Robert Welch of the John Birch Society said Houston and Los Angeles were his two strongest cities. Welch spoke to three thousand people in the Music Hall in 1961 (*Houston Post*, April 19, July 15, 1961; Morris, "Houston's Superpatriots," p. 49).

157. *Houston Post*, March 5, 1960.

158. Ibid., March 8–9, 25–26, 1960; Gray, *Report on Politics of Houston*, 5:16.

159. John M. Burnham, "Max Levine," Oral Business History Project, pp. 176–177.

160. *Houston Post*, January 28, 1961, February 1, March 8, 1962; *Houston Chronicle*, June 7, 1963.

161. *Houston Post*, July 17, 1963, January 28, July 6, 1964.

162. Ibid., November 13, 1965. T.S.U. began to integrate in 1955–1956 (*Houston Chronicle*, September 18, 1956).

163. *Houston Chronicle*, May 17–18, 1967; Bullock, *Houston Murder Problem*, pp. 69–82. Bill Helmer, writing for the *Texas Observer* (June 9–23, 1967, pp. 1–6), provided a thorough review of this 1967 riot in "Nightmare in Houston." In the face of conflicting reports, the movie taken by KHOU-TV cameraman Bob Wolfe was of particular interest. According to Helmer (p. 4), almost thirty minutes of unedited film revealed "more than a hundred students being treated with something less than courtesy, but nothing resembling brutality." He concluded, "No student who followed orders quickly and precisely could complain much about his treatment, but God help any of them who decided to be contrary."

164. "The Job Fair," *Newsweek*, May 27, 1968, 74B–75.

165. *Houston Post*, February 5, 1979, June 8, 1980; Phillips, "Housing for the Poor in Houston," p. 49.

166. *Houston Chronicle*, September 30, 1973.

167. *Houston Post*, March 3, 1979.

168. *Houston Chronicle*, April 6, 1980.

169. Ibid., July 7, 1963; *Houston Post*, January 28, 1964, June 15, 1969.

170. T. Coleman, "Francis Williams," Oral History Interview, September 21,

1974. See also Mildred Huber Meltzer, "Chapters in the Struggle for Negro Rights in Houston, 1944–1962."

171. *Houston Post*, June 6, 7, 24, 1965.

172. Louis Marchiafava, "Tatcho Mindeola," April 21, 1975, and "Lionel Castillo," Oral History Interview, March 7, 12, 1975; *Houston Chronicle*, September 14, 1973; *Houston Post*, May 21, 1978, June 12, 1979.

173. Mary Ellen Goodman, *The Mexican-American Population of Houston*, pp. 3–12.

174. *Houston Post*, September 9, 11, 12, 15, October 11, 1970, August 1, 1971, September 8, 1972.

175. Ibid., November 27, 1979, January 1, 1980.

176. Louis Marchiafava, "Betty Barnes," Oral History Interview, May 12, 1975.

177. *Houston Post*, February 10, December 4, 1973.

178. Ibid., May 18, 1976; Judith Jett Hendricks, "The Office of the Women's Advocate in Houston: An Attempt at Affirmative Action for Women," pp. 42–52.

179. *Houston Post*, May 31, July 17, December 4, 21, 1976, January 13, March 17, 29, 30, 31, October 25, 1977, January 6, 1978.

180. Ibid., November 19, 20, 21, 1977.

181. Ibid., January 4, June 29, 1946, November 17–21, 1949, September 26, October 1, 1950, October 14, 1951, December 20, 1959, April 7, 1960, July 19, 1962; "Rice Institute Has New President and Four Trustees," *Houston* 17 (January 1946): 58; "Rice's New Stadium Nearing Completion," *Houston* 21 (September 1950): 32; "Rice Given Atom Smasher by U.S.," *Houston* 22 (September 1951): 97; "Houston Gets Bowled Over," *Houston* 30 (October 1959): 44–45.

182. *Houston Post*, January 6, 1951, December 12, 1954, November 18, 1955, February 26, 1960, August 4, 1963; "J. S. Abercrombies Give $500,000 to Rice," *Houston* 20 (March 1947): 28; "Mrs. Wiess Gives Rice Large Gift," *Houston* 23 (February 1952): 50; "Rice Goes to Colleges," *Houston* 26 (January 1956): 42, 44.

183. *Houston Post*, February 18, March 10, 1964.

184. Ibid., March 10, 1964. The ruling was upheld by the Texas Supreme Court (ibid., February 23, 1967; "John B. Coffee et al. vs. William Marsh Rice University et al.," *South Western Reporter, Second Series* 408: 269–287).

185. *Houston Post*, May 2, 29, 1964.

186. Ibid., September 17, 1967.

187. Ibid., May 17, 1969, April 18, 1970; *Report of the President, 1980*, p. 16.

188. E. E. Oberholtzer, "The University of Houston Marches On!" *Houston* 7 (September 1936): 4–5.

189. *Houston Post*, March 25, 1938; "A Million Dollar Drive," *Houston* 11 (March 1938): 8; "Success of Houston University Assured with Gift of Arts and Culture Center," *Houston* 11 (April 1938): 5.

190. *Houston Post*, May 28, April 22, 1939.

191. Ibid., March 22, 1945, July 14, 1946.

192. "A Review of the Rapid Growth of University of Houston," *Houston* 18 (August 1946): 14–16; "Rice Institute to Build Two Buildings," *Houston* ibid., p. 13.

193. *Houston Post*, January 22, May 6, 1949.

194. Ibid., September 23, 1952, May 26, June 9, 1953; "Doctor Kemmerer Named Houston University Head," *Houston* 23 (May 1952): 25.

195. *Houston Post*, May 1, 1959.

196. Ibid., April 21, 1953, December 3, 1954.

197. Ibid., February 22–23, 1957; "Richly Endowed," *Houston* 28 (February 1957): 50.

198. *Houston Post*, May 31, 1961.

199. Ibid., November 21, 1953, January 15, 1955, March 15, 1957; "Neigh Yea," *Houston* 28 (May 1957): 34.

200. *Houston Post*, March 4, 1955.

201. Ibid., April 13, 1960; *The University of Houston and Full State Tax Support*, unpaged.

202. *Houston Post*, May 24, 1961.

203. Ibid., May 7, 8, 1970, May 4, 1971, April 29, 1973, December 14, 1977, May 16, September 7, 1978, November 6, 1979, June 17, 1980.

204. Ed Kilman and Theon Wright, *Hugh Roy Cullen*, pp. 39, 96–97, 105, 114–115, 142–143.

205. *Houston Post*, February 9, 1936.

206. Ibid., March 31, 1938.

207. "Cullen Gives $100,000 to Negro College Here," *Houston* 18 (February 1946): 42; "University Here for the Negroes," *Houston* 21 (August 1947): 58.

208. *Houston Post*, March 3–4, 8, 1945; "The H. R. Cullens Give $4,000,000 to Hospitals," *Houston* 17 (March 1945): 9, 24.

209. *Houston Post*, March 4, July 3–4, 1947, September 23, 1951, November 29, 1953; "Cullen to Give St. Joseph $1,000,000," *Houston* 20 (September 1949): 27.

210. *Houston Post*, March 4, 1955.

211. "Great Medical Center Being Created Here," *Houston* 14 (August 1943): 4; N. Don Macon, *Mr. John D. Freeman and Friends*, pp. 22–27, 42–43.

212. *Houston Chronicle*, March 18, 1942; *Houston Post*, March 18, 1942.

213. "Texas Dental College Merged with U. of T.," *Houston* 13 (September 1942): 7; "Baylor Branches South," *Houston* 14 (May 1943): 5.

214. Nicholas Lemann, "Super Medicine," *Texas Monthly* 7 (April 1979): 111, 200; *Houston Post*, April 5, 6, 8, 9, 11, May 7, 16, 18, 1969, July 3, 7, 13, 1976.

215. *Houston Post*, December 7, 1945, September 4, 1946, April 15, 1955, May 25, 1969, June 15, 1980; "City's $11,000,000 Naval Hospital Formally Opened," *Houston* 18 (September 1946): 20–21.

216. *Houston Post,* November 10, 1940, April 17, 1955, July 9, 1965, July 16, 1967.
217. Ibid., March 7, 1969, April 14, 1971, March 16, 1973.
218. *Houston Post-Dispatch,* October 16, 1930.
219. *Houston Post,* August 13, 1935.
220. Ibid., April 20, 1937.
221. "Modern Hospitals," *Houston* 11 (August 1940): 26–28.
222. *Houston Post,* July 21–22, 29, 1949.
223. Ibid., August 11, 1949, January 28–29, 1950.
224. Ibid., July 9–10, 1953.
225. Ibid., July 12, 1953.
226. Ibid., January 26, 1958 (see part 2, pp. 12–13).
227. Ibid., August 2, 1956.
228. Ibid., September 15, 1957.
229. Ibid., July 11, 1958.
230. Ibid., July 18, 28, 1958.
231. Ibid., March 22, April 2, May 15, 26, 1958.
232. Ibid., February 10, 1960.
233. Ibid., September 12, 1959, June 16, 1961.
234. From the book *The Hospital* by Jan de Hartog (published by Atheneum, copyright © 1964 by The Citizens Fund for Voluntary Nursing, reprinted by permission of Atheneum Publishers).
235. *Houston Post,* October 31, November 8, 1964.
236. Ibid., November 8, December 6, 1964.
237. Ibid., November 8, December 4, 1964.
238. Ibid., November 11–12, 1964.
239. Ibid., January 14, 1965.
240. Ibid., January 24, 1965.
241. Ibid., October 19, November 21, 1965.
242. Ibid., September 26, October 31, 1980.
243. Ibid., February 15, 1939, February 26, April 21, December 31, 1940, January 16, 1943, January 24, 1944, March 17, 1947.
244. "'Capital Record,' Says Capitol Records," *Houston* 29 (July 1958): 23; Hubert Roussel, *The Houston Symphony Orchestra, 1913–1971,* pp. 80–84.
245. *Houston Post,* March 4, 1964; *New York Times,* March 4, 1964; *New York Herald Tribune,* March 4, 1964.
246. Roussel, *Houston Symphony,* pp. 160, 205.
247. Ibid., pp. 218–219.
248. *Houston Post,* January 9, May 6, 18, 1969 (see Carl Cunningham, "The Private War of Andre Previn," *Tempo,* pp. 7–10).
249. Ibid., June 1, 1962; "Housing the Performing Arts," *Houston* 33 (August 1962): 44.
250. *Houston Post,* October 4, 1966; "Setting the Stage for Fine Arts," *Houston* 37 (October 1966): 61–62.
251. *New York Times,* October 4, 1966.

252. *Houston Post,* March 24, 1957 (see "Titled Texan" by Victor Junger); Francis Wrightman, "'Alley'—Theater Unusual," *Houston* 22 (August 1948): 25.

253. *Houston Post,* January 26, 1949 (see David Westheimer); "'Alley' . . . Everybody's Theatre," *Houston* 22 (October 1948): 88; "Alley Strewn with Stars," *Houston* 28 (November 1957): 25.

254. "Down the Alley," *Houston* 30 (March 1959): 30, 32; "Another Alley Accolade," *Houston* 30 (January 1960): 25; "Reaching New Levels," *Houston* 33 (December 1962): 28.

255. "Change of Scenes," *Houston* 33 (June 1962): 29; *Houston Post,* November 27, 1968.

256. *Houston Post,* February 1, 1948, September 27, 1953; "Museum Takes Wing," *Houston* 29 (October 1958): 25.

257. *Houston Post,* April 4, 1965, January 13, 1974.

258. Ibid., March 7, 1966; "Bayou Bends for Art," *Houston* 28 (February 1957): 49. Miss Ima Hogg, one of the most beloved patrons of cultural events in Houston, died in London in August 1975.

259. *Houston Post,* September 6, 1964, July 1, 1968.

260. Robert S. Vines, "Building Proposed for Science Museum," *Houston* 22 (February 1948): 36; "Star-Studded Show for Houston," *Houston* 35 (August 1964): 34, 36.

261. *Texas Public Library Statistics, 1966,* pp. 12–13, 18–19; *Texas Almanac, 1978–1979,* pp. 574–575.

262. *Houston Post,* September 24, 1954; "Houston: Cultural Profile . . ." *Houston* 32 (June 1961): 22–26, 28, 30, 32; "The Arts in Houston," *Houston* 34 (December 1963): 43.

263. U.S. Bureau of the Census, *Census of Business, 1963,* vol. 1, *Retail Trade—Summary Statistics,* part 5, pp. 7H-251, 7H-253, 7H-289, 7H-291; idem, *1977 Census of Retail Trade, Texas,* pp. 44-96, 44-97, 44-88, 44-89.

264. *Houston Post,* December 12, 1948, January 2, 1949.

265. "History Scene on TV Screen," *Houston* 26 (January 1956): 14–15.

266. *Houston Post,* March 23, 1953; "Network Television Comes to Houston," *Houston* 23 (July 1952): 96; "New HOUston TV," *Houston* 30 (July 1959): 76.

267. *Houston Post,* October 21, 1953, June 26, February 24, 1954.

268. Ibid., May 4, November 21, 1954; "History Scene on TV Screen," pp. 14–15.

269. *Houston Post,* January 6–7, 1967.

270. Ibid., December 1, June 22, 1953; Eddie Mack, "Epsom Downs Gets Ready for New Meet," *Houston* 7 (February 1936): 24; "Ice Hockey Has Arrived," *Houston* 18 (October 1946): 20, 56; "Apollos on Ice," *Houston* 36 (October 1965): 72, 75.

271. Marshall Monroe, "Cattlemen Plan Huge Revival of Industry," *Houston* 3 (March 1932): 19, 21; Maudeen Marks, "History of Houston Fat Stock Show and Rodeo, 1932–1953," varied paging (typescript).

272. *Houston Post*, January 15, 20–21, 1950, March 17, 1951, September 19, 21, 1952.
273. Ibid., August 3–4, 1959, September 19, 1960.
274. Ibid., January 8, 1979.
275. Ibid., June 12, 1969, June 28, 1971, November 1, 1973, November 3, 1975.
276. Ibid., August 3, October 20, 1960, January 18, 1961, December 10, 1964, May 14, June 6, 1965; "Colt .45s Pull the Trigger on April 10th," *Houston* 33 (April 1962): 52–53; "Here Comes the Judge—Again," *Newsweek*, May 27, 1968, pp. 74–74A.
277. *Houston Post*, January 15, 1950; *Inside the Astrodome*, p. 10.
278. *Houston Post*, June 21, July 28, 1958.
279. Ibid., January 18, 22, 1961.
280. Ibid., January 18, 27, 1961.
281. Ibid., January 27, February 1, 1961.
282. Ibid., May 27, 30, 1961, May 17, 29, 1962.
283. Ibid., December 23, 1962.
284. *Inside the Astrodome*, pp. 8–9, 13–14, 17, 23–24.
285. The rental figure of $750,000 can be found in the *Houston Post* (July 25, 1967), and "Houston's Miracle on South Main," *Houston* 36 (March 1965): 98.
286. *Houston Post*, April 10, 1965.
287. Ibid. In 1980 the Astros lost to Philadelphia in a race for the pennant (ibid., October 13, 1980).
288. Ibid., April 8–10, 1965.
289. Ibid., May 12, 1965.
290. Ibid., March 20, 1966; "Plastic Underfoot, Too," *Houston* 37 (May 1966): 76.
291. *Houston Post*, June 5, August 10, 1965, February 11, 1968.
292. Ibid., December 20, 1966, July 25, 1967.
293. Ibid., June 2, 1968.
294. Ibid., November 4, 1965.
295. Ibid., January 2, 18, 1970, May 26, September 24, 1976, October 29, November 8, 1980; Houston Chamber of Commerce, *Houston Facts '80*, p. 4.

EPILOGUE: HOUSTON AND AN URBAN RENAISSANCE

1. Phil Patton, "Philip Johnson: The Man Who Changed Houston's Skyline," *Houston City Magazine* 4 (January 1980): 46.
2. *Denver Post*, August 24, 1980.
3. *Houston Post*, October 22, 1978.
4. McFarland, "The Good, the Bad and the Ugly," p. 13.
5. *Houston Post*, May 21, 1980.
6. Ibid., April 10, May 7, November 1, 1980.
7. Ibid., August 6, 1980.

8. Ann Holmes, "Houston: The Second City for Art," *Art News* 74 (December 1975): 50–52.

9. *Houston Post*, November 9, 1980.

10. Ann Holmes, "The Rothko Chapel: Six Years Later," *Art News* 75 (December 1976): 35–37; *Houston Post*, May 29, August 21, 1969, March 31, 1980.

11. *Houston Post*, March 3, 1980.

12. West, "Only the Strong Survive," pp. 180–181.

13. *Houston Post*, May 16, 1980.

BIBLIOGRAPHY

UNPUBLISHED SOURCES

Oscar M. Addison Papers. University of Texas Archives, Austin, Texas.

Annual Report of the City Controller for the Year Ending December 31, 1904. City controller's office, Houston, Texas. (Bound, varied paging.)

Annual Report of the City Controller for the Year Ending February 28, 1907. City controller's office, Houston, Texas. (Bound, varied paging.)

Augustus C. Allen Papers. Texas State Archives, Austin, Texas. (Typescript.)

Barnes, William. Annual Reports of the British Consulate, Galveston, 1843–1879. San Jacinto Museum Library, Houston, Texas.

Berryman, Marsha Guant. "Houston and the Early Depression: 1929–1932." M.A. thesis, University of Houston, Houston, Texas, 1965.

Briscoe-Harris-Looscan Papers. San Jacinto Museum Library, Houston, Texas.

Burnham, John M. "Max Levine." Oral Business History Project, University of Texas, Austin, Texas, 1964.

Carleton, Don E. "A Crisis of Rapid Change: The Red Scare in Houston, 1949–1955." Ph.D. dissertation, University of Houston, Houston, Texas, 1978.

Central Houston Improvement Association. "Report on Bayou Utilization," April 12, 1951. Texas History Room, Houston Public Library, Houston, Texas.

Coleman, T. "Francis Williams." Oral History Interview, Houston Metropolitan Archives, Houston, Texas, September 21, 1974.

Deed Records of Harris County (County clerk's office, Houston). Vols. A, 668, 2011, 4508.

Dillon, Charles H. "A Story of the Telegraph and the Western Union and How They Reached the Southwest." University of Texas Archives, Austin, Texas.

Doswell, Adams and Company Papers. University of Texas Archives, Austin, Texas.

Kelsey H. Douglass Papers. University of Texas Archives, Austin, Texas.

Duke, Alan R. Letter, September 23, 1967.

Ellis, Louis Tuffly. "The Texas Cotton Compress Industry: A History." Ph.D. dissertation, University of Texas, Austin, Texas, 1964.

Fleming, Richard T. Interview, July 30, 1968.

Littleton Fowler Papers. University of Texas Archives, Austin, Texas.

Gustave Gerson Papers. Rosenberg Library Archives, Galveston, Texas.

Gillingham, Lawrence. "An Appraisal of Municipal Recreation in Houston, Texas." M.A. thesis, University of Chicago, Chicago, Illinois, 1954.

Gray, A. C. "Four Historical Talks." Vandale Collection. University of Texas Archives, Austin, Texas.

Groce Family Records. University of Texas Archives, Austin, Texas.

Grover, Henry C. "The Dissolution of T. W. House and Company." M.A. thesis, University of Houston, Houston, Texas, 1962.

William Job Hale Papers. University of Texas Archives, Austin, Texas.

Hamill, Allen W. "Spindletop, the Lucus Gusher." Oral History of the Oil Industry, Tape No. 84, September 2, 1952. University of Texas Archives, Austin, Texas. (Typescript.)

Harris County Health Department. "Progress Report, Stream and Air Pollution, December 1953 through December 1961." (Mimeographed.)

Pearl Hendricks Papers. University of Texas Archives, Austin, Texas.

Hendricks, Judith Jett. "The Office of the Women's Advocate in Houston: An Attempt at Affirmative Action for Women." M.A. thesis, University of Houston, Houston, Texas, 1977.

Hines, Gerald D. Letter, September 28, 1967.

Holmes, Harry D. "Boston Investment in the Buffalo Bayou, Brazos and Colorado Railway: A Study in Entrepreneurial Decision-Making." M.A. thesis, Louisiana State University, Baton Rouge, Louisiana, 1968.

Thomas W. House Papers. University of Texas Archives, Austin, Texas.

Houston–Harris County Economic Opportunity Organization. The Settegast Report. [Houston], 1966. (Mimeographed.)

Humason, Granville A. "Interview." Oral History of the Oil Industry, Tape No. 102, July 7, 1953. University of Texas Archives, Austin, Texas. (Multilithed.)

M. T. Jones Lumber Company Papers. University of Texas Archives, Austin, Texas.

Keller, Helen Katherine. "A History of Public Education in Houston, Texas." M.A. thesis, University of Texas, Austin, Texas, 1930.

Louis W. Kemp Collection. University of Texas Archives, Austin, Texas.

Kilgore, Linda Elaine. "The Ku Klux Klan and the Press in Texas, 1920–1927." M.J. thesis, University of Texas, Austin, Texas, 1964.

Thomas M. League Papers. Rosenberg Library Archives, Galveston, Texas.

Glenn McCarthy Biography File. Texas History Center, Austin, Texas.

McKee, Herbert C. "Air Pollution Survey of the Houston Area, 1964–1966, Final Report, Project No. 21-1587." Southwest Research Institute, San Antonio, October 1966.

Marchiafava, Louis J. "Institutional and Legal Aspects of the Growth of Professional Urban Police Service: The Houston Experience, 1878–1948." Ph.D. dissertation, University of Houston, Houston, Texas, 1976.

———. "Betty Barnes," "Lionel Castello," "Tatcho Mindeola," "Walter A. Quebedeaux" (with J. Mauer). Oral History Interviews, Houston Metropolitan Archives, Houston, Texas, 1975.

Marks, Maudeen. "History of Houston Fat Stock Show and Rodeo, 1932–1953." 1958. Texas History Room, Houston Public Library, Houston, Texas. Varied paging. (Typescript.)

"Mayors Book." Texas History Room, Houston Public Library, Houston, Texas.

Mays, Fayrene Neuman. "A History of Public Library Service to Negroes in Houston, Texas, 1907–1962." M.A. thesis, Atlanta University, Atlanta, Georgia, 1964.

Meltzer, Mildred Huber. "Chapters in the Struggle for Negro Rights in Houston, 1944–1962." M.A. thesis, University of Houston, Houston, Texas, 1963.

Merseburger, Marion. "A Political History of Houston, Texas, during the Reconstruction Period as Recorded by the Press: 1868–1873." M.A. thesis, Rice Institute, Houston, Texas, May 1950.

Milsaps, John. Diary. 73 vols. Texas History Room, Houston Public Library, Houston, Texas.

Minutes of the City Council of Houston. City secretary's office, Houston, Texas. Books A–R.

Minutes of the 11th District Court. District clerk's office, Houston, Texas. Books A–D.

Montgomery, William Edward. "The Depression in Houston during the Hoover Era, 1929–1932." M.A. thesis, University of Texas, Austin, Texas, 1966.

Muir, Andrew Forest. Interview, January 3, 1968.

O'Donnell, Sister Mary Brendan. "Annunciation Church—Catholic Motherchurch of Houston." M.A. thesis, University of Houston, Houston, Texas, 1965.

Ordinances of the City of Houston. City secretary's office, Houston, Texas. Vols. 2–5.

Phillips, Barbara R. "Housing for the Poor in Houston: Dynamic Factors." Report by the Southwest Center for Urban Research, Houston, Texas, August 1971. (Mimeographed.)

Pratt, Howard L. "Urban Public Services and Private Enterprise: Aspects of the Legal and Economic History of Houston, Texas, 1865–1905." Ph.D. dissertation, Rice University, Houston, Texas, 1974.

Record of Board of Commissioners and Election Returns, January 30, 1837, to January 25, 1866. County Commissioners' Court Records, Houston, Texas.

Rieber, Torkild. "Pioneers in Texas Oil." Oral History of the Oil Industry, Tape No. 146D, January 25, 1954. University of Texas Archives, Austin, Texas. (Multilithed.)

Sigafoos, Robert A., and Gerald A. Fox. "The Need for Governmental and Cultural-Convention Facilities in the Houston Civic Center to 1980." Stanford Research Institute, Stanford, California, May 1962.

Ashbel Smith Papers. University of Texas Archives, Austin, Texas.

Southwest Research Institute. "Air Pollution Survey of the Houston Area, Technical Report No. 5, Summary Report, Phase II, Project No. 566-1; for

the Houston Chamber of Commerce." San Antonio, Texas, July 1, 1958.
James Harper Starr Papers. University of Texas Archives, Austin, Texas.
United States Bureau of the Census. *Seventh Census of the United States,*
1850. Harris County, Texas, City of Houston, Free Schedule. (Microfilm.)
————. *Ninth Census of the United States, 1870. Harris County, Texas,*
Houston Schedule. (Microfilm.)
Weinberger, Abe Lincoln. "The History and Development of the Houston
Ship Channel and the Port of Houston." M.A. thesis, University of Texas,
Austin, Texas, 1940.
Zeigler, Robert E. "The Workingman in Houston, Texas, 1865–1914." Ph.D.
dissertation, Texas Tech University, Lubbock, Texas, 1972.

PUBLISHED SOURCES
Newspapers
Daily Houston Telegraph, January 1871–February 1871.
Daily Telegraph [Houston], February 1871–December 1871.
Denver Post, March 3, April 21, August 24, 1980.
Galveston Daily News [published in Houston throughout 1865], February
1865–December 1865; March 1873; September 1873–March 1874.
Houston Chronicle, October 1902 to present.
Houston Daily Telegram, April 1878–April 1879.
Houston Daily Telegraph, May 1874–July 1874, October 24, 1875, January
1, 11, March 3, 1876, April 1876–February 1877.
Houston Daily Union, May, July 1870, September 1871, May 29, 1872.
Houston Post [known variously as *Houston Post, Houston Daily Post,*
Daily Post, Houston Post-Dispatch], August 1880 to present.
Morning Star [Houston], April 1839–October 1844.
National Intelligencer [Houston], April 18, 1839.
New York Herald Tribune, March 4, 1964.
New York Times, March 4, 1964, October 4, 1966.
Telegraph and Texas Register [Houston] [known as *Democratic Telegraph*
and Texas Register, March 18, 1846–March 28, 1851; published in Co-
lumbia, August 2, 1836–April 11, 1837], August 1836–January 1853.
Tri-Weekly Telegraph [Houston], February 1856–October 1860, September
18, 1867.
Tri-Weekly Union, June, October 1869.
Weekly Houston Telegraph, April 1874–March 1876.
Weekly Telegraph [Houston], February 1856–October 1856, November
1860–February 1864, September 1867–October 1873.

Articles
"Additional Air Service." *Houston* 7 (September 1936): 18.
"'Alley' . . . Everybody's Theatre." *Houston* 22 (October 1948): 88.
"Alley Strewn with Stars." *Houston* 28 (November 1957): 25.
"Another Alley Accolade." *Houston* 30 (January 1960): 25.
"Apollos on Ice." *Houston* 36 (October 1965): 72, 75.
Arthur, Dora Fowler, ed. "Jottings from the Old Journal of Littleton Fowler."

Southwestern Historical Quarterly 2 (July 1898): 73–84.
"The Arts in Houston." *Houston* 34 (December 1963): 43–58.
Aswell, James. "How to Have Fun with 100 Million Dollars." *Collier's*, May 2, 1953, pp. 50–53.
Barrett, Claude B. "Houston—Growing Air Center." *Houston* 22 (November 1951): 12–13, 57.
"Battelstein's Opens River Oaks Store." *Houston* 24 (August 1953): 20–22.
"Baylor Branches South." *Houston* 14 (May 1943): 5.
"Bayou Bends for Art." *Houston* 28 (February 1957): 49.
"Bayport Expands Industrial Complex." *Houston* 35 (March 1964): 22–24.
"Better Luck This Time." *Forbes*, August 6, 1979, p. 78.
"Big and Little Inch Pipe Lines Purchased." *Houston* 20 (March 1947): 37.
"Big Time in Houston: Opening of the Shamrock Hotel." *Fortune* 39 (May 1949): 80–82.
"Blooming Prairie: Sharpstown." *Newsweek*, March 21, 1955, pp. 88, 90.
"Booming Gulf Surf." *Houston* 27 (November 1956): 40.
"Booming Houston." *Life*, October 21, 1946, 108–117.
Booth, Brown. "Texas Gas Goes East." *Houston* 22 (October 1948): 13.
"Brown Builds Ships for the Navy." *Houston* 14 (June 1943): 6–7.
"Buses on the Move." *Houston* 33 (April 1962): 58–59.
"Cameron Iron Works Honored." *Houston* 12 (August 1941): 22.
"'Capital Record,' Says Capitol Records." *Houston* 29 (July 1958): 23.
Carlson, Avery L. "The Expansion of Texas Banking: 1894–1929." *Texas Monthly* 5 (January 1930): 74–102.
———. "Laying the Foundations of Modern Banking in Texas: 1861–1893." *Texas Monthly* 4 (December 1929): 615–641.
"Central Industrial Park." *Houston* 34 (August 1963): 58.
"Change of Scenes." *Houston* 33 (June 1962): 29.
"Chemicals and Petrochemicals." *Houston* 33 (March 1962): 46–49.
"City Planning Needed." *Houston* 7 (October 1936): 14–15.
"City's $11,000,000 Naval Hospital Formally Opened." *Houston* 18 (September 1946): 20–21.
"City's Postwar Planning Group Makes Its Report." *Houston* 16 (June 1944): 20–21, 58–62.
"City's Water Supply to Be Increased 18,000,000 Gallons." *Houston* 17 (April 1945): 43, 73.
"City Triples Size, Adds Population by Annexation of Outlying Areas." *Houston* 22 (January 1949): 85.
"Clearing Decks for Action." *Houston* 27 (November 1956): 88, 90–91.
"Clear the Tracks." *Houston* 34 (January 1964): 22–23.
"Colt .45s Pull the Trigger on April 10th." *Houston* 33 (April 1962): 52–53.
"Comparative Statistics, Port of Houston." *Houston* 20 (May 1949): 7.
Cook, Charles Orson. "John Milsaps' Houston: 1910." *Houston Review* 1 (Spring 1979): 33–54.
"Correspondence—Cooped" (letter to editor from B. Hard), *Nation*, July 18, 1928, p. 63.
"A Costly Break for Illegal Aliens." *Newsweek*, August 4, 1980, p. 60.

"Cotton Greatest Contribution to Port Houston Growth." *Houston* 2 (May 1931): 26–28.

Cox, C. C. "Reminiscences of C. C. Cox." *Southwestern Historical Quarterly* 6 (October 1902): 113–138.

"Cullen Gives $100,000 to Negro College Here." *Houston* 18 (February 1946): 42.

"Cullen to Give St. Joseph $1,000,000." *Houston* 20 (September 1949): 27.

Dillon, Charles H. "The Arrival of the Telegraph in Texas." *Southwestern Historical Quarterly* 64 (October 1960): 200–211.

"Doctor Kemmerer Named Houston University Head." *Houston* 23 (May 1952): 25.

"Double Feature in Houston." *Time*, February 15, 1943, p. 80.

"Down the Alley." *Houston* 30 (March 1959): 30, 32.

"Down the Long Lines." *Houston* 37 (December 1966): 90–92.

"The Drab Side of Houston." *Civics for Houston* 1 (September 1928): 5, 10–11.

Dreyer, Martin. "An Era Ends for Old Union Station." *Texas Tempo Sunday Magazine, Houston Post*, September 24, 1967, pp. 5–7.

"18 Railroads Which Meet the Sea." *Houston* 22 (November 1951): 8–9, 35.

"$8,000,000 New Home Underway for Sakowitz." *Houston* 20 (September 1949): 29, 76.

Ellis, L. Tuffly. "The Revolutionizing of the Texas Cotton Trade, 1865–1885." *Southwestern Historical Quarterly* 73 (April 1970): 478–508.

"An Engineering Masterpiece." *Tangent* 1 (December 1911): 9–20.

"An Enlarged and Modernized Fashion Greets Public." *Houston* 21 (September 1947): 31.

"Extensive Port Improvements Planned for 1932." *Houston* 3 (February 1932): 27–29.

"Fannin Bank: A 'Texas-Size Annex.'" *Houston* 34 (April 1963): 50.

"Federated Foley's." *Newsweek*, November 3, 1947, pp. 60, 62.

"50 Biggest Metropolitan Areas." *U.S. News and World Report*, March 16, 1981.

"Focus of a Nation's Eyes." *Houston* 35 (July 1964): 29–30.

Frantz, Joe B., ed. "Moses Lapham: His Life and Some Selected Correspondence." *Southwestern Historical Quarterly* 54 (January 1951): 324–332; (April 1951): 462–475.

"Freeway Give-Away." *Houston* 28 (November 1957): 67.

"From Cow Pasture to Moon." *Houston* 37 (September 1966): 22–23.

"Full Time Mayor Succeeds City-Manager Form Here." *Houston* 21 (August 1947): 68.

"Galveston-Houston Electric Railway." *Pan American Magazine* 36 (October 1923): 181–182.

Garwood, Ellen. "Early Texas Inns: A Study in Social Relationships." *Southwestern Historical Quarterly* 60 (October 1956): 219–244.

Geiser, S. W. "Naturalists of the Frontier." *Southwest Review* 16 (Autumn 1930): 109–135.

Gibbon, Anthony. "Creator of Cargo Ships." *Houston* 14 (June 1943): 10–11, 46–47.

Gilbert, Charles E. "City Planning." *Houston* 8 (September 1937): 25.

"Goodyear Rubber Plant Opens November 17." *Houston* 15 (December 1943): 32.

Gottmann, Jean. "Why the Skyscraper?" *Geographical Review* 16 (April 1966): 190–212.

"A Great Airport Completed." *Houston* 11 (June 1940): 13–14.

"Great Medical Center Being Created Here." *Houston* 14 (August 1943): 4.

"A Growing Industry—in the Air." *Houston* 37 (August 1966): 62–63.

"The Growing Port." *Houston* 39 (August 1968): 36–37.

"Harvest in Houston." *Time*, March 30, 1953, p. 68.

Haskell, H. J. "City Government by a Board of Directors." *Outlook*, April 13, 1907, pp. 839–843.

Haynes, Robert V. "The Houston Mutiny and Riot of 1917." *Southwestern Historical Quarterly* 76 (April 1973): 418–439.

Helmer, Bill. "Nightmare in Houston." *Texas Observer*, June 9–23, 1967, pp. 1–6.

Hendricks, Pearl. "Builders of Old Houston." *Houston* 12 (July 1941): 2–4, 16–18, 23–27.

———. "Chamber 98 Years Old." *Houston* 9 (December 1938): 50–51.

"Here Comes the Judge—Again." *Newsweek*, May 27, 1968, pp. 74–74A.

"Hilton Rides Again." *Time*, April 9, 1954, p. 71.

"History Scene on TV Screen." *Houston* 26 (January 1956): 14–15.

Hogan, William Ransom. "Pamelia Mann, Texas Frontierswoman." *Southwest Review* 20 (Summer 1935): 360–370.

———. "Rampant Individualism in the Republic of Texas." *Southwestern Historical Quarterly* 44 (April 1941): 454–480.

Holmes, Ann. "Houston: The Second City for Art." *Art News* 74 (December 1975): 50–52.

———. "The Rothko Chapel: Six Years Later." *Art News* 75 (December 1976): 35–37.

Hoover, Edgar M. "The Economic Functions and Structure of the Metropolitan Region." In *Planning and the Urban Community: Essays on Urbanism and City Planning*, ed. Harvey S. Perloff, pp. 3–15. Pittsburgh: University of Pittsburgh, 1961.

"Housing the Performing Arts." *Houston* 33 (August 1962): 44.

"Houston: Cultural Profile . . ." *Houston* 32 (June 1961): 22–26, 28, 30, 32.

"Houston: Southwest Money Market." *Houston* 35 (October 1964): 61–64.

"Houston Billionaire." *Houston* 37 (September 1966): 42.

"Houston Gets Bowled Over." *Houston* 30 (October 1959): 44–45.

"Houston Goes Dutch." *Houston* 28 (May 1957): 59–60.

"Houston Leads Nation in Per Capita Building." *Houston* 20 (April 1949): 8.

"Houston Millionaire Beats Jones on Zoning." *Business Week*, February 14, 1948, p. 48.

"Houston's Freewheeling Freeways." *Houston* 36 (October 1965): 47–50.

"Houston's Greater Water Supply Near." *Houston* 23 (August 1952): 8–11.
"Houston's Miracle on South Main." *Houston* 36 (March 1965): 98, 100.
"Houston's Municipal Airport Formally Dedicated." *Houston* 11 (October 1940): 25.
"Houston's Quiet Victory." *Negro History Bulletin* 23 (January 1960): 75–79.
"Houston's Texas-size Land Grab." *Business Week*, July 23, 1960, pp. 54, 56.
"Houston 'Tops' Industrially." *Houston* 20 (April 1949): 24, 59, 86, 97.
"The H. R. Cullens Give $4,000,000 to Hospitals." *Houston* 17 (March 1945): 9, 24.
"Hugh Potter Tells of City's Post War Needs." *Houston* 14 (June 1943): 36.
"Humble Oil Research Center to Open Jan. 1st." *Houston* 24 (November 1953): 66.
Hutcheson, Palmer. "Earliest Effort to Secure 25 Foot Channel Described." *Houston* 8 (November 1937): 3–4.
"Ice Hockey Has Arrived." *Houston* 18 (October 1946): 20, 56.
"Insured for Growth." *Houston* 36 (September 1965): 21–23.
"International Air Gateway." *Houston* 18 (June 1946): 6–8, 53.
"J. K. Allen First Booster for Houston." *Houston* 11 (April 1940): 28.
"J. S. Abercrombies Give $500,000 to Rice." *Houston* 20 (March 1947): 28.
Jackson, Susan. "Movin' On: Mobility through Houston in the 1850s." *Southwestern Historical Quarterly* 81 (January 1968): 251–282.
"Jesse Holman Jones." *Houston* 11 (October 1940): 2–3.
"Jetero Groundbreaking." *Houston* 33 (September 1962): 76–77.
"Jetero Site Landed." *Houston* 31 (August 1960): 50.
Jewell, Larry. "The City-Manager Plan." *Houston* 13 (September 1942): 13.
Jewett, Dorothy. "Highways De Luxe." *Houston* 9 (November 1938): 62–64.
"The Job Fair." *Newsweek*, May 27, 1968, 74B–75.
"John B. Coffee et al. vs. William Marsh Rice University et al." *South Western Reporter, Second Series* 408:269–287.
Jordan, Gilbert J., ed. and trans. "W. Steinert's View of Texas in 1849." *Southwestern Historical Quarterly* 80 (April 1977): 399–416.
Kemp, L. W. "Early Days in Milam County, Reminiscences of Susan Turham McCown." *Southwestern Historical Quarterly* 50 (January 1947): 367–376.
Kiper, James C. "Monsanto Supplies Styrene." *Houston* 14 (July 1943): 28–29.
Lawrence, Jennifer. "The City in Worldly Perspective." *Houston* 50 (February 1979): 49–52, 91.
Ledbetter, Nan Thompson. "The Muddy Brazos in Early Texas." *Southwestern Historical Quarterly* 63 (October 1959): 238–262.
Lemann, Nicholas. "Super Medicine." *Texas Monthly* 7 (April 1979): 111–126, 184–218.
Letson, John W. "Controversy in Houston." *National Educational Association Journal* 44 (January 1955): 45–46.
Looscan, Adele B. "Harris County 1822–1845." *Southwestern Historical*

Quarterly 18 (October 1914): 195–207, (January 1915): 261–286, (April 1915): 399–409; 19 (July 1915): 37–64.

McCraven, William. "On the Yellow Fever of Houston, Texas, in 1847." *New Orleans Medical & Surgical Journal* 5 (1848–1849): 227–235; 6 (1849–1850): 60–64.

"McEvoy Makes Tripods." *Houston* 12 (June 1941): 13.

McFarland, Gay. "The Good, the Bad and the Ugly." *Houston* 44 (August 1975): 12–13.

Mack, Eddie. "Epsom Downs Gets Ready for New Meet." *Houston* 7 (February 1936): 24.

"Metropolitan America: How It's Changed since '39." *Sales Management*, November 10, 1950, pp. 136–218.

Miller, Harvey C. "First Houston S.S. Line Began in August." *Houston* 3 (August 1932): 13, 20.

"Million Day." *Houston* 25 (July 1954): 18–19.

"A Million Dollar Drive." *Houston* 11 (March 1938): 8.

"Million Dollar Laboratory Being Built Here by Shell." *Houston* 17 (November 1945): 10.

"Modern Apartments Replace Schrimpf Alley Slum Area." *Houston* 23 (April 1952): 38.

"Modern Hospitals." *Houston* 11 (August 1940): 26–28.

"Money in the Spaghetti Bowl." *Houston* 29 (April 1958): 16–17.

Monroe, Marshall. "Cattlemen Plan Huge Revival of Industry." *Houston* 3 (March 1932): 19, 21.

"Monument to Money." *Houston* 32 (March 1961): 40–41.

Morris, Willie. "Houston's Superpatriots." *Harper's Magazine* 223 (October 1962): 48–56.

"Mr. Fred of the Lazari." *Fortune* 37 (March 1948): 108–115ff.

"Mrs. Wiess Gives Rice Large Gift." *Houston* 23 (February 1952): 50.

Muir, Andrew Forest. "The Destiny of Buffalo Bayou." *Southwestern Historical Quarterly* 47 (October 1943): 91–106.

———, ed. "Diary of a Young Man in Houston, 1838." *Southwestern Historical Quarterly* 53 (January 1950): 276–307.

———. "The Free Negro in Harris County, Texas." *Southwestern Historical Quarterly* 46 (January 1943): 214–238.

———. "The Municipality of Harrisburg, 1835–1836." *Southwestern Historical Quarterly* 56 (July 1952): 36–50.

———. "The Night Carry Nation Smashed a Houston Saloon." *Texas Tempo Sunday Magazine, Houston Post*, January 7, 1968, pp. 16–17.

———. "Railroad Enterprise in Texas, 1836–1841." *Southwestern Historical Quarterly* 47 (October 1943): 339–370.

———. "Railroads Come to Houston, 1857–1861." *Southwestern Historical Quarterly* 64 (July 1960): 42–63.

———. "William Marsh Rice, Houstonian." *East Texas Historical Journal* 2 (February 1964): 32–39.

"Murdertown, USA." *Time*, February 3, 1958, p. 17.

"Museum Takes Wing." *Houston* 29 (October 1958): 25.

"Neigh Yea." *Houston* 28 (May 1957): 34.

"Network Television Comes to Houston." *Houston* 23 (July 1952): 96.

"The New Battelstein's Formally Opens in March." *Houston* 21 (March 1950): 10–11, 36.

"New Channel Improvement Assures Added Business." *Houston* 6 (July 1935): 26–27.

"New Dams to Bring Profit and Safety." *Houston* 22 (September 1948): 38, 103.

"New Highway Tunnel Is South's Largest: Washburn Tunnel." *American City* 65 (July 1950): 72–73.

"New HOUston TV." *Houston* 30 (July 1959): 76.

"Nine Modern Bus Lines Serve City." *Houston* 21 (January 1951): 19, 57, 59, 60.

"Nine Surveys Made to Locate Tunnels." *Houston* 17 (February 1945): 27.

"Nobody Here But Us Texans . . ." *Forbes*, February 1, 1977, pp. 52–54.

"Now Comes Rubber." *Houston* 14 (June 1943): 26–27.

"Now It's Joske's." *Houston* 22 (September 1948): 26–27.

"No. 1 Industry." *Houston* 14 (April 1943): 7–11.

Oates, Stephen B. "NASA's Manned Spacecraft Center at Houston, Texas." *Southwestern Historical Quarterly* 67 (January 1964): 350–375.

Oberholtzer, E. E. "Houston . . . Passes Rigid School Test." *Houston* 2 (September 1931): 4–5.

———. "The University of Houston Marches On!" *Houston* 7 (September 1936): 4–5.

"Objet d'Art." *Houston* 35 (November 1964): 36.

"Office Space Race." *Houston* 34 (December 1963): 23–25.

"The Old Makes Way for the New." *Houston* 20 (July 1949): 6–8, 30–33.

"114,000 Employed in Houston's Busy Industrial Plants." *Houston* 14 (April 1943): 4.

"100-mph Zone Ahead." *Houston* 31 (November 1960): 44, 47.

"One Million Plus." *Houston* 32 (January 1962): 62.

"Open: The New Tennessee Building." *Houston* 34 (June 1963): 75–76.

"Opening: Cullen Center." *Houston* 34 (March 1963): 38.

"Passenger Buses of Today." *Houston* 21 (November 1947): 33, 35, 37.

Patton, Phil. "Philip Johnson: The Man Who Changed Houston's Skyline." *Houston City Magazine* 4 (January 1980): 36–47.

"Plastics: Will They Boost the Boom?" *Houston* 28 (April 1957): 16–17.

"Plastic Underfoot, Too." *Houston* 37 (May 1966): 76.

Porter, Eugene O. "Railroad Enterprises in the Republic of Texas." *Southwestern Historical Quarterly* 59 (January 1956): 363–371.

"A Port Fights Back." *Houston* 29 (June 1958): 69.

"Port Houston Second in U.S." *Houston* 20 (January 1950): 24.

"Prudential to Build $6,000,000 Home." *Houston* 21 (April 1950): 6–7, 27, 96–97.

"Reach for the Sky." *Houston* 28 (November 1957): 81–82.

"Reaching New Levels." *Houston* 33 (December 1962): 28.

Red, William S., ed. "Allen's Reminiscences of Texas, 1838–1842." *Southwestern Historical Quarterly* 17 (January 1913): 283–305; 18 (January 1915): 287–304.

Reed, S. G. "A Romance of the Rails." *Houston* 8 (January 1938): 12, 30–36.

Reeder, George K. "The Port's Salesman." *Houston* 22 (May 1951): 13, 57.

Reese, James V. "The Early History of Labor Organizations in Texas, 1838–1876." *Southwestern Historical Quarterly* 72 (July 1968): 1–20.

"A Review of the Rapid Growth of University of Houston." *Houston* 18 (August 1946): 14–16.

Reynolds, Lewis B. "Big Chemical Companies Spending $300 Million on the Gulf Coast." *Houston* 19 (April 1947): 53–54.

"Rice Given Atom Smasher by U.S." *Houston* 22 (September 1951): 97.

"Rice Goes to Colleges." *Houston* 26 (January 1956): 42, 44.

"The Rice Institute." *Tangent* 2 (October 1912): 5–12.

"Rice Institute Has New President and Four Trustees." *Houston* 17 (January 1946): 58.

"Rice Institute to Build Two Buildings." *Houston* 18 (August 1946): 12–13.

"Rice's New Stadium Nearing Completion." *Houston* 21 (September 1950): 32.

"Richly Endowed." *Houston* 28 (February 1957): 50.

Ridley, J. Kent. "Petroleum Refining." *Houston* 1 (June 1930): 18.

Roberts, Merrill J. "The Motor Transportation Revolution." *Business History Review* 30 (March 1956): 57–95.

Rule, Burt. "Motor Truck Supplants Horse Power in Houston." *Houston* [Young Men's Business League] 2 (February 1920): 18–21.

Scott, J. Virgil. "Houston Banks Grow." *Houston* 15 (September 1943): 6–7.

"Sears $1,000,000 Store Opens Soon." *Houston* 10 (November 1939): 10.

"Securing Our Future." *Houston* 38 (November 1967): 68–70.

"Setting the Pace." *Houston* 28 (July 1957): 80–81.

"Setting the Stage for Fine Arts." *Houston* 37 (October 1966): 61–62.

"$17,000,000 Steel Mill for Houston." *Houston* 12 (February 1941): 2.

"Shamrock Opens." *Houston* 20 (February 1949): 6, 9, 11, 20, 23.

"Shamrock Opens with a Bang." *Newsweek*, March 28, 1949, p. 64.

Shepherd, J. C. "Houston and Steel." *Houston* 14 (April 1944): 6.

Shuffler, R. Henderson. "Decimus et Ultimus Barziza." *Southwestern Historical Quarterly* 66 (April 1963): 501–512.

Siddall, William R. "Wholesale-Retail Trade Ratios as Indices of Urban Centrality." *Economic Geography* 37 (April 1961): 124–132.

"Sinclair's $24,000,000 Butadiene Plant." *Houston* 14 (July 1943): 46–47.

"$6,000,000 Foley Bros. Home." *Houston* 17 (June 1945): 17.

"$16,000,000 Community Center to Be Built." *Houston* 17 (June 1945): 26.

"SMSA Promises More Prosperity." *Houston* 36 (May 1965): 34–35.

Snyder, A. W. "Twenty Years of Aviation Progress." *Houston* 21 (November 1947): 20–22.

"So-Pac Pulls 'Switch.'" *Houston* 27 (February 1956): 95–97.

"Southwest's Prudential." *Houston* 23 (July 1952): 25, 27–28.

"Southwest's Tallest Skyscraper." *Houston* 34 (April 1963): 34.
"Space-Age Impact on Houston." *Houston* 33 (September 1962): 26, 29–30, 33–34, 37.
Stanley, Richard. "Three Decades of Freeways, and Still Pouring." *Houston* 50 (May 1979): 14–15, 17.
"Star-Studded Show for Houston." *Houston* 35 (August 1964): 34–36.
"Steel: Strip-mine to Strip-mill." *Houston* 27 (July 1956): 68, 70–72.
Stewart, Frank M. "Mayor Oscar F. Holcombe of Houston." *National Municipal Review* 17 (June 1928): 317–321.
Stokes, Barbara. "The Next Hurricane." *Houston* 50 (July 1979): 20–21, 23.
"Success of Houston University Assured with Gift of Arts and Culture Center." *Houston* 11 (April 1938): 5.
Suman, John R. "Amazing Facts about Texas Oil Industry." *Houston* 6 (May 1935): 19.
———. "Importance of Oil and Gas Industry to Houston." *Houston* 11 (April 1940): 50–52.
"Symphony Society." *Houston* 22 (February 1948): 12–13.
"Taking a Scientific Sniff." *Houston* 27 (June 1956): 56, 58–59.
"Ten on Eleven." *Houston* 35 (November 1964): 34.
"Test Tube Riches." *Houston* 37 (February 1966): 26–27.
"Texas: King of the Wildcatters." *Time*, February 13, 1950, pp. 18–21.
"Texas Dental College Merged with U. of T." *Houston* 13 (September 1942): 7.
"Texas Gas Now in the Chips." *Houston* 21 (October 1950): 14–15, 40–43.
This Week in Houston, September 2–8, 1923, p. 26.
Thomson, Franklin O. "Houston Makes Giant Strides." *Houston* 7 (January 1937): 9.
"Thousands Attend as Humble Celebrates." *Houston* 16 (January 1945): 24–25, 28.
"300th Warship Built by Brown Launched." *Houston* 17 (April 1945): 27.
"Todd Shipbuilding Corp. Returns." *Houston* 20 (May 1949): 35.
"Togetherness for Federal Offices." *Houston* 30 (December 1959): 35.
"Tough & Growing." *Houston* 37 (February 1966): 23–25.
"Tranquility Park." *Houston* 50 (August 1979): 21–22.
"Trucking Transport." *Houston* 33 (January 1963): 19–21.
"$12,000,000 Gulfgate to Soon Get Underway." *Houston* 24 (June 1953): 36.
"$21 Million Hotel Opens: Shamrock." *Life*, March 28, 1949, pp. 27–31.
"$256,000,000 for Gulf Coast." *Houston* 12 (February 1941): 6–7.
"University Here for the Negroes." *Houston* 21 (August 1947): 58.
"The Unusual Development of Chemicals on the Gulf Coast of Texas." *Houston* 22 (June 1948): 6–8, 10.
"Usable Depth 34 Feet Assured Ship Channel." *Houston* 6 (September 1935): 25.
"Utilities: Water." *Houston* 27 (March 1956): 9.
Van London, W. J. "Modern Expressways Under Way in Houston." *Houston* 21 (November 1947): 19, 100.
"Victory in Air Power." *Houston* 32 (April 1961): 52–53.

Vines, Robert S. "Building Proposed for Science Museum." *Houston* 22 (February 1948): 36.

"Visitors to Landing." *Houston* 37 (October 1966): 79.

Wagoner, Ed. "Subsidence: Can It Be Stopped." *Houston* 47 (November 1976): 27, 60.

Waide, C. D. "When Psychology Failed." *Houston Gargoyle*, May 15, 1928, pp. 5–6; May 22, 1928, pp. 5–6; May 29, 1928, pp. 10–11; June 5, 1928, pp. 11–12; June 12, 1928, pp. 10–11.

Walter, M. Emmett. "City Planning Progress." *Houston* 21 (June 1950): 16, 48–49.

"War Needs . . . Houston." *Architectural Record* 91 (April 1942): 47–50.

Washburn, Harry L. "Flood Control and Protection for Texas' Greatest Port." *Houston* 9 (February 1938): 12, 25–27.

"A Washington Columnist Pays Jesse H. Jones a Real Tribute." *Houston* 16 (June 1944): 26.

Weinstein, James. "Organized Business and the City Commission and Manager Movements." *Journal of Southern History* 28 (May 1962): 166–182.

West, Richard. "Only the Strong Survive." *Texas Monthly* 7 (February 1979): 94–105, 170–181.

"What Do We Do Next." *Houston* 28 (July 1957): 20–22, 24–25, 27.

"What Is . . . Houston's *Real* Water Picture?" *Houston* 28 (April 1957): 24–25, 27, 29.

"What We Need—And Why." *Houston* 30 (April 1959): 84, 86–87, 89–90, 92.

"When Houston Was Young." *Tangent* 3 (February 1913): 9–17, 43–44.

"Where Do We Stand?" *Houston* 28 (July 1957): 68–71.

"Where Houston's Ships Come In." *Houston* 37 (August 1966): 22–23.

"Where the City Plays." *Houston* 29 (September 1958): 16–17.

Whitcomb, Gail. "Allen's Landing Park . . . Another C of C Project." *Houston* 37 (June 1966): 96.

Williams, Crawford. "Here's a Houston Firm You Should Know." *Houston* 6 (June 1935): 27, 29–32.

"Woolworth Store Opens." *Houston* 20 (November 1949): 14–16, 50.

"World Trade Center." *Houston* 33 (February 1962): 64.

"WPA Aids Deserving, $4,245,000 Spent in Houston Area." *Houston* 7 (October 1936): 8–9.

Wrightman, Francis. "'Alley'—Theater Unusual." *Houston* 22 (August 1948): 25.

N.B. Volume numbers for *Houston* were revised January–February 1949.

Books

Albion, Robert Greenhalgh, and Jennie Barnes Pope. *The Rise of New York Port, 1815–1860.* New York: Charles Scribner's Sons, 1939.

Alexander, Charles C. *Crusade for Conformity: The Ku Klux Klan in Texas, 1920–1930.* [Houston]: Texas Gulf Coast Historical Association, 1962.

Allen, Ruth. *Chapters in the History of Organized Labor in Texas.* University of Texas publications, no. 4143. Austin: University of Texas Press, 1941.

Babcock, Richard F. *The Zoning Game: Municipal Practices and Policies.* Madison: University of Wisconsin Press, 1966.

Ball, Thomas H. *The Port of Houston: How It Came to Pass.* Houston, n.d.

Barker, Eugene C. *The Life of Stephen F. Austin.* Austin: Texas State Historical Association, 1949.

Barnstone, Howard. *The Architecture of John F. Staub: Houston and the South.* Austin: University of Texas Press, 1979.

Baughman, James P. *Charles Morgan and the Development of Southern Transportation.* Nashville: Vanderbilt University Press, 1968.

Blake, Nelson Manfred. *Water for the Cities.* Syracuse, N.Y.: Syracuse University Press, 1956.

Board of Education [Houston]. *High Spots in Houston Public Schools.* Houston, 1927.

Bogy, Eroll R. *Houston in Brief.* Houston: E. R. Bogy, 1932.

Brady, William. *Glimpses of Texas, Its Divisions, Resources, Development, and Prospects.* Houston, 1871.

Brown, John Henry. *Indian Wars and Pioneers of Texas.* Austin: L. E. Daniell, 1890[?].

Bullock, Henry Allen. *The Houston Murder Problem: Its Nature, Apparent Causes and Probable Cures.* Houston, 1961.

Burchard, John, and Albert Bush-Brown. *The Architecture of America: A Social and Cultural History.* Boston: Little, Brown and Co., 1961, 1966.

Carroll, B. H., Jr. *Standard History of Houston, Texas.* Knoxville, Tenn.: H. W. Crew, 1912.

CBD Today. Houston: City Planning Department, 1964.

Chamber of Commerce. *Houston.* Houston, 1929.

The Charter of the City of Houston Together with the Revised Code of Ordinances. Houston: Smallwood, Dealy & Baker, 1886.

Comey, Arthur C. *Houston: Tentative Plans for Its Development, Report to the Park Commission.* Boston: Geo. H. Ellis Co., 1913.

Cooley, Charles H. *The Theory of Transportation.* Baltimore: Weil and Co., 1894.

de Hartog, Jan. *The Hospital.* New York: Atheneum, 1964.

Department of Traffic and Transportation. *Economic Evaluation of the Gulf Freeway.* [Houston]: City of Houston, 1949.

Domenech, Abbé E. H. D. *Missionary Adventures in Texas and Mexico.* London: Longman, Brown, Green, Longmans, and Roberts, 1858.

Dresel, Gustav. *Houston Journal: Adventures in North America and Texas, 1837–1841.* Translated by Max Freund. Austin: University of Texas Press, 1954.

Fleming, Lamar, Jr. *Growth of the Business of Anderson, Clayton & Co.* Ed. James A. Tinsley. [Houston]: Texas Gulf Coast Historical Association, 1966.

Fornell, Earl Wesley. *The Galveston Era: The Texas Crescent on the Eve of Secession.* Austin: University of Texas Press, 1961.

Fuermann, George. *Houston: Land of the Big Rich*. Garden City: Double-day, 1951.

Gallegly, Joseph. *Footlights on the Border: The Galveston and Houston Stage before 1900*. The Hague: Mouton and Co., 1962.

Gammel, H. P. N., comp. *The Laws of Texas, 1822–1897*. 10 vols. Austin: Gammel Book Co., 1898.

Gates, Paul W. *Agriculture and the Civil War*. New York: Alfred A. Knopf, 1965.

Geib, H. V. *Soil Survey of Harris County, Texas*. U.S. Department of Agriculture, Bureau of Soils. Washington, D.C.: U.S. Government Printing Office, 1928.

Glaab, Charles N., and A. Theodore Brown. *A History of Urban America*. New York: The Macmillan Co., 1967.

Goodman, Mary Ellen. *The Mexican-American Population of Houston: A Survey in the Field, 1965–1970*. Houston: Rice University Studies, 1971.

Gray, E. N. *Memories of Old Houston*. Houston, 1940.

Gray, Kenneth E. *A Report on the Politics of Houston*. 2 vols. Cambridge: Joint Center of Urban Studies of the Massachusetts Institute of Technology and Harvard University, 1960.

Gray, Millie Richards. *The Diary of Millie Gray, 1832–1840*. Houston: Fletcher Young Publishing Co. for the Rosenberg Library Press, 1967.

Green, Charles D. *Fire Fighters of Houston, 1838–1915*. Houston: Dealy-Adey Co., 1915.

Grimes, Louis Howard. *Cloud of Witnesses: A History of First Methodist Church, Houston, Texas*. Houston, 1951.

Gulick, Charles Adams, Jr., ed. *The Papers of Mirabeau Buonaparte Lamar*. 6 vols. Austin: Texas State Library, 1922.

Hardy, Dermot H., and Ingham S. Roberts. *Historical Review of South-East Texas*. 2 vols. Chicago: Lewis Publishing Co., 1910.

Hatch, Orin Walker. *Lyceum to Library: A Chapter in the Cultural History of Houston*. [Houston]: Texas Gulf Coast Historical Association, 1965.

Hatcher, Mattie Austin. *Letters of an Early American Traveller*. Dallas: Southwest Press, 1933.

Hautier, J. G., comp. *Revised Code of Ordinances of the City of Houston of 1922*. Houston, 1922.

Haynes, Robert V. *A Night of Violence: The Houston Riot of 1917*. Baton Rouge: Louisiana State University Press, 1976.

Hill, Charles J. *A Brief History of ILA Local 872*. [Houston?: International Longshoremen's Association, Local 872, 1959?].

History of Texas, Together with a Biographical History of the Cities of Houston and Galveston . . . Chicago: Lewis Publishing Co., 1895.

Houston, Sam. *Writings*. See Williams, Amelia.

Houston Chamber of Commerce. *Houston Facts '80*. Houston: Chamber of Commerce, 1980.

Houston City Planning Commission. *Comprehensive Plan—Houston Urban Area*. 3 vols. [Houston], 1958.

Houstoun, Matilda Charlotte. *Texas and the Gulf of Mexico; or Yachting in the New World.* 2 vols. London: J. Murray, 1844.

Hurley, Marvin. *Decisive Years for Houston.* Houston: Houston Magazine, 1966.

Inside the Astrodome. Houston: Houston Sports Association, 1965.

Jacobs, Jane. *The Death and Life of Great American Cities.* New York: Vintage Books, 1961.

Johnston, Marguerite. *A Happy Worldly Abode: Christ Church Cathedral, 1839–1964.* Houston: Cathedral Press, 1964.

Jones, Julia. *Houston: 1836–1940.* Houston, 1941.

Journal of the House of Representatives, Republic of Texas, First Congress, First Session. Houston: Telegraph, 1838.

Kilman, Ed, and Theon Wright. *Hugh Roy Cullen: A Story of American Opportunity.* New York: Prentice-Hall, Inc., 1954.

King, John O. *The Early History of the Houston Oil Company of Texas, 1901–1908.* [Houston]: Texas Gulf Coast Historical Association, 1959.

Lasswell, Mary. *John Henry Kirby, Prince of the Pines.* Austin: Encino Press, 1967.

Leonard, W. A., comp. *Houston City Directory for 1866.* Houston: Gray, Strickland & Co., 1866.

————. *Houston City Directory for 1867–'8.* Houston: Gray, Smallwood and Co., 1867.

Living in River Oaks. Houston: River Oaks Corp., 1941.

Lösch, August. *The Economics of Location.* New Haven: Yale University Press, 1954.

Lubbock, Francis R. *Six Decades in Texas.* Edited by C. W. Rains. Austin: Ben C. Jones & Co., 1900.

Macon, N. Don. *Mr. John D. Freeman and Friends: A Story of the Texas Medical Center and How It Began.* Houston: Texas Medical Center, 1973.

Maxwell, Robert S. *Whistle in the Piney Woods: Paul Bremond and the Houston East and West Texas Railway.* [Houston]: Texas Gulf Coast Historical Association, 1963.

Morrison and Fourmy's General Directory of the City of Houston, 1882–1883. [Houston]: Morrison and Fourmy, 1882.

Muir, Andrew Forest, ed. *Texas in 1837: An Anonymous, Contemporary Narrative.* Austin: University of Texas Press, 1958.

National Education Association of the United States. *Houston, Texas: A Study of Factors Related to Educational Unrest in a Large School System.* December 1954.

Nimmo, Joseph, Jr. *Report on the Internal Commerce of the United States* (1879), *House Executive Documents.* 45th Congress, 3rd Session (Serial No. 1857), Document No. 32, part 3. Washington, D.C.: Government Printing Office, 1879.

Olmsted, Frederick Law. *Journey through Texas.* Edited by James Howard. Austin: Von Boeckmann-Jones Press, 1962.

Origins and History of Houston Lighting and Power Company. Houston, 1940.

Putnam, Frank. *City Government in Europe.* Houston: City of Houston, 1913.

Rankin, G. C. *The Story of My Life.* Nashville: Smith and Lamar, 1912.

Reader, Earl J. *Houston Traffic Survey, City of Houston, 1939.* Works Progress Administration, 1939.

Red, Samuel C. *A Brief History of First Presbyterian Church, Houston, Texas, 1839–1939.* Houston: Wilson Stationery and Printing Co., 1939.

The Red Book of Houston. Houston: Sotex Publishing Co., [1915].

Reed, S. G. *A History of Texas Railroads.* Houston: St. Clair Publishing Co., 1941.

Report of the City Planning Commission. Houston: Forum of Civics, [1929].

Report of the President, 1980. Houston: Rice University, 1980.

Riddle, Don. *River Oaks: A Pictorial Presentation of Houston's Residential Park.* Houston: River Oaks Corp., 1929.

Riis, Jacob. *How the Other Half Lives.* New York: Hill and Wang, 1957.

Ripley, Eliza McHatton. *From Flag to Flag: A Woman's Adventures and Experiences in the South during the War, in Mexico, and in Cuba.* New York: D. Appleton and Co., 1896.

Roemer, Ferdinand. *Texas: With Particular Reference to German Immigration and Physical Appearance of the Country.* Translated by Oswald Mueller. San Antonio: Standard Printing Co., 1935.

Rose, Warren. *The Economic Impact of the Port of Houston, 1958–1963.* Houston, 1965.

Rostow, W. W. *The Stages of Economic Growth.* Cambridge: At the University Press, 1960.

Roussel, Hubert. *The Houston Symphony Orchestra, 1913–1971.* Austin: University of Texas Press, 1972.

Rules and Regulations. Houston: Houston Independent School District, n.d.

Sharpe, Ernest A. *G. B. Dealey of the Dallas News.* New York: Henry Holt and Co., 1955.

Sibley, Marilyn McAdams. *The Port of Houston: A History.* Austin: University of Texas Press, 1968.

Smith, Jesse Guy. *Heroes of the Saddle Bags: A History of Christian Denominations in the Republic of Texas.* San Antonio: Naylor Co., 1951.

Southern Transcontinental Service Case, Exhibits before the U.S. Civil Aeronautics Board, Docket No. 7984 et al. [Houston]: City of Houston and Houston Chamber of Commerce, 1959.

Spratt, John S. *The Road to Spindletop: Economic Change in Texas, 1875–1901.* Dallas: Southern Methodist University Press, 1955.

The Standard Blue Book of Texas: Who's Who. Houston: Who's Who Publishing Co., 1907.

The Statistical History of the United States from Colonial Times to the Present. Stamford, Conn.: Fairfield Publishers, 1965.

Texas Almanac and State Industrial Guide, 1911. Dallas: A. H. Belo & Co., 1911.

Texas Almanac and State Industrial Guide, 1925. Dallas: A. H. Belo & Co., 1925.

Texas Almanac and State Industrial Guide, 1931. Dallas: A. H. Belo Corp., 1931.

Texas Almanac and State Industrial Guide, 1941–1942. Dallas: A. H. Belo Corp., 1941.

Texas Almanac and State Industrial Guide, 1951–1952. Dallas: A. H. Belo Corp., 1951.

Texas Almanac and State Industrial Guide, 1966–1967. Dallas: A. H. Belo Corp., 1966.

Texas Almanac and State Industrial Guide, 1978–1979. Dallas: A. H. Belo Corp., 1978.

Texas Newspapers, 1813–1939: A Union List of Newspaper Files Available in Offices of Publishers, Libraries, and a Number of Private Collections. Houston: San Jacinto Museum of History Association, 1941.

Texas Public Library Statistics, 1966. Austin: Texas State Library, 1967.

Tiling, Moritz. *History of the German Element in Texas.* Houston: Moritz Tiling, 1913.

Timmons, Bascom N. *Jesse H. Jones.* New York: Henry Holt and Co., 1956.

United States Bureau of the Census. *Eighth Census, Manufactures of the United States in 1860.* Washington, D.C.: Government Printing Office, 1865.

———. *Eighth Census of the United States, Population.* Washington, D.C.: Government Printing Office, 1864.

———. *Ninth Census.* Vol. III, *The Statistics of the Wealth and Industry of the United States . . .* Washington, D.C.: Government Printing Office, 1872.

———. *Tenth Census of the United States: 1880, Statistics of the Population of the United States.* Washington, D.C.: Government Printing Office, 1883.

———. *Report on the Manufactures of the United States at the Tenth Census.* Washington, D.C.: Government Printing Office, 1883.

———. *Fifteenth Census of the United States: 1929, Manufacturers.* Vol. III. Washington, D.C.: U.S. Government Printing Office, 1933.

———. *Fifteenth Census of the United States: 1930, Distribution.* Vols. I, II. Washington, D.C.: U.S. Government Printing Office, 1934.

———. *Fifteenth Census of the United States: 1930, Population.* Vols. I, IV. Washington, D.C.: U.S. Government Printing Office, 1931, 1933.

———. *Census of Business, 1963.* Vol. I, *Retail Trade—Summary Statistics,* part 5. Washington, D.C.: U.S. Government Printing Office, 1966.

———. *County and City Data Book, 1967.* Washington, D.C.: U.S. Government Printing Office, 1967.

———. *County and City Data Book, 1977.* Washington, D.C.: U.S. Government Printing Office, 1978.

———. *1977 Census of Retail Trade, Texas.* Washington, D.C.: U.S. Government Printing Office, 1979.

————. *Statistical Abstract of the United States, 1979.* Washington, D.C.: U.S. Government Printing Office, 1979.

————. *Preliminary Reports, 1980 Census of Population and Houston, Texas.* Washington, D.C.: U.S. Government Printing Office, 1981.

United States Engineering Department. *Houston Ship Channel, Texas.* Washington, D.C.: U.S. Government Printing Office, 1929.

The University of Houston and Full State Tax Support. [Houston]: University of Houston, 1960.

Wade, Richard C. *Slavery in the Cities.* New York: Oxford University Press, 1964.

————. *The Urban Frontier.* Cambridge, Mass.: Harvard University Press, 1959.

Wallis, Jonnie Lockhart, and Laurance L. Hill. *Sixty Years on the Brazos: The Life and Letters of Dr. John Washington Lockhart.* Los Angeles: Dunn Bros., 1930.

Warner, C. A. *Texas Oil and Gas since 1543.* Houston: Gulf Publishing Co., 1939.

Webb, Walter Prescott, ed. *The Handbook of Texas.* 2 vols. Austin: Texas State Historical Association, 1952.

Williams, Amelia W., and Eugene C. Barker, eds. *The Writings of Sam Houston, 1813–1863.* 8 vols. Austin: University of Texas Press, 1938–1943.

Williams, David E., ed. *Houston Eight Million.* Houston: University of Houston, College of Architecture, 1965.

The World Almanac and Book of Facts, 1945. Edited by E. Eastman Irvine. New York: New York World Telegram, 1945.

The World Almanac and Book of Facts, 1967. Edited by Luman H. Long. New York: Newspaper Enterprise Association, Inc., 1966.

Writers' Program, Work Projects Administration. *Houston: A History and Guide.* Houston: Anson Jones Press, 1942.

INDEX

Abercrombie, James: 81, 174
Academy Bldg.: 3, 41
Adams, Lt. H. M.: 33
Adams, K. S. "Bud": 186, 189
Aeros: 187
AFL-CIO Council: 188
African Methodist Church: 41
Agee, William: 194
Agricultural, Mechanical, & Blood
  Stock Assn. of Texas: 44
agriculture: 38
air conditioning: 5, 192
Air France: 118
airport, municipal: 75, 117, 118–119,
  137, 141, 189
air transport: 75, 117–119
Allen, Augustus C.: 9–12, 14–16, 26,
  30, 66, 200 n. 19
Allen, Charlotte: 11, 12
Allen, E. A.: 74
Allen, Ebenezer: 27
Allen, Henry R.: 36
Allen, John K.: 9–12, 14–16, 30–31, 66,
  200 n. 19, 205 n. 118
Allen, William Y.: 50
Allen Parkway: 137, 162, 192
Allen's Landing: 160–161
Alley Theatre: 184, 193
Allied Bank Bldg.: 134, 135
Altfeld, Bob and Vivian: 184
Alvord, Burdick, & Howson: 146
Amateis, Louis: 100
American Airlines: 117
American Brewing Assn.: 79
American Civil Liberties Union: 169
American College of Physicians: 180
American College of Surgeons: 180

American General Life Insurance Bldg.:
  137
American Government: 164
American Hospital Assn.: 180
American Maid Flour Co.: 81
American Medical Assn.: 180
American Rolling Mill Co.: 130
Amoco: 129
Ancient Order of Hibernians: 100
Anderson, Frank E.: 77
Anderson, Monroe D.: 77, 177
Anderson, Clayton & Co.: 77, 177
Andrew, John L.: 160
Andrews, Ben C.: 97
Andrews, Jesse: 157
Andrews, John D.: 32
annexation: 139–142, 143. *See also* ex-
  pansion
Anti-Saloon League: 107
Arabia Temple Crippled Children's
  Clinic: 177
architecture: 4, 97–98, 101–102,
  132–136, 184, 185, 188, 191–192
Armco: 149
Armour: 81
Armstrong, Neil: 143
army engineers: 33–34, 65–66, 91, 120,
  146
Army-Navy "E": 131
Arnold, Daniel C.: 181
artesian wells: 89, 90, 91, 145, 147
arts: 38–39, 41, 101, 185, 193–194
Ashby, Lynn: 192–193
Astrodome: 4, 187–188
Astros: 137, 187, 188
AstroTurf: 189
Astroworld: 189